JIBS Special Collections

Series Editor
Academy of International Business
Michigan State University
East Lansing, MI, USA

Technical Series Editor: Alain Verbeke is a Professor of International Business Strategy and holds the McCaig Research Chair in Management at the Haskayne School of Business, University of Calgary (Canada). He was elected as the Inaugural Alan M. Rugman Memorial Fellow at the Henley Business School, University of Reading (UK), and is Editor-in-Chief of the *Journal of International Business Studies.* He is also an Adjunct Professor at the Solvay Business School, Vrije Universiteit Brussel (Belgium). He is an elected Fellow of the Academy of International Business and has served as Secretary and Treasurer of the Fellows. He is also an elected Fellow of the European International Business Academy.

***Journal of International Business Studies* (*JIBS*)** is an official publication of the Academy of International Business and is the top-ranked journal in the field of international business. The goal of *JIBS* is to publish insightful, innovative and impactful research on international business. *JIBS* is multidisciplinary in scope and interdisciplinary in content and methodology. For more information, visit www.jibs.net.

Academy of International Business (AIB) is the leading association of scholars and specialists in the field of international business. A global community for the creation and dissemination of knowledge about international business and policy issues, the AIB transcends the boundaries of single academic disciplines and managerial functions to enhance business education and practice. For more information, visit aib.msu.edu.

More information about this series at
http://www.palgrave.com/gp/series/15231

Murad A. Mithani
Rajneesh Narula • Irina Surdu
Alain Verbeke
Editors

Crises and Disruptions in International Business

How Multinational Enterprises Respond to Crises

palgrave
macmillan

Editors
Murad A. Mithani
School of Business
Rutgers University at Camden
Camden, NJ, USA

Rajneesh Narula
Henley Business School
University of Reading
Reading, UK

Irina Surdu
Warwick Business School
University of Warwick
Coventry, UK

Alain Verbeke
Haskayne School of Business
University of Calgary
Calgary, AB, Canada

Henley Business School
University of Reading
Reading, UK

Solvay Business School
Vrije Universiteit Brussel
Brussels, Belgium

ISSN 2397-8775 ISSN 2397-8783 (electronic)
JIBS Special Collections
ISBN 978-3-030-80382-7 ISBN 978-3-030-80383-4 (eBook)
https://doi.org/10.1007/978-3-030-80383-4

This Palgrave Macmillan imprint is published by the registered company Springer Nature Switzerland AG.
The registered company address is: Gewerbestrasse 11, 6330 Cham, Switzerland

Contents

List of Figures

List of Tables

Part I

Introduction

1

Unique Implications of Crises and Disruptions for International Business: How Established MNEs Are Exposed to Crises and Mitigate Their Effects

Murad A. Mithani, Rajneesh Narula, Irina Surdu, and Alain Verbeke

Environmental crises and disruptions come in various forms: economic recessions, disease outbreaks, as well as terrorist attacks (Meyer, 1982; Quarantelli, 1988; Weick, 1993). A common theme across these threats is that they are difficult to predict, cannot be fully avoided, and impose nontrivial costs (Hällgren et al., 2018; McKnight & Linnenluecke,

M. A. Mithani (✉)
School of Business, Rutgers University at Camden, Camden, NJ, USA
e-mail: murad.mithani@rutgers.edu

R. Narula
Henley Business School, University of Reading, Reading, UK
e-mail: r.narula@henley.ac.uk

I. Surdu
Warwick Business School, University of Warwick, Coventry, UK
e-mail: irina.surdu@wbs.ac.uk

M. A. Mithani et al. (eds.), *Crises and Disruptions in International Business*, JIBS Special Collections, https://doi.org/10.1007/978-3-030-80383-4_1

2019). Crises and disruptions can be associated with fundamental changes in the economic, social and institutional environments of firms and pose unique challenges to the established multinational enterprise (MNE) due to its multi-market exposure.

As this collection showcases, research in international business focuses on the implications of crises and disruptions for the MNE, and the ways in which a multinational firm is affected differently compared to a firm with a primarily domestic footprint. At the same time, MNEs may also command a greater capability to respond to crises and disruptions relative to domestic firms. Despite the progress made, the field of international business lacks a descriptive overview of how the established MNE's unique structural and operational functioning characteristics lead to unique exposures and capacities to respond to crises and disruptions.

The COVID-19 pandemic has generated a renewed sense of urgency to synthesize the essence of this prior research. The present collection therefore brings together selected articles previously published in *JIBS* and that are especially insightful. Each article is complemented by a brief Commentary that extends the analysis conducted in the original paper. These Commentaries by content experts (including in some cases, the original authors) offer a state-of-the-art update of the received knowledge on the topic. The Commentaries provide a forward-looking perspective on both the current and expected future importance of the type of crisis or disruption discussed in the original article.

The analyses presented in this volume recognize that MNEs are increasingly exposed to "extremes" and yet, we know very little about the antecedents, consequences, and perhaps even the opportunities associated with different types of crises and disruptions. Past scholarly research in

---

A. Verbeke
Haskayne School of Business, University of Calgary, Calgary, AB, Canada

Henley Business School, University of Reading, Reading, UK

Solvay Business School, Vrije Universiteit Brussel, Brussels, Belgium
e-mail: alain.verbeke@haskayne.ucalgary.ca

the broad management and strategy arenas has tended to overgeneralize both the threats that are disruptive to domestic firms, and the optimal responses to these threats; over time, assumptions made about domestic firms' responses to crises, have been extended to MNEs. However, this collection series shows that MNEs are affected by – and respond to – crises and disruptions differently than domestic firms. These differences arise because established MNEs with geographically dispersed operations are, on the one hand, more vulnerable to these threats, but on the other, have accumulated a wider range of experiences from operating in distinct environments, and rarely face existential threats from a crisis arising in a single host country. MNEs typically have greater flexibility to 'avoid' locations characterized by crises and disruptions, and when affected, have the capacity to deploy a broader and more refined range of responses than their domestic companies, including the capacity to exit a location when it becomes unattractive.

We therefore classify in a stylized way the unique MNE vulnerabilities and responses to crises and disruptions. First, we proposed that there are the unique exposures and capabilities resulting from MNE *structural characteristics*, especially aspects such as an MNE's geographic diversification. Second, there are the unique exposures and capabilities resulting from MNE characteristics in the realm of *operational functioning* in host markets. Table 1.1 summarizes the proposed exposures and capabilities resulting from MNE structural characteristics and MNE operational functioning characteristics. Broadly, we highlight the implications of crises and disruptions for MNEs in terms of higher *exposures* to threats, but also the (potentially) greater *capabilities* needed to mitigate such threats relative to domestic firms. We therefore describe the distinct characteristics of established MNEs vis-à-vis standard domestic incumbents without international operations and note that the extent to which these often-observed features will actually affect MNE exposures and capabilities in the real world and as compared to domestic companies, will be country-, industry- and firm-specific.

Table 1.1 Unique implications of crises and disruptions for established MNEs

	Exposures based on MNE structural characteristics	**Exposures bases on characteristics of MNE operational functioning**
1	Higher frequency (+)	Constrained local autonomy to respond (+)
2	Higher variety (+)	Greater visibility to hostile local stakeholders (+)
3	More wide-ranging stakeholder expectations (+)	Higher threats of exploitation and local stakeholder criticism (+)
4	Combinatorial effects of threats (+)	Greater cautiousness in addressing institutional constraints (+)
	Capabilities based on MNE structural characteristics	**Capabilities bases on characteristics of MNE operational functioning**
1	Ease of exit (+)	Firm-specific advantages allowing a wider portfolio of anticipatory and remedial actions (+)
2	Relative autonomy vis-à-vis host market institutions (+)	Access to internal slack resources (+)
3	Dispersed distribution of revenues (+)	Better procurement of innovations and other resources from the global environment (+)
4	Experiential knowledge from wide array of crisis responses (+)	Potential to build relational capabilities (+)

The symbol "+" reflects the fact that the parameter considered increases the MNE's exposure to crises and disruptions, or creates potential to improve its capabilities to manage this exposure

MNEs, Crises, and Disruptions

Crises and disruptions generally represent local events unfolding within social and ecological contours that geographically divide countries and regions. For instance, natural disasters are typically bound by physical terrains and their effects are usually confined to regions that are in the immediate vicinity of the threat (Quarantelli, 2000). On occasion, local disturbances are so massive or impactful that they turn into global events. Both the 9/11 terrorist attacks and the 2007–2008 financial crisis are examples of an initially localized crisis that turned out to have significant global implications. More specifically, although both crises began as local events in the United States, their global ramifications appeared soon after (Brounen & Derwall, 2010; Helleiner, 2011).

Events that remain local (as well as those that transition to become globally significant) affect MNEs because of structural characteristics, such as their level of diversification and the firm's accumulation of experiential knowledge. The severity of the impact usually depends upon the extent to which the MNE is embedded in countries affected by the exogenous threat or shock, at least in the initial period. In rare cases, disruptions represent global occurrences from the start, with their effects transpiring throughout the world. Climate change is one such example. Importantly, even though the effects of climate change are unevenly distributed across the globe, the ways in which MNEs are affected may have less to do with their overall international diversification levels, and more with choices regarding their operational functioning, such as their preference for engaging in highly asset-specific investments in particular host market locations. Below, we discuss in more detail how MNE structural and operational functioning characteristics affect these firms' exposure and capabilities.

MNE Structural Characteristics

Exposure to Crises and Disruptions

The geographic diversification of MNEs leads to differences in their exposure to disruptive events as compared to firms that have a narrower geographic scope. Perhaps most importantly, higher diversification leads quasi-automatically to increases in exposure to the frequency and diversity of threats. A higher frequency of threats reflects the fact that firms present in multiple markets are less likely to experience randomness or luck, and more likely to experience the average effects of *inter alia* sudden financial, social, and ecological changes across those different market environments. Although judicious location choices may include investments in regions that pose fewer predictable financial or social hazards, these investments do not eliminate the potential impact of ecological disasters, or other types of local events that can morph into global disruptions. Moreover, the nature of crises differs across countries. For instance, some locations may be more vulnerable to social upheaval, and other ones to financial challenges (Abadie & Gardeazabal, 2003). Greater geographic diversification therefore increases the MNE's overall exposure to a wide range of crises and subsequent disruptions.

A major consequence of greater geographic diversification is that MNEs are also exposed to a broader range of stakeholder demands. Although, as we discuss below, each of these localized demands may be less salient than for domestic companies due to weaker business and social ties and a lower impact on the overall core business, they also increase the difficulty of optimal responsiveness. Corporate head offices are responsible for allocating resources to address stakeholder concerns and related challenges across regions, and this may lead to geography-driven prioritization. One such example is the use of philanthropy. While MNEs may be particularly generous when a local natural disaster occurs, they have also been shown to act less generously when a disaster affects multiple countries simultaneously (Mithani, 2017; Muller & Whiteman, 2009).

Exposure to frequent and diverse threats, and to a wide array of geographically distributed stakeholder concerns, may have subsequent combined effects on the overall scale and scope of the vulnerabilities that the MNE is likely to face. While threats may initially be specific to localized markets, new vulnerabilities can emanate from the interplay among multiple markets. For instance, the overall impact on an MNE exposed to a natural disaster in one market and a reputational crisis in another, is not merely a sum of the challenges specific to each market. These threats can also interact in ways that are difficult to predict in advance (Andriani & McKelvey, 2007). The combinatorial effects of various exposures distributed across geographic space can translate into consequences that go far beyond the directly affected local milieus. Fortunately, the outcome for the MNE is not solely determined by the combined vulnerabilities it faces, but also by its capacity to address these simultaneously.

Capabilities to Manage Crises and Disruptions

The diversified operations that expose MNEs to a variety of spatially distributed threats also broaden the ways in which they can respond to crises and disruptions. Whether threats exist locally or globally, the response portfolio of MNEs is typically broader than that of a domestic firm of equivalent size.

First, there is the potential for MNEs to reduce exposure through market exit and divestment (Dai et al., 2013). For instance, foreign market exit is one of the most effective strategies the MNE can adopt when the institutional environment offers little guarantee that existential threats to a subsidiary can be avoided or mitigated in the future (Oh & Oetzel, 2011). In turn, the ease with which MNEs can exit from a location may be determined by the firm's presence in other institutional environments (e.g., locations of alternative supply sources or potential customers). The capacity to exit relatively easily when faced with a crisis, could be viewed as a distinct MNE capability.

Second, and relatedly, MNEs are typically less constrained, relative to domestic incumbents, by preferences voiced by host market stakeholders. Exit from one host country location may be associated with an entry into another, more attractive foreign milieu, thereby reducing, at least to some extent, potential negative impacts on MNE operations.

A third advantage of the MNE over a domestic firm when addressing crises and disruptions is that the geographic dispersion of input streams and revenue streams across a wide range of market environments, makes the firm relatively less vulnerable to local threats occurring in any given market or region. Even though the subsidiary in a market may be significantly affected, the MNE as a whole is typically less vulnerable when facing localized threats.

Fourth, MNEs that have experience with a broader array of crises and disruptions, and across a wider range of countries, are likely to be better prepared to address new threats. The MNE is able to transfer resources, personnel and capabilities across geographic space to address challenges, and possibly to improve the 'rate of recovery'. The use of emergency response teams is now common in large MNEs such as IBM, P&G, and Unilever. These teams can be quickly deployed, capitalize on past experiences, and transfer the much needed capabilities to affected subsidiaries, and where relevant, to local communities (Green & Kolesar, 2004; McNutt & Leshner, 2013).

MNE Characteristics of Operational Functioning

Exposure to Crises and Disruptions

In addition to the impact of its structural characteristics, an MNE's exposure to threats and its capabilities to respond effectively to such threats is also determined by its operational functioning characteristics.

First, given their more limited local ties relative to domestic firms in host environments and the need to work closely with the corporate head office, MNE subsidiaries may not have as much latitude as domestic companies to respond to local threats. This explains why local threats of crises and disruptions lead to MNE departures from affected markets, rather than to more local engagement (Wang & Li, 2019).

Second and relatedly, MNEs tend to be comparatively large, resource-rich and thus highly visible which in turn expose their host country operations to greater local scrutiny. Due to their visibility, MNEs may also become a target of local activists and social movements (Zhang & Luo, 2013). As a result, MNEs will tend to prioritize greater local engagement and stronger compliance with local expectations only in those markets which are viewed as strategically important.

Third, comparatively weaker local ties may also increase MNE vulnerabilities to various expressions of manipulation, particularly by political and social actors (e.g., local NGOs). In the event of a threat, these actors can capitalize on the MNE's comparatively weaker local ties and more limited understanding of the local informal and formal institutions. Even though such local actors can serve as efficiency-enhancing intermediaries, they can also use their relationship with the MNE as a platform to foster their own interests (Henisz & Zelner, 2010). This can lead to exploitation, undue exposure to hostile stakeholders, and distraction from needed efforts for recovery during and after a crisis.

Fourth, in times of crises, MNE subsidiary operations will typically be more cautious than domestic firms when addressing dysfunctional institutional constraints, in order to avert a backlash (Khanna & Palepu, 2013). Effective responses to crises and disruptions often require circumventing or going against formal and informal institutional constraints and introducing new principles of operational functioning. In turn, circumventing institutional constraints may often prove difficult for MNE subsidiaries that tend to face a liability of foreigness compared to local firms. If foreign firms circumvent or oppose what they may perceive as flawed institutional rules and are perceived to do so inappropriately, this may expose them to strong criticism, especially if their actions are perceived to somehow negatively affect local stakeholders. The lack of deep knowledge about the local environment and the resulting cautiousness, can limit the extent to which MNE resources are deployed effectively in host markets to anticipate or mitigate the effects of crises and disruptions.

Capabilities to Manage Crises and Disruptions

Whilst facing higher threats, established MNEs are also better equipped than domestic firms to respond to crises and disruptions because their geographic scope endows them with a larger set of capabilities.

First, MNEs typically command non-location-bound capabilities that are critical during crises and in the aftermath of crises. These include not only firm-specific advantages in managing cross-border value chains, but also common environmental and corporate social responsibility safeguards shared by the entire network, the capacity to deploy emergency response teams, the ability to coordinate with disaster recovery organizations, and expertise in community development projects. Older and larger MNEs are more likely to have experienced, and learned from, crises and disruptions in different markets, and to have developed the distinct competences needed to manage such threats.

Second, crises and disruptions generally constrain the extent to which slack resources in the affected geographic milieu can be made available for immediate deployment. Compared to local firms, MNE subsidiaries tend to have access to slack resources available at the head office and other resources embedded in the remainder of the MNE network. Strong linkages with the head office (including good personal relationships between subsidiary and head office managers) can increase a subsidiary's capacity to deploy material resources in local markets when needed to contribute to recovery efforts.

Third, in addition to commanding internationally deployable firm-specific advantages and material resources, MNEs are typically also more competent in identifying and purchasing outside innovations and other valuable resources from any location in the world, and that can be useful during times of crises. Such procurement may include inputs as diverse as outside substitute production capacity and advanced machinery as well as specialized services to facilitate crisis mitigation and recovery efforts (e.g., Un, 2016). Access to innovations and other valuable resources procured externally do not only improve the MNE's capacity to manage threats but can also complement efforts by local governments and civil society to address the outcomes of crises and disruptions.

Fourth, crises and disruptions offer the potential to participate proactively in local mitigation and recovery efforts, thereby allowing MNEs to strengthen existing relationships and build new ones. MNEs interested in local relationship building are given the opportunity to build relational capabilities, which implies reduced liabilities of outsidership associated with foreign ownership and control (Mithani, 2017).

The collection of papers included in this volume provides a broad overview of the effects of crises and disruptions on internationally operating firms. These effects include not only heightened exposure to risks, but also opportunities for capability deployment and augmentation. The various chapters highlight how MNEs' geographic diversification brings higher exposure to crises and disruptions, but also opens up new pathways for crafting and deploying location-bound and internationally transferable capabilities.

Volume Content: Conceptualizing Crises and Disruptions in International Business

The *JIBS* articles included in this volume were selected because they highlight common challenges arising from MNEs' exposure to crises and disruptions, as well as the management and outcomes thereof. Each chapter included in this volume represents a step forward towards advancing our understanding of how MNEs are affected differently than domestic firms by crises and disruptions. The insightful Commentaries accompanying each chapter deliver forward-looking ideas to augment extant international business theory and practice.

We organized this volume into six distinct Parts. With the exception of the *Introduction* (Part I) and the *Conclusions* chapter (Part VI), each Part contains two original *JIBS* articles on a particular topic published between 2005 and 2020. Each *JIBS* article is followed by a Commentary from one or more experts. These experts provide a fresh, contemporary perspective on the specific crisis and disruption examined in the original article. In some cases, we invited one or more authors of the original *JIBS* article to reflect on their own work with future research directions in mind.

As Editors of this volume, we reflected carefully on which *JIBS* articles to include. We used several criteria to select the articles, including quantitative measures of impact such as the total citation count and the total citation count per year, as well as several qualitative elements. First, we wanted each article to represent a distinct approach to examining either the *behavior* of MNEs around crises and disruptions or the performance *outcomes* thereof. Second, we wanted to include articles that address a type of crisis relevant to the challenges facing MNEs today such as climate change, political unrest or the Covid-19 pandemic. Third, we recognized the need to acknowledge diversity and context in our selection. For instance, the way in which MNEs manage a political conflict may be very different in a developed market versus a developing one. Overall, the studies in our volume focus on different empirical contexts and timelines within which different types of crises and disruptions unfolded.

Part II (Chaps. 2, 3, 4, 5 and 6) addresses specifically the political dimension of crises and disruptions and how pressures from different stakeholders have the potential to influence MNE responses. In their Commentary on Chap. 2, "Speculation in international crises: Report from the Gulf", by Weiner (2005), W. Travis Selmier and Chang Hoon Oh argue that it is important to recognize how organizations – in their analysis, oil MNEs – may or may not benefit from crises (in the article the focus was mainly on the Gulf crisis). At the same time, the authors of the commentary point out that the economic, technological, and social environments of firms have changed since the 2005 *JIBS* article was published. There may be stronger macro-level institutions, better access to markets, and more professional corporate risk management, but, as the commentary highlights, speculative behavior and a variety of exposures have also increased in financial trading and international business. The continued influence of politics on market volatility following a crisis is categorized as important in this respect.

Also in Part II, we delve deeper into how firms respond strategically to political conflict, with Oetzel and Getz's (2012) original *JIBS* article entitled "Why and how might firms respond strategically to political conflict". In Chap. 5, we have the first commentary written by Jennifer Oetzel herself, where she recognizes that research on crises, disruptions, and violent conflict has grown substantially since the article was published. She explains why the greatest challenge to advancing research on managing violence, and crises and political risk more generally, is the need to focus on the managerial mindset around risk rather than on introducing sophisticated methodologies. Oetzel concludes that crises and disruptions can negatively affect MNEs, but MNEs can (intentionally or unintentionally) aggravate conditions that cause crises and disruptions. In Chap. 6, Caroline Witte zooms in on the role of the firm in managing political conflict (the thesis of "peace through commerce"), and on the ways in which conflict may give rise to conflict-profiting firms. It appears that insider firms can benefit significantly from conflict by engaging in informal government deals to secure licenses and valuable resources.

Part III (Chaps. 7, 8, 9 and 10) builds further on the theme of political conflict, with a particular emphasis on the consequences for firms. Lorraine Eden summarizes and augments the insights from Chap. 7, "Place, space, and geographical exposure: Foreign subsidiary survival in conflict zones" by Dai, Eden and Beamish (2013). Her Commentary in Chap. 8 suggests that the research question of how exposure to a conflict zone will influence the stay-versus-exit decision is a multi-disciplinary one, fascinatingly positioned at the crossroads of international business, economic geography, political science, and physics. In Rakesh Sambharya's commentary on Chap. 9, "Impact of historical conflict on FDI location and performance: Japanese investment in China", by Gao, Wang and Che (2018), Sambharya also points to the theoretical complexity required to understand crises and disruptions. He specifically suggests that the risks MNEs are exposed to when internationalizing, are often interdependent. Sambharya offers a number of ideas around a multidimensional conceptualization of risk. For example, he explains how different types of risks (political, economic, technological, ecological) have become interdependent due to the globalization of finance, the spread of information technology, and the growth of international trade along with deregulation and privatization.

In Part IV (Chaps. 11, 12, 13 and 14), we shift focus towards a different type of crisis and disruption, namely that resulting from climate change and the related exposure incurred by MNEs. In Chap. 12, Ans Kolk and Francesca Ciulli offer an updated view on the effects of climate change on firm strategy and capability development, initially discussed in the original *JIBS* article by Ans Kolk and Jonatan Pinkse (2008), entitled "A perspective on multinational enterprises and climate change: learning from 'an inconvenient truth'". Kolk and Ciulli consider how MNEs may aggravate the problem of climate change versus bringing solutions to it. They also discuss how the issue can affect MNE strategies, performance and growth. Specifically, the authors connect the concept of firm-specific advantages (FSAs) developed in their original *JIBS* article to the business model construct. They conceptualize firm-level resources in terms of a business model-related specific advantage (BMSA). "Green" FSAs, they argue, may not only be embedded in a specific technology or narrow capability, but can also encompass a "configuration" of activities. Next, in Chap. 14, Martina Linnenluecke offers a Commentary on the article entitled "The impact of climate risk on firm performance and financing choices: An international comparison" by Huang, Kerstein and Wang (2018). In her Commentary, Linnenluecke seeks to advance the debate on climate risk, *inter alia* by highlighting the need to develop better and more consistent methods to empirically examine climate change risk and to reduce the prediction uncertainty of current modelling techniques.

In Part V (Chaps. 15, 16, 17 and 18), we discuss some of the ways in which MNEs may seek to adapt and gain legitimacy in host markets. In Chap. 16, Murad Mithani discusses the questions that remained unanswered in his original *JIBS* article published in 2017 and entitled, "Liability of foreignness, natural disasters, and corporate philanthropy". These include the need to understand how crises introduce changes in societies and value systems, the nature and modalities of informal groups that emerge in the event of a crisis, and the extent to which foreign (or domestic) firms' participation in recovery and relief efforts may be informed by moral versus economic considerations. In Chap. 18, Kamel Mellahi and David Collings comment on the *JIBS* editorial "International HRM insights for navigating the COVID-19 pandemic: Implications for future research and practice" by Caligiuri, De Cieri, Minbaeva, Verbeke and Zimmermann (2020). The authors of the commentary praise the article's review of the relevant literature on international HRM practice themes such as the selection, training and employee support; management of health and safety; international leadership in MNEs; virtual international collaboration; and global talent management. Importantly, the commentators emphasize the importance of focusing not just on tactical responses to a crisis such as the COVID-19 pandemic. Current HR responses are recognized to have resulted in temporary fixes to immediate challenges, while at the same time, such responses are unlikely to represent effective, long term solutions.

Finally, in Part VI (Chap. 19) of this volume, we included an important contribution by Jonathan Doh and Mirko Benischke that takes a 'big picture' view of the subject and key themes included in this volume. Doh and Benischke recognize that one recurring theme in research on crises and disruptions relates to the varying uses of the constructs of "risk" and "uncertainty". They find that studies vary in their conceptualization of the relationship between risk and uncertainty, with the main difference being whether risk and uncertainty are (or should be) treated as separate constructs or not. In this concluding chapter, the authors introduce and discuss their framework for consideration of crises and disruptions through the lens of risk and uncertainty.

References

Abadie, A., & Gardeazabal, J. (2003). The economic costs of conflict: A case study of the Basque Country. *American Economic Review*, 113–132.

Andriani, P., & McKelvey, B. (2007). Beyond Gaussian averages: Redirecting international business and management research toward extreme events and power laws. *Journal of International Business Studies, 38*, 1212–1230.

Brounen, D., & Derwall, J. (2010). The impact of terrorist attacks on international stock markets: The impact of terrorist attacks on international stock markets. *European Financial Management, 16*(4), 585–598.

Dai, L., Eden, L., & Beamish, P. W. (2013). Place, space, and geographical exposure: Foreign subsidiary survival in conflict zones. *Journal of International Business Studies, 44*(6), 554–578.

Green, L. V., & Kolesar, P. J. (2004). Improving emergency responsiveness with management science. *Management Science, 50*(8), 1001–1014.

Hällgren, M., Rouleau, L., & De Rond, M. (2018). A matter of life or death: How extreme context research matters for management and organization studies. *Academy of Management Annals, 12*(1), 111–153.

Helleiner, E. (2011). Understanding the 2007–2008 global financial crisis: Lessons for scholars of international political economy. *Annual Review of Political Science, 14*(1), 67–87.

Henisz, W. J., & Zelner, B. A. (2010). The hidden risks in emerging markets. *Harvard Business Review, 88*(4), 88–95.

Khanna, T., & Palepu, K. G. (2013). *Winning in emerging markets: A road map for strategy and execution*. Harvard Business Press.

McKnight, B., & Linnenluecke, M. K. (2019). Patterns of firm responses to different types of natural disasters. *Business & Society, 58*(4), 813–840.

McNutt, M., & Leshner, A. (2013). Preparing for disasters. *Science, 341*(6146), 592–592.

Meyer, A. D. (1982). Adapting to environmental jolts. *Administrative Science Quarterly*, 515–537.

Mithani, M. A. (2017). Liability of foreignness, natural disasters, and corporate philanthropy. *Journal of International Business Studies, 48*(8), 941–963.

Muller, A., & Whiteman, G. (2009). Exploring the geography of corporate philanthropic disaster response: A study of fortune global 500 firms. *Journal of Business Ethics, 84*(4), 589–603.

Oh, C. H., & Oetzel, J. (2011). Multinationals' response to major disasters: How does subsidiary investment vary in response to the type of disaster and the quality of country governance? *Strategic Management Journal, 32*(6), 658–681.

Quarantelli, E. L. (1988). Disaster crisis management: A summary of research findings. *Journal of Management Studies, 25*(4), 373–385.

Quarantelli, E. L. (2000). Disaster research. In H. E. F. Borgatta & R. J. V. Montgomery (Eds.), *Encyclopedia of sociology* (2nd ed., pp. 681–688). Macmillan.

Un, C. A. (2016). The liability of localness in innovation. *Journal of International Business Studies, 47*(1), 44–67.

Wang, S. L., & Li, D. (2019). Responding to public disclosure of corporate social irresponsibility in host countries: Information control and ownership control. *Journal of International Business Studies, 50*, 1283–1309.

Weick, K. E. (1993). The collapse of sensemaking in organizations: The Mann Gulch disaster. *Administrative Science Quarterly*, 628–652.

Zhang, J., & Luo, X. R. (2013). Dared to care: Organizational vulnerability, institutional logics, and MNCs' social responsiveness in emerging markets. *Organization Science, 24*(6), 1742–1764.

Part II

Multi-Stakeholder Pressures and Political Conflict

2

Speculation in International Crises: Report from the Gulf

Robert J. Weiner

Introduction

Globalization has been associated with a variety of controversies and discontents, but none so dramatic as the financial crises that have become a feature of the international landscape. Just as MNEs have received scrutiny for labor and environmental practices, so too have traders and speculators become targets of government officials and the antiglobalization

Accepted by Lorraine Eden, Department Editor, 21 December 2004. This paper has been with the author for two revisions.

R. J. Weiner (✉)
International Business Department, George Washington University, Washington, DC, USA

GREEN (Group de Recherche en Économie de l'Énergie et des Ressources Naturelles), Département d'économique, Université Laval, Québec, QC, Canada
e-mail: rweiner@gwu.edu

M. A. Mithani et al. (eds.), *Crises and Disruptions in International Business*, JIBS Special Collections, https://doi.org/10.1007/978-3-030-80383-4_2

movement for causing, or at least exacerbating, market turmoil in these crises.

Buckley and Ghauri (2004, 81) suggest that globalization is one of the 'big questions which arise from empirical developments in the world economy' on which IB research should focus. The IB literature focuses on implications of globalization in two areas:

1. MNEs' competitive strategies (recent examples include: Ghemawat, 2003; Buckley & Ghauri, 2004; Rugman & Verbeke, 2004); and
2. interactions between MNEs and nation-states (see, e.g., the papers collected in the Symposium on 'Multinationals: The Janus Face of Globalization', 2001).

In contrast, discussion of globalization of financial markets in the IB literature is sparse (e.g., Foerster & Karolyi, 1993; Ghemawat, 2003).[1] The body of IB research that examines market turmoil in particular is surprisingly limited, despite the fact that economic and financial crises exemplify Buckley's 'key empirical factors in the global economy which need to be explained' (Buckley, 2002, 370) that have motivated successful research in international business. The small literature focuses on the *effects* of volatility (e.g., Miller & Reuer, 1998; Glaum et al., 2000; Pantzalis et al., 2001).

Speculation has been neglected in IB research, despite its prevalence in international markets, and the concerns regarding its role in financial crises. Speculator behavior tends to be difficult to observe and explain, making it a ready scapegoat for fundamental problems. Notwithstanding its neglect in the IB literature, speculation as a *cause* of volatility has attracted unfavorable attention from policymakers and the public as sources of instability in the international financial system.

Speculators, particularly hedge funds, have been blamed in several crises, including the worldwide stock market crash of October 1987, the

---

[1] In contrast to IB, there is an active literature in economics on financial globalization. This literature, however, focuses primarily on measurement of international capital mobility, and integration of LDCs into the international financial system, with attendant increased volatility of capital flows (see the recent survey in Schmukler, 2004). Obstfeld and Taylor (2003) provide historical perspectives on financial globalization.

Gulf Crisis of 1990–91, the breakdown of the European Exchange Rate Mechanism (ERM) in 1992–93, the Tequila crisis and the Asian financial crisis of the 1990s, and the Russian crisis and collapse of LTCM of 1998. For example, the Prime Minister of Malaysia was widely quoted as blaming the Asian crisis on foreign speculators, and restricted trading of the Malaysian ringgit (Mahathir, 1997).

Derivative instruments (swaps, options, futures, etc.) have been singled out as particularly damaging, as they facilitate speculation by reducing its cost (see, e.g., Hill, 2003), and have been a lightning rod for criticism during periods of market volatility, particularly in the cases of the stock market crash, the ERM breakdown, the Asian crisis, and the LTCM collapse. Little research has been undertaken, however, on the role of derivatives in exacerbating or ameliorating crises.[2]

In principle, speculation could either exacerbate or dampen market volatility arising from changes in supply and demand. In practice, disentangling the effects of trading and changes in fundamentals is difficult. For example, in the foreign-exchange (FX) market, controversy has been generated by a 'Tobin Tax' on speculative activity, proposed by Nobel-prize winner James Tobin with the objective of reducing FX trading through 'throwing sand in the wheels of international finance' (Eichengreen et al., 1995; ul Haq et al., 1996).[3]

This paper contrasts with the small IB literature noted above by examining the *causes* of market volatility, rather than its *effects*. The objective of the paper is to assess what role, if any, trading played in contributing to, or even causing, market volatility The paper presents a case study[4] of the Gulf Conflict of 1990–91 (referred to as the 'Gulf Crisis' below), when the Iraqi invasion of Kuwait, and Operations Desert Shield (stationing of

[2] Dodd (2002) discusses derivatives in the Asian crisis, concluding that 'Derivatives played a key role in the East Asian financial crisis of 1997… derivatives first made the economy more susceptible to financial crisis and then quickened and deepened the downturn once the crisis began' (p. 447), but provides no empirical evidence or analysis. Ghysels and Seon (2005) examine the crash of the Korean stock market during the Asian crisis, focusing on the role of index futures trading on the Korean Stock Exchange.

[3] Similarly, Shiller (2000, 2003) claims that equity markets demonstrate 'massive excess volatility' (2003, 14) as a result of the 'irrational exuberance' of speculators.

[4] Shenkar (2004, 168) suggests the use of case-study methodology as a research strategy in rejuvenating IB's contributions to knowledge as a field.

foreign troops in the Middle East under UN aegis) and Desert Storm (air attack on Iraq, and subsequent ground war, by the United States (US) and its allies) made front-page news for several months.

Over the course of the Crisis, the price of crude oil roughly doubled (from around $20 per barrel to around $40) and then returned to its initial level. Oil-price volatility reached unprecedented levels, yet changes in underlying market fundamentals were not readily apparent. The 'derivatives trading causes volatility theory' was widely advanced during the Crisis, motivating proposals for closing the petroleum derivatives markets, analogous to the US shutdown of wheat trading for a 'cooling-off' period after the Soviet grain embargo in 1980, and the German shutdown of futures trading to reduce market volatility in 1897–1900.

The Gulf Crisis is a natural experiment for scrutinizing trading and volatility, for several reasons. First, it sheds light on the relationships between political conflict and international markets, a subject that has not received much attention in IB research, despite renewed interest since the 11 September 2001 terrorist attacks, as well as the Iraq conflict. Second, the Gulf Crisis's primary impact was on the world oil market, where supply and demand fundamentals are more straightforward than for markets such as FX and stocks, where valuation is more complex. For example, it is difficult to know when trading may be influencing currency values, as existing models are limited in their ability to relate currency valuation to the underlying fundamentals (Hopper, 1997). Third, the crisis has a well-defined and unanticipated start and end, unlike the conflict in Iraq, yielding an unusually clean natural experiment. Finally, the geographical dimension of the conflict is critical to disentangling the role of speculation, which makes for a nice fit with the strengths of IB research.

In addition to providing a natural laboratory for examining market behavior in a crisis, the oil market is of interest in IB in its own right. Petroleum is the largest single item by value in international trade, accounting for 5–20% of world trade in the last three decades.[5] Governments play a major role in the oil sector, from ownership of

[5] Figures exclude intra-FSU trade. The share of petroleum in total trade is closely related to oil prices, and thus can fluctuate greatly from year to year. See International Monetary Fund (various years) for trade data, and Oil and Gas Journal (1995) for petroleum data. Petroleum reached 39% of US imports in 1980, falling to about 5% by the mid-1990s.

reserves, to regulation, to management of petroleum SOEs, to foreign policy, raising political economy issues (see, e.g., Makhija, 1993). Oil is closely related to the economic health of many nations, and its importance was offered as a justification for military intervention in the Gulf Crisis.

Historically, oil-price volatility has substantially exceeded that of interest rates, exchange rates, and most other commodities in international trade. Oil-price shocks have been followed by recessions in the industrialized countries and oil-importing LDCs.[6] To the extent that speculation contributed to market turmoil, the actions of speculators can have far-reaching consequences.

The remainder of this paper is organized as follows. The next section provides a brief account of the Gulf Crisis, focusing on oil-market behavior. Following that, we present the empirical approach, and then report the results from applying it to the Gulf Crisis. Finally, conclusions and implications for international business are offered.

The Gulf Crisis: A Brief Nonmilitary Account[7]

On 2 August 1990, Iraq invaded its neighbor Kuwait, setting off the Gulf Crisis. As part of the diplomatic response to the invasion, the United Nations embargoed oil exports from the two countries, resulting in a supply disruption of 4.3 million barrels per day (mmbd), at the time equivalent to roughly 8% of oil consumption outside the former communist bloc (which was largely insulated from the world oil market).

Because of oil already loaded and transit times on the order of a month from the Gulf to refining centers, the full supply disruption did not register until September 1990. Increased production from other oil-exporting countries rapidly reduced the magnitude of the disruption,

[6] See Jones and Kaul (1996) on the impact of oil price shocks on Canada, Japan, the UK, and the USA.

[7] This brief account of the Gulf Crisis focuses on aspects salient to the oil market. General diplomatic, military, political, and economic aspects of the Crisis are widely available in the popular press (e.g., Ridgeway, 1991), and will be touched upon here only insofar as they influenced the market.

however, and then offset it. The US Energy Information Administration estimated the size of the disruption as 3.4 mmbd in September 1990, 0.7 mmbd in October 1990, and close to zero thereafter (US Energy Information Administration, 1990).

The fall of 1990 was characterized by diplomatic efforts to resolve the Crisis through persuading the Iraqi government to remove its army from Kuwait, by a major military build-up by the US and its allies in the Middle East, and by threats of force on both sides. Despite last-minute efforts to negotiate a settlement, diplomacy eventually failed. Allied military intervention in the Crisis commenced with air strikes on 16 January 1991. The ground war started on 24 February 1991. A unilateral cease fire was declared by the allies on 28 February 1991.

Figure 2.1 displays crude-oil prices for the period 1989–91.[8] Despite the relatively brief duration of the disruption, oil prices climbed dramatically, jumping about 10% on the news of the invasion on 2 August, and reached a maximum of $41.10 per barrel (an increase of almost 100%)

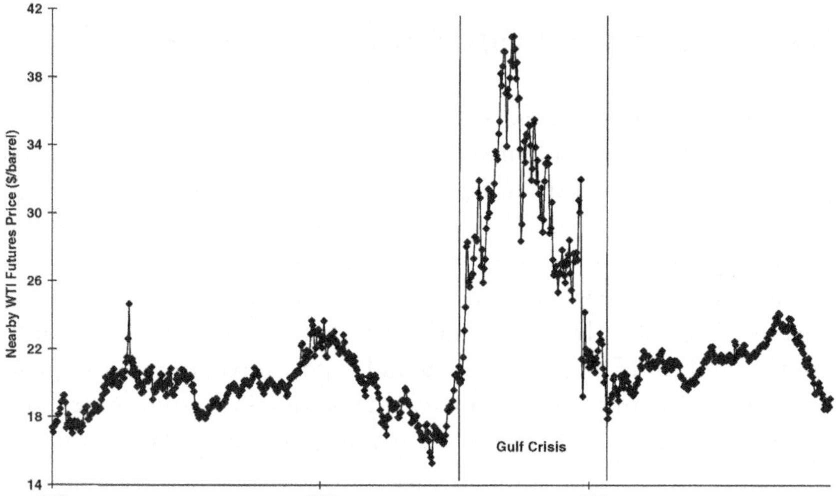

Fig. 2.1 Crude-oil prices, 1989–91

[8] Shown are closing prices on the New York Mercantile Exchange for the nearby WTI crude oil futures contract. These prices and spot prices are virtually identical as a result of delivery logistics.

on 11 October. On 29 November, the UN Security Council approved a resolution authorizing the use of force if Iraq did not withdraw from Kuwait by 15 January; crude-oil prices fell more than $4 per barrel the next day. When the air war broke out, oil prices fell about one-third in a single day, bringing them back to pre-invasion levels.

The widespread availability of, and active trading in, derivative markets is what sets the Gulf Crisis apart from earlier oil supply shocks; by 1990, crude oil traded on the New York Mercantile Exchange (NYMEX) had become the world's most active futures contract outside of purely financial instruments.[9]

The controversial issues raised by derivatives trading and oil-price behavior during the Crisis are several. Why did crude-oil futures prices rise so rapidly, and to such a high level, when the physical supply disruption itself was relatively modest? Why did prices decline so sharply in the middle of the Crisis? How can the unprecedented volatility in the oil market be explained? Was the presence of derivatives trading responsible for this volatility? Or was there underlying volatility present in the market, which was exacerbated by derivatives trading? Or did derivatives markets mitigate, or have no effect on underlying price volatility?[10]

Derivatives Trading and Oil-Price Volatility in the Gulf Crisis: Empirical Approach

The question of the role of the trading process in market stability is an old one. During financial crises, derivatives trading activity rises. Trading could be a response to increased volatility, as market participants attempt

[9] Although NYMEX introduced heating-oil contracts in 1978 and crude-oil contracts in 1983, futures trading was negligible during the Iran shock of 1978–80 and oil price collapse in early 1986.

[10] As in earlier shocks, the behavior of oil prices during the Gulf Crisis generated considerable controversy, but relatively little scholarly research. Foster (1996) compared price adjustment in spot and futures markets. Malliaris and Urrutia (1995) examined the impact on international stock prices. Melick and Thomas (1997) looked at market expectations regarding likely future price behavior. For research on earlier oil shocks, see, for example, Frankel (1958) on the Suez Crisis; Vernon (1976), Verleger (1979, 1982), Badger (1984), and Adelman (1995) on the shocks of the 1970s; and Gately (1986) and Weiner (1994) on the 1986 price collapse.

to hedge or speculate, but it could also exacerbate the volatility arising from shifts in underlying fundamentals.

Critics of derivatives markets have pointed to the enormous price spike that accompanied the Gulf Crisis (see Fig. 2.1), despite the fact that the lost production was quickly made up from other sources, as discussed above. The critics' view is that most, if not all, of the price run-up was due to speculation on derivatives markets. Such views are widespread,[11] and the basic intuition is straightforward.

The presence of derivatives markets makes speculation less expensive. In the oil crises of the 1970s and 1980s, speculation on oil-price changes entailed buying and storing physical cargoes, and selling them at a later time. With derivatives markets, one need only buy 'paper barrels', and pay only a part of the cost ('margin'), which opens up speculation to many more participants. If the speculators who enter the market as a result of the reduced cost of trading are less knowledgeable about market fundamentals than those already in the market, the result can be increased price volatility.[12]

Over the last decade, researchers have addressed this question by comparing price volatility for a given asset, typically measured by standard deviations of returns, between periods when the exchange is open and closed. The idea behind this methodology is straightforward, and runs as follows. There are two types of reason why asset prices might fluctuate. The first is 'news' – shorthand for the arrival into the market of new information regarding future supply and demand fundamentals.

For example, if Iraq had invaded Saudi Arabia, a supply disruption of unprecedented magnitude would very likely have ensued. In anticipation of the future reduction in supply, inventories would have been built up, resulting in an immediate price increase. Such a price increase would fall into the category of response to news about market fundamentals, and would occur irrespective of the presence of derivatives markets.

[11] Many of the experts who submitted testimony to the US Senate hearings on the Gulf Crisis shared this view, as did the senators at the hearings. See US Senate (1991).

[12] The literature refers to such uninformed speculators as 'noise traders'. See the Spring 1990 issue of the *Journal of Economic Perspectives*, especially Flood and Hodrick (1990) and Shleifer and Summers (1990).

The second possible source of price fluctuation is the trading process itself. If speculators drive prices up and down as a result of their trading activity, then volatility need not be the result of news (see, e.g., Black, 1986). Two possible channels for the trading process to affect volatility can be consistent with rational behavior. The first is 'noise trading', based on extrapolation of past price trends (a popular trading strategy, known as 'technical analysis', or 'charting'), rather than on anticipated changes in market fundamentals. The second is 'herding', wherein less-informed traders attempt to watch better-informed traders, and to copy their trading strategies. Either case may lead to periodic 'contagion' or 'stampedes', wherein a large group of traders all attempt to move in the same direction at the same time, resulting in increased price volatility.[13]

Of course, these two sources need not be mutually exclusive; most derivatives market detractors claim not that the trading process creates volatility out of thin air, but rather that it exacerbates volatility arising from changes in fundamentals. The empirical approach below compares price volatility during periods when exchanges are open, and thus both news and trading effects are present, with periods when they are closed, so that only the news effect is present. If the news effect is the same during trading and non-trading periods, then any observed differences in volatility can be ascribed to the trading process itself.[14]

This methodology can be applied to prices of crude-oil futures contracts to shed light on the issue addressed in this paper – the role of derivatives trading in the oil-price shock attending the Gulf Crisis. This section compares the volatility of WTI crude-oil prices during the period when the NYMEX is open for trading crude-oil futures – 9:45 AM to

[13] Decomposition of asset prices into 'news' and 'noise' was introduced in the FX market by Frenkel (1981). For an assessment of trading rules based on technical analysis in the crude oil futures market, see Dominguez (1991). Shleifer and Summers (1990) and Flood and Hodrick (1990) provide an introduction to the finance literature on noise trading. Herding behavior is surveyed in Devenow and Welch (1996). Evidence on herding in oil futures markets is presented in Weiner (2002).

[14] French and Roll (1986) were the first to use this approach: examining US stock prices over the period 1963–82, they found the variance of daily returns much higher when the stock exchanges were open than over weekends and holidays. Results from a variety of market settings generally support their findings: there is a consensus in the literature that asset-price volatility, at least for the case of stock and currency markets, is substantially greater during periods when trading takes place than during non-trading periods (overnight, weekends, holidays, and business days or parts thereof when the relevant exchange is closed).

3:10 PM Eastern time, Monday through Friday, except holidays – with price volatility when the exchange is closed.[15]

The methodology is particularly effective here due to geography. During a supply shock, news about market fundamentals is associated primarily with possible changes in oil production and exports, rather than consumption, which adjusts gradually. Thus, during the Gulf Crisis, news was most likely to be coming out of the Middle East, whether in the form of actions or threats thereof by Iraq or the allies, or of oil-related or military announcements in Saudi Arabia, or of effects upon the Kuwaiti oil sector. For example, the Iraqi invasion of Kuwait, the allied air attack, the start of the ground war, and the ceasefire, all occurred either at night or over the weekend, while the NYMEX was closed.

Because of time differences with the US East Coast (Riyadh, Baghdad, and Kuwait City are 7 h ahead of New York in the summer, 8 h ahead in the winter), news from the Gulf was almost certain to arrive in the oil market while the NYMEX was closed. News released during normal business hours in the Gulf will not overlap with NYMEX trading hours.[16] Daytime (i.e., when the exchange is open) price fluctuations during the Gulf Crisis can be associated primarily with the trading process, and overnight fluctuations with news. This leads to a straightforward way to test the effect of trading on price volatility: simply compare open-to-close and close-to-open return variance. The greater the ratio of trading-time to non-trading-time variance, the greater the contribution of trading to price volatility.[17]

---

[15] Eastern time is 5 h behind GMT; the last Sunday in October through the first Sunday in April, 4 h behind the rest of the year. After-hours electronic trading, which would complicate the analysis, started well after this period.

[16] Business hours in the Gulf vary some by country and season, but government ministries, which are open Saturday through Wednesday, plus a half-day Thursday, close at latest by 3 pm in Iraq, 2 pm in Saudi Arabia, and 1:30 pm in Kuwait. Shops reopen in the early evening after afternoon prayers, but government ministries and banks do not.

[17] If some news reaches traders while the exchange is open, this should not affect the validity of the approach, which depends on the comparison between exchange trading and non-trading hours. Note also that existence of price limits (trading halts when prices move sharply in a single day) on all futures contracts except the nearby will tend to bias comparisons of daytime and nighttime volatility, making the former appear too small, and the latter, too large. To avoid this problem, a list of days on which price limits were reached was obtained from NYMEX. When the closing price on a contract represents a limit move, that contract's day-return and the succeeding night-return were

Results

Table 2.1 presents a comparison of trading-time and overnight volatility of futures prices, broken down by time period. Price volatility is measured in the same way as in the studies in the literature discussed

Table 2.1 Intraday volatility results

Contract maturity (number of observations)	Standard deviation of daytime return[a]	Standard deviation of nighttime return[a]	Variance ratio: day/night	Robust F-test
Pre-Crisis: 1 January 1989–1 August 1990				
One (398,397)[b]	1.80	0.82	4.80[c]	141[c]
Two (397,396)	1.45	0.79	3.32[c]	99[c]
Three (397,396)	1.34	0.72	3.52[c]	98[c]
Four (398,397)	1.27	0.67	3.61[c]	96[c]
Five (398,397)	1.24	0.62	3.96[c]	99[c]
Six (399,398)	1.21	0.62	3.80[c]	84[c]
Crisis & War: 2 August 1990–28 February 1991				
One (143,142)	3.71	3.13	1.40	3.20
Two (120,112)	3.06	2.69	1.29	0.94
Three (118,110)	2.81	2.31	1.47[d]	1.94
Four (122,116)	2.76	3.41	0.65[d]	0.07
Five (126,122)	2.69	3.42	0.62[c]	0.00
Six (127,122)	2.69	3.19	0.71	0.04
Immediate Aftermath: 1 March 1991–31 December 1991				
One (212,212)	1.26	0.93	1.83[c]	25[c]
Two (212,212)	1.21	0.88	1.91[c]	26[c]
Three (212,212)	1.11	0.80	1.92[c]	28[c]
Four (212,212)	1.04	0.76	1.86[c]	27[c]
Five (212,212)	0.99	0.73	1.85[c]	26[c]
Six (212,212)	0.95	0.61	2.41[c]	30[c]

[a]Standard deviations in percent per day
[b](Number of intraday returns, number of overnight returns) in sample period
[c]Significantly different from one at 1% level, two-tailed test. F-test critical points are 0.62, 1.61. Robust F-test critical points are 3.94 (5%) and 6.90 (1%)
[d]Significantly different from one at 5% level, two-tailed test. F-test critical points are 0.70, 1.43

dropped from the calculations. If in addition the limit on that day was reached at the opening price, the contract's preceding night-return was dropped as well.

above – standard deviations of returns, that is, percentage change in prices.[18] The hypothesis that trading is the main source of price volatility implies that returns should be more variable during the daytime, when the exchange is open, than at night, when it is closed. As measured in this paper, the standard deviation of daytime returns should exceed that of overnight returns.

To ascertain whether the oil market behaved abnormally during the Crisis, the return calculations were performed for the period before the Crisis and the period immediately following the Crisis, as well as for the Crisis period itself. In order to keep the lengths of the various periods of the same order of magnitude, the pre-Crisis period was taken somewhat arbitrarily as starting at the beginning of 1989, rather than from the beginning of NYMEX crude-oil trading in March 1983. The immediate aftermath period extends through the end of 1991.[19]

Table 2.1 presents the key results of this paper. For the first- through sixth-month contracts (the ones with virtually all of the futures-market liquidity), the table displays the standard deviations of daytime and nighttime returns for three non-overlapping periods: pre-Crisis, Crisis & War, and Immediate Aftermath. The table also displays in parentheses the number of observations on which the calculations are based.

As shown in the table, prices were more volatile during trading hours *before* the Crisis started. For example, the standard deviations of returns on the nearby contract were 1.80% per day during trading hours, and only 0.82% per day during non-trading hours. Note also that volatility tends to decline with contract length, indicating mean-reversion – market participants expect the effects of shocks to diminish over time.[20]

The rightmost columns of the table provide significance figures necessary to test whether the daytime and nighttime returns are likely to be truly different, or just differ due to random chance. If intraday and overnight returns are normally distributed, then the ratio of sample variances has an F distribution with $n_{\text{day}^{-1}}$ and $n_{\text{night}^{-1}}$ degrees of freedom, where

[18] This paper follows the literature by measuring returns as logarithmic price relatives, rather than literal percentage changes.

[19] The 3-year period following the immediate aftermath was also examined, but the results are nearly identical to the immediate aftermath, and are not reported here.

[20] See Schwartz (1997) on mean reversion, which is typical of commodity prices.

n_{day} and n_{night} are the number of intraday and overnight returns, respectively, in each sample period.

The F-test will reject the null hypothesis of equal daytime and nighttime price variance, if the ratio of the sample daytime and nighttime variances is too high or too low relative to tabulated critical values, which are provided in the footnotes to the table.[21] During the pre-Crisis period, the variance of daytime returns was 4.8 times that of nighttime returns for the nearby contract. We can be (far) more than 99% sure that this difference is statistically significant (i.e., not due to random factors), because 4.8 (greatly) exceeds the 1% critical value of 1.61.

During the Crisis & War period, return standard deviations more than doubled, reflecting the increased volatility in the market. Note, however, that nighttime volatility increased far more than daytime volatility, so much more, in fact, that daytime volatility became *less* than nighttime volatility for the fourth- through sixth-month contracts. During the Crisis, return variability was about the same during trading and non-trading hours. For the immediate aftermath period, the pattern is the same as the pre-Crisis period; daytime returns are more volatile, at a high level of statistical significance.

Likely deviations from normality, however, imply that these F-tests are probably biased towards rejection of the null hypothesis of equal daytime and nighttime variances. The empirical literature suggests that asset returns tend to be leptokurtic, that is, have distributions heavier-tailed than the normal. Thus, Table 2.1 also presents results from the Brown–Forsythe modified Levene robust F-test, based on mean absolute deviations from sample medians.[22] The results of the robust F-test are stronger than those for the ordinary F-test: daytime variance exceeds nighttime variance, with high statistical significance in both the

---

[21] Because the variance is the square of the standard deviation, the 'variance ratio' column of the table is obtained by squaring the ratio of the figures in the two columns to the left; for example, $(1.80/0.82)^2 = 4.80$.

[22] See the discussion and references in Lockwood and Linn (1990), who indicate that, in experiments with various methods of testing for heteroskedasticity, the Brown–Forsythe modified Levene test is 'among the most powerful and is robust regarding departure of the underlying data from normality.' This test was the most powerful when the underlying data were generated from leptokurtic distributions. The test statistic is:

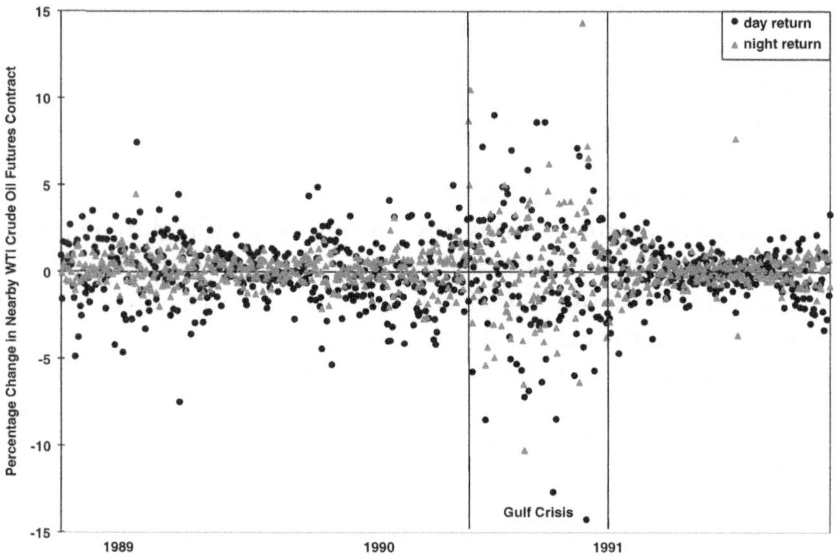

Fig. 2.2 Daytime and nighttime returns, 1989–91

pre-Crisis and post-War periods. In sharp contrast, there are no significant differences in daytime and nighttime variance during the Crisis & War period.

Figure 2.2 plots daytime and nighttime returns over the 1989–91 period, which serves to illustrate these volatility patterns. Both before and after the Crisis, the points representing daytime returns tend to lie

---

$$F_{\text{robust}} = \left[\frac{n_{\text{day}} \left(D^*_{\text{day}} - D^* \right)^2 + n_{\text{night}} \left(D^*_{\text{night}} - D^* \right)^2}{\sum_i \left(D_{i,\text{day}} - D^*_{\text{day}} \right)^2 + \sum_i \left(D_{i,\text{night}} - D^*_{\text{night}} \right)^2} \right] \times (n-2)$$

where subscripts indexing contracts and time period have been omitted for clarity of presentation, $D_{i,\text{day}}=|r_{i,\text{day}}-m_{\text{day}}|$ is the absolute deviation of the return on day i from the median day-return for the contract and period, D_{day}^* is the mean absolute deviation from the median day-return for the period and contract (the night variables are analogous), $n=n_{\text{day}}+n_{\text{night}}$ is the total number of observations for the contract and period, and $D^*=(n_{\text{day}}D_{\text{day}}^*+n_{\text{night}}D_{\text{night}}^*)/n$ is the grand mean absolute deviation. The test statistic F_{robust} is distributed $F_{1,n-2}$.

outside those representing nighttime returns; during the Crisis, in contrast, the points are more dispersed (reflecting the higher volatility level), but no clear pattern is evident.

Conclusion: Interpretation and Implications for International Business

The interpretation of these results is straightforward – futures trading activity contributed *less* to price volatility during the Gulf Crisis than during normal periods. The primary source of market fluctuations was news about fundamentals coming out of the Gulf area while the exchange was closed. For those concerned about the role of derivatives during crises, the evidence is that, at least for the 'case-study Crisis' examined here, derivatives markets worked relatively *better* (in the sense of adding volatility to the market beyond that attributable to movements in supply and demand fundamentals) during the Crisis than before or afterward. Perhaps, during crises news about fundamentals is easier to interpret and loud enough to dominate the typical 'background noise' affecting speculation in derivatives markets.[23]

This conclusion begs a critical question: if the disruption turned out to be small, why then did prices rise so sharply? After all, if the 'fundamentals' of current supply and demand were little changed during the Crisis, and derivatives trading was not responsible for the dramatic price increase and equally steep decline, then what was behind market behavior?

The key is geopolitics – during the Crisis, Iraq tried to exploit its army's entrenched position in Kuwait to pressure Saudi Arabia and other Gulf states to reduce their production and raise prices. These states are large oil producers with small populations, weak militaries, and ill-defined borders. This pressure was consistent with Iraq's previously stated grievances against the Gulf producers for maintaining high production levels and low prices, thereby hindering Iraq's ability to obtain the revenue needed to rebuild after its extended war with Iran during the 1980s. Moreover,

[23] I am grateful to an anonymous referee for this point.

the possibility that the Iraqi military would continue the short distance across the Kuwaiti border into Saudi Arabia could not easily be discounted.

The fact that, in hindsight, UN forces were able to overcome the Iraqi military easily, and to restore the political *status quo ante* in the Gulf, is of limited relevance for analyzing market behavior at the time, when Iraq was viewed as a formidable regional power, with a huge army that had already attacked two of its neighbors in the recent past. Nor could the allies' ability to cooperative effectively in the Gulf have been easily anticipated. Diplomatic and ideological tensions between the US and Soviet Union had for decades constrained East and West in undertaking political and military activity in the Middle East. Furthermore, the US experience in Vietnam, and the desire of Western European countries to maintain good relations with the Arab world, both pointed to reluctance toward extended military action.

Implications for Governments and Multilaterals

The finding that what drives the market during a crisis is news about fundamentals, rather than trading on the exchange, has several implications. First, closing down the market, either for an indefinite time, as supported by some of the critics of derivatives trading in US Senate (1991), or until the implementation of sales from strategic reserves,[24] as suggested by Verleger (1991), would not have served to reduce price volatility.[25]

Second, efforts to reduce volatility must be aimed at influencing market fundamentals, and expectations thereof. For example, an announcement of forthcoming strategic-reserve releases is news of additional future supply. In the case of the Gulf Crisis, however, the International Energy

[24] OECD countries hold strategic petroleum reserves as part of International Energy Agency membership.

[25] A policy of halting petroleum trading on the NYMEX at the time crude oil prices soared to over $40 per barrel was considered by the CFTC, the US futures regulator (Petroleum Intelligence Weekly, 1990). The finding here echoes that of a 1901 statistical study of the German market shutdown: 'The conditions existent at Berlin during the suspension of the produce exchange … have not imparted greater stability to … prices if, indeed, they have not exercised a deleterious effect…' (quoted in Bakken, 1953, 139).

Agency (the OECD agency that deals with oil crises) and its member governments did just the opposite. The announcement that oil would not be released from government reserves was just as 'newsworthy' as events in the Middle East, signaling to market participants that OECD governments expected the situation in the Gulf to deteriorate, and were holding back their oil against the prospect of reduced future supply.

Implications for Companies

A central determinant of trade and FDI flows is world economic performance. Oil shocks have been closely linked to such performance – for example, all but one of the US recessions since World War II have followed an oil shock (Hamilton, 1983, 2003). Similarly, oil shocks have hurt economic performance in the other large oil-importing OECD countries that are the primary home countries for FDI (Jiménez-Rodríguez & Sánchez, 2004). Oil shocks have also been found to have adverse effects on expected profitability of companies listed on the stock exchanges in the USA, UK, Japan, and Canada, as seen by their negative effect on stock prices (Jones & Kaul, 1996). The start of the Gulf Crisis had negative effects on equity markets in 16 nations in North America, Western Europe, and East Asia (Malliaris & Urrutia, 1995).

Competition in energy-intensive industries (e.g., air freight transport, aluminum, chemicals) is likely to be especially affected by oil shocks, particularly when product prices are fixed in advance, as in air passenger transport. Companies with weak balance sheets may cease to be effective competitors: witness the bankruptcy of Pan American World Airways and Eastern Airlines in the early 1990s. Competition is also likely to be affected in industries where the energy intensity of the product differs greatly among companies: for example, the rise of fuel-efficient Japanese autos in the North American market following the oil shock of the early 1970s.

Turning to political economy, oil shocks may affect the bargaining power of multinational oil companies and governments and state-owned oil companies of oil-exporting countries, especially those considered to be remote from the sources of likely shocks. The efforts by petroleum

MNEs to undertake FDI in West Africa and Central Asia, and the changing terms and incidence of corruption they have encountered, provide good examples.[26]

Given the systemic effects of oil shocks, understanding the factors that cause or exacerbate them is important, both for predicting their occurrence, and for mitigating their effects. The finding that it is fundamentals rather than speculation that drive oil-price volatility implies that companies and governments should focus on these fundamentals, and not seek to blame speculation, or discourage it (*à la* Tobin Tax discussed above).

Conclusion

The continuing dramatic growth and visibility of derivatives markets and speculation has made them natural targets for those seeking to assign responsibility for the crises that regularly appear on the international financial stage. Too often, strong claims and policy proposals are made without supporting analysis. This paper has provided an analytical view of one such crisis, and found that derivatives trading contributed less to market volatility during the crisis than before or afterward. The presence of a market system that works well, properly used, can be a boon to governments and companies in times of crisis.

Acknowledgements I thank Mirna Hussein, Régis Veillet, Gulcin Afres, Emidio Checcone, Marissa Martinez, and Wenyi Xu for able research assistance, three anonymous referees of this journal, Departmental Editor Lorraine Eden, William Hogan, Tim Krehbiel, Henry Lee, Michael Lynch, John Peterson, Richard Schmalensee, Stephen Smith, and participants at the annual meetings of the Academy of International Business, the American Economics Association, the Financial Management Association, the Multinational Finance Society, and the South Dakota International Business Conference, as well as the Ninth International Symposium on Petroleum Economics, Québec, the 10th Journées du GREEN, the FRB Atlanta/Georgia State/Virginia Tech Conference on

[26] Petroleum Intelligence Weekly (2004a, b) discusses recent developments in Kazakhstan and Russia; MNEs' experience in Russia is covered in Considine and Kerr (2002). On West Africa, see Gary and Karl (2003).

Derivatives and Systemic Risk, and the MIT Seminar on Political Economy of Global Energy for comments, the GW Center for the Study of Globalization and the US Department of Energy for support, and the New York Mercantile Exchange for data. Responsibility for the contents of the paper is solely the author's.

References

Adelman, M. A. (1995). *The genie out of the bottle: World oil since 1970*. MIT Press.

Badger, D. B. (1984). The anatomy of a 'minor disruption': Missed opportunities. In A. L. Alm & R. J. Weiner (Eds.), *Oil shock* (pp. 33–53). Ballinger.

Bakken, H. H. (1953). *Theory of markets and marketing*. Mimir.

Black, F. (1986). Noise. *Journal of Finance, 41*(3), 529–543.

Buckley, P. J. (2002). Is the international business research agenda running out of steam? *Journal of International Business Studies, 33*(2), 365–373.

Buckley, P. J., & Ghauri, P. N. (2004). Globalization, economic geography, and the strategy of multinational enterprises. *Journal of International Business Studies, 35*(2), 81–98.

Considine, J. I., & Kerr, W. A. (2002). *The Russian oil economy*. Edward Elgar.

Devenow, A., & Welch, I. (1996). Rational herding in financial economics. *European Economic Review, 40*(3–5), 603–615.

Dodd, R. (2002). The role of derivatives in the east Asian financial crisis. In J. Eatwell & L. Taylor (Eds.), *International capital markets: Systems in Transition* (pp. 447–473). Oxford University Press.

Dominguez, K. M. (1991). Trading strategies in oil financial markets. In K. M. Dominguez, W. W. Hogan, B. Mossavar-Rahmani, G. M. Phillips, & R. J. Weiner (Eds.), *Oil markets in a turbulent era* (pp. 48–97). President and Fellows of Harvard College.

Eichengreen, B., Tobin, J., & Wyplosz, C. (1995). Two cases for sand in the wheels of international finance. *Economic Journal, 105*, 162–172.

Flood, R. P., & Hodrick, R. J. (1990). On testing for speculative bubbles. *Journal of Economic Perspectives, 4*(2), 85–101.

Foerster, S. R., & Karolyi, G. A. (1993). International listings of stocks: The case of Canada and the US. *Journal of International Business Studies, 24*(4), 763–784.

Foster, A. J. (1996). Price discovery in oil markets: A time varying analysis of the 1990–91 Gulf conflict. *Energy Economics, 18*(3), 231–246.

Frankel, P. H. (1958). Oil supplies during the Suez crisis. *Journal of Industrial Economics, 6*(2), 85–100.
French, K. R., & Roll, R. (1986). Stock return variances: The arrival of information and the reaction of traders. *Journal of Financial Economics, 17*(1), 5–26.
Frenkel, J. A. (1981). Flexible exchange rates, prices, and the role of 'news': Lessons from the 1970s. *Journal of Political Economy, 89*(4), 665–705.
Gary, I., & Karl, T. L. (2003). *Bottom of the barrel: Africa's oil boom and the poor.* Catholic Relief Services.
Gately, D. (1986). Lessons from the 1986 oil price collapse. *Brookings Papers on Economic Activity, 2*, 237–271.
Ghemawat, P. (2003). Semiglobalization and international business strategy. *Journal of International Business Studies, 34*(2), 138–152.
Ghysels, E., & Seon, J. (2005). The Asian financial crisis: The role of derivative securities trading and foreign investors in Korea. *Journal of International Money and Finance, 24*(4), 607–630.
Glaum, M., Brunner, M., & Himmel, H. (2000). The DAX and the dollar: The economic exchange rate exposure of German corporations. *Journal of International Business Studies, 31*(4), 715–724.
Hamilton, J. D. (1983). Oil and the macroeconomy since World War II. *Journal of Political Economy, 91*(5), 228–248.
Hamilton, J. D. (2003). What is an oil shock? *Journal of Econometrics, 113*(2), 363–398.
Hill, A. (2003, March 4). Buffett likens derivatives to weapons of mass destruction. *Financial Times*, p. 21.
Hopper, G. P. (1997). What determines the exchange rate: Economic factors or market sentiment? *Federal Reserve Bank of Philadelphia Business Review, September/October*, 17–29.
International Monetary Fund. (various years). *Direction of trade statistics yearbook.*
Jiménez-Rodríguez, R., & Sánchez, M. (2004, May). *Oil price shocks and real GDP growth: Empirical evidence from OECD countries* (European Central Bank Working Paper 362).
Jones, C. M., & Kaul, G. (1996). Oil and the stock markets. *Journal of Finance, 51*(2), 463–491.
Lockwood, L. J., & Linn, S. C. (1990). An examination of stock market return volatility during overnight and intraday periods, 1964–1989. *Journal of Finance, 45*(2), 591–601.
Mahathir, M. (1997). Highwaymen of the global economy. *The Wall Street Journal, 23*(September), A22.

Makhija, M. V. (1993). Government intervention in the Venezuelan petroleum industry: An empirical investigation of political risk. *Journal of International Business Studies, 24*(3), 531–555.

Malliaris, A. G., & Urrutia, J. L. (1995). The impact of the Persian Gulf crisis on national equity markets. *Advances in International Banking and Finance, 1*, 43–65.

Melick, W. R., & Thomas, C. P. (1997). Recovering an asset's implied PDF from option prices: An application to crude oil during the Gulf crisis. *Journal of Financial and Quantitative Analysis, 32*(1), 91–115.

Miller, K. R., & Reuer, J. J. (1998). Firm strategy and economic exposure to foreign exchange rate movements. *Journal of International Business Studies, 29*(3), 469–492.

Obstfeld, M., & Taylor, A. M. (2003). Globalization and capital markets. In M. D. Bordo, A. M. Taylor, & J. G. Williamson (Eds.), *Globalization in historical perspective*. University of Chicago Press.

Oil and Gas Journal. (1995). *Energy statistics sourcebook* (10th ed.). Pennwell.

Pantzalis, C., Simkins, B. J., & Laux, P. A. (2001). Operational hedges and the foreign exchange exposure of US multinational corporations. *Journal of International Business Studies, 32*(4), 793–812.

Petroleum Intelligence Weekly. (1990, November 5). Marketview: future shock for NYMEX?, *29*(45), 9.

Petroleum Intelligence Weekly. (2004a, August 9). Kazakhs put their partners under pressure, *43*(32), 4–5.

Petroleum Intelligence Weekly. (2004b, August 9). Russians risk rise, reserves remain cheap, *43*(32), 1–2.

Ridgeway, J. (1991). *The March to war*. Four Walls Eight Windows.

Rugman, A. M., & Verbeke, A. (2004). A perspective on regional and global strategies of multinational enterprises. *Journal of International Business Studies, 35*(1), 3–18.

Schmukler, S. L. (2004). Financial globalization: Gain and pain for developing countries. *Federal Reserve Bank of Atlanta Economic Review, 89*(2), 39–66.

Schwartz, E. (1997). The stochastic behavior of commodity prices: Implications for valuation and hedging. *Journal of Finance, 52*(3), 923–973.

Shenkar, O. (2004). One more time: International business in a global economy. *Journal of International Business Studies, 35*(2), 161–171.

Shiller, R. J. (2000). *Irrational exuberance*. Princeton University Press.

Shiller, R. J. (2003). *The new financial order: Risk in the 21st century*. Princeton University Press.

Shleifer, A., & Summers, L. H. (1990). The noise trader approach to finance. *Journal of Economic Perspectives, 4*(2), 19–33.
Symposium. (2001). Multinationals: The Janus face of globalization. *Journal of International Business Studies, 32*(3), 383–518.
ul Haq, M., Kaul, I., & Grunberg, I. (1996). *The Tobin tax: Coping with financial volatility*. Oxford University Press.
United States Energy Information Administration. (1990, November). *Petroleum prices and profits in the 90 days following the invasion of Kuwait*, SR/0A/90-01.
United States Senate and Committee on Governmental Affairs. (1991). *Oil prices and supplies during the Persian Gulf crisis, hearings, 101st congress, 2nd session*. US Government Printing Office.
Verleger, P. K. (1979). The US petroleum crisis of 1979. *Brookings Papers on Economic Activity, 2*, 463–475.
Verleger, P. K. (1982). *Oil markets in turmoil*. Ballinger.
Verleger, P. K. (1991). *Impact of the embargo on exports of oil from Iraq and Kuwait. Statement before the Joint Economic Committee, 8 August 1990, in United States House of Representatives, Committee on Foreign Affairs, The Persian Gulf Crisis, Hearings, 101st Congress*, 2nd Session. Washington, DC: US GPO.
Vernon, R. L. (Ed.). (1976). *The oil crisis*. Norton.
Weiner, R. J. (1994). Default, market microstructure, and changing trade patterns in forward markets: Case study of North-Sea oil. *Journal of Banking and Finance, 18*(5), 955–977.
Weiner, R. J. (2002). Sheep in wolves' clothing? Speculators and price volatility in petroleum futures. *Quarterly Review of Economics and Finance, 42*(2), 391–400.

3

Global Closure, Crises and Financial Markets: A Commentary

W. Travis Selmier II and Chang Hoon Oh

Introduction

In the paper titled "Speculation in international crises: report from the Gulf", Weiner (2005) analyzes oil futures trading on the New York Mercantile Exchange [NYMEX] during the Gulf Crisis (1990–1991) to address several issues critical to financial trading, national security policy, and the impacts of crises. Splitting price movements of futures contracts into Day (trading occurring when NYMEX is open) and Night (contract price changes which occur between market close and the following day's opening price), the author searches to identify the causes of market volatility rather than merely symptoms of volatility. The paper essentially

W. T. Selmier II (✉)
Indiana University, Bloomington, IN, USA
e-mail: wselmier@indiana.edu

C. H. Oh
University of Kansas School of Business, Lawrence, KS, USA
e-mail: changhoon_oh@ku.edu

M. A. Mithani et al. (eds.), *Crises and Disruptions in International Business*, JIBS Special Collections, https://doi.org/10.1007/978-3-030-80383-4_3

questions whether trading and speculation cause greater market volatility. He argues that politics and market fundamentals are more impactful progenitors of market volatility rather than speculation *per se*. Herein, we argue that changes in technologies and markets since the [first] Gulf Crisis have perhaps strengthened his conclusion, but with an important twist. While there are deeper institutional frameworks, more access to markets, and stronger corporate risk management, speculative behavior and variety of risks have also increased in financial trading and international business.

Weiner (2005, 577) notes four reasons why "[t]he Gulf Crisis is a natural experiment for scrutinizing trading and volatility", namely (1) there is a clear link between political conflict and international markets; (2) the global impact on the oil market wherein defined, direct results are evident; (3) the Crisis' beginning and end are clearly defined temporally; and (4) both the Crisis and the futures market [NYMEX] are geographically distinct. We concur with these ideas, but we also feel Weiner undersells his "natural experiment." Some market participants were familiar – in some cases extremely adept – at dealing with crises and understood how those crises affected oil markets at that time. Given a long history of wars and conflict (in the Middle East and elsewhere), some oil MNEs were already quite experienced in risk management, in some cases even profiting from crises. Their strong institutional memories had already been established with a product that has always been political. Hence, a fifth reason why the Gulf Crisis may be a useful natural experiment to scrutinize market volatility is that the oil MNEs – which were active traders of both physical (oil and its downstream products) and futures – could count among their numbers true exemplars of what has become known as "non-market strategy" in the decades following the Gulf Crisis. Oil MNEs were early employers of technology and non-market strategies to manage political and business risk.[1]

[1] Yergin (1992: 129–133) provides a fascinating vignette into how oil MNEs weighed market and non-market strategies in the aftermath of the revolutionary Baku oil riots in 1905. Yergin argues this was "the first time… a violent upheaval had interrupted the flow of oil, threatening to make a vast investment worthless." Paris-based Rothschilds decided to lower their Russia-concentrated oil interests; whereas Royal Dutch/Shell, seeking to diversify supplies, paid in stock for the Baku assets. The Rothschilds became the largest shareholders of both Shell and Royal Dutch stock, considerably diversifying away from Russian oil assets into a global oil company, while Royal Dutch/Shell diver-

In another paper published during the Gulf Crisis, Weiner (1991) made a fascinating, controversial claim that the "world oil market is by no means unified. Almost half of the region-pairs (11 out of 23) are in different geographic markets more than half the time" ([based on price fluctuation analytics) (1991: 105). As strong proponents of regionalization we recognize this, but add an important caveat, which constitutes a sixth reason underpinning his "natural experiment": The oil market may not be (or have been then) "one great pool", but oil MNEs arbitraged around these region-pairs. Oil MNEs recognized the idea of "global closure" (a term coined in 1904 by British Member of Parliament and geographer Halford Mackinder, often called the "Father of Geopolitics"); i.e. the idea was that world transport routes were being knitted together by the coming of the railroad era which were then linking markets, people and armies globally.

The Interaction Between Technology, Traders and International Business

We take Weiner's "natural experiment", using three quotes from his 2005 paper, to point out that technology, traders and international business dynamically interact in sometimes cooperative, sometimes conflictual, ways. First, Weiner notes (2005: 578): "The question of the role of the trading process in market stability is an old one." Yes indeed, this question literally goes back millennia: Cicero complained that "the credit of the Roman money market is intimately bound up with the prosperity of Asia; a disaster cannot occur there without shaking our credit to its foundations" (Frank, 1992, quoting from Teggart, 1939: 74, fn. 40). Traders conveyed the effects of Asian booms and busts to the Roman money market, causing political leaders like Cicero to express concern and occasional hostility. Osaka rice merchants in Edogawa Japan developed bonds, then a form of futures contracts in rice during the seventeenth century

---

sified their oil assets by adding Baku to their portfolio. Both sides weighed the political risks of the developing Russia revolutionary movements against their respective needs for oil assets, coming to this agreement in 1912.

CE, but were constantly criticized for weakening market stability; "futures trading, the market in 'book transactions ... was said to be nothing but gambling' by the government" (Schaede, 1989: 494). The latter nineteenth century introduction of intercontinental telegraph networks resulted in share-pricing differentials between London and New York Stock Exchanges shrinking from ten days before the Atlantic Cable was installed in 1867 to "zero days" (Hoag, 2006). To take advantage of this emergent technology, British merchant bank Samuel Montagu & Co. began siting their offices next to telegraph facilities in the 1870s (Chapman, 1984: 47). Later that decade, Chicago-traded commodity prices reacted to Indian climate disasters within hours through the transmission of the news via several intercontinental cables (Odlyzko, 2000: 96–97), leading to considerable outcry against traders from farmers and from the US government. These three examples illustrate not only the political pressures on trading mechanisms, but also that, while developments in techniques and technology – expansion of long-distance trading, financial contract sophistication, and telecommunications advances – created pressures on existing markets, the abovementioned market developments were primarily responses to demand for goods over geographic space and time.

Second, as Weiner states (2005: 577), "Speculators, particularly hedge funds, have been blamed in several crises, including the worldwide stock market crash of October 1987, the Gulf Crisis of 1990–1991, the breakdown of the European Exchange Rate Mechanism (ERM) in 1992–1993, the Tequila crisis and the Asian financial crisis of the 1990s, and the Russian crisis and collapse of LTCM of 1998." And these were only the crises occurring just before and after the Gulf Crisis of 1990–1991. We can look back just a decade before to find a powerful source of this blame which influenced policymakers during the Gulf Crisis: the infamous Hunt Brothers' attempt to corner the silver market in the late 1970s. Initially buying physical silver, the Brothers' shifted to futures markets and borrowed heavily, even arranging warehouse space so that when their futures contracts expired, they could demand physical silver in payment rather than simply settle their futures contracts at expiry for the profits (Abolafia & Kilduff, 1988). Silver prices shot up in the resulting "squeeze", affecting film producers and other MNEs dependent on silver, as well as other commodities such as gold and platinum (Selmier, 2017: 229–231). This memory was very fresh on the minds of regulators and non-financial MNE managers during the Gulf Crisis as the Hunt Brothers were finally fined and banned from trading just at the end of 1989 (Eichenwald, 1989). In effect, the Brothers' example proved that old adage stating that one scandal cancels out a thousand good deeds, and their attempts considerably damaged speculators' reputations and set the stage for policymakers' overreactions during the Gulf Crisis, overreactions which Weiner deflates (2005: 582–583). But over the last century of financial markets, the Brothers' perfidy was a rarer occurrence. As Weiner points out, closing or severely restricting markets does not end speculation except in criminal cases such as the one illustrated by the Hunt Brothers.

Third, Weiner correctly argues that "[t]oo often, strong claims and policy proposals are made without supporting analysis"; in this case of the Gulf Crisis, governments may "influenc[e] market fundamentals, and expectations … [through] an announcement of forthcoming strategic-reserve releases" (2005: 583). Unfortunately, policymakers sometimes panic (Weiner notes some government-tied reserves were purposefully not released, causing further panic). In 2009, economist and former Bundesbank Director Beatrice Weder di Mauro (2009) pointed out another relevant policy-linked problem when she summed up post-Global Financial Crises challenges facing policymakers: "As soon as crisis strikes, the optimal choice for policymakers differs from the pre-announced policy, the authorities will usually offer support. The banks anticipate this behaviour and run even more risks as a result." Either closing down the market, or offering too much unquestioned support, signals a lack of balance. Weiner (2005) and Weder di Mauro (2009) acknowledge additional problems without explicitly stating them. One is that policymaking almost never exists in a *tabula rasa* form; already codified, policy *changes* must often be made rather than policy newly written. Another problem is that a complex pastiche of policymakers interacts with policymaking, which clutters, complicates, and even confuses responses. In contrast, the corporate form was created, in part, to form a more hierarchical, in many cases, command economy nature with defined boundaries. A third problem is that technology may move faster within markets rather than within governments. This is particularly so with financial markets. In 2009, technology consultancy Gartner Group pointed out that financial firms spend more globally on technology that any other institutional grouping – 20% more than industrial firms, and 60% more than all governments at that time (Economist, 2009). This leads to considerable information asymmetry across and even within industries.

Oil MNEs – The Winners of the Gulf Crisis?

When engaging in policy analyses, analytics must include estimations of who benefits and who is harmed *ceteris paribus*. Analytics requires information, but information is only one necessary condition. In Weiner's *problematique*, oil MNEs were among the biggest winners of this Gulf Crisis. Adrian Throop of the Federal Reserve Bank of San Francisco (1991) estimated that American oil companies garnered *additional* overseas profits of $8 and $9 billion in the 4th quarter of 1990 and 1st quarter of 1991 respectively, which he attributes to the oil price increase caused by the Gulf Crisis. Since the Gulf Crisis, the boundaries between non-financial MNEs with oil operations and financial firms have become blurred. Hache and Lantz (2013), Zhang (2012) and others point out the increase in non-commercial trading volume in the "noughties" from perhaps 20% of trading volume to more than 60%. Goldman Sachs, for instance, now trades in both physical and futures, having arranged considerable storage facilities. Natural resource MNEs such as Glencore and Trafigura engage in so much financial trading that they have been compared to large financial firms through engendering systemic risk. Trafigura commissioned Craig Pirrong (2015), a prominent natural resources economist specializing in hedging strategies, to argue they were not "too big to fail."

We differ in part with Weiner's assertion "Daytime (i.e., when the exchange is open) price fluctuations during the Gulf Crisis can be associated primarily with the trading process, and overnight fluctuations with news" (580). The operative word is "primarily". No doubt if a reaction to the Crisis were forthcoming, it would have been led by the US, so news was also created during the trading day. Attributing the "gapping" that occurred – where future contract trading begins with a gap between opening and previous day's close –to "news" is not inaccurate, though. Oil companies could and did trade both physical and derivatives, as they had done for decades; physical traded 24/7 during the Crisis. But NYMEX was the only game in town for those who could not trade physical. SIMEX (Singapore International Monetary Exchange) began trading oil futures during October 1989, while TOCOM (Tokyo Commodity Exchange) did not begin trading similar contracts until September 10, 2001. To critics who might argue that Weiner (2005) ignored SIMEX, volumes were so low that Victor Yu, in the energy group of Refco (then perhaps the world's largest risk management consultancy), said during the Crisis that "SIMEX is kind of a joke, the IPE [SIMEX oil futures] just doesn't have the liquidity that you really need" (see Beveridge, 1991).

Is Weiner's 2005 Paper Dated?

We, with an obvious bent toward economic history, are not unbiased judges. The readers will have to decide, and they will need to consider how technology developments in international business, trading and risk management dynamically change over time. America's Strategic Petroleum Reserve was established after the oil crises in 1973–1974. NYMEX' decision to extend oil futures' trading hours began during the Crisis. Glance back up at the times when SIMEX and TOCOM introduced oil futures – a few months before the Gulf Crisis, and the day before 9/11, respectively. Global closure, we argue, is an ongoing, dynamic process, but it is processed in fits and starts. International strategic management inherently accepts this; notably, Oh and Oetzel pointed out (2017) that MNEs develop institutional memories through experiential learning to manage risk but much of that learning results from experiencing, and overcoming, events such as crises, conflicts and disasters. Passing through trying periods catalyzes institutional changes, and the above-mentioned blurring of lines between financial and non-financial firms in resource markets underscore this.

In conclusion, we note that Weiner's (2005) analytics show us four important, and timeless lessons: (1) crises, which are inevitable and repetitive, may occur without adequate risk-management tools; (2) blame may be apportioned without fundamental analysis, which likely leads to (3) incomplete, inadequate and often off-target policy responses, all of which implicitly require (4) well-structured non-market strategies which consider both potential crises and inherent asymmetric information sets.

References

Abolafia, M. F., & Kilduff, M. (1988). Enacting market crisis: The social construction of a speculative bubble. *Administrative Science Quarterly, 33*(2), 177–193.

Beveridge, D. (1991, November 7). Oil market seeks round-the-clock trading. *AP News*. Downloaded November 17, 2020 @ https://apnews.com/article/79d83de27260365a253a6d64f3d6d950

Chapman, S. D. (1984). *The rise of merchant banking*. George Allen & Unwin.

Economist. (2009, December 3). Banks and information technology: Silo but deadly.

Eichenwald, K. (1989, December 21). 2 hunts fined and banned from trades. *The New York Times*.

Frank, A. G. (1992). *The centrality of Central Asia*. VU University Press.

Hache, E., & Lantz, F. (2013). Speculative trading and oil price dynamic: A study of the WTI market. *Energy Economics, 36*, 334–340.

Hoag, C. (2006). The Atlantic telegraph cable and capital market information flows. *Journal of Economic History, 66*(2), 342–353.

Mackinder, H. J. (1904). The geographical pivot of history. *The Geographical Journal, 23*(4), 421–437.

Odlyzko, A. (2000, June 16). *The history of communications and its implications for the Internet*. http://papers.ssrn.com/sol3/papers.cfm?abstract_id=235284

Oh, C. H., & Oetzel, J. (2017). Once bitten twice shy? Experience managing violent conflict risk and MNC subsidiary-level investment and expansion. *Strategic Management Journal, 38*(3), 714–731.

Pirrong, C. (2015). *NOT TOO BIG TO FAIL: Systemic risk, regulation, and the economics of commodity trading firms*. Trafigura. Downloaded June 1, 2016, at http://www.trafigura.com/media/2366/trafigura-pirrong-not-too-big-to-fail-systemic-risk-white-paper.pdf

Schaede, U. (1989). Forwards and futures in Tokugawa-period Japan: A new perspective on the Dōjima rice market. *Journal of Banking & Finance, 13*(4–5), 487–513.

Selmier, W. T. (2017). An institutional perspective on governance, power, and politics of financial risk. *Business and Politics, 19*(2), 215–240.

Throop, A. W. (1991, September 13). The Gulf war and the U.S. economy. *FRBSF Weekly Letter*, pp. 91–31.

Weder di Mauro, B. (2009, October 1). The dog that didn't bark. *The Economist*. http://www.economist.com/node/14539774

Weiner, R. J. (1991). Is the world oil market "One Great Pool"? *The Energy Journal, 12*(3), 95–107.

Weiner, R. J. (2005). Speculation in international crises: Report from the Gulf. *Journal of International Business Studies, 36*, 576–587.

Yergin, D. (1992). *The prize: The epic quest for oil, money, and power*. Simon & Schuster.

Zhang, Y. J. (2012). Speculative trading and WTI crude oil futures price movement: An empirical analysis. *Applied Energy, 107*, 394–402.

4

Why and How Might Firms Respond Strategically to Violent Conflict?

Jennifer Oetzel and Kathleen Getz

Introduction

For as long as companies have been operating, there has been an interest in understanding how firms can reduce or manage the external risks they face. Formulating appropriate firm responses to external threats in the operating environment is a salient and complex challenge for firms engaged in international business. While managers will generally avoid operating in high-risk environments, avoidance is not always possible, feasible, or even desirable (Delios & Henisz, 2003; Dunning, 1998). Not all risks can be anticipated or avoided, especially since many business

Accepted by Ishtiaq Mahmood, Area Editor, 11 September 2011. This paper has been with the authors for two revisions.

J. Oetzel (✉)
Kogod School of Business, American University, Washington, DC, USA
e-mail: oetzelj@american.edu

K. Getz
Graduate School of Business, Loyola University Chicago, Chicago, USA

M. A. Mithani et al. (eds.), *Crises and Disruptions in International Business*, JIBS Special Collections, https://doi.org/10.1007/978-3-030-80383-4_4

investments have a long-term time horizon. In situations such as these, where companies have large sunk costs or firm-specific assets in place, if risk levels increase, managers must decide how best to protect their firms and employees, and possibly reduce the overall level of risk in the environment.

Of course, the initial impetus to respond to complex risks is not always the result of top management initiative. At times, various stakeholder groups may bring issues – and perhaps possible solutions – to the attention of the firm. Issues that are outside the "dominant logic" and experience of the firm – issues that may require radical new ways of thinking and responding – may be raised by groups or individuals not entrenched in the normal approach to doing business, or which have alternative perspectives on issues (Prahalad & Bettis, 1986). For example, avoidance of risk may be a common firm response, but attempting to actively reduce risk, particularly if that involves engaging participants in a violent conflict, is outside the norm for many managers. Stakeholders may influence firms to engage with nontraditional actors by increasing the salience of issues, as well as the means for addressing them. Understanding the role that perceived stakeholder pressure has on firms' likely strategic response is a primary objective of this study.

For their part, when addressing complex issues such as violent conflict, firms must increasingly respond to, engage with, and try to influence a broader set of actors (Gladwin & Walter, 1980; Luo, 2006). Each of the actors – or stakeholders – involved may have different views about the violent conflict, and the need to resolve it. Examining these actors enables us to better understand the salience of the stakeholder to the firm, and the likelihood that firms will respond to stakeholder pressure (Eesley & Lenox, 2006). When examining firm response to violent conflict risk, it is interesting to consider stakeholders in terms of their location or proximity to the conflict. Multinational enterprises (MNEs) face pressure from both home- and host-country stakeholders. At times, purely local firms can also receive international stakeholder pressure. When local issues become global concerns, international stakeholders may attempt to influence international and local firm behavior.

For these reasons, it is important to understand better that stakeholder salience may vary, based on stakeholder location. Thus we seek to extend the research on firm response to risk by drawing on insights from the strategic response to risk and stakeholder literatures. We do so by examining the relative salience of internationally and locally based stakeholders, and how the proximity of stakeholders can affect the type of strategy firms are likely to adopt in response to violent conflict risk. By drawing on these two literatures, we aim to contribute to the empirical research on how firms respond to stakeholder demands (Berman et al., 1999; Christmann, 2004), as well as gain a better understanding of how firms might respond to violent conflict risk. Thus the specific research questions of interest are:

1. How do international and local stakeholder groups differ in terms of their ability to influence firms to engage in various forms of violent conflict resolution?
2. If firms do decide to act to reduce risk, do the sources of stakeholder pressure influence the strategies and tactics that firms are likely to adopt?

To our knowledge, this exploratory analysis presents the first empirical study of these issues.

Survey and archival data on respondents from 471 multinational and local firms operating in 80 countries were used to explore these issues. The sample of firms was drawn from the population of United Nations Global Compact (UNGC) members. Results of our regression analyses indicate these important findings:

1. Local stakeholder pressure is associated with the likelihood that firms will respond directly to violent conflict, and collaborate with other organizations or work alone when doing so.
2. International stakeholder pressure is associated with the likelihood that firms will respond indirectly to violent conflict, collaborating with other organizations or working alone.

Although not the key focus of our study, we also find that firm and industry characteristics are generally not significantly related to the likelihood that firms will respond to violent conflict.

Given that the impetus for firms to address other social issues began, at least in part, with stakeholder pressure to engage, it may be that our findings regarding stakeholder pressures and firm response suggest a long-term trend toward greater pressure for firms to respond to violent conflict.[1] As with other difficult societal problems, firms might see proactive responsiveness to violent conflict as strategically important for their profitability and legitimacy. Although engaging in conflict reduction is still relatively novel for managers, certainly there is evidence that MNEs are increasingly recognizing the problem of violent conflict (Jamali & Mirshak, 2010; Kolk & Lenfant, 2010). In a study of MNEs operating in three conflict-prone countries in Central Africa, Kolk and Lenfant (2010) investigate how MNEs are reporting on violent conflict, among other issues. The scholars found that although firms are beginning to acknowledge the risks they face from violent conflict in their corporate statements, only a few openly discuss their role in addressing conflict issues. We seek to extend this growing body of research by looking at how a variety of company types operating across 80 countries may be likely to respond to violent conflict.

Theory and Hypotheses

Firm Response to Violent Conflict Risk

Violent conflict, defined as the organized and sustained use of physical force that results in injury or death to persons and/or damage or destruction to property (Getz & Oetzel, 2010), may include war, revolution, rebellion, insurgency, and sustained campaigns of violence or terrorism, but not episodic and less organized forms of violence, such as crime. Unfortunately, violent conflicts are not rare occurrences. According to the Heidelberg Institute for International Conflict Research, in 2008 there were 254 intrastate conflicts in the world, with 49.6% of them

[1] Of course it may also be that managers are increasingly aware of the role that businesses play in the wider society, and more motivated to make a positive impact on the communities and nation-states in which they operate. We thank one of our anonymous reviewers for this insight.

characterized by sporadic or continuous violence. Many of these conflicts occurred in countries that are important locations for business, such as Russia, India, Nigeria, Thailand, and Mexico (HIIK, 2008).

When companies decide that avoidance of, or exit from, conflict-prone environments is too costly, or is not feasible, they take steps to safeguard their investments. In addition to increasing security or insurance coverage, an array of firm responses is possible. Companies may take a direct approach that focuses on the particular situation of violence. A direct approach, as defined here, has the intention of stopping violence or preventing a situation with a clear capacity for violence from becoming violent. As research on firm political strategies has argued, a direct approach may be aimed at influencing key actors by lobbying host governments to act (Boddewyn & Brewer, 1994; Hillman & Hitt, 1999) or speaking out publicly against violence (Diamond & McDonald, 1996; Lieberfeld, 2002). At times, companies may actually engage with parties to the conflict to facilitate negotiations, arbitration or mediation between combatants, government leaders, and other groups (Ballentine & Nitzschke, 2004; Berman, 2000; Gerson & Colletta, 2002; Kriesburg, 1998; Oetzel et al., 2007). There is evidence that firms are doing so (Banfield et al., 2006; Guáqueta, 2008; Lieberfeld, 2002). Anglo-American Mining Company, for one, is credited with facilitating negotiations between the African National Congress (ANC) and the South African government between 1984 and 1990 (Lieberfeld, 2002). For its part, Anglo-American was concerned about the company's inability to access foreign capital, and the overall threat to its profitability and survival amidst the conflict in South Africa. As South Africa's most prominent corporation at the time, Anglo-American used its leverage to bring the ANC and the South African government to the negotiating table in Zambia (Lieberfeld, 2002).

Alternatively, firms may act indirectly to address challenges related to the conflict. As defined here, an indirect approach involves efforts to mitigate root causes so that a situation becomes less violence-prone, or to soften the adverse effects of violence. For example, they may adopt human resource policies or supplementary activities aimed at minimizing societal tensions that are a key factor in fueling civil war in a country such as Côte d'Ivoire. Protina, a small beverage company in Abidjan, Côte d'Ivoire, employs people from Burkina Faso and its home country in the same facility. High levels of xenophobia in the wider social environment in Côte d'Ivoire spilled over into the workplace, and created serious internal tensions within the firm. To resolve this problem, the company organized dinners to bring all employees together and diffuse tensions. The dinners were held between the day and night shifts, and enabled workers to voice their concerns and resolve differences. According to Protina, the company's efforts yielded valuable benefits, including an ability to maintain a diverse workforce, high customer satisfaction, and the ability to continue to operate despite wider conflict in the country at large.[2]

Other tactics that firms may adopt include supporting small business development in post-conflict settings through microfinance, skills training, and the like, withholding payments or refraining from selling to those who facilitate conflict (Collier, 2007), verifying that participants in the supply chain are not aggravating the conflict, adopting industry codes of conduct aimed at ending conflict (e.g., Kimberley Process, which is aimed at ending the trade in conflict diamonds; Bennett, 2002; Dunfee & Fort, 2003), and engaging in philanthropic activities to aid victims of the conflict (Luo, 2006; van Tulder & Kolk, 2001).

Firms that respond to violent conflict risk must also decide whether to act alone or join forces with other groups or organizations. Both direct and indirect responses may be undertaken unilaterally or collaboratively. The choice may be affected by the firm's need for the knowledge, skills, or access that collaboration partners may provide, along with the availability of potential partners. Collaborative action in response to a variety of social issues is becoming more commonplace (Doh & Teegen, 2003; Smith & Feldman, 2003; Teegen et al., 2004). Potential partners include other private sector organizations, non-governmental organizations (NGOs), and even inter-governmental organizations or agencies of the local government. There are a number of obstacles to and facilitators of inter-organizational collaboration (Gray, 1985). One facilitator is the interest that potential collaboration partners have in reducing the risks associated with taking action in areas where organizations of their type typically do not act. These risks are many, but include the potential for

[2] The example of Protina is from the UNGC 2009 series, "Case Studies in Business Responses to Violent Conflict". Dissemination of findings has begun; publication is in progress.

failure attributable to the organization's limited experience as well as the inherent difficulties of the problem to be addressed. In such situations, collaboration provides at least two benefits. First, the combination of the different skill sets and knowledge bases of collaborating organizations may increase the probability of success. In conflict settings, a firm might seek a partner that has expertise in addressing the social, cultural, or political concerns that are drivers of conflict. Second, collaboration provides opportunities for blame-shifting in the event of failure (see also Kaufman et al., 1993). Cost is a key obstacle to collaboration. These costs, which include screening potential partners and developing and maintaining partner relationships, may be high (see also Konczak, 2001).

Stakeholder Pressure and Firm Strategic Response to Violent Conflict

Although a variety of factors are likely to influence whether or not firms respond to violent conflict, and which strategies and tactics firms adopt, here we focus our attention on the role played by stakeholder pressure. Stakeholders – individuals or groups that can affect, or are affected by, a firm and its actions (Freeman, 1984) – can have a significant influence on the likelihood that firms will respond to pressure, on the type of strategies firms adopt, and, more generally, on how firms respond to events in the wider operating environment (Eesley & Lenox, 2006). A growing body of research empirically demonstrates that, in response to certain types of stakeholder pressure, firms are likely to change policies or practices (Eesley & Lenox, 2006; Kassinis & Vafeas, 2006). Although this is certainly not the first study to examine how stakeholder pressure may influence firm response, relatively few studies of firm response to risk have examined the role that stakeholders play in firm response to violent conflict.

As Mitchell, Agle and Wood (1997) suggest, and others have affirmed through empirical research (e.g., Agle et al., 1999; Magness, 2008), firms respond to stakeholders that succeed in demonstrating that their issues are salient. Salience is based on a firm's perception of the legitimacy, power, and urgency of the stakeholder. With respect to these three attributes and the issue of violent conflict, we distinguish between local and international stakeholders. Local stakeholders are those who reside within the country of operations. They include employees, the immediate community, local consumers, and so on. International stakeholders reside outside the country of operations. They include international NGOs, foreign governments, and multilateral organizations. For multinational firms, international stakeholders also include home-country shareholders, government, and others. These groups of stakeholders are sufficiently different that firms may respond differently to the pressure they exert.

Although international stakeholders may be highly salient at times, in the case of violent conflict salience may be higher among local stakeholders, owing to their expected levels of power, legitimacy, and urgency. Local stakeholder power may be coercive, utilitarian, and normative (Mitchell et al., 1997). Local stakeholders who are belligerents in the conflict may threaten the firm's personnel or property, for example, by engaging in kidnapping or sabotage (coercive power). They may withhold important resources, by striking or boycotting the firm's outputs (utilitarian power). The local government or those who can influence the government may threaten to withdraw the firm's license to operate or to enforce existing laws more stringently (utilitarian power). More generally, some stakeholders may have the ability to influence the firm's acceptance locally (normative power). Many local stakeholders (other than the belligerents themselves) have high legitimacy; firms may perceive or believe that they truly represent local interests because they know and understand the local situation better than the firm itself, and better than international stakeholders. Finally, the perceived urgency of their claims is also likely to be high, because a delay in addressing the issue would allow the violence to continue.

Because companies are likely to attribute high salience to local stakeholders, managers have "a clear and immediate mandate to attend to and give priority to [the] stakeholder's claim" (Mitchell et al., 1997: 878; see also Phillips, 2003; Szwajkowski, 2000). This imperative is likely to lead to responses that address the stakeholder's concerns directly. That is, because local stakeholders probably want to see an end to the violence and the conflict that drives it, companies may consider that their responses should be overtly oriented toward just that. Thus firms might adopt direct actions that focus on stopping violence as it is occurring, or on preventing an imminent outbreak of violence. Further, companies may want to show that they are striving for effective responses to these high-salience stakeholders. To enhance effectiveness, companies would need to have a deep understanding of the stakeholder's needs and of the environment in which action is to take place. Therefore firms would be likely to seek knowledgeable collaboration partners, particularly those with complementary knowledge bases, in developing their responses to local stakeholders (Gray, 1985; Schermerhorn, 1975; Stern & Hicks, 2000).

Efforts to end protracted or chronic violence can be risky for firms, because they may be (at best) only partly successful. Among high-salience stakeholders, the reputational and other consequences associated with perceived failure would be highly detrimental, as these stakeholders might use their power against the firm. For example, the firm might be concerned about potential legal action. This fear is not unfounded, as activities seen as interfering with the local government's sovereignty have sometimes been vigorously repudiated by government and other stakeholders (Kline, 2000; Winston, 2003). In fact, fear of litigation is often cited as a potential deterrent to any activities beyond the essential functions of business (Goodpaster, 2004). This potential risk is not likely to affect whether a response is direct or indirect, since that choice is driven by stakeholders' perceived needs. However, with high-salience stakeholders, such risk may induce firms to work together with other firms or organizations. Collaborative efforts minimize the risk to any one firm by obscuring the roles of particular participants (Gray, 1985). Thus:

Hypothesis 1 Local stakeholder pressure is positively associated with the likelihood that firms will adopt tactics that respond directly to violent conflict, and will do so in collaboration with other firms or organizations. Pressure from international stakeholders may elicit other types of response from firms because their salience may be lower. They have some power, but do not have high levels of legitimacy or urgency as compared with local stakeholders. Mitchell, Agle and Wood (1997) label such stakeholders "latent". The sources of international stakeholders' power are primarily utilitarian or normative. For example, consumer groups may boycott a firm's products, and investor groups may sell their stock in the firm (utilitarian power). These actions might occur in reaction to activism by NGOs to publicize negatively the firm's presence in a violent country (normative power). However, international stakeholders would be unlikely to use physical force against the firm (e.g., kidnapping or sabotage). Firms may be skeptical regarding the legitimacy of international stakeholders' claims, because they may believe that the stakeholders do not understand the situation as well as local stakeholders do. Similarly, the urgency of their claims is likely to be lower than that of local stakeholders, as they are not directly affected by the violence.

Although firms often do not respond to latent stakeholders (Mitchell et al., 1997), we suggest that managers might opt to respond unilaterally and indirectly. Activities might include philanthropic efforts, support of educational programs, implementing training programs aimed at reducing conflict within the firms, or other activities (Jamali & Mirshak, 2010; Kolk & Lenfant, 2010). Such actions may result in positive outcomes for stakeholders (e.g., reduction in the conflict that drives violence), and at the same time may shield the firm from an escalation of stakeholder pressure while allowing it to retain discretion in its response activities (see, e.g., Carroll, 2000). These responses may even yield direct benefits for the firms as their reputations are enhanced among both international and local stakeholders, providing additional reasons to act unilaterally rather than collaboratively. For these reasons, we suggest the following hypothesis:

Hypothesis 2 International stakeholder pressure is positively associated with the likelihood that firms will adopt tactics that respond indirectly to violent conflict, and will do so acting alone.

Methods

Sample

Survey and archival data were collected from a cross-sectional sample of UNGC member firms. The UNGC is a global corporate citizenship and sustainability initiative founded and managed by the United Nations. The program, initiated in July 2000, includes organizations from the private, public, and civil society sectors. At the time of our study in April of

2008, the UNGC had more than 5000 participants, including approximately 4000 businesses operating in 120 countries around the world. A key reason for choosing this sample is that businesses that participate in the UNGC include a wide variety of firms (e.g., member firms include domestic and multinational firms, global Fortune 500 firms, small local businesses, and firms operating in a wide variety of industries) operating in diverse geographic locations (developed and developing countries). These factors were important for our study, since we wanted to be able to control for other factors that might affect the likelihood that firms would adopt strategies in response to violent conflict. Additionally, with UNGC member firms we could be certain that some firms would have a presence in countries that are experiencing, or have experienced, conflict – a critical factor for this study.

Due to resource constraints and the time limitations of our collaborators, we were unable to translate the survey into multiple languages. For this reason, since the survey was conducted only in English, the UNGC did not send the survey to member firms in Portugal, Spain, France, and China that were known not to have English-speaking Focal Points. The UNGC made this decision based on their knowledge of respondents' ability to answer an English-only survey. Although firms from these countries may be relatively underrepresented, all of these countries are included in our final sample.

Out of the 4000 UNGC member firms in the spring of 2008, our survey was sent to 2154 active and non-communicating members. Non-communicating members are those that have not submitted the annual Communication on Progress report that is required of all active UNGC member firms. Firms that have been non-communicating for one year or more are delisted from the UNGC website. Of the 2154 companies that received the survey, 1078 were small to medium-sized enterprises (firms with <250 employees). The other half of the sample ($n = 1076$) consisted of 102 Global Fortune 500 companies and another 431 companies that include Financial Times 500 firms. The remaining 543 firms included other large companies located in Nordic and European countries (excluding Spain, France, and Portugal). Out of these 1076 large companies, 258 companies had more than 10,000 employees and 343 had more than 5000 employees.

Across the variety of dimensions listed above, the sample firms are largely representative of the population of UNGC firms. Thus we expect their exposure to violent conflict to be similar to that of UNGC firms not in our sample. A distinctive characteristic of UNGC member firms is that they have pledged to implement the UNGC's core principles, which focus on protecting human rights, avoiding labor abuses, protecting the environment, and refraining from corruption. Very little research has been done regarding the extent to which the UNGC directly affects business behavior. One study, which had only 29 respondents, found that UNGC participation significantly increased the number of responsible environmental projects implemented by firms (Cetindamar & Husoy, 2007). In contrast, in a comparative case study in the telecommunications industry, Runhar and Lafferty (2009) found the UNGC's effect to be marginal. Even if UNGC membership affects the tendency of business to behave in a socially responsible way, its impact on response to violent conflict and the presence of a concomitant social desirability bias is likely to be minimal, since none of the UNGC principles directly addresses the issue of violent conflict.[3] Future research is necessary to empirically assess the impact of UNGC membership on firms.

Data Collection

Following Dillman's (2000) guidelines, we developed a questionnaire in collaboration with the UNGC office and International Alert in London. International Alert is an independent, non-profit organization that specializes in conflict reduction and peace-building efforts around the world. Since we could not rely on previously tested measures for our study, we developed several new scales based on strategies and tactics identified in the literature on stakeholder management, firm political strategies, and conflict risk management, which is largely grounded in political science (Bennett, 2002; Christmann, 2004; Collier, 2007; Dunfee & Fort, 2003; Fisher, 1997; Fisher & Ury, 1991; Galtung, 1996; Gerson & Colletta,

[3] Exactly how firms can best avoid complicity in abuses – for example, whether it is better to withdraw from the country or continue operations – is still a subject of debate. We thank one of our anonymous reviewers for raising this issue.

2002; Hillman, 2003; Hillman & Hitt, 1999; Kriesburg, 1998; Miall et al., 2008; Montville, 1992; Oetzel et al., 2007).

To enhance the reliability of our measures, our scales were then exhaustively pre-tested with academic experts, MBA students, and practitioners in International Alert and the UNGC. As part of this process we asked master's students in international studies and business, doctoral students in business, academics who have published in the field, and practitioners in the field of business and conflict resolution at International Alert and the UN Global Compact to respond to a set of questions on how well various indicators measure each of our main constructs. This iterative process of developing the scales took approximately 12 months to complete.

Given the number of countries represented in the sample (more than 80), we determined that an electronic survey was most appropriate for reaching respondents. We developed an online survey using Survey Monkey software. A link to the survey was sent to respondents via email. From the total population of 4000 UN Global Compact member businesses in April 2008, our survey was initially sent to 2154 English-speaking respondents at an equal number of unique firms. The individuals who responded to our survey serve as "Focal Points" for the UN Global Compact. Focal Points are individuals who are selected by their company, are generally high ranking within their organization (information we were able to corroborate between the survey and archival data from the UNGC), and are responsible for communicating with the UNGC. Thus, although they are our single informant, they were not someone selected at random. In fact, they are people chosen by their firm to speak publicly for the company on corporate strategy and activities.

These respondents included both active and non-communicating members. Our survey response rate from this initial sample was 29.25%, given 630 initial survey responses. Of the 630 responses we received, 471 surveys were completed and used in the analysis, for an effective response rate of 21.87% (see Tables 4.1 and 4.2 for a summary of the sample characteristics). Our response rate is consistent with or slightly higher than that obtained in other cross-country surveys (e.g., Husted & Allen, 2006; Venaik et al., 2005).

To determine whether non-response biased our data, we compared early and late respondents using *t*-tests (Armstrong & Overton, 1977). Tests revealed no significant differences between early responders and late

Table 4.1 Sample description

Variable	Number	Percentage of sample
Firm type		
Headquarters firm	175	37.2
Local firm	222	47.1
Subsidiary	74	15.7
Publicly held	182	38.6
Firm size		
<100 employees	119	25.3
100–999 employees	121	25.7
1000–9999 employees	122	25.9
10,000 or more employees	109	23.1
Industry		
Utilities	58	12.3
Extractive firms	57	12.1
Finance/banking	65	13.8
Manufacturing	124	26.3
Pharmaceutical	6	1.3
Entertainment/hotel/food/service/recreation	16	3.4
Media/marketing/advertising/PR	18	3.8
Retailer/distributor/wholesaler	34	7.2
Others	93	19.7
Respondent title		
Chief Executive Officer (CEO)	56	11.9
Vice President (VP), General Manager (GM)	116	24.6
Chief Financial Officer (CFO), Controller	15	3.2
Technical staff	58	12.3
Middle managers, consultants, and others	226	48.0

responders in terms of the four dependent variables, the stakeholder measures, and other key firm characteristics (e.g., industry, publicly held or not, firm size, etc.). Thus results of the *t*-tests suggest that the data do not suffer from non-response bias.

Measures

Dependent Variable: Firm Response

Based on the literature (specifically insights from the political strategy, stakeholder management, and conflict risk management literatures discussed earlier), we developed four response types – unilateral-direct,

Table 4.2 Countries represented in the sample

Australia and Pacific Islands	*Central and Southern Asia*	*Eastern Asia*	*Western Europe*
Australia	Bangladesh[a]	China	Austria
New Zealand	India[a,b]	Japan	Belgium
	Indonesia[a,b]	Republic of Korea	Denmark
Central America and Caribbean	Kazakhstan		Finland
Dominican Republic	Malaysia	*Middle East and North Africa*	France
Panama	Nepal[a,b]	Armenia[c]	Germany
	Pakistan[a,b]	Bahrain	Greece
Central and Southern Africa	Philippines[a,b]	Cyprus	Italy
Ivory Coast[a,b]	Singapore	Egypt	Latvia
Kenya[a,b]	Sri Lanka[a,b]	Georgia[b]	Luxembourg
Madagascar[a]	Thailand[b]	Tunisia	Netherlands
Mauritius	Vietnam	Turkey[b]	Norway
Mozambique		United Arab Emirates	Portugal
Namibia	*Eastern Europe*		Slovenia
Nigeria[a,b]	Albania	*North America*	Spain[b]
South Africa	Belarus	Canada	Sweden
Sudan[a,b]	Bulgaria	Mexico[a,b]	Switzerland
Uganda[a,b]	Croatia	United States[b]	United Kingdom[b]
	Latvia		
	Lithuania	*South America*	
	Kosovo	Argentina	
	Macedonia	Bolivia[a]	
	Moldova[b]	Brazil[a,b]	
	Poland	Chile	
	Romania	Colombia[a,b]	
	Russia[b]	Ecuador[a]	
	Serbia	Paraguay	
	Ukraine	Peru[b]	

Note: 80 countries

[a]Indicates countries that experienced communal and organized armed conflict where *none* of the parties is the government of a state between 2000 and 2008 (Uppsala University, UCDP Non-State Conflict Dataset v. 2.3–2010)

[b]Indicates countries that experienced one or more conflicts between 2000 and 2008 where at least one party to the conflict is the government of a state (Uppsala University, Uppsala Conflict Database Categorical Variables 1989–2008)

[c]Armenia is at times referred to as Central Europe or the Middle East

unilateral-indirect, collaborative-direct, and collaborative-indirect – and measures to identify them. To do this, we employed two seven-point Likert scales (with randomized items) to measure our four constructs of interest, and then created factor-based scales as shown in Appendix 1. It is important to note that neither our indirect-direct scale nor our unilateral-collaborative scale represents different ends of a continuum in the sense that a respondent who scores highly on indirect will necessarily score lower on direct, or vice versa (likewise for the unilateral-collaborative measure). Respondents' actions are not mutually exclusive. Thus some companies may be willing to act both directly and indirectly (and unilaterally or collaboratively) to respond to violent conflict.

First, we sought to assess the likelihood that firms might act directly or indirectly to respond strategically to violent conflict. Five items were initially used to assess the likelihood of a *Direct Strategic Response*. One item was dropped (see Appendix 1) because, in the factor analysis, it did not load onto the *Direct Strategic Response* construct. The reliability (Cronbach's α) for the resulting four-item measure was 0.81. To measure *Indirect Strategic Response* we used six items. Factor analytic results indicated that one item should be dropped (see Appendix 1) since it loaded onto both factors. The reliability (Cronbach's α) for the resulting five-item measure was 0.84.

The purpose of our second scale was to determine the likelihood that firms would respond to violent conflict unilaterally or in collaboration with other organizations. The constructs were assessed with six items each. Factor analytic results indicated that all items loaded onto *Unilateral Strategic Response* as expected except one, which was dropped (see Appendix 1). The reliability (Cronbach's α) for the resulting five-item measure was 0.68. Factor analytic results indicated that all six items loaded onto *Collaborative Strategic Response* as expected. The reliability (Cronbach's α) for the resulting six-item measure was 0.80.

The last step in the construction of the dependent variables was to create the factor-based scales that corresponded to the four theoretical measures of interest: indirect and collaborative, indirect and unilateral, direct and collaborative, and direct and unilateral (Kim & Mueller, 1978). All items loaded onto each of the theoretical measures of interest, with corresponding Cronbach's αs for each factor-based scale as follows: indirect collaborative ($\alpha = 0.82$), indirect and unilateral ($\alpha = 0.78$), direct and collaborative ($\alpha = 0.81$), and direct and unilateral ($\alpha = 0.6$). See Appendix 2 for a list of the items included in each of the four dependent variable measures.

Independent Variables

Our two independent variables measured the degree of local and international stakeholder pressure experienced by the respondents. Each of these variables was measured using a seven-point Likert scale (with randomized items). The factor analytic results are shown in Appendix 3.

1. *Local stakeholders.* Seven items were used to measure the degree to which respondents experienced local sources of stakeholder pressure (pressure from within the country where they are operating) to respond to violent conflict (see Appendix 3). Factor analysis revealed that one item (shareholders) should be dropped. The reliability (Cronbach's α) for the resulting six-item measure was 0.93.
2. *International stakeholders.* Six items were used to measure the degree to which respondents experienced international sources of stakeholder pressure (pressure from outside the country where they are operating) (see Appendix 3). Factor analysis revealed that all items should be retained. The reliability (Cronbach's α) for the six-item measure was 0.94.

Control Variables

We controlled for the following factors:

1. the respondent's level in the organization (respondents at different levels might have dissimilar understandings of their company's likelihood of responding);
2. whether the firm was publicly held (public ownership has been associated with strategy and strategic intent in other studies);
3. region (geographic differences might affect the likelihood of firm response);

4. firm size;
5. industry; and
6. firm type/ownership structure – specifically corporate headquarters, multinational subsidiary, or locally owned firm.

These variables were obtained from two sources: survey responses, and archival data from the UNGC. Using these two sources enabled us to corroborate the validity of the findings between the survey responses and membership data from the UN Global Compact. Survey responses were nearly perfectly correlated with data from the UN.

A dichotomous variable was used to measure public ownership. For respondent position, dummy variables were used to distinguish between different titles, with consultant and "other" combined as the reference variable. Region was also measured with dummy variables; North America (Canada, Mexico, and the United States) served as the reference variable. Firm size was measured using five categories:

1. <100 employees;
2. 100–999 employees;
3. 1000–4999 employees;
4. 5000–9999 employees; and
5. 10,000 or more.

For the purpose of the analysis, Groups 3 and 4 were combined, and Group 1 served as the reference group. For firm industry, survey respondents were asked to identify the industry that best reflected their company's primary business activity. For the analysis, dummy variables were used to measure the different industry categories (with "other" as the reference group), including:

1. utilities (transportation, utilities, communications);
2. extractive firms (agriculture, forestry, mining, oil, and gas);
3. finance and banking (finance, banking, accounting, insurance, real estate); and
4. manufacturing and pharmaceutical firms.

Other firms in the reference group generally include services such as entertainment, healthcare/medical, legal services, media/marketing/advertising, and engineering and architecture. Finally, in terms of firm type or ownership structure, we differentiated between respondents working at their:

1. corporate headquarters;
2. multinational subsidiary; and
3. a local (non-multinational) enterprise.

Dummy variables were used to identify the organization types. Multinational subsidiaries were used as the reference.

Analysis and Results

To ensure that our data did not suffer from multicollinearity we employed two diagnostic tests; variance inflation factor (VIF) and tolerance (1/VIF). The mean VIF value was 1.85, and all VIF values were below 4, well under the recommended cutoff of 10 (Belsey et al., 1980). All measures of tolerance were above the recommended 0.10 cutoff (Belsey et al., 1980). Next, we took steps to ensure that our data did not suffer from common method bias. First, for a number of our independent variables we were able to corroborate respondents' answers with archival data from the UNGC. We found that the survey responses and UNGC data were largely consistent. Second, since we did not have archival sources for all of our variables, particularly our measures of stakeholder pressure, we applied Harman's single-factor test to assess the potential for common method bias (Podsakoff et al., 2003). We loaded all of the study variables into a factor analysis and examined the unrotated solution to determine the number of factors that were necessary to explain the variables (Podsakoff et al., 2003: 889). Results revealed five factors with Eigenvalues greater than 1.0. The first factor accounted for only 16% of the variance, suggesting that common method bias is not a problem in the data.

Ordinary least-squares robust regression analysis was used when estimating our four models:

$$Y_{1,2,3,4} = \beta X_1 + \beta X_2 + \beta X_3 + \ldots + \beta X_{26} + \varepsilon \tag{4.1}$$

The dependent variables for strategic response are represented by Y_1 to Y_4: Y_1 represents direct/unilateral, Y_2 direct/collaborative, Y_3 indirect/unilateral, and Y_4 indirect/collaborative. Each of the X variables refers to one of the independent variables described in the measurement section. Finally, ε represents the error term. Results of the correlation analysis are shown in Table 4.3.

Results of the regression analysis are shown in Table 4.4. The F-tests for all four models are significant, indicating that the models are a good fit with the data. The variance explained ranged from 14% to 18%. Support was found for both hypotheses, although whether the firm acts alone or in collaboration with other organizations does not appear to be a critical differentiating factor. Findings indicate that the firm-level variables were not significant predictors of firms' likelihood of responding to violent conflict. Rather, external pressures arising from domestic and international stakeholders tended to be more important predictors of firm response to violent conflict.

With respect to Hypothesis 1, local stakeholder pressure was positively and significantly associated with both types of direct strategic response variables (see Table 4.4). Results suggest that local pressure is associated with the likelihood that firms will directly engage in violent conflict resolution, and will do so either unilaterally or in collaboration with other firms or organizations (see Table 4.4). Thus, although Hypothesis 1 was supported in terms of the likelihood that firms will adopt direct strategic responses, it appears that firms are as likely to do so alone as in collaboration with other organizations.

Hypothesis 2 predicted that international stakeholder pressure would be positively associated with indirect approaches to violent conflict resolution, and that firms would probably act unilaterally when doing so. Findings suggest that international pressure is positively and significantly associated with the likelihood that firms will adopt strategies that indirectly address violent conflict. Again, however, results indicate that firms are equally likely to engage alone or with others. Although it was not significant at $p < 0.05$, it is important to recognize that international

Table 4.3 Descriptive statistics and correlation matrix

Variable	Mean	s.d.	1	2	3	4	5	6	7	8	9	10
1. Headquarters	0.37	0.48	1.00									
2. Local firm	0.47	0.50	−0.73	1.00								
3. Local stakeholder pressure	1.54	1.64	−0.03	0.01	1.00							
4. International stakeholder pressure	1.42	1.56	0.03	−0.04	0.77	1.00						
5. Publicly held	0.39	0.49	0.37	−0.37	−0.06	0.01	1.00					
6. 100–999 employees	0.26	0.44	−0.23	0.17	0.04	−0.01	−0.20	1.00				
7. 1000–9999 employees	0.26	0.44	0.05	−0.15	0.01	0.07	0.11	−0.35	1.00			
8. 10,000 or more employees	0.23	0.42	0.46	−0.38	−0.05	−0.00	0.46	−0.32	−0.32	1.00		
9. Utilities	0.12	0.33	0.06	−0.00	0.03	0.08	0.03	−0.01	−0.02	0.09	1.00	
10. Extractive	0.12	0.33	0.12	−0.13	−0.01	0.03	0.08	−0.07	0.09	0.03	−0.14	1.00
11. Finance and banking	0.14	0.35	−0.09	0.05	−0.04	−0.04	0.04	−0.02	0.05	0.06	−0.15	−0.15
12. Manufacturing	0.26	0.44	−0.03	−0.00	0.00	0.00	0.04	0.12	−0.07	0.00	−0.22	−0.22
13. Pharmaceutical	0.01	0.11	−0.01	−0.03	−0.05	−0.00	0.14	−0.02	0.11	−0.02	−0.04	0.02
14. Australia/New Zealand	0.01	0.11	−0.05	0.05	−0.01	−0.03	−0.01	−0.03	−0.07	−0.02	−0.04	−0.04
15. Central America	0.02	0.15	−0.02	0.01	0.03	−0.04	−0.06	−0.02	−0.06	0.01	−0.06	0.08
16. Central and Southern Africa	0.06	0.24	−0.02	0.03	−0.01	−0.06	0.03	−0.03	−0.01	0.17	0.04	−0.04

(continued)

Table 4.3 (continued)

Variable	Mean	s.d.	1	2	3	4	5	6	7	8	9	10
17. *Central and Southern Asia*	*0.11*	*0.32*	*0.05*	*−0.03*	*0.12*	*0.15*	*0.04*	*−0.01*	*0.11*	*−0.02*	*0.04*	*−0.05*
18. Eastern Europe	0.12	0.33	−0.09	0.05	−0.06	−0.06	−0.08	0.02	−0.07	−0.06	−0.04	0.02
19. East Asia	0.05	0.23	−0.00	0.06	0.02	0.05	0.01	0.03	0.03	0.01	−0.00	−0.09
20. Middle East and North Africa	0.07	0.26	−0.04	0.06	−0.01	−0.02	−0.03	0.07	−0.01	−0.05	0.07	−0.00
21. South America	0.12	0.33	−0.04	−0.03	0.09	0.04	−0.01	−0.01	0.04	0.05	−0.04	0.00
22. Western Europe	0.35	0.48	0.10	−0.07	−0.08	−0.04	0.09	−0.03	0.02	0.03	0.00	0.06
23. Title: CEO	0.12	0.32	−0.12	0.18	0.06	−0.03	−0.18	−0.04	−0.14	−0.17	−0.08	0.01
24. Title: VP, GM	0.25	0.43	−0.05	0.00	−0.05	0.01	0.02	−0.03	0.03	0.01	0.01	−0.00
25. Title: CFO, Controller	0.03	0.18	−0.06	0.02	0.01	0.03	−0.09	0.03	−0.05	−0.07	−0.03	0.01
26. Title: Technical staff	0.12	0.33	−0.01	0.07	−0.05	−0.04	−0.01	0.00	−0.00	−0.01	0.04	0.02
27. Direct/ collaborative	12.4	11.3	−0.05	0.04	0.30	0.27	−0.01	0.10	−0.03	−0.03	−0.07	−0.01
28. Direct/ unilateral	6.44	6.51	−0.06	0.02	0.26	0.25	0.01	0.08	0.02	−0.02	−0.09	0.02
29. Indirect/ collaborative	19.3	14.6	0.06	−0.03	0.24	0.26	0.08	0.03	0.03	0.06	−0.01	−0.02
30. Indirect/ unilateral	9.81	8.26	0.03	−0.03	0.21	0.24	0.06	0.03	0.08	0.04	−0.05	0.02

Variable	11	12	13	14	15	16	17	18	19	20
1. Headquarters										
2. Local firm										
3. Local stakeholder pressure										
4. International stakeholder pressure										
5. Publicly held										
6. 100–999 employees										
7. 1000–9999 employees										
8. 10,000 or more employees										
9. Utilities										
10. Extractive										
11. Finance and banking	1.00									
12. Manufacturing	–0.24	1.00								
13. Pharmaceutical	–0.05	–0.07	1.00							
14. Australia/New Zealand	0.01	0.02	–0.01	1.00						
15. Central America	0.03	–0.02	–0.02	–0.02	1.00					

(continued)

Table 4.3 (continued)

Variable	11	12	13	14	15	16	17	18	19	20
16. Central and Southern Africa	0.00	0.03	0.05	−0.03	−0.04	1.00				
17. Central and Southern Asia	−0.02	0.04	0.02	−0.04	−0.05	−0.09	1.00			
18. Eastern Europe	0.00	−0.05	0.02	−0.04	−0.06	−0.10	−0.133	1.00		
19. East Asia	−0.01	0.12	−0.03	−0.03	−0.04	−0.06	−0.085	−0.090	1.00	
20. Middle East and North Africa	0.01	−0.05	−0.03	−0.03	−0.04	−0.07	−0.098	−0.105	−0.067	1.00
21. South America	0.05	−0.04	0.08	−0.04	−0.06	−0.09	−0.131	−0.139	−0.089	−0.103
22. Western Europe	−0.01	−0.01	−0.04	−0.08	−0.11	−0.19	−0.259	−0.276	−0.176	−0.204
23. Title: CEO	−0.03	0.00	0.08	0.07	0.08	0.07	−0.026	0.001	−0.031	−0.001
24. Title: VP, GM	−0.03	0.07	−0.02	−0.02	0.02	−0.04	0.037	−0.079	0.062	0.094
25. Title: CFO, Controller	−0.00	0.00	−0.02	−0.02	−0.03	0.00	0.091	−0.032	−0.044	−0.004
26. Title: Technical staff	0.09	−0.03	−0.04	−0.04	−0.06	−0.07	−0.024	0.065	−0.059	0.027
27. Direct/ collaborative	−0.02	0.03	0.06	0.15	0.02	0.08	0.049	0.085	0.006	−0.093
28. Direct/ unilateral	−0.07	0.03	0.14	0.05	−0.00	0.05	0.019	0.098	0.053	−0.066
29. Indirect/ collaborative	−0.01	0.03	0.06	0.14	−0.01	0.07	0.081	0.041	−0.038	−0.088
30. Indirect/ unilateral	−0.06	0.03	0.16	0.03	−0.02	0.04	0.056	0.071	0.009	−0.066

Variable	21	22	23	24	25	26	27	28	29	30
1. Headquarters										
2. Local firm										
3. Local stakeholder pressure										
4. International stakeholder pressure										
5. Publicly held										
6. 100–999 employees										
7. 1000–9999 employees										
8. 10,000 or more employees										
9. Utilities										
10. Extractive										
11. Finance and banking										
12. Manufacturing										
13. Pharmaceutical										
14. Australia/New Zealand										
15. Central America										

(*continued*)

Table 4.3 (continued)

Variable	21	22	23	24	25	26	27	28	29	30
16. Central and Southern Africa										
17. Central and Southern Asia										
18. Eastern Europe										
19. East Asia										
20. Middle East and North Africa										
21. South America	1.00									
22. Western Europe	−0.270	1.00								
23. Title: CEO	−0.035	−0.021	1.00							
24. Title: VP, GM	−0.088	0.045	−0.210	1.00						
25. Title: CFO, Controller	−0.030	0.046	−0.067	−0.104	1.00					
26. Title: Technical staff	0.029	0.040	−0.138	−0.214	−0.068	1.00				
27. Direct/ collaborative	0.023	−0.155	0.000	−0.008	0.010	0.021	1.00			
28. Direct/ unilateral	0.016	−0.132	0.002	−0.006	0.009	−0.019	0.778	1.00		
29. Indirect/ collaborative	0.005	−0.105	0.005	−0.047	0.014	−0.002	0.822	0.575	1.00	
30. Indirect/ unilateral	0.007	−0.099	0.008	−0.041	0.028	−0.052	0.612	0.836	0.698	1.00

Notes: Number of observations is 471. Correlations >±0.09 are significant at the 0.05 level or greater

Table 4.4 Regression results

	Strategic response variables			
	Direct/collaborative (1)	Direct/unilateral (2)	Indirect/collaborative (3)	Indirect/unilateral (4)
Local stakeholder pressure	1.32**	0.69**	0.95	0.35
	(0.50)	(0.27)	(0.61)	(0.31)
International stakeholder pressure	1.04[a]	0.56[a]	1.65**	1.03**
	(0.55)	(0.30)	(0.64)	(0.35)
100–999 employees	3.60*	2.15**	4.95**	3.18**
	(1.48)	(0.80)	(1.85)	1.01
1000–9999 employees	1.11	1.66*	4.37*	4.10***
	(1.48)	(0.85)	(1.98)	(1.10)
10,000 or more employees	1.40	1.91[a]	4.93*	4.18***
	(1.82)	(1.00)	(2.36)	(1.25)
Utilities	-2.78[a]	-2.34**	-0.84	-1.91[a]
	(1.57)	(0.86)	(2.05)	(1.06)
Extractive	-0.79	-0.22	-1.13	-0.67
	(1.62)	(1.00)	(2.09)	(1.19)
Finance and banking	-1.20	-1.91*	-0.21	-2.11[a]
	(1.68)	(0.86)	(2.23)	(1.17)
Manufacturing	-0.93	-0.70	-0.03	-0.56
	(1.36)	(0.78)	(1.75)	1.04
Pharmaceutical	5.81	7.67[a]	6.19	9.71*
	(4.70)	(4.14)	(4.66)	(4.26)
Headquarters	0.10	-0.78	2.36	0.28
	(1.55)	(1.01)	(1.97)	(1.25)
Local firm	1.05	0.30	2.63	1.28

(continued)

Table 4.4 (continued)

	Strategic response variables			
	Direct/collaborative (1)	Direct/unilateral (2)	Indirect/collaborative (3)	Indirect/unilateral (4)
	(1.49)	(0.89)	(1.95)	(1.17)
Publicly held firm	0.36	0.00	1.21	0.09
	(1.23)	(0.70)	(1.59)	(0.92)
Australia/New Zealand	13.99**	2.89	16.89*	2.27
	(5.41)	(2.97)	(7.38)	(3.20)
Central America	-0.15	-0.69	-1.49	-1.38
	(2.9)	(1.51)	(4.06)	(1.94)
Central and Southern Africa	2.59	0.58	1.51	-0.28
	(2.89)	(1.29)	(3.53)	(1.76)
Central and Southern Asia	-1.87	-1.54	-1.90	-1.71
	(2.35)	(1.14)	(2.98)	(1.50)
Eastern Europe	1.16	0.97	0.12	0.68
	(2.31)	(1.17)	(2.96)	(1.58)
Eastern Asia	-2.42	0.037	-6.72[a]	-2.16
	(3.23)	(2.29)	(3.82)	(2.54)
Middle East and North Africa	-5.78**	-2.37[a]	-7.17*	-3.16[a]
	(2.28)	(1.32)	(3.24)	1.79
South America	-2.06	-1.45	-3.60	-2.28
	(2.19)	(1.14)	(2.91)	(1.52)
Western Europe	-3.94*	-1.94*	-4.72[a]	-2.55*
	(1.84)	(0.88)	(2.50)	(1.23)
Title: CEO	-0.039	0.14	1.68	1.07
	(1.56)	(0.90)	(2.22)	(1.20)
Title: VP, GM	1.47	0.51	0.25	-0.20
	(1.28)	(0.80)	(1.67)	(1.03)

Title: CFO, Controller	1.76	1.04	3.26	2.36
	(2.79)	(1.43)	(3.95)	(2.22)
Title: Technical staff	2.39	0.68	0.87	-0.43
	(1.78)	(0.93)	(2.10)	(1.05)
$F(26, 432)$	3.87***	3.23***	3.15***	3.48***
N	459	459	459	459
R^2	0.18	0.16	0.14	0.14

[a]$p < 0.10$; *$p < 0.05$; **$p < 0.01$; ***$p < 0.001$. Robust standard errors are in parentheses

stakeholder pressure is weakly associated with both types (i.e., collaborative and unilateral) of direct strategic responses at $p < 0.10$.

In terms of the control variables, few significant results were found. There was no significant relationship between respondent's title and the likelihood of adopting one of the strategic response strategies. Publicly held firms were no more likely to respond to violent conflict than privately held companies. Respondents from a multinational's corporate headquarters, and solely local firms, were no more likely to respond than multinational's foreign subsidiaries.

There is some indication that regional differences may be associated with the type of likely firm response. Compared with our reference region, companies in North America (United States, Canada, and Mexico), companies in Australia and New Zealand were significantly more likely to respond directly and indirectly to conflict, and to do so in collaboration with others. Firms in the Middle East and North Africa tended to be significantly less likely to engage, particularly in collaboration with other organizations. Likewise, firms from Western Europe also tended to be less likely to engage. For robustness checks, we (1) tested the coefficients for region and found that they were significantly different from one another, and (2) re-estimated our models with an interaction term between collaboration and region. None of the interaction terms was significant for any of our models, but the results for the other key variables of interest were generally consistent with the original results. Results are available upon request.

In another robustness check, we used data from the Uppsala Conflict Data Program from Uppsala University in Sweden (http://www.pcr.uu.se/research/ucdp/), and more specifically the "Uppsala Conflict Database Categorical Variables 1989–2008" and the "UCDP Non-State Conflict Dataset v. 2.3–2010" to identify which countries in our sample had experienced violent conflict since 2000 (see Table 4.2). Based on this information, we added a dummy variable to reflect operation in a country that had experienced conflict (1) since 2000, and (2) since 2003. Results of this analysis indicated that neither variable was significant; there was no significant difference between respondents operating in a conflict-prone country and those that did not.

Beyond the finding that firms larger than 100 employees were significantly more likely to respond strategically to violent conflict than smaller firms, firm size was not a key differentiating factor. There was no significant relationship between respondent's title and the likelihood of adopting one of the strategic response strategies. This suggests that the respondent's level in the organization did not affect his/her response about the firm's likelihood of engagement. In terms of industry, utility firms were significantly less likely than other firms to respond to violent conflict across three of the four types of response strategies. Only firms in the pharmaceutical industry were significantly more likely to respond indirectly to violent conflict. No other significant findings were associated with industry.

Discussion

Our objectives in this study were to investigate whether or not MNEs and local firms would be likely to engage in efforts to reduce violent conflict, and to understand better the relationship between stakeholder pressure and likely firm strategic response to violent conflict. Regarding the first objective, findings from our survey suggest that, contrary to popular wisdom and much of the research on firm response to risk, a substantial number of firms indicated a willingness to engage in violent conflict reduction (interestingly, there was no significant difference between respondents at local firms, MNE subsidiaries, and MNE headquarters in terms of likelihood of engaging). Generally, it is assumed that managers will avoid taking actions like the ones we discuss in our paper, but our findings suggest that this may not be the case. Given the complexity of risks faced by firms today, managers may be willing to adopt nontraditional, or what are assumed to be nontraditional, strategies for minimizing risk to the firm.

In addition, we examined how the geographic source of stakeholder pressure – that is, internationally or locally based – affected firm response choice. The results of our study indicate that local stakeholder pressure is associated with the likelihood that firms will respond directly to violent conflict, collaborating with other organizations or working alone when doing so. International stakeholder pressure is related to the likelihood that firms will respond indirectly to violent conflict, either working alone or in collaboration with others. Thus, while international stakeholder pressure is often extremely influential, as noted throughout the stakeholder literature, in the specific case of spurring firms to engage *directly* in violent conflict resolution, local stakeholders may be more influential. Understanding who these local stakeholders are, and when they are likely to act, is clearly of importance to managers.

We suggest that differences between international and local stakeholder pressure are tied to variations in stakeholder salience, which reflects the firm's perception of the stakeholder's power, legitimacy, and urgency. With respect to violent conflict, salience is likely higher among local than international stakeholders. The power of some local stakeholders may be higher than that of international stakeholders; local employees who fear physical attacks, kidnapping and the like may refuse to work, local government may withhold permits, and the local community and activists may initiate legal action against a firm thought to be contributing to violent conflict. Further, because they are local, their legitimacy in truly representing local interests and having a genuine understanding of the situation is high. Finally, because local stakeholders are directly affected by conflict and violence, their urgency in seeking or demanding a response from a firm is likely to be higher than that of international stakeholders.

With high salience, "managers have a clear and immediate mandate to attend to and give priority to that stakeholder's claim" (Mitchell et al., 1997: 878). We suggest that this imperative is likely to lead to responses that address the stakeholders' concerns directly, because local stakeholders are likely to want to see an end to the violence and the conflict that drives it. Thus responsive firms might adopt direct actions that focus on stopping violence as it is occurring, or on preventing an imminent outbreak of violence.

We suggested that high salience, along with the reputational risks associated with certain kinds of direct responses, would lead firms to use collaborative responses to local stakeholder pressure; however, we found that unilateral responses were as likely as collaborative responses. Similarly, we hypothesized that firms' responses to international stakeholders would be unilateral, rather than collaborative. Again, we found that either type was equally likely. These unanticipated results may be attributable to the fact that firms tend to support a portfolio of responses to difficult social and political problems, including the problem of violent conflict. It may be important to firms to collaborate so as to have access to the knowledge and skills of collaboration partners, and so as to (at least in some cases) diffuse the risk associated with potential unanticipated consequences of the response. Yet it may also be important for the firm to take some actions unilaterally, so that it need not share credit for successes, or be burdened by the time and effort associated with developing and implementing collaborative relationships.

With respect to firm size, the finding that firms with 100 employees or fewer were significantly less likely to strategically respond to violent conflict was not particularly surprising, since firms smaller than 100 employees may lack the capacity or resources to respond strategically. One interesting aspect of the findings on firm size was that larger firms were not more likely than the smallest firms to respond directly and collaboratively to violent conflict. Additional research is necessary to determine whether the finding holds across other samples and in other settings, and why these firms are less likely to respond in this way.

Our study contributes to the work of others who have looked at firms' willingness to respond (or their actual response) to violent conflict (Gladwin & Walter, 1980; Jamali & Mirshak, 2010; Kolk & Lenfant, 2010). More specifically, studies have shown that MNEs operating in countries such as Angola, the Democratic Republic of Congo, and Lebanon are well aware of the connection between business, conflict, and peace (Jamali & Mirshak, 2010; Kolk & Lenfant, 2010). Indeed, there is evidence that, increasingly, firms feel a responsibility to respond to violence in the countries where they do business (Kolk & Lenfant, 2010). As Fort and others have argued, businesses can play a significant role in reducing violence and promoting peace and stability in countries where they operate (Fort, 2007; Fort & Schipani, 2004). Likewise, firms may also be able to reduce the risks they face from violent conflict, and even obtain long-term competitive advantage and/or positive financial outcomes from responding effectively to adversity and conflict (Branzei & Abdelnour, 2010).

Even in the absence of stakeholder pressure, the prevalence of conflict and adversity in many countries around the world suggests that managers should begin to consider how they and their firms might respond. Many firms cannot or will not leave the countries in which they operate, even in the face of conflict. A recent study of seven MNEs operating in Lebanon revealed that none left the country after the 2006 war, despite suspension of operations and extensive disruption to business (Jamali & Mirshak, 2010). This example is repeated across many countries experiencing violence and conflict. For this reason, firms should consider *a priori* what factors may lead them to respond, what strategic options are available, and how they might respond.

Limitations and Future Directions

As with all empirical research, certain limitations of this study should be acknowledged. First, owing to the high costs of translation and the time constraints of our survey partners, the survey was distributed only to UNGC members who were known to have top managers (potential respondents) fluent in reading and writing English. Thus some potential respondents were unable to participate. Nonetheless, the sample included locally owned and subsidiary-level firms from all regions, including those where English is not the primary business language. Since the final sample of respondents represented firms operating across 80 different countries, we do not believe that this created a substantial bias.

Second, although there is no evidence that firms that are members of the UNGC may be more likely to experience or respond to violent conflict, it is possible that the sample firms differ from firms that are not UNGC members. For example, it may be that UNGC members are more likely than other firms to adopt, or suggest that they will adopt, actions that are viewed as socially responsible. To the extent that they perceive firm response to violent conflict as a socially responsible activity, they may be more likely to report a higher likelihood of response. Future research should examine the impact of UNGC membership to answer this question.

A third limitation is that we attribute the association between stakeholder pressure and firm response to stakeholder salience. Most extant empirical research that considers stakeholder salience assesses power, legitimacy, and urgency using archival and secondary sources (e.g., Friedman & Mason, 2004; Magness, 2008; Ryan & Schneider, 2003), but no standard measures have been developed. For this reason, and because of the exploratory nature of our research, we opted not to measure the three aspects of salience directly. Future research should probe more deeply the rationale for firms' responses. Specifically, researchers should develop questions to learn about stakeholders' use of coercive, utilitarian and normative power, as well as about firms' perceptions of stakeholders' legitimacy and urgency. Perhaps some of these aspects of salience are more important than others. For example, firms may be more likely to respond when perceived urgency is high or when stakeholders exercise utilitarian power.

Fourth, our study measures the likelihood that firms will respond to violent conflict, not firms' actual responses to conflict. Although we asked respondents about the likelihood that their firm might experience negative effects from violent conflict, and found that a substantial percentage of firms did see violence as a threat to their operations,[4] it is possible that respondents overestimate or underestimate the likelihood that their firms will adopt one of the strategies described in our study. In addition, respondents who have not experienced a conflict may be not able to predict their actual behavior reliably. Given these limitations, we suggest that future research replicate this study with other types of firms, including those that may have been excluded because of language, and those that are not UNGC members. Further, future research should measure firms' actual responses to violent conflict, although this is not always possible in the midst of a conflict.

[4]When asked about the likelihood that their company would be negatively affected by violent conflict, respondents indicated that they would be moderately or very likely to experience (or require): (a) increased insurance costs (53.4%); (b) increased security (55.7%); (c) disruptions to their supply chains (49.4%); and (d) reductions in firm output (47.3%). In another question, respondents replied that their firm was at a moderate to very high risk of: (a) [an] attack on communities surrounding the company (23%); (b) direct attacks on [the] company's premises (16.4%); (c) physical attacks on employees (21.9%); (d) kidnapping of employees (19%); and (e) unintentional damage to company premises when the company was not the target (21.8%).

We also suggest research to extend this study. For example, future research should explore firms' motivations for selecting particular response strategies. Aguilera et al. (2007), for example, proposed that instrumental, relational, and moral motivations may influence firms to engage in social change. Given that stakeholder pressure is significantly related to the likelihood of firm response to conflict, it would be valuable to better understand firms' rationale for responding to these pressures. Is the rationale primarily instrumental – that is, to avoid negative publicity or financial loss to the firm; is it more relational in nature, arising from a desire to increase the perceived legitimacy of the firm and respond to stakeholder concerns; or is it moral, reflecting a sense of collective responsibility for important public interest objectives?

Our exploratory empirical analysis of how firms respond to violent conflict suggests that qualitative research designs that enable scholars to explore these and similar questions more deeply would enlighten our understanding of firm response to violent conflict. It would be valuable to understand how many firms operating across a variety of industries respond to one specific conflict. For instance, by studying firm reaction to a specific conflict, scholars can control for the characteristics of a specific conflict, measure its impact, and assess how and why firms in the vicinity of conflict respond or not. A field study during a period of conflict might yield important insights into firm behavior.

Another avenue for future research is to consider how violent conflict resolution activities impact on firms' financial performance. While the research linking social responsibility to financial performance has been inconclusive (Margolis & Walsh, 2001), it is conceptually and methodologically possible to link specific activities undertaken by a firm with its financial performance (Hillman & Keim, 2001), through, for example, considerations of risk management (e.g., Orlitzky & Benjamin, 2001) or effects on consumers' or investors' decisions (e.g., Waddock & Graves, 1997). Research on the impact of conflict and responses to it on firm financial performance could clarify the extent to which there is a business case to engage in conflict resolution activities. We are also interested in exploring the relationship between firm strategy and the reduction of (1) risk to the firm, and (2) violence/conflict in society.

Our research considered how stakeholder pressures affect firm response to violent conflict. Perhaps the relationships are more complex than we present. For example, parent organizations (headquarters) may impose new requirements on their subsidiaries in response to stakeholder pressure.[5] Similarly, companies may react to stakeholder pressure by imposing new requirements on firms in their supply chain. Further, factors other than stakeholder pressure may also influence a firm's decision to respond. For example, cultural differences may result in variations across regions. Local attitudes toward foreign businesses and the private sector more generally may affect firms' willingness and ability to respond. There may also be differences in response patterns, based on the characteristics and geographic location of the conflict (Getz & Oetzel, 2010; Jamali & Mirshak, 2010; Kolk & Lenfant, 2010). Perhaps culture and/or country of origin play a role in determining whether firms are more likely to act alone, collaborate with other organizations, and respond directly or indirectly to violent conflict. Future research should compare firm responses in different types of settings, and with different conflict characteristics.

Implications for Theory and Practice

To the extent that firms are actually addressing violent conflict, practitioners may be ahead of scholars in their consideration of big issues that are sometimes seen as outside the domain of business – while scholars might question whether firms should respond to violent conflict, many of the firms in our study report that they are likely to go ahead and do it. While much more research on this topic is needed, there are some immediate implications for management practice. The most fundamental implication is that firms operating in settings of violent conflict need not be passive observers or victims. Further, conflict need not be avoided at any cost. Firms may respond proactively, and may potentially help to reduce conflict. Many firms are already engaging in such activities. Among MNEs, a firm that voluntarily responds to violent conflict, especially one seen as a first-mover, may establish a position that strengthens its

[5] We thank one of our anonymous reviewers for this insight.

legitimacy and ultimately leads to a long-term competitive advantage in the host country. When the situation in the country improves, the firm may have advantages stemming from good relations with local stakeholders and activists. The appreciation of the host government and general community might lead to greater access and preferential opportunities for expansion. A further advantage to the firm that voluntarily undertakes responses to violent conflict is that the experience may lead to a competitive advantage in high-risk environments (Delios & Henisz, 2003). Firm competence in managing risk may be a valuable, rare, costly-to-imitate resource that the MNE can leverage in a variety of operating environments to outperform competitors.

Conclusion

Our findings show that many businesses operating in areas affected by violent conflict both acknowledge the difficulties violence creates for business and are likely to accept the proactive roles that firms may undertake for reducing the problem. To a large extent, it appears that stakeholder pressure is a key factor in moving firms from the acknowledgement of the problem to responsive action. These observations suggest that even reluctant firms may make contributions to reducing violent conflict. In addition to the theoretical and empirical contributions, this study is expected to contribute to practice and policy. A better understanding of firms' responses to violent conflict can help all those affected by violent conflict – firms themselves, governments, and others – develop strategies aimed at reducing violence and its devastating negative consequences.

Acknowledgements We would like to thank Melissa Powell and Da Woon Chung from the United Nations Global Compact, and Canan Gündüz from mediatEUr (formerly from International Alert), for their valuable and productive partnership, without which this paper would not have been possible. We also want to acknowledge three reviewers for their valuable comments on our paper, and Parthiban David for helpful comments and suggestions on an earlier version of this manuscript.

Appendix 1

Scales for Dependent Variables

Scale Measuring Direct and Indirect Strategic Responses

Think about the conflict-prone countries where you operate. How likely is your company to engage in any of the following activities in those countries?

1. Lobby the government to actively resolve the conflict.
2. Speak out publicly against violence and/or its causes.
3. Mediate interactions between parties to the conflict.
4. Organize negotiations among the conflict parties.
5. Conform to relevant global multilateral agreements.
6. Cut ties with actors involved in human rights violations.
7. Adopt human resource policies that avoid aggravating social and ethnic tensions in the society.
8. Verify that the participants in our supply chain have not contributed to the conflict.
9. Adopt industry codes of conduct for operating in conflict areas.
10. Donate resources to respond to local humanitarian crises.
11. Provide human rights training to private security guards.

(Items 6 and 11 were dropped from the scale, since they did not load onto the constructs of interest.)

The reliability (Cronbach's α) for the resulting nine-item scale assessing likelihood of working directly or indirectly to respond to violent conflict was 0.86.

Scale Measuring Collaborative or Unilateral action

Please indicate your level of agreement with the following statements: "My company is likely to work in the following ways to address violent conflict ..."

1. Work independently of other organizations to respond to conflict.
2. My company would be unlikely to work with another company.
3. My company would be unlikely to work with a non-government organization.
4. Develop response strategy without consulting with others outside the firm.
5. My company would be unlikely to work with multilateral organizations.
6. *Independently determine our firm's response objectives.*
7. Participate in industry association activities.
8. Cooperate with NGOs.
9. Work with the national government.
10. Work with a multinational company.
11. Collaborate with a local company in the host country.
12. Cooperate with other organizations in planning a response strategy.

(Item 6 was dropped from the scale since it did not load onto the construct of interest.)

The reliability (Cronbach's α) for the resulting 11-item scale assessing likelihood of working unilaterally or collaboration was 0.74.

Appendix 2

Measures Derived From Factor-Based Scales

Indirect and Collaborative Response

1. Conform to relevant global multilateral agreements.
2. Adopt human resource policies that avoid aggravating social and ethnic tensions in the society.
3. Verify that the participants in our supply chain have not contributed to the conflict.
4. Adopt industry codes of conduct for operating in conflict areas.
5. Donate resources to respond to local humanitarian crises.
6. Participate in industry association activities.

7. Cooperate with NGOs.
8. Work with the national government.
9. Work with a multinational company.
10. Collaborate with a local company in the host country.
11. Cooperate with other organizations in planning a response strategy.

The reliability (Cronbach's α) for the resulting 11-item measure was 0.82.

Indirect and Unilateral Response

1. Conform to relevant global multilateral agreements.
2. Adopt human resource policies that avoid aggravating social and ethnic tensions in the society.
3. Verify that the participants in our supply chain have not contributed to the conflict.
4. Adopt industry codes of conduct for operating in conflict areas.
5. Donate resources to respond to local humanitarian crises.
6. Work independently of other organizations to respond to conflict.
7. My company would be unlikely to work with another company.
8. My company would be unlikely to work with a NGO.
9. Develop response strategy without consulting with others outside the firm.
10. My company would be unlikely to work with multilateral organizations.

The reliability (Cronbach's α) for the resulting ten-item measure was 0.78.

Direct and Collaborative Response

1. Lobby the government to actively resolve the conflict.
2. Speak out publicly against violence and/or its causes.
3. Mediate interactions between parties to the conflict.
4. Organize negotiations among the conflict parties.

5. Participate in industry association activities.
6. Cooperate with NGOs.
7. Work with the national government.
8. Work with a multinational company.
9. Collaborate with a local company in the host country.
10. Cooperate with other organizations in planning a response strategy.

The reliability (Cronbach's α) for the resulting ten-item measure was 0.81.

Direct and Unilateral Response

1. Lobby the government to actively resolve the conflict.
2. Speak out publicly against violence and/or its causes.
3. Mediate interactions between parties to the conflict.
4. Organize negotiations among the conflict parties.
5. Work independently of other organizations to respond to conflict.
6. My company would be unlikely to work with another company.
7. My company would be unlikely to work with a NGO.
8. Develop response strategy without consulting with others outside the firm.
9. My company would be unlikely to work with multilateral organizations.

The reliability (Cronbach's α for the resulting nine-item measure was 0.61.

Appendix 3

Scales for Independent Variables

Scale for Local Stakeholders

To what degree have you been pressured by the following stakeholders to respond to violent conflict in any of the countries where you have operations? For this set of responses, consider national sources of pressure (pressure from *within* the country):

1. local consumers;
2. local employees;
3. local community leaders;
4. local NGOs;
5. national government; and
6. local media.

The reliability (Cronbach's α) for the resulting six-item measure was 0.93.

Scale for International Stakeholders

Factor analysis revealed that six items should be retained.

To what degree have you been pressured by the following stakeholders to respond to violent conflict in any of the countries where you have operations? For this set of responses, consider international sources of pressure (pressure from *outside* the country):

1. the government of your company's headquarters;
2. international NGOs;
3. shareholders;
4. international media;
5. consumers from your company's home country; and
6. multilateral organizations.

The reliability (Cronbach's α) for the six-item measure was 0.94.

References

Agle, B. R., Mitchell, R. K., & Sonnenfeld, J. A. (1999). Who matters to CEOs? An investigation of stakeholder attributes and salience, corporate performance, and CEO values. *Academy of Management Journal, 42*(5), 507–525.

Aguilera, R. V., Rupp, D. E., Williams, C. A., & Ganapathi, J. (2007). Putting the S back in corporate social responsibility: A multilevel theory of social change in organizations. *Academy of Management Review, 32*(3), 836–863.
Armstrong, J. S., & Overton, T. S. (1977). Estimating nonresponse bias in mail surveys. *Journal of Marketing Research, 14*(3), 396–402.
Ballentine, K., & Nitzschke, H. (2004). Business and armed conflict: An assessment of issues and options. *Die Friedens-Warte, 79*(1–2), 35–56.
Banfield, J., Gündüz, C., & Killick, N. (Eds.). (2006). *Local business, local peace: The peacebuilding potential of the domestic private sector*. International Alert.
Belsey, D. A., Kuh, E., & Welsch, R. E. (1980). *Regression diagnostics*. Wiley.
Bennett, J. (2002). Multinational corporations, social responsibility and conflict. *Journal of International Affairs, 55*(2), 393–410.
Berman, J. (2000). Boardrooms and bombs: Strategies of multinational corporations in conflict areas. *Harvard International Review, 22*(3), 28–32.
Berman, S. L., Wicks, A. C., Kotha, S., & Jones, T. M. (1999). Does stakeholder orientation matter? The relationship between stakeholder management models and firm financial performance. *Academy of Management Journal, 42*(5), 488–506.
Boddewyn, J., & Brewer, T. (1994). International-business political behavior: New theoretical dimensions. *Academy of Management Review, 19*(1), 119–143.
Branzei, O., & Abdelnour, S. (2010). Another day, another dollar: Enterprise resilience under terrorism in developing countries. *Journal of International Business Studies, 41*(5), 804–825.
Carroll, A. B. (2000). A commentary and an overview of key questions on corporate social performance measurement. *Business & Society, 39*(4), 466–478.
Cetindamar, D., & Husoy, K. (2007). Corporate social responsibility practices and environmentally responsible behavior: The case of the United Nations Global Compact. *Journal of Business Ethics, 76*(2), 63–176.
Christmann, P. (2004). Multinational companies and the natural environment: Determinants of global environmental policy standardization. *Academy of Management Journal, 47*(5), 747–760.
Collier, P. (2007). Economic causes of civil conflict and their implications for policy. In C. A. Crocker, F. O. Hampson, & P. Aall (Eds.), *Leashing the dogs of war: Conflict management in a divided world* (pp. 197–218). United States Institute of Peace.
Delios, A., & Henisz, W. J. (2003). Political hazards, experience, and sequential entry strategies: The international expansion of Japanese firms, 1980–1998. *Strategic Management Journal, 24*(11), 1153–1164.

Diamond, L., & McDonald, J. W. (1996). *Multi-track diplomacy: A systems approach to peace*. Kumarian Press.

Dillman, D. A. (2000). *Mail and internet surveys: The tailored design method*. Wiley.

Doh, J. P., & Teegen, H. (Eds.). (2003). *Globalization and NGOs: Transforming business, government, and society*. Praeger.

Dunfee, T., & Fort, T. L. (2003). Corporate hypergoals, sustainable peace, and the adapted firm. *Vanderbilt Journal of Transnational Law, 36*(2), 563–617.

Dunning, J. (1998). Location and the multinational enterprise: A neglected factor? *Journal of International Business Studies, 29*(1), 45–66.

Eesley, C., & Lenox, M. J. (2006). Firm responses to secondary stakeholder action. *Strategic Management Journal, 27*(8), 765–781.

Fisher, R. (1997). *Interactive conflict resolution*. Syracuse University Press.

Fisher, R., & Ury, W. (1991). *Getting to yes: Negotiating an agreement without giving in*. Penguin Books.

Fort, T. L. (2007). *Business, integrity, and peace: Beyond geopolitical and disciplinary boundaries*. Cambridge University Press.

Fort, T. L., & Schipani, C. A. (2004). *The role of business in fostering peaceful societies*. Cambridge University Press.

Freeman, R. E. (1984). *Strategic management: A stakeholder approach*. Pitman.

Friedman, M. T., & Mason, D. S. (2004). A stakeholder approach to understanding economic development decision making: Public subsidies for professional sports facilities. *Economic Development Quarterly, 18*(3), 236–254.

Galtung, J. (1996). *Peace by peaceful means: Peace and conflict, development and civilization*. Sage.

Gerson, A., & Colletta, N. (2002). *Privatizing peace: From conflict to security*. Transnational Publishers.

Getz, K. A., & Oetzel, J. (2010). MNE strategic intervention in violent conflict: Variations based on conflict characteristics. *Journal of Business Ethics, 89*(4), 375–386.

Gladwin, T., & Walter, I. (1980). How multinationals can manage social and political forces. *Journal of Business Strategy, 1*(1), 54–68.

Goodpaster, K. E. (2004). *Creating corporate conscience: American Refining Group and Caux Round Table self assessment and improvement process*. Paper presented at the International Conference on Voluntary Codes of Conduct for Multinational Corporations: Promises and Challenges, New York.

Gray, B. (1985). Conditions facilitating interorganizational collaboration. *Human Relations, 38*(10), 911–936.

Guáqueta, A. (2008). Occidental petroleum, Cerrejon, and NGO partnerships in Colombia: Lessons learned. In O. F. Williams (Ed.), *Peace through commerce: Responsible corporate citizenship and the ideals of the United Nations Global Compact* (pp. 381–402). University of Notre Dame Press.

Heidelberg Institute for International Conflict Research (HIIK). (2008). *Conflict barometer 2008*. http://www.hiik.de/en/konfliktbarometer/pdf/ConflictBarometer_2008.pdf. Accessed 5 Feb 2009.

Hillman, A. J. (2003). Determinants of political strategies in US multinationals. *Business & Society, 42*(4), 455–484.

Hillman, A., & Hitt, M. (1999). Corporate political strategy formulation: A model of approach, participation, and strategy decisions. *Academy of Management Review, 24*(4), 825–842.

Hillman, A., & Keim, G. (2001). Shareholder value, stakeholder management, and social issues: What's the bottom line? *Strategic Management Journal, 22*(2), 125–141.

Husted, B. W., & Allen, D. B. (2006). Corporate social responsibility in the multinational enterprise: Strategic and institutional approaches. *Journal of International Business Studies, 37*(6), 838–849.

Jamali, D., & Mirshak, R. (2010). Business-conflict linkages: Revisiting MNCs, CSR, and conflict. *Journal of Business Ethics, 93*(3), 443–464.

Kassinis, G., & Vafeas, N. (2006). Stakeholder pressures and environmental performance. *Academy of Management Journal, 49*(1), 145–159.

Kaufman, A. M., Englander, E. J., & Marcus, A. A. (1993). Selecting an organizational structure for implementing issues management: A transaction costs and agency theory perspective. In B. M. Mitnick (Ed.), *Corporate political agency* (pp. 148–168). Sage.

Kim, J., & Mueller, C. W. (1978). *Factor analysis: Statistical methods and practical issues*. Sage.

Kline, J. M. (2000). Business codes and conduct in a global political economy. In O. F. Williams (Ed.), *Global codes of conduct: An idea whose time has come* (pp. 39–56). University of Notre Dame Press.

Kolk, A., & Lenfant, F. (2010). MNC reporting on CSR and conflict in Central Africa. *Journal of Business Ethics, 93*(2), 241–255.

Konczak, L. (2001). Review of the process of business/environmental collaborations: Partnering for sustainability. *Personnel Psychology, 54*(2), 515–518.

Kriesburg, L. (1998). *Constructive conflicts: From escalation to resolution*. Rowman & Littlefield Publishers.

Lieberfeld, D. (2002). Evaluating the contributions of track-two diplomacy to conflict termination in South Africa, 1984–90. *Journal of Peace Research, 39*(3), 355–372.

Luo, Y. (2006). Political behavior, social responsibility, and perceived corruption: A structuration perspective. *Journal of International Business Studies, 37*(6), 747–766.

Magness, V. (2008). Who are the stakeholders now? An empirical examination of the Mitchell, Agle, and Wood theory of stakeholder salience. *Journal of Business Ethics, 83*(2), 177–192.

Margolis, J. D., & Walsh, J. P. (2001). *People and profits? The search for a link between a company's social and financial performance*. Lawrence Erlbaum Associates.

Miall, H., Ramsbotham, O., & Woodhouse, T. (2008). *Contemporary conflict resolution*. Polity Press.

Mitchell, R. K., Agle, B. R., & Wood, D. J. (1997). Toward a theory of stakeholder identification and salience: Defining the principle of who and what really counts. *Academy of Management Review, 22*(4), 853–886.

Montville, J. V. (1992). Transnationalism and the role of track-two diplomacy. In W. S. Thompson, K. M. Jensen, R. N. Smith, & K. M. Schraub (Eds.), *Approaches to peace: An intellectual map* (pp. 253–270). United States Institute for Peace.

Oetzel, J., Getz, K., & Ladek, S. (2007). The role of multinational enterprises in responding to violent conflict: A conceptual model and framework for research. *American Business Law Journal, 44*(2), 331–358.

Orlitzky, M., & Benjamin, J. D. (2001). Corporate social performance and firm risk: A meta-analytic review. *Business & Society, 40*(4), 369–396.

Phillips, R. (2003). *Stakeholder theory and organizational ethics*. Berrett-Koehler Publishers.

Podsakoff, P. M., MacKenzie, S. B., Lee, J. Y., & Podsakoff, N. P. (2003). Common method biases in behavioral research: A critical review of the literature and recommended remedies. *Journal of Applied Psychology, 88*(5), 879–903.

Prahalad, C. K., & Bettis, R. A. (1986). The dominant logic: A new linkage between diversity and performance. *Strategic Management Journal, 7*(6), 485–501.

Runhar, H., & Lafferty, H. (2009). Governing corporate social responsibility: An assessment of the contribution of the UN Global Compact to CSR strategies in the telecommunications industry. *Journal of Business Ethics, 84*(4), 479–495.

Ryan, L. V., & Schneider, M. (2003). Institutional investor power and heterogeneity: Implications for agency and stakeholder theories. *Business & Society, 42*(4), 398–429.

Schermerhorn, J. R., Jr. (1975). Determinants of interorganizational cooperation. *Academy of Management Journal, 18*(4), 846–856.

Smith, G., & Feldman, D. (2003). *Company codes of conduct and international standards: An analytical comparison*. World Bank.

Stern, A. J., & Hicks, T. (2000). *The process of business/environmental collaborations: Partnering for sustainability*. Quorum.

Szwajkowski, E. (2000). Simplifying the principles of stakeholder management: The three most important principles. *Business & Society, 39*(4), 379–396.

Teegen, H., Doh, J. P., & Vachani, S. (2004). The importance of nongovernmental organizations (NGOs) in global governance and value creation: An international business research agenda. *Journal of International Business Studies, 35*(6), 463–483.

van Tulder, R., & Kolk, A. (2001). Multinationality and corporate ethics: Codes of conduct in the sporting goods industry. *Journal of International Business Studies, 32*(2), 267–283.

Venaik, S., Midgley, D. F., & Devinney, T. M. (2005). Dual paths to performance: The impact of global pressures on MNC subsidiary conduct and performance. *Journal of International Business Studies, 36*(6), 655–675.

Waddock, S. A., & Graves, S. B. (1997). The corporate social performance – Financial performance link. *Strategic Management Journal, 18*(4), 303–319.

Winston, M. (2003). Corporate responsibility for preventing human rights abuses in conflict areas. In J. Frynas & S. Pegg (Eds.), *Transnational corporations and human rights* (pp. 70–99). Palgrave Macmillan.

5

New 'Dominant Logic' on How Firms Respond to Crises: A Commentary

Jennifer Oetzel

Oetzel and Getz (2012) Original Research Motivation

When we first began thinking about this project on how managers and their MNEs might respond to political risk and crises abroad, a "dominant logic" (Prahalad & Bettis, 1986) at the time was bargaining power theory. A key tenet of bargaining power theory is that, before MNEs invested in a particular location, they should seek to extract protections and investment incentives from host country governments. The rationale being that after MNEs' investment was on the ground their bargaining

It is an honor for Kathleen Getzand I to have our co-authored article chosen for the book, "Crises and Disruptions in International Business," to be published in the JIBS Collection Series by Palgrave Macmillan. We would like to thank Murad Mithani, Rajneesh Narula, Irina Surdu, and Alain Verbeke for selecting our article for this volume. It is particularly gratifying since the project was an extremely rewarding one for both of us.

J. Oetzel (✉)
Kogod School of Business, American University, Washington, DC, USA
e-mail: oetzelj@american.edu

M. A. Mithani et al. (eds.), *Crises and Disruptions in International Business*, JIBS Special Collections, https://doi.org/10.1007/978-3-030-80383-4_5

power would diminish and they would become subject to the whims of the host country government. While that approach yielded some safeguards, it tied MNEs to unsavory, authoritarian governments that sought to maximize their own personal interests rather than those of their country. Under this model, MNEs might gain some short-term advantages, but in the long-term, MNEs were associated with, and even perceived to be complicit in, the actions of corrupt political regimes.

Although similar situations existed in different parts of the world, a watershed moment for MNE-host country relations occurred in 1998 in Indonesia. MNEs that had done business with President Suharto and his family – a requirement for doing business in Indonesia - had benefited for years from the regime's favors and investment protections. The fall of the military dictatorship, however, exposed the MNE-government alliance as a shady partnership that provided protection only while the regime lasted. Once Suharto and his family were removed, companies suffered severe losses and it became clear that MNEs had tied their fortunes to a government engaged in crony capitalism and systematic human rights abuses.

A few years following the events in Indonesia, my co-author and I started to consider the ways in which MNEs might be able to fundamentally reduce conflict, simultaneously benefitting the firms' themselves as well as the host country stakeholders more broadly. We developed a typology of MNE responses to violent conflict, that would seek to address risk through direct or indirect actions; and actions that could be conducted by firms alone or in collaboration with others (Oetzel et al., 2007). We then set a research agenda on the topic which led to a partnership with the United Nations Global Compact (UNGC) and later the Institute for Economics and Peace (IEP),[1] resulting in our 2012 JIBS article.

For understandable reasons, business schools rarely, if ever, train managers of MNEs to address political risk by reducing violence or conflict at its source. We therefore turned to the research in political science to gain insights into conflict dynamics, Track II interventions, and an understanding of the political dynamics fueling conflict. One example that stood out was the case of violent conflict in Northern Ireland. In 1994,

[1] The author is a member of the Research Committee at IEP.

the Northern Ireland Confederation of British Industry (CBI) prepared a document that is colloquially known as the "Peace Dividend Paper" (Günduz et al., 2006: 438–439). In this document, business leaders argued that if violence ceased, the money currently spent on law, order and protective services (some $1.42 billion in 1994)," could be redirected to other sectors such as education and infrastructure, as well as the general promotion of social and economic development in the region. A subsequent ceasefire supported these arguments: *"[d]uring the period of nonviolence, tourism rose 20 percent in a year and unemployment dropped by 11.5 percent, its lowest level in 14 years. Over the following six months, $48 million in new investment ventures where announced" (*Günduz, et al., 2006*: 439).* Given the potential power and influence of businesses in many countries, we sought to examine whether and how MNEs would engage in efforts to reduce violence in the host countries where they operate.

Our findings indicated that local stakeholder pressure was associated with an increased likelihood that MNEs would be willing to respond directly to violent conflict, and that MNEs would collaborate with other organizations, or work alone, when doing so. Direct responses to crises involved actions such as lobbying the government to resolve the conflict, mediating interactions between the parties involved in a conflict (as Anglo-American Mining reportedly did during Apartheid in South Africa (Lieberfeld, 2002)), or working through industry associations to effect change, among other strategies and tactics. International stakeholder pressure was associated with the likelihood that firms would respond indirectly to violent conflict, collaborating with other organizations or working alone. Indirect responses included adopting industry codes of conduct, donating resources to respond to crises, or other actions to modify human resource policies to avoid aggravating social and/or ethnic tensions.

In contrast to prior studies that focused on the impact of international stakeholders on MNE behaviors, we found that local stakeholders were more likely to influence MNE responses. We explained that local stakeholder influence may be more salient because "local stakeholders are directly affected by conflict and violence, [so] their urgency in seeking or demanding a response from a firm is likely to be higher than that of international stakeholders" (page 179). Local stakeholders may be in a better position to understand conflict dynamics and which MNE actions may be most effective to reduce conflict.

One of the insights from our study was that "contrary to popular wisdom and much of the research on firm response to risk, a substantial number of firms indicated a willingness to engage in violent conflict reduction" (page 179). While, until then, research tended to assume that managers would avoid taking actions to reduce risk at its origin, our findings suggested that managers may be willing to adopt non-traditional strategies for minimizing risk to the firm and improving host country conditions.

State-of-the-Field on Crises and Disruptions

Given world events, there is substantial research interest in how violence, terrorism, and political risk affect MNEs and their subsidiaries in the host countries in which they operate (see Branzei & Abdelnour, 2010; Czinkota et al., 2010; Dai et al., 2013; Darendeli & Hill, 2016; Li & Vashchilko, 2010; Meyer & Thein, 2014; Oh & Oetzel, 2017; Surdu et al., 2019; Witte et al., 2017). Scholars explore different approaches and perspectives in an effort to generate new insights into how best to manage risk.

In particular, one study to bring novel insights into managing political risk was the study by Darendeli and Hill (2016). In their article, the authors tackled the dilemma around how to manage political risk in the context of operating in Libya. Although MNEs needed to maintain ties with Qadhafi to operate in Libya, those firms that "invested in social-benefit projects" and formed "social ties with families with few ties to Qadhafi," enjoyed increased legitimacy in the country and were able to survive the fall of the Qadhafi regime (Darendeli & Hill, 2016: 68). The implications of the study are that what is good for the host country, its local firms, and institutions, can also be risk reducing and good business for MNEs.

In other studies, researchers are explicitly embracing stakeholder theory with an eye towards understanding MNE – stakeholder relationships

(Buysse & Verbeke, 2003; Crilly, 2011) and their impact on MNEs. One study suggests that MNEs may focus on rights- rather than standards-based CSR when stakeholders possess a greater level of power; thus, influential stakeholders can move MNEs to address substantive issues (Rathert, 2016). Consequently, by making substantive contributions to improving labor and human rights, MNEs are expected to benefit themselves and the communities in which they operate (Rathert, 2016; Wettstein et al., 2019). In the same vein, scholars argued specifically for the financial value of positive stakeholder relationships (in addition to the high cost of conflict with key stakeholders) (Dorobantu et al., 2017; Henisz et al., 2014).

Also notable, in a 2006 JIBS article, Husted & Allen (2006: 838) explained that "institutional pressures rather than strategic analysis of social issues and stakeholders, [were] guiding decision-making with respect to CSR". Since that paper was published, stakeholder influence has become increasingly salient. Even so, we are not yet at the point that substantive issues around human rights, and the positive economic and social impact that MNEs can have on conflict-affected countries, are considered part and parcel of addressing (and possibly preempting) crises and disruptions. Moreover, we know little about whether MNE efforts to positively contribute to host country environments are, indeed, effective. A comprehensive bibliometric mapping of research on this issue suggests that, by and large, socially responsible strategies are not having the intended impact (Barnett et al., 2020). Moreover, benefits typically accrue to "specific stakeholders rather than to wider society" (Barnett et al., 2020: 937). One way to move research forward on MNE response to crises and disruptions is to reconsider our "dominant logic" (Prahalad & Bettis, 1986) around the role of the MNE in society (Lall & Narula, 2004; Oetzel & Doh, 2009).

A New Mindset for Managing Risk?

There is a general sense of crisis and disruption in many parts of the world, triggered, in part, by the Covid-19 pandemic. MNEs have substantial economic power and political influence and, as a result, their actions can affect the locations in which they operate. As we focus on how MNEs can manage political risk and contribute to the countries in which they operate, we must also recognize that MNEs can engage in irresponsible corporate practices that undermine host country institutions, aggravate inequality, and ultimately increase political and social risk. MNEs may also seek legitimacy in their home countries but transfer illegitimate or even illegal practices abroad (Surroca, Tribo, & Zahra, 2013).

Crises and disruptions can negatively affect MNEs, but MNEs can (intentionally or unintentionally) aggravate conditions that cause crises and disruptions. As such: how do we integrate these ideas into our future research? Without understanding the complexity of MNE behavior, we may very well be the proverbial blind men, each one studying only one part of an elephant yet believing they fully understand what stands in front of them. Approaching the "elephant" in a business-as-usual manner can unintentionally worsen conflicts and crises, as well as undermine peace dynamics in fragile locations. While MNEs can generate economic growth, engage in life saving research and development, create good jobs and enhance livelihoods, support strong institutions, and make valuable contributions to society, there is no expectation or requirement that they do so, especially in the absence of external pressures (Oetzel & Miklian, 2017).

In light of the gross socio-economic inequities laid bare by the Covid-19 pandemic, and the role that some businesses like Facebook, Twitter, and others have played in exacerbating socio-political weaknesses for profit, we, as international business scholars and educators, have the opportunity to reconsider 'business-as-usual'. Do we take for granted or simply accept that in some cases MNEs are aggravating socioeconomic inequality and abetting human rights abuses? For instance, "prestigious" placements for new MBAs like Facebook, YouTube, Twitter, McKinsey & Co., have been linked to instances of widely reported human rights abuses in the U.S. and around the world. Yet, business schools have been relatively silent on cases of serious corporate misconduct (Benner et al., 2018; Bogdanich & Forsythe, 2020). Moreover, is Facebook's refusal to curb hate speech, even in the face of advertiser boycotts, simply a strategic choice or is it an irresponsible corporate practice (Graham, 2020)? In

2016, Goldman Sachs agreed to pay more than $5 billion dollars as part of a settlement with the Department of Justice (2016) over its sale of mortgage-backed securities in 2005–2007. The, company's actions affected "distressed borrowers" and entire communities. Such actions undermine the social fabric, increase inequality, and ultimately undermine the environment for business. Effective responses to crises and disruptions often require a change in our "dominant logic." For those of us who are seasoned researchers, positioned to challenge norms, an important question remains: What role do we play in addressing today's socioeconomic challenges and how do we make a positive contribution to the next era of "best business practices?"

References

Barnett, M. L., Henriques, I., & Husted, B. W. (2020). Beyond good intentions: Designing CSR initiatives for greater social impact. *Journal of Management, 46*(6), 937–964.

Benner, K., Mazzetti, M., Hubbard, B., & Isaac, M. (2018, October 20). Saudis' image makers: A troll army and a Twitter insider. *New York Times.*

Bogdanich, W., & Forsythe, M. (2020, December 1). McKinsey proposed paying pharmacy companies rebates for oxycontin overdoses. *New York Times.*

Branzei, O., & Abdelnour, S. (2010). Another day, another dollar: Enterprise resilience under terrorism in developing countries. *Journal of International Business Studies, 41*(5), 804–825.

Buysse, K., & Verbeke, A. (2003). Proactive environmental strategies: A stakeholder management perspective. *Strategic Management Journal, 24*(5), 453–470.

Crilly, D. (2011). Predicting stakeholder orientation in the multinational enterprise: A mid-range theory. *Journal of International Business Studies, 42*, 694–717.

Czinkota, M. R., Knight, G., Liesch, P. W., & Steen, J. (2010). Terrorism and international business: A research agenda. *Journal of International Business Studies, 41*, 826–843.

Dai, L., Eden, L., & Beamish, P. W. (2013). Place, space, and geographical exposure: Foreign subsidiary survival in conflict zones. *Journal of International Business Studies, 44*(6), 554–578.

Darendeli, I. S., & Hill, T. L. (2016). Uncovering the complex relationships between political risk and MNE firm legitimacy: Insights from Libya. *Journal of International Business Studies, 47*, 68–92.

Department of Justice. (2016, April 11). Goldman Sachs agrees to pay more than $5 billion in connection with its sale of residential mortgage backed securities. https://www.justice.gov/opa/pr/goldman-sachs-agrees-pay-more-5-billion-connection-its-sale-residential-mortgage-backed. Accessed 10 Dec 2020.

Dorobantu, S., Henisz, W. J., & Nartey, L. (2017). Not all sparks light a fire: Stakeholder and shareholder reactions to critical events in contested markets. *Administrative Science Quarterly, 62*(3), 561–597.

Graham, M. (2020, August 6). Zuckerberg was right: Ad boycotts don't hurt Facebook that much. *CNBC.* https://www.cnbc.com/2020/08/04/some-major-companies-will-keep-pausing-facebook-ads-as-boycott-ends.html. Accessed 10 Dec 2020.

Günduz, C., Banfield, J., & Killick, N. (Eds.). (2006). *Local business, local peace: The peacebuilding potential of the domestic private sector.* International Alert.

Henisz, W. J., Dorobantu, S., & Nartey, L. J. (2014). Spinning gold: The financial returns to stakeholder engagement. *Strategic Management Journal, 35*(12), 1727–1748.

Husted, B. W., & Allen, D. B. (2006). Corporate social responsibility in the multinational business enterprise: Strategic and institutional approaches. *Journal of International Business Studies, 37*, 838–849.

Lall, S., & Narula, R. (2004). Foreign direct investment and its role in economic development: Do we need a new agenda? *The European Journal of Development Research, 16*(3), 447–464.

Li, Q., & Vashchilko, T. (2010). Dyadic military conflict, security alliances, and bilateral FDI flows. *Journal of International Business Studies, 41*, 765–782.

Lieberfeld, D. (2002). Evaluating the contributions of track-two diplomacy to conflict termination in South Africa, 1984–90. *Journal of Peace Research, 39*(3), 355–372.

Meyer, K., & Thein, H. H. (2014). Business under adverse home country institutions: The case of international sanctions against Myanmar. *Journal of World Business, 49*(1), 156–171.

Oetzel, J., & Doh, J. (2009). Multinational enterprise in developing countries: Spillovers, liabilities and resource complementarity. *Journal of World Business, 44*(2), 108–120.

Oetzel, J., & Getz, K. (2012). Why and how might firms respond strategically to violent conflict? *Journal of International Business Studies, 43*, 166–186.

Oetzel, J., Getz, K., & Ladek, S. (2007). The role of multinational enterprises in responding to violent conflict: A conceptual model and framework for research. *American Business Law Journal, 44*(2), 331–358.

Oetzel, J., & Miklian, J. (2017). Multinational enterprises, risk management, and the business and economics of peace (invited perspective piece). *Multinational Business Review, 25*(4), 270–286.

Oh, C. H., & Oetzel, J. (2017). Once bitten twice shy? Experience managing violent conflict risk and MNC subsidiary-level investment and expansion. *Strategic Management Journal, 38*(3), 714–731.

Prahalad, C. K., & Bettis, R. A. (1986). The dominant logic: A new linkage between diversity and performance. *Strategic Management Journal, 7*(6), 485–501.

Rathert, N. (2016). Strategies of legitimation: MNEs and the adoption of CSR in response to host-country institutions. *Journal of International Business Studies, 47*, 858–879.

Surdu, I., Mellahi, K., & Glaister, K. W. (2019). Once bitten, not necessarily shy? Determinants of foreign market re-entry commitment strategies. *Journal of International Business Studies, 50*, 393–422.

Surroca, J., Tribo, J. A., & Zahra, S. A. (2013). Stakeholder pressure on MNEs and the transfer of socially irresponsible practices to subsidiaries. *Academy of Management Review, 56*(2), 549–572.

Wettstein, F., Giuliani, E., Santangelo, G. D., & Stahl, G. K. (2019). International business and human rights: A research agenda. *Journal of International Business Studies, 54*(1), 54–65.

Witte, C. T., Burger, M. J., Ianchovichina, E. I., & Pennings, E. (2017). Dodging bullets: The heterogeneous effect of political violence on greenfield FDI. *Journal of International Business Studies, 48*, 862–892.

6

Why and How Might the Modern MNE Respond Strategically to Violent Conflict: A Commentary

Caroline Witte

Introduction

Despite the history of international business scholars trying to understand political risk, for long we have left the topic of violent conflict almost untouched. This might be due to the implicit assumption that multinational enterprises (MNEs) will try to avoid having to deal with this type of high impact risk at almost all costs. However, if anything, the last decade has proven that firms cannot anticipate all risks. Some of the events that have the highest impact on firms also seem to the hardest to predict, whether it is a pandemic, a climate related disaster or a violent conflict.

The study by Jennifer Oetzel and Katherine Getz (2012) is one of the first and continues to be one the few that study the strategic response of firms to violent conflict. Their article continues to play an important role

C. Witte (✉)
Rotterdam School of Management, Erasmus University,
Rotterdam, The Netherlands
e-mail: witte@rsm.nl

M. A. Mithani et al. (eds.), *Crises and Disruptions in International Business*, JIBS Special Collections, https://doi.org/10.1007/978-3-030-80383-4_6

in nuancing how we think about conflict and the role firms play in it. It moves away from the simplistic idea that all firms can and will avoid conflict and instead forces us to think about how firms themselves might affect conflict. This commentary will review how the literature on firms and violent conflict has developed in the nine years since the publication of Oetzel and Getz's (2012) article. From this, I will discuss future research directions related to (1) the effect of MNE strategy on conflict risk, (2) conflict-profiting MNEs and (3) institution-building in conflict countries.

Where Do We Stand? Divestment and Investment in the Face of Violent Conflict

Oetzel and Getz (2012) note that '(u)nfortunately, violent conflicts are not rare occurrences' (p. 168). Since the publication of the article, they have become even less rare. Whilst in 2010, the Uppsala Conflict Data Program (the main datacenter for armed conflict) recognized thirty-one violent conflicts; in 2019 they recognized fifty-four conflicts. Part of this increase is due to the conflicts following the Arab Spring, but there have also been outbursts of violence in other parts of the world such as Africa (e.g., South Sudan) and Europe (i.e., Ukraine). Hence, more firms are exposed to violent conflict. Compared to corruption or the risk of expropriation, violent conflict poses a more discontinuous risk; conflicts tend to be episodic and difficult to anticipate (Oetzel & Oh, 2014), as exemplified by the Arab Spring conflicts (Gause, 2011). The uncertainty associated with violent conflicts makes it considerably harder for MNEs to avoid them. Of course, MNEs can divest subsidiaries, when the region in which they are located is unexpectedly exposed to violent conflict. Dai, Eden and Beamish (2013; 2017) study under which conditions these exits are most likely to take place; not surprisingly, the distance from the conflict's epicenter plays an important role, so that the closer the subsidiary is to intense fighting, the more likely it is that the MNE decides to exit that region. Yet, many firms might be unwilling to exit conflict regions due to the high sunk costs related to exiting (e.g., losing an important business license) or business opportunities related to staying (e.g., real options related to business expansion). Dai et al. (2017) find that resilience - an index capturing experience with conflict and political risk - and MNE sales, are positively related to firms staying in a conflict host region.

Modern MNEs have, indeed, a new mindset for managing risk. Some firms might not only decide not to close a subsidiary when a conflict starts in the region, but actively invest in conflict zones. While on average greenfield FDI flows decrease when conflict breaks out in a country, there are many firms that will nevertheless invest in these places (see Witte et al., 2017). Further, it is not necessarily surprising that FDI from MNEs in the natural resource sector is insensitive to violent conflict. Not only are the economic rents in this sector high enough to offset conflict risk, but they are also constrained by the limited number of locations where the resource is available. In addition, firms that are large enough to diversify risk, are willing to invest in conflict regions, with the most geographically diversified firms even being attracted to these locations. Hence, it may be that for those MNEs that can manage the risk conflict poses, there are significant opportunities in these locations.

In addition to geographic diversification, I highlight that experience with violent conflict might allow firms to gain a competitive advantage in conflict regions. In turn, because conflict is for many firms a rare event on which the MNE is perceived not to have a direct influence, it is not guaranteed that these experiences result into useful and improved organizational routines (Buckley et al., 2020). Driffield, Jones and Crotty (2013) find that firms originating from countries with high levels of political risk (e.g., India) are more likely to invest in a conflict region. This might be due to the (dis)approval that firms might receive from their home government for their involvement in conflict countries or the experience that firms accumulate in dealing with high-risk institutional settings.

In a relatively more recent study, Oh and Oetzel (2017) find that only country-specific experience with managing conflict is beneficial for promoting investment into conflict countries. This suggests that the capabilities needed to successfully manage a subsidiary in a conflict zone are idiosyncratic and may not easily be leveraged from one conflict to another. The effect of experience in conflict regions on future investment is also expected to be relatively short-lived, in that the experience may only affect the probability of investment in the year following the violent conflict (Oh et al., 2021). The reduced effects of experience might be due to the institutional volatility in conflict countries; the political and economic contexts change rapidly, and hence the value of experience is transient.

The Effect of MNE Strategy on Conflict Risk?

The market and non-market strategies of MNEs also affect conflict risk. Oetzel and Getz (2012) focus primarily on risk management initiatives that might reduce conflict risk. These initiatives correspond mainly with MNE non-market strategies and include: (1) indirect and collaborative responses such as cooperating with NGOs; (2) indirect and unilateral responses such as donating resources; (3) direct and collaborative responses such as mediation interactions between parties to the conflict; and (4) direct and unilateral responses such as speaking out publicly against the acts of violence.

However, I emphasize here that MNEs' market strategies might also reduce conflict risk. This is the core idea behind the 'peace through commerce' thesis. As a result of its bilateral nature, FDI creates dependencies between countries, which are likely to decrease the probability of international conflict (Bussmann, 2010; Polachek & Seiglie, 2007). With regards to civil conflict, the root causes are often economic (Blattman & Miguel, 2010) and firms might thus reduce conflict risk by enhancing local growth, transferring technologies and improving employment. Manufacturing and service FDI might, for example, help raise the level of human capital and infrastructure, meaning that FDI could play an important role in the reconstruction of internet connectivity, ports and roads. This is especially valuable if the domestic private sector has shrunk significantly as a result of the conflict and hence, the risk of crowding out domestic firms is limited. Such an understanding of MNE market strategies may pave the way for reconsidering the role of the MNE in the broader societies of host locations entered.

Importantly also, the extent to which MNEs enhance economic development in the local communities surrounding them may be highly dependent on the initial stock of absorptive capacity (Görg & Greenaway, 2004). In the case of conflict countries, this absorptive capacity is most likely missing, because financial markets, human capital and institutional quality are depreciated due to conflict. MNEs might, for example, make extensive use of expatriates instead of employing local staff.

Consequently, with regards to the consequences of the different strategies adopted by MNEs in the economies of conflicted-affected countries, more research is needed. The international community has repeatedly sanctioned countries experiencing war. These sanctions severely disrupt the activities of MNEs active there, often leading to divestments (Bais & Huijser, 2005). Yet, as long as the negative effect of MNE involvement in conflict countries is not systematically verified, these sanctions might only increase economic suffering in these countries.

Conflict-Profiting Firms

While most firms benefit from a reduction in conflict risk (Witte et al., 2017), others may also benefit from the instability and chaos in the conflict environment of the host market. Conflict is likely to weaken the institutions that restrict discretionary actions by the government and reduce the transparency of transactions (Guidolin & La Ferrara, 2007). Firms that are considered insiders can benefit from this by engaging in informal government deals to secure licenses or other valuable resources. These informal deals might be particularly important for firms in the resource sector, which tend to be dependent on exploration and exploitation licenses. It is thus not surprising that resource firms are not deterred from, and possibly even attracted to, conflict regions (Skovoroda et al., 2019; Witte et al., 2017). Guidolin and La Ferrara (2007) find that abnormal returns of diamond firms in Angola decreased after a sudden end of a bloody civil war. They interpret these findings in light of conflict-generated entry barriers, decreased government bargaining power, and opacity in the licensing process. In addition, Reade et al. (2019) argue that firms in the resource sector might face relatively little stakeholder pressure to respond responsibly to conflict; in turn, the presence of MNEs in the natural resource sector may, indeed, exacerbate conflict risk (Mihalache-O'Keef 2018).

How can these findings be integrated into future research? The current research on divestment or investment in conflict countries cannot distinguish between firms that are located in a conflict country because of violent conflict and those that are there despite conflict. Those that invest because of war face incentives to prolong conflict and their investments might hence be detrimental to the country's development. In contrast, firms that invest despite war might be inclined to adopt conflict sensitive practices, such as those proposed by Oetzel and Getz (2012). Of course, firms that willingly prolong conflict could lose their license to operate, but this strategy is not always observable to external stakeholders. Future research should shed light on the determinants of corporate social irresponsibility in conflict zones. This would also support the development of policies that disincentivize entry by MNEs that profit from conflict and incentivize entry by MNEs willing to engage in peacebuilding initiatives.

Non-market Strategy and Institution Building

Institutions also matter. Because violent conflicts concern the distribution of power and economic resources, institutions that govern these resources in conflict zones tend to be characterized by constant change (Bucheli & Kim, 2012). Independent of whether we consider conflict-profiting or peace-profiting MNEs, there are considerable advantages in influencing how host country institutions develop during a conflict or right after the termination of a conflict. For example, when Mittal Steel set up an iron extraction sight in Liberia after the end of a bloody civil war, it was able to influence government policies regarding resource extraction so that the company received a five-year tax holiday and complete control over the amount of royalties paid to the government (Global Witness, 2006).

It is not surprising that being an insider in the political context can increase an MNE's influence on institutional change and reduce the related uncertainty (Luiz et al., 2019). Firms can become an insider by having strong ties to the political regime, but they can also benefit from macro-level home-host ties (e.g., Li et al., 2018; Witte et al., 2020). However, the political instability that is inherent in armed conflict can significantly devaluate these ties. As also briefly mentioned in Chapter 5, Darendeli and Hill (2016) document how Turkish construction MNEs needed ties to the Qadhafi family to survive in Libya before the Arab Spring, while after the Arab Spring, these same ties led to a loss of legitimacy; in turn, the study also showed that MNEs that invested in social-benefit projects and social ties were better able to overcome conflict. Because what is good for the host location might also benefit the firm (and vice-versa), I propose that more research is needed specifically on how firms can affect the development of institutions in conflict-affected countries and what the optimal strategies are for contributing to institution building and upgrading in the post-conflict environment.

Final Remarks

While Oetzel and Getz's (2012) article is about how to strategically *respond to* and *manage* conflict risk, most subsequent studies look at divestment and investment in conflict countries instead of examining various strategies to optimally manage conflict risk. On the one hand, this is understandable. Studying firm responses to conflict is not easy due to limited availability of secondary data on firms' activities in conflict-affected regions and the security risks related to collecting primary data in these regions. On the other hand, insights on effective risk management strategies are much needed considering the number of firms exposed to this risk and the effect they might have on the intensity of a conflict. In this commentary, I focused on three themes on which big questions remain unanswered:

1. How do the strategies of MNEs affect conflict risk?
2. Under which conditions do firms profit from violent conflict?
3. How do firms influence institution-building in conflict and post-conflict countries?

It is my hope that econometric analyses will be complemented with other innovative research designs, such as archival studies into past conflicts, field studies on current conflicts and experimental set-ups.

References

Bais, K., & Huijser, M. (2005). The profit of peace: Corporate responsibility in conflict regions. Greenleaf Publishing, Sheffield.

Blattman, C., & Miguel, E. (2010). Civil war. *Journal of Economic Literature, 48*(1), 3–57.

Bucheli, M., & Kim, M. (2012). Political institutional change, obsolescing legitimacy, and multinational corporations: The case of the Central America banana industry. *Management International Review, 52*(6), 847–877.

Buckley, P. J., Chen, L., Clegg, L. J., & Voss, H. (2020). The role of endogenous and exogenous risk in FDI entry choices. *Journal of World Business, 55*(1), 101040.

Bussmann, M. (2010). Foreign direct investment and militarized international conflict. *Journal of Peace Research, 47*(2), 143–153.

Dai, L., Eden, L., & Beamish, P. W. (2013). Place, space, and geographical exposure: Foreign subsidiary survival in conflict zones. *Journal of International Business Studies, 44*(6), 554–578.

Dai, L., Eden, L., & Beamish, P. W. (2017). Caught in the crossfire: Dimensions of vulnerability and foreign multinationals' exit from war-afflicted countries. *Strategic Management Journal, 38*(7), 1478–1498.

Darendeli, I. S., & Hill, T. L. (2016). Uncovering the complex relationships between political risk and MNE firm legitimacy: Insights from Libya. *Journal of International Business Studies, 47*(1), 68–92.

Driffield, N., Jones, C., & Crotty, J. (2013). International business research and risky investments, an analysis of FDI in conflict zones. *International business review, 22*(1), 140–155.

Gause, G. F., III. (2011). Why Middle East studies missed the Arab spring. *Foreign Affairs, 90*, 81–90.

Global Witness. (2006). *Heavy Mittal? A state within a state: The inequitable mineral development agreement between the government of Liberia and Mittal Steel Holdings NV.* Available at: https://www.business-humanrights.org/pt/últimas-not%C3%ADcias/pdf-full-report-heavy-mittal-a-state-within-a-state-the-inequitable-mineral-development-agreement-between-the-government-of-liberia-and-mittal-steel-holdings-nv/

Görg, H., & Greenaway, D. (2004). Much ado about nothing? Do domestic firms really benefit from foreign direct investment? *The World Bank Research Observer, 19*(2), 171–197.

Guidolin, M., & La Ferrara, E. (2007). Diamonds are forever, wars are not: Is conflict bad for private firms? *American Economic Review, 97*(5), 1978–1993.

Li, J., Meyer, K. E., Zhang, H., & Ding, Y. (2018). Diplomatic and corporate networks: Bridges to foreign locations. *Journal of International Business Studies, 49*(6), 659–683.

Luiz, J. M., Ganson, B., & Wennmann, A. (2019). Business environment reforms in fragile and conflict-affected states: From a transactions towards a systems approach. *Journal of International Business Policy, 2*(3), 217–236.

Mihalache-O'Keef, A. S. (2018). Whose greed, whose grievance, and whose opportunity? Effects of foreign direct investments (FDI) on internal conflict. *World Development, 106*, 187–206.

Oetzel, J., & Getz, K. (2012). Why and how might firms respond strategically to violent conflict?. *Journal of International Business Studies, 43*(2), 166–186.

Oh, C. H., & Oetzel, J. (2017). Once bitten twice shy? Experience managing violent conflict risk and MNC subsidiary-level investment and expansion. *Strategic Management Journal, 38*(3), 714–731.

Oh, C. H., Shin, J., & Oetzel, J. (2021). How does experience change firms' foreign investment decisions to non-market events? *Journal of International Management, 27*(1), 100802.

Polachek, S., & Seiglie, C. (2007). Trade, democracy and peace. In K. Hartley & T. Sandler (Eds.), *Handbook of defense economics* (Vol. 2). North-Holland-Elsevier.

Reade, C., McKenna, M., & Oetzel, J. (2019). Unmanaged migration and the role of MNEs in reducing push factors and promoting peace: A strategic HRM perspective. *Journal of International Business Policy, 2*(4), 377–396.

Skovoroda, R., Goldfinch, S., DeRouen, K., & Buck, T. (2019). The attraction of FDI to conflicted states: The counter-intuitive case of US oil and gas. *Management International Review, 59*(2), 229–251.

Witte, C., Burger, M., Ianchovichina, E., & Pennings, E. (2017). Dodging bullets: The heterogeneous effect of political violence on greenfield FDI. *Journal of International Business Studies, 48*(7), 862–892.

Witte, C. T., Burger, M. J., & Pennings, E. (2020). When political instability devaluates home-host ties. *Journal of World Business, 55*(4), 101077.

Part III

Conflict Zones, Firm Strategy and MNE Performance Outcomes

7

Place, Space, and Geographical Exposure: Foreign Subsidiary Survival in Conflict Zones

Li Dai, Lorraine Eden, and Paul W. Beamish

Introduction

With far-flung operations often located in unstable host countries, multinational enterprises (MNEs) are regularly exposed to geographically defined threats; however, geography has typically been neglected by international business scholars who study the MNE. This neglect is problematic, because changes in the global economy have made the location (L)

Accepted by Ram Mudambi and Sjoerd Beugelsdijk, Guest Editors, 24 February 2013. This chapter has been with the authors for three revisions.

L. Dai (✉)
Department of Management, College of Business Administration, Loyola Marymount University, Los Angeles, CA, USA
e-mail: li.dai@lmu.edu

L. Eden
Department of Management, Mays Business School, Texas A&M University, College Station, TX, USA
e-mail: LEden@mays.tamu.edu

M. A. Mithani et al. (eds.), *Crises and Disruptions in International Business*, JIBS Special Collections, https://doi.org/10.1007/978-3-030-80383-4_7

component of the OLI paradigm "an increasingly important determinant of the scope, pattern, form, and growth of MNE activity" (Dunning, 2009: 26). At the same time, geographers who study aspects of geography such as location, distance, and connectivity have largely ignored the MNE (McCann & Mudambi, 2004, 2005).

Recently, however, scholars from both international business and economic geography have begun to analyze the geography of the MNE. Notably, Beugelsdijk, McCann, and Mudambi (2010) have reorganized the OLI paradigm in an attempt to make geography more central within MNE theory. While "ownership" and "internalization" are merged into an "organization" factor, "location" is decomposed into two separate factors: "place" and "space." *Place* refers to location-specific attributes, and *space* emphasizes geographic distance and network characteristics (McCann, 2011). Place and space therefore have the potential to become core geographic concepts, enabling international business scholars to better understand the MNE as an organizational form within the global economy.

In the international business literature the notions of place and space have been used to examine MNE social responsibility at a global level (Devinney, 2011), place-specific firm value extraction (Zaheer & Nachum, 2011), headquarters resource allocation to subsidiaries (Dellestrand & Kappen, 2012), and the paradox of distance with respect to knowledge transfer (Zaheer & Hernandez, 2011). While these papers do examine MNE strategy in a spatial context, their conceptualization of place and space as beneficial or at best neutral for the MNE overlooks the potential downsides of geography. MNEs face a variety of location-specific hazards, particularly when parent firms set up subsidiaries in politically unstable host countries. We therefore argue that there is distinct value in empirically establishing a link between the place–space nexus and MNE responses to geographic threats such as political conflicts. As Piscitello (2011) points out, in addition to exploiting the

P. W. Beamish
Richard Ivey School of Business, The University of Western Ontario,
London, ON, Canada

benefits of differences between locations, the essence of strategy for MNEs also involves avoiding locational hazards.

Our paper builds on Beugelsdijk et al. (2010) by examining how place and space affect MNEs in highly risky locations. We develop sophisticated treatments of geography to address why certain MNEs stay in and other leave conflict zones. Defined as "regions of war, insurgency, or severe lawlessness" (Anderson et al., 2010), conflict zones pose irrevocable threats to the operations and employees of MNEs. According to GlobalSecurity, a US-based public policy organization, there were approximately 40 conflict zones worldwide in 2008 (Anderson et al., 2010). Moreover, a record of 388 conflicts ravaged the world in 2011 alone, 38 of which were deemed to be highly violent (HIIK, 2011).

Beugelsdijk et al. (2010: 489) assert that an integrative analysis of "firm organizational issues with the characteristics of the subnational region is essential for understanding the interplay between the MNE and its spatial environment." This holds true especially in the context of conflict zones. For example, the Chechen War in 1995 was confined to a relatively small and peripheral part of Russia, while the Democratic Republic of Congo in 2007 experienced two distinct civil wars that took place in different parts of the country (Gleditsch & Weidmann, 2012). To account for firm-level heterogeneity at the subnational level, we develop street-level measures to capture precisely the subnational variation in conflict zone coverage and subsidiary activity.

Because MNEs may exit from conflict-prone environments (e.g., if they decide that measures to safeguard investments are too expensive), geographic exposure to political conflicts constitutes a significant problem for subsidiary survival abroad. Our paper helps to open up the "black box" of MNE strategy in adverse conditions by focusing explicitly on the relationship between the MNE's exit-vs-stay decision and its geographic location. Our study contributes to the existing literatures in international business and economic geography by offering insights into physical threats – including their geographical antecedents – and subsidiary survival, in conjunction with a novel analysis of geographical factors. While we know much about subsidiary survival, there has been little research on its geographical determinants in turbulent environments. Our paper also adds to extant knowledge on MNEs by developing subnational theory and testing it with a unique, fine-grained geographic information system (GIS) data set that is able to reveal the critical roles played by geography in MNE strategy.

Theory and Hypotheses

Threat and Exposure

An analysis of whether MNEs can survive in conflict zones should begin with the question of why MNEs might want to stay in such hostile locations. Locating in a conflict zone is likely to cause major disruptions for firms in terms of bombings, disruptions in supply chain activities and network structures, harm to employees, and other political hazards (Henisz, 2000). Political conflicts thus affect the most fundamental goals of a firm, and constitute threats producing "negative situations in which loss is likely and over which one has relatively little control" (Dutton & Jackson, 1987: 80).

It is important to distinguish between a general threat that is faced by all firms in a conflict-ridden country, and a specific threat, which reflects an individual firm's likelihood of encountering violence from a conflict in a particular location. Because conflicts can be geographically delimited (Buhaug & Gates, 2002), we characterize the level of specific threat experienced by a given subsidiary in terms of its *exposure*, which geographically captures the extent to which the subsidiary may be in contact with, or subject to, a specific threat (Adger, 2000).

Relevant both at the level of socioeconomic groups such as MNEs and across time and space (Turvey, 2007), the concept of exposure has emerged as a cross-cutting theme in many research traditions. Examples include the human dimensions of global environmental change (Gallopin, 2006), socioeconomic differentials in physical and mental health (Baum, Garofalo, & Yali, 1999), race differences in substance abuse (Wallace & Muroff, 2002), gender differences in work stress (Roxburgh, 1996), and socioeconomic differences in susceptibility to life events (McLeod & Kessler, 1990).

Exposure is conceived of in our paper as a geographical mechanism governing the exit-vs-stay decisions of multinationals located in conflict-prone

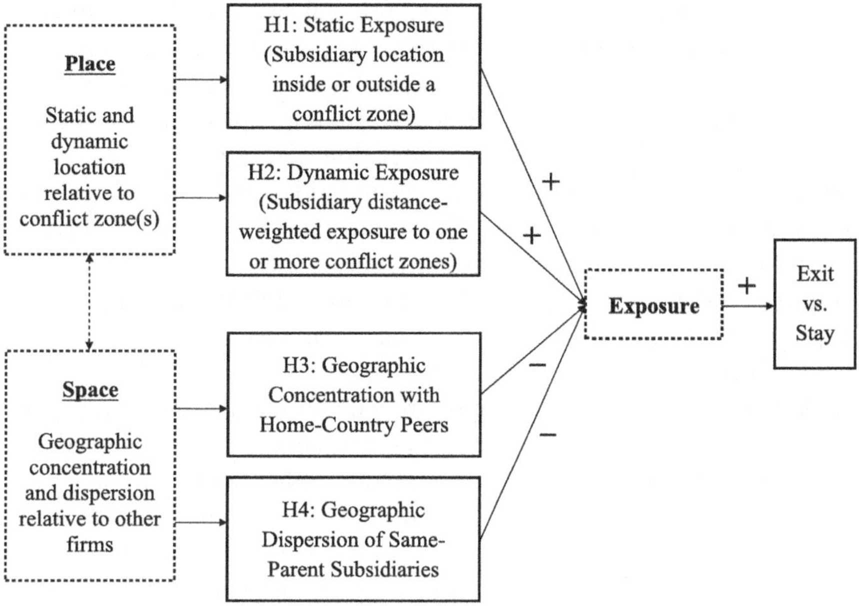

Fig. 7.1 Impact of geography on foreign subsidiary survival in conflict zones

countries. We argue that increased exposure raises the probability of subsidiary exit (reduces the likelihood of survival). Given the unique form of the MNE, with parent and subsidiary operations that traverse multiple country borders, we argue that geographic exposure is experienced differently by each subsidiary based on its location, and that therefore the subsidiary's exit-vs-stay response will vary across national and subnational locations. Figure 7.1 illustrates our conceptual framework, explaining how place and space affect a foreign subsidiary's exposure to conflict zones and its exit-vs-stay decision. We explore these arguments below.

Conflict Zones as Subnational Geographic Places

In the international business literature, *place* refers to the inherent attributes of the physical locations that affect MNE strategy and performance (Zaheer & Hernandez, 2011). Places have distinctive geographic characteristics, which can be natural (e.g., climate, minerals, elevation) or man-made (e.g., buildings, language, political systems). In the international business literature, place has typically been treated as synonymous with country, to the neglect of subnational differences (Beugelsdijk et al., 2010; Phelps & Fuller, 2000). We believe this is inappropriate. As Buckley and Ghauri (2004: 83) point out, "the nation state as the possessor of the sense of identity is being replaced by subnations and internal regions." Country-level analysis is especially problematic for our study, because political conflicts are usually concentrated in specific locations inside a country, and therefore "place" in terms of political conflicts is more appropriately examined using a subnational perspective (Buhaug & Gates, 2002).

We view conflict zones as important subnational places that, depending on their geographic characteristics, can affect a foreign subsidiary's exit-vs-stay decision in the host country. Conflict zones pose a specific threat to the foreign subsidiary: the more the subsidiary is exposed, the less likely it is to stay. In effect, political conflict is the "ultimate" hassle facing the firm (Schotter & Beamish, 2013). Our baseline arguments with respect to *place* focus on the characteristics of the conflict zone as experienced by the foreign subsidiary. We argue that a subsidiary's exposure to conflict depends on geographic factors such as the location, size, and number of conflict zones in a host country in a particular year. These geographic factors matter in the same way that an individual's susceptibility to the flu virus depends on his or her location relative to the location and number of infected individuals, and the severity of their illness.

In our theory development, we differentiate between *static exposure* (whether the subsidiary is located inside a conflict zone) and *dynamic exposure* (a compound measure of exposure that takes into account location, distance, zone size, and number of conflict zones). Static exposure captures the actual and immediate threat faced by the subsidiary if it is located inside a conflict zone. Dynamic exposure captures the compound potential threat to the subsidiary posed by its location in a conflict-ridden host country, as determined by a combination of factors, such as size and number of the conflict zones, and the subsidiary's distance from the center of these zones. As static and dynamic exposure increase, we hypothesize that the foreign subsidiary is more likely to leave (less likely to survive), *ceteris paribus*.

Static exposure

To the extent that geographic proximity to knowledge and markets is a strong predictor of MNE location (Nachum et al., 2008), proximity to political conflict should encourage a foreign MNE to reevaluate its location choice. A case in point is Shell, which first decided to leave Nigeria because of violent conflict in the Niger Delta, despite the rich petroleum reserves that originally attracted its entry (Feil et al., 2008).[1]

The counterfactual argument is that outside the boundaries of a conflict zone a firm faces less exposure, and therefore has more willingness to stay and a higher likelihood of survival if it does stay in the host country. Similarly, when a political conflict is confined to the periphery or border areas, the conflict is less likely to generate physical harm to firms located elsewhere in the host country (Berman, 2000): therefore the MNE may not need or want to exit (Li, 2006). For example, the majority of foreign subsidiaries were unaffected by the Algerian civil war (1991–2002), because they were in the southern parts of the country, removed from the conflict zone, which was in the north (Berman, 2000).

Because violence in political conflicts is more selective than indiscriminate, and bounded by the control of belligerents over a specific territory (Kalyvas, 2003), we argue that the exposure – as well as the survival – of a subsidiary will be affected by its location relative to (i.e., inside or outside) a conflict zone in the host country. When the foreign subsidiary is located inside the boundaries of a conflict zone, we argue that the firm faces *static exposure*, and predict that:

Hypothesis 1
A foreign subsidiary will be more likely to exit (less likely to survive) if it is located inside rather than outside a conflict zone in the host country.

Dynamic Exposure

In addition to addressing the question of whether a foreign subsidiary is located inside or outside a conflict zone, there are a variety of "place"

[1] Shell later chose to exit only partially, evacuating non-essential personnel and cutting back on oil production and exports.

characteristics that can affect the subsidiary's total exposure to political conflict, and therefore influence the firm's exit (survival) decision.

A subsidiary's exposure is contingent not only on its location *vis-à-vis* a conflict zone, but also on the firm's distance from the zone and the size of the zone. Berman (2000), for example, argues that conflict zone size is positively linked with persistent and intense combat. Often involving large, organized opposition groups (Buhaug, 2010), a conflict covering a broader geographic area even at a low intensity can be more destabilizing than a confined but more destructive conflict in one location (O'Loughlin & Witmer, 2010). Just as gravity is influenced by size and distance, we expect that a firm's exposure to political conflict will be higher (lower), the larger (smaller) the geographic size of the conflict zone(s) and the closer (further away) the firm is from these zones.

Conflict zones can also expand and contract over time, affecting the firm's exposure to political conflict (Gleditsch & Weidmann, 2012). Because the distance between a subsidiary and a conflict zone will change with the annual expansion and contraction of these zones, place must be construed not only as static (in or out of the conflict zone) but also in terms of dynamic time–space. In measuring the combined effects of exposure, which we call *dynamic exposure*, we therefore need to treat conflict zones as "stretchable, shrinkable spaces" (Abler, Adams, & Gould, 1971: 82). Even in the case of a single conflict zone, dynamic exposure will vary over time, based on the location of the subsidiary, its distance to the conflict zone, and the size of the zone.

Moreover, there may be more than one conflict zone in a host country in a given year. When there are multiple conflict zones in the host country, a focal subsidiary is faced with several different exposures to place-specific threats. In considering the combined impact of these implied threats, we draw on insights from our solar system to model dynamic exposure. According to Coulomb's law,[2] the gravitational forces of attraction and repulsion among the planets are roughly a function of the relative sizes and distances of the planets from one another, which illustrates

[2] Coulomb's law states that "the magnitude of the electrostatics force of interaction between two point charges is directly proportional to the scalar multiplication of the magnitudes of charges and inversely proportional to the square of the distances between them" (http://en.wikipedia.org/wiki/Coulomb's_Law and http://regentsprep.org/Regents/physics/phys03/acoulomb/default.htm).

the loss-of-strength gradient principle of "the further the weaker" (Boulding, 1962: 78). The combined effects of gravity on a focal body (e.g., the earth) that is generated by its surrounding bodies (e.g., other planets, moons, and the sun) is a function of their location, distance, and size, which together determine the attraction/repulsion of the earth to these other bodies.

Taking a given subsidiary as the focal body, we can visualize multiple conflict zones as planets of different sizes and at various distances from the subsidiary. Using Coulomb's law, we can therefore predict that the combined gravitational force (i.e., the *dynamic exposure*) faced by the focal subsidiary should depend on the locations, distances, and sizes of the conflict zones relative to the subsidiary, each of which can vary from year to year. Using our gravitational analogy and Coulomb's law, we argue that a subsidiary's dynamic exposure will be magnified if it is near such conflict zones, and diminished if it is far from them. In any given year, the forces of attraction may dominate, and the focal subsidiary stays or survives in its place; in another year the forces of repulsion could dominate, and the subsidiary exits. Because *place* is *dynamic and evolutionary* (Lorenzen & Mudambi, 2013), we propose the following:

Hypothesis 2
A foreign subsidiary will be more likely to exit (less likely to survive) as its dynamic exposure to political conflict inside the host country increases.

Concentration and Dispersion of Firms in Geographic Space

If *places* are distinctive, nonempty geographic locations – that is, "they have content" (Taylor, 1999: 10) – *spaces* are relational.[3] Whereas place is somewhere, space is everywhere (Taylor, 1999). Space can be conceptualized as the variety of relationships linking two or more places, examples

[3] The distinction between place and space can be drawn too finely. Taylor (1999: 12), for example, argues that "the same location can be both place and space depending on whose perspective is involved": that is, there can be spatial relationships (distance, proximity, ties) within a place such as a city or country.

of which include distance, connectivity or shared ties, and spatial dependence. As Agnew and Duncan (1989: 2) put it, "space emphasizes the location of things in relationship to other things, and how things are *distributed*."

In the international business literature, space has been represented primarily as the distance between home and host countries (Dunning, 1988; Piscitello, 2011). Empirically, scholars have found that increasing levels of cultural, institutional, and geographic distance not only lead to lower levels of foreign direct investment (FDI) (Beugelsdijk & Frijns, 2010), but also exert different effects on market-seeking vs efficiency-seeking FDI (Slangen & Beugelsdijk, 2010). Distance can also reduce spillovers (Adams & Jaffe, 1996; Beugelsdijk & Cornet, 2002), even as geographic dispersion increases product-specific efficiencies and organizational learning (Audia, Sorenson, & Hage, 2001). For MNEs, geographically dispersed interfirm networks are particularly influential in spreading knowledge (Mowery, Oxley, & Silverman, 1996), and beneficial for subsidiary reconfiguring of value-chain activities during economic crises (Chung et al., 2010), but disadvantageous for resource allocation from headquarters to subsidiaries (Dellestrand & Kappen, 2012).

The opposite of distance – variables such as proximity (Zipf, 1949), shared borders (Starr, 2005), and connectivity (Lorenzen & Mudambi, 2013) – has also been shown to be an important influence on MNE behavior. While geographic clusters may develop as a result of historic factors and co-location advantages (Mudambi & Swift, 2012; Zucker et al., 1998), the functionality of clusters may be conditioned by different types of connectivity, such as personal relationships, pipelines, or a mix of both (Lorenzen & Mudambi, 2013), and networks of alliances (Markusen, 1999). Research suggests that firms can reduce the liability of foreignness by expanding to geographically proximate countries (Hymer, 1960) and co-locating with other home-country firms (Zaheer & Mosakowski, 1997). The clustering phenomenon has also been used to show a positive relationship between spatial proximity and knowledge spillovers (Cantwell & Piscitello, 2005) and the impact of proximity with collaborators and competitors on firm performance (Chang & Xu, 2008).

Thus space in the international business literature has been characterized in terms of centrifugal forces (the distance or dispersion of firms or countries from one another) and centripetal forces (the clustering or concentration of firms or countries with one another). In our work, we extend this earlier literature by examining how the centrifugal and centripetal forces of other firms inside the host country can affect a focal subsidiary's exit/survival response to exposure to conflict zones.

We differentiate between two groups of such firms: *home-country peers* (firms from the same home country as the focal firm) and *same-parent subsidiaries* (sister subsidiaries of the focal firm). We argue that centripetal forces (e.g., concentration) are important for home-country peers, whereas centrifugal forces (e.g., dispersion) are important for same-parent (sister) subsidiaries, in terms of their relative impacts on the focal firm's likelihood of survival in a conflict-afflicted host country.

Specifically, we hypothesize that geographic concentration of home-country peers with the focal firm in the host country reduces the focal firm's exposure to political conflict. We hypothesize also that geographic dispersion of same-parent subsidiaries (i.e., the overall geographic breadth of the MNE's network) inside the host country reduces the focal subsidiary's exposure to conflict zones. Our theory therefore predicts that both geographic concentration and dispersion with respect to home-country firms can help decrease a subsidiary's exposure to conflict zones, and increase its chances for survival.

Geographic Concentration of Home-country Peers

Following McCann and Mudambi (2004), we examine the centripetal effect of *geographic concentration* that stems from home-country peer firms aggregating in a particular location. Theories of agglomeration economies suggest that the potential for growth in a location becomes more salient with geographic proximity and attendant externalities found in specialized workers, suppliers, and infrastructure (Krugman, 1991). By locating in proximity to one another, firms can benefit from self-reinforcing agglomeration economies such as close supplier–customer relationships and the use of common technologies and specialized labor pools. We argue that such concentration makes it less likely that the focal firm will exit from a conflict-afflicted host country.

Not only is a location more likely to attract subsequent firms once agglomeration economies are established (McCann & Mudambi, 2004), but incumbent firms are also less likely to leave, owing to endowment effects. The concept of endowment effects predicts that people tend to value what they already own more than comparable things that they do not own (Kahneman et al., 1991). In geographical terms, endowment effects suggest that MNEs should attribute a higher value to a location once they have established a subsidiary in that location. We furthermore argue that such attachment to a location increases with the proximity of peers from the same home country, given the shared investment in and use of local amenities (e.g., schools, grocery stores), labor training systems and labor pools, and just-in-time delivery systems that require spatial concentration of manufacturing plants and strict production flow control by suppliers (Head et al., 1995). The geographic concentration of home-country peers in a location therefore has the potential to induce and reinforce hysteresis – that is, the reluctance to divest subsidiaries, even under adverse circumstances (Belderbos & Zou, 2009).

Geographical proximity to home-country peers that likewise experience endowment effects should therefore increase a subsidiary's willingness to stay in a location, given the competitive pressure and constant comparison that occur among geographically co-located firms (Porter, 2000). Since the number of firms in a location proxies for the underlying economic efficiency of the location (Sorenson & Audia, 2000), a focal firm should attach a loss to relinquishing its position within a cluster of competitors greater than the benefits it would perceive from finding another location elsewhere. The resulting interdependence of the decisions of co-located peers amounts to herding behavior, which in foreign MNEs is motivated primarily by the need to prevent competitors from gaining advantage in a host country (Flowers, 1976), especially if those competitors can threaten interests back at home (Knickerbocker, 1973). In leaving a location, an MNE therefore not only forsakes its own locational advantages, but also contributes to the strategic position of its competitors. This has been the case in the Philippines, where foreign MNEs that have stayed through the conflicts (e.g., Honda and Toyota) now reap the benefits of profitability, while those that have left (e.g., Ford, Opel, Chevrolet) find it difficult to regain market share.

In addition to increasing the motivation of MNEs to stay, geographic concentration with home-country peers can also increase the capability of MNEs to stay. To the extent that distance increases difficulties in coordination (Ghemawat, 2001; Sorenson & Stuart, 2001), and proximity lowers the cost and risk of contracting for services (Bania et al., 1992), the co-location of home-country peers can give rise to locational economies of scale, such as joint hiring of private security and joint lobbying of the host-country government. Even though co-location does not inherently lead to interaction (McCann & Mudambi, 2005), proximity has the potential to facilitate collective action. Moreover, geographic concentration of home-country peers increases their visibility and collective weight, making it more feasible for them to lobby jointly for shelter from the violence (Hillman & Hitt, 1999).

Therefore we argue that:

Hypothesis 3
A foreign subsidiary is less likely to exit (more likely to survive) in response to political conflict in a host country, the greater the geographic concentration of home-country peers with the focal subsidiary.

Geographic Dispersion of Same-parent Subsidiaries

Space, as it pertains to the MNE, also emphasizes how its own subsidiaries are distributed within the host country. Whereas in Hypothesis 3 we argued that centripetal forces (concentration) are important for home-country peers, here we argue that centrifugal forces (dispersion) are important for same-parent (sister) subsidiaries, in terms of their relative impacts on the focal firm's likelihood of survival.

Geographic dispersion of same-parent subsidiaries within the host country should reduce exposure for an MNE, for several reasons. First, if the MNE's subsidiaries are widely dispersed within the host country, having access to sister subsidiaries (siblings) located elsewhere should help to reduce the focal firm's exposure to a conflict zone or zones, since firms with ties outside a particular district, rather than within a local vicinity, are more likely to survive crises (Lazerson & Lorenzoni, 1999).

Subsidiaries located elsewhere in the host country may be able to provide critical support akin to – or indeed better than – that available from the parent firm. Geographic remoteness compromises a parent firm's capacity to alleviate the impact of external threats on its subsidiaries abroad in terms of providing advice and resources (Boeh & Beamish, 2011). In the same vein, subsidiaries in conflict zones face difficulties in relaying sensitive local information back home and making decisions based on parent feedback (Ghemawat, 2001). Thus the flow of communications and resources between a parent firm and its focal subsidiary is likely to be disrupted during political conflict. On the other hand, as Kim, Lu, and Rhee (2012) show, the experience of sister subsidiaries can be a valuable source of survival-enhancing learning about a subsidiary's operating environment, and help in revising its operating practices.

To the extent that greater MNE network dispersion provides operational flexibility (Allen & Pantzalis, 1996; Chung et al., 2008), a focal subsidiary may be able to move expatriates and critical resources elsewhere in the MNE's host-country network. Ingram and Baum (1997), for example, show in a domestic context that the operation of geographically dispersed units allows firms to weather idiosyncratic risks associated with particular locations. Dispersed subsidiaries, which are far enough away to be shielded from the violence but closer to the focal subsidiary than their parent firm, can provide assistance such as temporary refuge for conflict zone employees. The focal subsidiary may therefore not have to shut down, but rather needs only to reduce production temporarily, and shift employees elsewhere in the MNE's host-country network until the conflict subsides. We therefore expect that dispersed same-parent subsidiaries can provide critical resources and support during political conflicts abroad, perhaps more easily and quickly than the parent firm, enhancing the likelihood of survival. Formally stated:

Hypothesis 4

A foreign subsidiary is less likely to exit (more likely to survive) in response to political conflict in a host country, the greater the geographic dispersion of same-parent subsidiaries inside the host country.

Methodology

Sample

We tested our hypotheses on a sample of Japanese MNEs from several editions of *Kaigai Shinshutsu Kigyou Souran, Kuni-Betsu* (Japanese Overseas Investments, by Country), a Japanese-language directory of FDI information published by Toyo Keizai (TK data set hereafter). Given the context of our study, a Japanese sample was appropriate for several reasons. First, the extensive time and country distribution in the data set offer considerable variance in the exit-vs-stay outcomes of MNEs. In addition, the data set covers activity across Asia, Africa, and the Middle East, which represent almost all of the conflict zones during this period worldwide. Finally, Japan is less involved in international politics than countries such as the United States and China (Calder, 1988), so our sample also provides a platform for studying MNE behavior where the home-country's influence on the outcome is negligible.

To ensure that the exit-vs-stay decision could be attributed to a single parent firm, we selected wholly owned subsidiaries and international joint ventures where there was a local partner or partners, but only one foreign (Japanese) parent. After listwise deletion of missing values, the sample consisted of 5643 observations from 670 foreign subsidiaries of 433 Japanese parent firms in 25 countries and 54 industries operating between 1987 and 2006. Parent firm data drawn from the *Nikkei Economic Electronic Databank* of Nihon Keizai Shimbun, Inc. were matched with parent firm names in the TK data. Industry-level data were derived from the *Analyst's Guide* of the Daiwa Institute of Research. Unless otherwise noted, country-level controls were from the World Bank's *World Development Indicators*.

The data on political conflicts, along with GIS latitude and longitude data for each conflict zone, were compiled from the *UCDP-PRIO Armed Conflict Dataset*, which is a collaborative project between the Uppsala Conflict Data Program and the International Peace Research Institute. The data set has been widely used by both researchers and policymakers

Table 7.1 Host countries and Japanese subsidiary exits

Number	Country	Number of observations	Distribution of observations (%)	Number of foreign subsidiary exits	Distribution of foreign subsidiary exits (%)
1	Angola	9	0.2	0	0
2	Ecuador	6	0.1	0	0
3	Egypt	13	0.2	1	0.8
4	Ethiopia	28	0.5	2	1.5
5	India	442	7.8	13	9.5
6	Indonesia	1271	22.5	26	19.0
7	Iran	43	0.8	2	1.5
8	Israel	13	0.2	1	0.7
9	Kuwait	2	0	0	0
10	Liberia	18	0.3	0	0
11	Mexico	127	2.3	5	3.7
12	Nepal	7	0.1	0	0
13	Nigeria	26	0.5	1	0.7
14	Pakistan	107	1.9	1	0.7
15	Panama	17	0.3	0	0
16	Paraguay	1	0	0	0
17	Peru	3	0	0	0
18	Philippines	1519	26.9	43	31.4
19	Russia	48	0.9	3	2.2
20	Spain	44	0.8	1	0.7
21	Sri Lanka	38	0.7	2	1.5
22	Thailand	1773	31.4	32	23.4
23	Turkey	75	1.3	3	2.2
24	Uganda	5	0.1	1	0.7
25	Venezuela	8	0.1	0	0
	Total	5643	100	137	100

(Miguel et al., 2004). Conflicts in this data set are defined to have a minimum threshold of 25 battle-related deaths (Uppsala, 2011).

A list of the host countries represented in our sample is provided in Table 7.1. As an illustration of our data set, Fig. 7.2 provides a GIS-based map showing the location of conflict zones and Japanese subsidiaries in West Africa. The zones are represented as circles, and the subsidiaries as either airplanes (they exited) or pins (they stayed).

Because our binary dependent variable of exit contains many more zeros (5506) than ones (137), we followed Sorenson and Stuart (2001) in

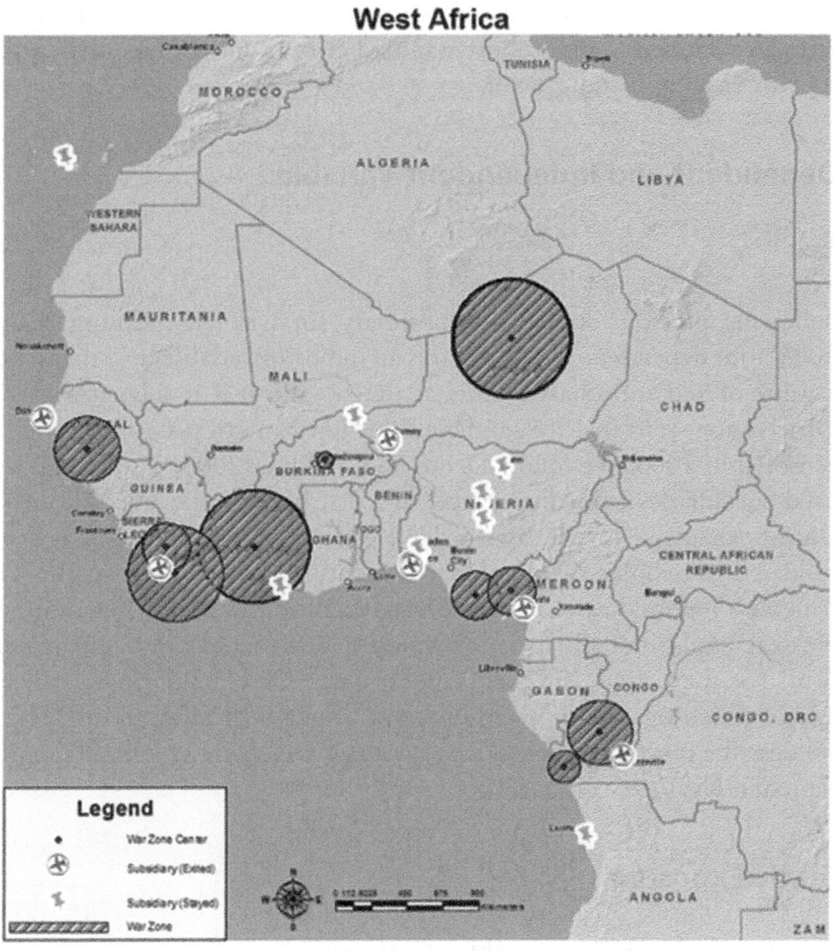

Fig. 7.2 Subsidiary exit-vs-stay decisions in conflict zones: West Africa

modeling our data using rare-event logistic regression to ensure that large numbers of repeat observations for each subsidiary did not result in underestimated standard errors.[4] Tomz's (2001) STATA procedure was used to estimate the rare-event logit models. To account for

[4] King and Zeng (2001) have shown that conventional logistic regression underestimates the probability of rare events (approximately < 5% of the data), producing biased coefficients. Please also note that STATA's RElogit command does not report goodness-of-fit statistics.

heteroskedasticity and correlated exit patterns within host countries, we estimated Huber–White robust standard errors adjusted for intra-country clustering of firm behavior.

Dependent and Independent Variables

Exit

Following previous studies on subsidiary survival (e.g., Chung et al., 2008), our dependent variable *Exit* is an indicator variable, E_{xt}, that takes a value of 1 if subsidiary *x* exits at time *t*, and 0 if it stays (survives). Observations start in 1987, and continue until an exit occurs, or is right-censored in 2006. We follow Delios and Makino (2003) in treating delisted subsidiaries from the sample as exits, because the TK data set is almost exhaustive for all cases of Japanese FDI. Our approach has been validated by scholars who compared identified cases of exit in the TK data with reported cases of exit (Delios & Beamish, 2004). In addition, we treat a sell-off of all Japanese ownership as an act of exit by the parent firm. For the period 1987–2006 there were 137 exits during conflicts, 123 of which were physical closures and 14 of which were sell-offs. Next, we describe our four independent variables, which are graphically represented in Fig. 7.3.

Static Exposure

Our first independent variable, *Static exposure*, is a dummy variable identifying whether a focal subsidiary is located inside a conflict zone or not. To obtain a precise measure for this subnational geographic place variable (Beugelsdijk et al., 2010), we began by searching for Japanese subsidiaries' street addresses in their respective host countries.[5] Then, using a GIS approach, we geo-coded each subsidiary's

[5] To our knowledge, with the exception of Boeh and Beamish (2012), no prior international business research has been carried out at this level of analysis. We first searched for foreign subsidiary street addresses on various Internet sites using information on parent name, subsidiary phone number, industry, founding year, and host country. We also searched old news articles for the addresses

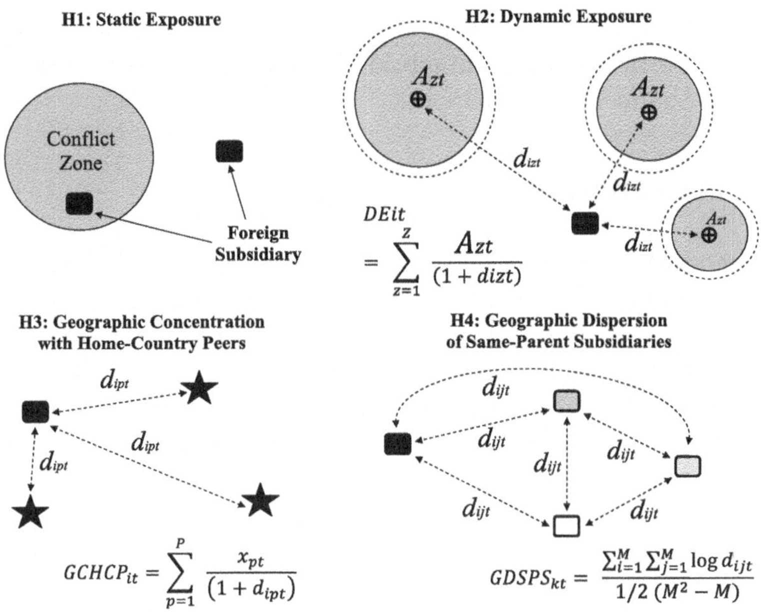

Fig. 7.3 Graphical representations of place and space variables

address with its latitude and longitude. Conflict zones were similarly geo-coded with center-point coordinates as the smallest circle that surrounds all violent events in a given country and year, with a radius variable to denote their spatial extent (Buhaug & Gates, 2002). Next, we applied the great-circle distance formula to the latitude and longitude of both the subsidiary and the center of its nearest conflict zone to calculate the distance between them. To determine whether a subsidiary was inside or outside a conflict zone, we subtracted the radius from the distance. If the result is negative, then the subsidiary is inside the perimeter of a conflict zone (dummy variable equals 1), and vice versa. For a subsidiary in a country with multiple conflict zones, we subtracted the corresponding radius of each conflict zone from the distance of its center to the subsidiary to determine whether the

of the subsidiaries that had already exited. We then identified the latitude and longitude of the subsidiary's address using the website http://itouchmap.com/latlong.html

subsidiary was inside any of the conflict zones – either near or far (i.e., as indicated by a negative number) – in which case this variable was assigned a value of 1 for that year.

Dynamic Exposure

To determine a subsidiary's overall geographic exposure to political conflict in a host country in a given year, we need to capture the time and space dimensions of the subsidiary's geographical context. *Dynamic exposure* reflects the combined impact of the focal subsidiary's location relative to the center of each conflict zone, the number of conflict zones, and the size of the zone(s). Following Coulomb's law for determining the gravitational pull/push of multiple bodies,

$$DE_{it} = \sum_{Z=1}^{Z} \frac{A_{Zt}}{1 + d_{iZt}} \tag{1}$$

where DE_{it} is the dynamic exposure faced by foreign subsidiary i, d_{izt} is the distance of subsidiary i to conflict zone z ($z = 1, \ldots, Z$), and A_{zt} is the size of conflict zone z, all measured in year t, we calculate A_{zt}, "the geographic domain of the conflict zone, measured as the circular area centered on the conflict center and covering all significant battle zones" (Buhaug & Gates, 2002: 421), by applying the πr^2 formula for the area of a circle to the radius for each conflict zone. Each area size is then adjusted by its distance d_{izt} from the focal subsidiary, and the result is summed over N conflict zones in a host country in a given year. This measure of exposure is dynamic, in that it varies over time as the number and size of conflict zones rise and fall in a host country.[6] By considering the distance from a focal subsidiary to the conflict zone(s), our gravitational formula adjusts for their respective area(s) by showing that their effective sizes decrease as their distance from the subsidiary increases, and vice versa.

[6] In the case of a single conflict zone, Eq. (1) collapses to $A_{zt}/(1+d_{izt})$. Our measure of dynamic exposure therefore incorporates situations where the focal subsidiary faces exposure to a single conflict zone (z=1), as well as to multiple conflict zones (z>1).

Geographic Concentration of Home-country Peers

To test the exposure-reducing benefits of co-locating near home-country peers, we follow Sorenson and Audia (2000) in weighting for each foreign subsidiary i the contribution of its home-country peers j ($j = 1, \ldots, N$) according to the inverse of their distance from the focal subsidiary, for each year t, using the formula

$$GCHCP_{it} = \sum_{p=1}^{P} \frac{X_{pt}}{1 + d_{ipt}} \tag{2}$$

where $GCHCP_{it}$ is the geographic concentration of home-country peers ($p = 1, \ldots, P$) *vis-à-vis* focal subsidiary i, and x can be any variable being weighted over a distance (for simplicity, we assign a vector of 1 s to x).[7] We aggregate the weighted contributions across all home-country peers to determine their extent of geographic concentration with a focal subsidiary. If there are no home-country peers, $GCHCP_{it}$ is 0; this variable increases as the number of peers and their proximity to the subsidiary increase.

Geographic Dispersion of Same-parent Subsidiaries

This variable captures the overall size or average dispersion of the MNE's network of affiliates (i.e., sister subsidiaries) within the host country. Following Audia et al. (2001), we calculate the distance between each pair (dyad) of subsidiaries i and j, and log and average their distances across all possible dyads for each parent firm k.[8] The formula for the geographic dispersion of an MNE's network of M subsidiaries in a host country in a given year t is

[7] Note the similarity with Eq. (1), where A is the "weight" (the area of the conflict zone).

[8] The log form accounts for the fact that transportation costs, in terms of both time and money, do not increase linearly over geographic space (Sorenson & Audia, 2000).

$$GDSPS_{kt} = \frac{\sum_{i=1}^{M}\sum_{j=1}^{M} \log d_{ijt}}{1/2\left(M^2 - M\right)} \quad (3)$$

where a double sum is taken over all possible dyads of subsidiaries for a parent *k*, with d_{ij} being the distance between the *i*th and *j*th same-parent subsidiaries. Applying the combinations formula, there are $1/2(M^2 - M)$ dyads for any given parent firm. If the MNE has only one subsidiary, $GDSPS_{kt}$ is 0; larger values of this variable indicate greater degrees of dispersion of an MNE's network within the host country.

Control Variables

We control for a variety of other factors that could possibly influence the probability of foreign subsidiary exit (survival), and therefore could confound our results. First, at the subsidiary level, *Subsidiary age* is employed to control for the possible effect on subsidiary survival of the liability of newness, as well as for the ability of older subsidiaries to adapt to host-country conditions. We measure subsidiary age as the number of years a subsidiary has operated since its date of establishment in the host country. We control for *Subsidiary size*, measured by the total number of employees, because studies have shown a positive relationship between the size and survival of foreign subsidiaries (Li, 1995). Because an MNE may seek alternative uses for poorly performing assets (Barney, 1997), we control for *Subsidiary performance* lagged by 1 year to account for the possible effect of financial performance on subsidiary survival. With the advantage of bypassing different national accounting rules that can complicate the comparison of financial performance across countries, this variable – based on managerial reports – has three ordinal levels: 1 for gain (the reference category), 2 for break-even, and 3 for loss; we therefore include *Financial break-even* and *Financial loss.*

At the parent firm level, because strategic considerations such as the need to focus on core activities can affect the divestment of foreign subsidiaries (Benito, 1997), we include a dummy variable *Same industry as parent* to capture whether the subsidiary is in the parent's core industry. Because there is a nonlinear and asymmetrical relationship between an MNE parent's percentage of equity and subsidiary survival (Dhanaraj & Beamish, 2004), we control for *Parent ownership level* as the percentage of the focal subsidiary's equity owned by the Japanese parent. The relationship between parent size and subsidiary survival has been mixed (Li, 1995); larger firms with higher sales can withstand more setbacks abroad, but at the same time give less weight to the survival of individual subsidiaries (Chung & Beamish, 2005). We therefore control for *Parent sales*, annual worldwide sales of the parent firm.

We also include control variables at the industry and country levels. To account for industry effects, we include dummy variables for *Primary*, *Manufacturing*, and *Wholesale industry* (service is the reference category). Per capita gross domestic product (GDP) and percentage change in GDP were used to control for *Host market size* and *Host market potential*. In considering other risks associated with conflict-prone countries, we control for levels of political, economic, and financial risk with the *Host composite risk* variable.[9] To control for increased exposure to physical atrocities (e.g., kidnapping and torture) and violent political oppression specific to conflict zones, we employed Amnesty International's Political Terror Scale[10] (Vergne, 2012). *Host political terror* ranges from 1 to 5, with the two highest scores capturing conditions where "murders, disappearances, and torture are a common part of life" and "terror has expanded to the whole population."

We also control for several types of ties between the home country (Japan) and each host country, on the grounds that home–host-country ties may affect foreign subsidiary survival. To proxy for the extent to which Japan is an ally of a host country, and may therefore intervene in its political conflict, we measure the two countries' ideological and diplomatic affinity with the *Home–host diplomatic ties* variable. As a proxy for diplomatic ties, we use Gartzke's (2006) Affinity of Nations index,[11]

---

[9] The Composite Political Risk Rating from International Political Risk Services includes 12 weighted variables: see http://www.prsgroup.com/ICRG_Methodology.aspx/

[10] The Political Terror Scale is available at http://www.politicalterrorscale.org

[11] The Affinity of Nations Index is available at http://dss.ucsd.edu/~egartzke/htmlpages/data.html

which is based on voting behavior in the United Nations (UN) General Assembly. The index is constructed such that the affinity between any two nations at any point in time falls in the interval from −1 to 1, where −1 means that the two political positions are completely dissimilar (i.e., voting contrary in each instance) and 1 means that they are identical (i.e., voting identically in each instance). Political scientists have found that UN General Assembly votes provide a good approximation for political allegiance and even colonial ties (Brams, 1966; Gartzke, 2006). Similarly, because *Bilateral investment treaties (BITs)* have been found to guard against expropriation (Egger & Pfaffermayr, 2004), we use *Home–Host BIT* to control for the presence of a BIT between Japan and the host country, coded as 1 if there is a BIT and 0 otherwise.[12]

Extant studies have found that MNEs are less likely to locate value-creating activity in countries at greater cultural distance from their home country (Delios & Henisz, 2003). We therefore control for *Home–host cultural distance* using the Kogut and Singh (1988) index, based on Hofstede's (1980) four dimensions of national culture: power distance, individualism, uncertainty avoidance, and masculinity. Because geographic distance between home and host countries makes it more difficult for the MNE to exert control over threats abroad (Boeh & Beamish, 2011), we account for *Home–host geographic distance* by computing the great-circle distance between the capital cities of the home and host countries.

Lastly, because MNEs tend to learn from and mimic firms from the same industry and home country (Kim et al., 2010), we control for *Peer industry exits* to measure the prevalence of mimetic isomorphism (Greve, 1995). This variable is measured as the number of home-country subsidiaries, in the same industry as the focal firm, that exited from the host country 1 year earlier (Henisz & Delios, 2004).

Results

Hierarchical regression analysis was used to analyze the effects of our four main-effect variables (static and dynamic exposure, geographic concentration of home-country peers, and geographic dispersion of same-parent

[12] BIT data are available at http://www.unctad.org/Templates/Page.asp?intItemID=2344%lang=1/

subsidiaries) on foreign subsidiary survival in conflict-prone countries. Table 7.2 presents summary statistics and correlations. Table 7.3 presents standardized regression coefficients for the rare-event logit models testing the likelihood of MNE exit. All variance inflation factor (VIF) values are below 8, and the mean VIF is below 3 for all models, suggesting that multicollinearity is not a problem in our regressions.

Model 1 of Table 7.3 includes only the control variables. The coefficients for financial loss, parent ownership, parent sales, host market size, diplomatic relations, geographic distance, and peer industry exits variables are statistically significant at the $p < 0.05$ level or higher, with largely expected signs. As a conservative test of statistical significance, we use two-tailed *t*-tests. Models 2–5 each add an independent variable, while Model 6 represents the full model. Models 2–6 have better overall model fit than Model 1, given their larger log likelihoods, and lower Akaike information criterion (AIC) and Bayesian information criterion (BIC) (Cleves, Gould, & Gutierrez, 2010). Following Newson (2004), we computed the statistical power to be approximately 0.86 (α=0.05; effect size=log ratio of 0.35), which exceeds Cohen's (1988) recommended standard for a minimum power of 0.80.

Our first hypothesis states that foreign subsidiaries are more likely to exit (less likely to survive) if they are located inside a conflict zone. The coefficient on the static exposure variable is positive and significant (0.421, $p < 0.001$) in Model 6, providing strong support for Hypothesis 1. Hypothesis 2 predicts that subsidiary exit is also positively related to dynamic exposure; the coefficient is positive and significant (0.082, $p < 0.05$), providing support for this hypothesis. Since the coefficients are standardized, we can also see that the present and immediate threat of locating inside a conflict zone (static exposure) is much stronger than the potential compound threat posed by dynamic exposure (0.421 vs 0.082) in terms of their impact on the subsidiary's exit-vs-stay decision, *ceteris paribus*.

Hypothesis 3 argues that the focal subsidiary is less likely to exit (more likely to survive) if concentrated in a space with same-country peers. The coefficient for geographic concentration of same-country peers is negative and significant (−0.511, $p < 0.001$), providing support for Hypothesis 3. Our results for Hypothesis 4 are the opposite of what we predicted,

Table 7.2 Descriptive statistics and correlations

	Variable	Mean	SD	1	2	3	4	5	6	7	8	9	10
1.	Exit	0.02	0.15										
2.	Subsidiary age	15.97	8.99	0.04									
3.	Subsidiary size	463.47	929.95	-0.01	0.14								
4.	Financial breakeven	0.19	0.39	0.00	-0.02	-0.08							
5.	Financial loss	0.13	0.34	0.03	-0.11	-0.06	-0.18						
6.	Same industry as parent	0.65	0.48	-0.04	0.06	0.07	0.02	-0.04					
7.	Parent ownership level (%)	50.98	29.65	-0.08	-0.07	0.10	0.02	0.00	-0.07				
8.	Parent sales (millions)	0.96	2.54	0.07	0.06	0.03	-0.01	0.01	-0.26	-0.09			
9.	Primary industry	0.22	0.42	0.01	0.14	-0.01	0.03	-0.05	0.07	-0.09	0.05		
10.	Manufacturing industry	0.56	0.50	-0.02	-0.08	0.16	-0.03	0.03	0.17	0.11	-0.10	-0.60	
11.	Wholesale industry	0.13	0.33	0.01	-0.03	-0.16	0.04	0.01	-0.12	-0.02	0.01	-0.20	-0.43
12.	Host market size (billions)	3.77	7.55	0.00	0.00	0.00	0.01	0.01	-0.02	0.08	-0.04	-0.06	0.01
13.	Host market potential (%)	0.21	4.18	0.00	0.01	0.00	0.00	-0.03	-0.01	-0.01	-0.03	-0.02	0.03
14.	Host composite risk	66.35	8.13	0.02	-0.10	-0.03	0.01	0.02	-0.05	0.12	-0.06	-0.11	0.02
15.	Host political terror	3.70	0.52	0.01	0.12	0.03	-0.01	-0.02	0.00	-0.04	0.00	0.03	0.02
16.	Home–host diplomatic ties	0.71	0.09	-0.02	-0.16	-0.06	0.01	0.03	-0.03	0.02	0.04	0.04	-0.10
17.	Home–host BIT	0.03	0.17	0.01	-0.04	-0.04	-0.01	-0.01	-0.05	-0.08	0.04	0.02	-0.04
18.	Home–host cultural distance	0.10	0.60	0.01	-0.13	-0.10	0.08	-0.01	-0.04	0.08	0.03	0.04	-0.14
19.	Home–host geographic distance	5.08	2.07	0.01	0.07	0.02	0.03	-0.01	0.00	-0.07	0.08	0.01	-0.01
20.	Peer industry exits	20.06	20.80	0.02	0.01	-0.02	0.03	0.02	-0.07	0.13	-0.10	-0.07	0.00
21.	Static exposure	0.19	0.39	0.03	-0.13	-0.05	0.04	0.02	-0.02	0.06	-0.01	-0.03	-0.03
22.	Dynamic exposure	0.47	2.70	0.00	-0.04	-0.03	0.04	0.00	0.02	0.02	-0.02	-0.04	-0.04
23.	Geographic concentration with home-country peers	0.43	0.42	-0.01	0.14	-0.08	0.05	-0.03	-0.09	0.04	-0.03	0.13	-0.30
24.	Geographic dispersion of same-parent subsidiaries	0.14	0.73	0.03	-0.02	0.16	-0.05	-0.04	0.01	0.01	0.07	-0.05	0.04

	Variable	11	12	13	14	15	16	17	18	19	20	21	22	23
12.	Host market size (billions)	0.04												
13.	Host market potential (%)	0.03	0.04											
14.	Host composite risk	0.13	0.16	0.53										
15.	Host political terror	-0.08	-0.08	-0.20	-0.41									
16.	Home–host diplomatic ties	0.09	0.04	-0.26	0.07	-0.40								
17.	Home–host BIT	-0.02	0.03	0.03	-0.12	0.11	0.06							
18.	Home–host cultural distance	0.10	-0.07	-0.17	0.01	-0.15	0.34	0.18						
19.	Home–host geographic distance	-0.03	0.05	-0.17	-0.37	0.10	-0.06	0.21	-0.30					
20.	Peer industry exits	0.07	0.15	0.20	0.45	-0.20	0.08	-0.15	-0.09	-0.26				
21.	Static exposure	0.07	-0.10	-0.13	-0.03	0.05	0.06	0.11	0.44	-0.15	-0.12			
22.	Dynamic exposure	0.06	-0.01	-0.05	-0.14	0.01	-0.03	-0.01	0.02	0.19	-0.07	0.21		
23.	Geographic concentration with home-country peers	0.16	0.13	0.16	0.37	-0.16	0.12	-0.17	-0.03	-0.30	0.50	-0.14	-0.06	
24.	Geographic dispersion of same-parent subsidiaries	0.02	-0.01	0.00	0.02	0.06	-0.05	0.01	-0.07	0.02	-0.05	-0.02	-0.01	-0.10

Correlations are based on the format used in regressions; correlations greater than or equal to 0.03 are significant at $p < 0.05$ (two-tailed). All distances used are in thousands of kilometers and account for the curvature of the earth (i.e., great-circle distances)

Table 7.3 Rare-event logistic regressions for foreign subsidiary exits from conflict-prone countries (standardized coefficients)

Variable	Model 1		Model 2		Model 3		Model 4		Model 5		Model 6	
Subsidiary age	0.013†	(0.008)	0.024**	(0.008)	0.023**	(0.008)	0.026***	(0.007)	0.024***	(0.007)	0.030***	(0.007)
Subsidiary size	0.030	(0.076)	-0.026	(0.152)	-0.031	(0.151)	-0.049	(0.163)	-0.089	(0.156)	-0.105	(0.167)
Financial breakeven	0.337†	(0.182)	0.051	(0.118)	0.040	(0.117)	0.043	(0.127)	0.039	(0.117)	0.062	(0.127)
Financial loss	0.551***	(0.106)	0.519***	(0.130)	0.522***	(0.127)	0.505***	(0.131)	0.538***	(0.132)	0.519***	(0.140)
Same industry as parent	-0.222	(0.175)	-0.392**	(0.148)	-0.386**	(0.149)	-0.405**	(0.136)	-0.396**	(0.153)	-0.421**	(0.139)
Parent ownership level	-0.015***	(0.003)	-0.021***	(0.004)	-0.022***	(0.003)	-0.022***	(0.004)	-0.022***	(0.004)	-0.021***	(0.004)
Parent sales	0.068***	(0.014)	0.069***	(0.018)	0.069***	(0.020)	0.069***	(0.019)	0.064***	(0.019)	0.062***	(0.017)
Primary industry	0.098	(0.174)	0.225	(0.243)	0.230	(0.242)	0.189	(0.240)	0.249	(0.251)	0.192	(0.235)
Manufacturing industry	-0.293†	(0.156)	-0.028	(0.180)	0.008	(0.181)	-0.164	(0.190)	0.002	(0.181)	-0.209	(0.185)
Wholesale industry	-0.042	(0.248)	0.032	(0.403)	0.104	(0.394)	0.032	(0.412)	0.061	(0.392)	-0.084	(0.415)
Host market size	-0.008**	(0.003)	-0.023***	(0.003)	-0.019***	(0.003)	-0.035***	(0.004)	-0.021***	(0.003)	-0.053***	(0.005)
Host market potential	-0.026	(0.017)	-0.041	(0.028)	-0.051†	(0.029)	-0.053†	(0.029)	-0.050†	(0.029)	-0.040	(0.028)
Host composite risk	0.018	(0.014)	0.043**	(0.015)	0.044**	(0.015)	0.051***	(0.015)	0.043**	(0.016)	0.046**	(0.015)
Host political terror	-0.006	(0.119)	0.110	(0.166)	0.113	(0.153)	0.103	(0.148)	0.080	(0.157)	0.045	(0.158)
Home–host diplomatic ties	-1.657*	(0.674)	-2.594**	(1.005)	-2.871**	(1.039)	-2.781**	(0.100)	-2.932**	(1.079)	-2.437*	(1.063)
Home–host BIT	0.701	(0.452)	0.129	(0.387)	0.191	(0.511)	0.149	(0.481)	0.171	(0.513)	0.115	(0.394)

Home–host cultural distance		0.284	(0.192)	0.244	(0.155)	0.385†	(0.207)	0.372*	(0.190)	0.438*	(0.210)	0.279†	(0.153)
Home–host geographic distance		0.062*	(0.031)	0.105***	(0.028)	0.090*	(0.037)	0.081*	(0.034)	0.089*	(0.038)	0.112**	(0.028)
Peer industry exits		0.012***	(0.003)	0.012***	(0.003)	0.011***	(0.003)	0.017***	(0.002)	0.012***	(0.003)	0.020***	(0.002)
Static exposure	H1			0.499***	(0.130)							0.421***	(0.122)
Dynamic exposure	H2					0.056†	(0.030)					0.082*	(0.042)
Geographic concentration with home-country peers	H3							-0.605***	(0.148)			-0.511***	(0.146)
Geographic dispersion of same-parent peers	H4									0.186***	(0.042)	0.181***	(0.037)
Constant		-3.575*	(1.640)	-5.387***	(1.628)	-5.131***	(1.611)	-5.286***	(1.513)	-4.856**	(1.672)	-5.316***	(1.515)
Number of subsidiary years		6400		5645		5653		5653		5651		5643	
Number of subsidiaries		825		670		671		671		671		670	
AIC		1731.110		1232.014		1241.287		1235.709		1236.998		1228.602	
BIC		1866.391		1371.423		1380.726		1375.148		1376.430		1387.918	
Log likelihood		-845.555		-595.007		-599.644		-596.854		-597.499		-590.301	

Standardized coefficients are reported, with robust standard errors clustered by country in brackets

†, *, **, *** show significance at the $p < 0.10$, $p < 0.05$, $p < 0.01$, $p < 0.001$, respectively (two-tailed)

however, since the coefficient for geographic dispersion of same-parent subsidiaries is positive and significant (0.181, $p < 0.001$). Given standardized coefficients, the impact of geographic concentration with peers appears to have a stronger impact on the focal firm's exit-vs-stay decision than dispersion of the MNE's network (-0.511 vs 0.181).

In Table 7.4, we present our rare-event logistic results using odds ratios in order to demonstrate the practical significance of our findings. We turn first to our two "place" hypotheses. On the basis of the odds ratio (1.524, $p < 0.001$) for static exposure in Model 6, we estimate that the probability of exit is 52% higher if the subsidiary is located inside rather than outside a conflict zone in the host country. Turning to dynamic exposure, the odds ratio (1.085, $p < 0.05$) implies that a one standard deviation increase in the level of this variable (based on the number and size of the conflict zones and their distance from the focal firm) produces a 9% increase in the likelihood of foreign subsidiary exit. Both results demonstrate the potentially severe impact on subsidiary survival when countries are faced with political conflicts; the results are nonetheless much stronger inside one "hot spot" compared with near several "hot spots" (52% vs 9%), *ceteris paribus*.

Our two "space" hypotheses also have practical significance, as demonstrated by their odds ratios in Table 7.4. The odds ratio for geographic concentration with home-country peers (0.600, $p < 0.001$) implies that a one standard deviation increase in geographic concentration of same-country peers with the focal firm increases its survival probability by 40%. Lastly, the odds ratio for geographic dispersion of same-parent subsidiaries (1.199, $p < 0.001$) implies that a one standard deviation increase in geographic dispersion of the MNE's network inside the host country increases the likelihood of the focal subsidiary's exit (reduces its chances of survival) by 20%. In terms of practical significance, concentrating with home-country peers therefore has twice the impact (but opposite in direction) as dispersion of the MNE's host-country network (40% vs 20%), *ceteris paribus*.

Table 7.4 Rare-event logistic regressions for foreign subsidiary exits from conflict-prone countries (odds ratio estimates)

Variable	Model 1		Model 2		Model 3		Model 4		Model 5		Model 6	
Subsidiary age	1.013†	(0.008)	1.024**	(0.008)	1.023**	(0.008)	1.027***	(0.008)	1.024***	(0.007)	1.028***	(0.007)
Subsidiary size	1.030	(0.078)	0.974	(0.149)	0.970	(0.147)	0.953	(0.155)	0.915	(0.142)	0.900	(0.151)
Financial breakeven	1.400†	(0.255)	1.053	(0.124)	1.041	(0.122)	1.044	(0.134)	1.039	(0.122)	1.064	(0.136)
Financial loss	1.735***	(0.183)	1.681***	(0.218)	1.686***	(0.214)	1.657***	(0.216)	1.713***	(0.226)	1.680***	(0.236)
Same industry as parent	0.801	(0.140)	0.675**	(0.100)	0.680**	(0.101)	0.667**	(0.091)	0.673**	(0.103)	0.656**	(0.091)
Parent ownership level	0.986***	(0.003)	0.979***	(0.004)	0.978***	(0.004)	0.978***	(0.004)	0.978***	(0.004)	0.979***	(0.004)
Parent sales	1.070***	(0.015)	1.071***	(0.020)	1.072***	(0.021)	1.072***	(0.020)	1.066***	(0.021)	1.064***	(0.018)
Primary industry	1.103	(0.192)	1.252	(0.305)	1.258	(0.305)	1.209	(0.290)	1.283	(0.322)	1.211	(0.284)
Manufacturing industry	0.732†	(0.116)	0.972	(0.175)	1.008	(0.182)	0.849	(0.161)	1.002	(0.181)	0.811	(0.150)
Wholesale industry	0.959	(0.238)	1.033	(0.417)	1.109	(0.437)	1.032	(0.425)	1.063	(0.417)	0.920	(0.381)
Host market size	0.992**	(0.003)	0.977***	(0.003)	0.981***	(0.003)	0.966***	(0.004)	0.979***	(0.003)	0.948***	(0.005)
Host market potential	0.974	(0.017)	0.959	(0.027)	0.951†	(0.027)	0.947†	(0.027)	0.952†	(0.028)	0.960	(0.027)
Host composite risk	1.108	(0.014)	1.044**	(0.015)	1.045**	(0.016)	1.052***	(0.016)	1.043**	(0.017)	1.048**	(0.016)
Host political terror	0.994	(0.118)	1.117	(0.186)	1.120	(0.172)	1.109	(0.164)	1.083	(0.170)	1.046	(0.165)
Home–host diplomatic ties	0.191*	(0.129)	0.075**	(0.075)	0.057**	(0.059)	0.062**	(0.068)	0.053**	(0.058)	0.078*	(0.093)
Home–host BIT	2.016	(0.911)	1.137	(0.441)	1.211	(0.620)	1.161	(0.558)	1.186	(0.609)	1.112	(0.442)
Home–host cultural distance	1.329	(0.256)	1.276	(0.198)	1.470†	(0.304)	1.451*	(0.276)	1.550*	(0.326)	1.322†	(0.202)

(continued)

Table 7.4 (continued)

Variable		Model 1		Model 2		Model 3		Model 4		Model 5		Model 6	
Home–host geographic distance		1.064*	(0.033)	1.111***	(0.031)	1.094*	(0.041)	0.085*	(0.037)	1.093*	(0.041)	1.118**	(0.032)
Peer industry exits		1.012***	(0.003)	1.012***	(0.003)	1.011***	(0.003)	1.017***	(0.002)	1.012***	(0.003)	1.020***	(0.002)
Static exposure	H1			1.647***	(0.225)							1.524***	(0.186)
Dynamic exposure	H2					1.058†	(0.032)					1.085*	(0.045)
Geographic concentration with home-country peers	H3							0.546***	(0.081)			0.600***	(0.087)
Geographic dispersion of same-parent subsidiaries	H4									1.204***	(0.051)	1.199***	(0.044)
Constant		0.028*	(0.046)	0.005***	(0.007)	0.006***	(0.010)	0.005***	(0.008)	0.008**	(0.013)	0.005***	(0.007)
Number of subsidiary years		6400		5645		5653		5653		5651		5643	
Number of subsidiaries		825		670		671		671		671		670	
AIC		1731.110		1232.014		1241.287		1235.709		1236.998		1228.602	
BIC		1866.391		1371.423		1380.726		1375.148		1376.430		1387.918	
Log likelihood		-845.555		-595.007		-599.644		-596.854		-597.499		-590.301	

Odds ratios are reported, with robust standard errors clustered by country in brackets

†, *, **, *** show significance at the $p < 0.10$, $p < 0.05$, $p < 0.01$, $p < 0.001$, respectively (two-tailed)

Robustness Tests

To check the robustness of our results, we conducted additional tests. First, we explored alternate measures of the "space" variables. Because managers are defined by their shared industry mental models as well as their shared national culture (Pouder & St John, 1996), we created a geographic concentration with home-country peers variable using only firms in the same industry as the focal firm. All independent variables retained their signs and remained significant at the $p < 0.001$ level, with only the dynamic exposure variable now marginally significant ($p < 0.10$).

To accommodate alternate assumptions for geographic dispersion of the MNE's host-country network, we reconstructed this variable by adding the dyadic distances between a focal subsidiary and each of its sister subsidiaries in the host country. To take account of differences in host-country size, we created two more measures of relative dispersion of same-parent subsidiaries by dividing our original geographic dispersion variable by the host country's circumference and area, respectively. All three alternate measures of dispersion had the same sign and significance level as our original variable, and left the results for the other independent variables intact.

We also employed alternate measures for our control variables. As a substitute for the political terror variable, we created a battle deaths density variable by dividing the number of battle-related deaths over all concomitant conflicts[13] in a host country by its population for a given year. In addition, because subsidiaries may not be divested because of poor performance unless subject to a lengthy period of observation, we constructed subsidiary performance variables lagged by 2, 3, and 5 years, respectively. All substantive results remained unchanged.

Next, we tested the sensitivity of our results to assumptions concerning home-country involvement, exit specifics, conflict landscape, and MNE activity. To account for Japan's possible intervention in regional conflicts, additional models were run for a subsample of subsidiaries in the Asia-Pacific region. The dynamic exposure variable lost its significance, which

[13] In the sample, 73% of the cases involved more than one conflict in a host country in a given year. If there was only one conflict in a given year for the host country, this step was omitted.

may be explained by the reduction in variance of this variable. Using the Philippines as an example, owing to the extensive coverage of the conflict zones, almost all the sampled subsidiaries were similarly exposed.

In addition, because the majority of the foreign subsidiary exits in our sample were closures (90%) rather than sell-offs of Japanese capital (10%), we re-ran our models, treating only closures as exits. To see that geographic landscape matters for subsidiary survival (Berman, 2000), we also conducted analyses using rural and urban subsamples. We similarly looked at whether survival likelihoods differed for market-seeking and efficiency-seeking FDI (Slangen & Beugelsdijk, 2010). All results in these alternate models remained substantively the same.

We then considered characteristics of the conflicts. The distribution of conflicts in our sample was 3.9% interstate, 90.6% intrastate, and 5.5% both inter- and intrastate. We re-ran our models using only subsidiaries that encountered intrastate conflicts; the results were not substantively affected. To determine whether the cause of the conflict affects subsidiary survival, we included a control variable for whether the conflict was a territorial or government dispute; again, our results were as expected.

Lastly, given the fact that 88.7% of the subsidiaries in our sample were accounted for by four countries (India, Indonesia, the Philippines, and Thailand), we examined the robustness of our findings by repeating all regression analyses using data only from these countries. This subsample analysis yielded matching significance levels for all the independent variables except the geographic concentration of home-country peers variable, which retained marginal significance ($p < 0.10$). To allay concerns regarding causality, we also re-ran our models using the variables lagged by 1 year. All results remained basically the same.

Post-Hoc Analysis

To determine why the geographic dispersion of same-parent subsidiaries variable had an unexpected sign (0.181, $p < 0.001$ in Model 6 of Table 7.5), we conducted a *post-hoc* analysis running Model 6 on subsamples of subsidiaries located inside and outside conflict zone(s), respectively, as shown in Table 7.5.

Table 7.5 Results by foreign subsidiary location inside and outside conflict zone(s)

Variable	Inside conflict zone		Outside conflict zone	
Subsidiary age	0.033*	(0.014)	0.025**	(0.009)
Subsidiary size	0.308	(0.243)	-0.139	(0.208)
Financial breakeven	-0.942**	(0.343)	0.394†	(0.225)
Financial loss	0.192	(0.552)	0.729**	(0.268)
Same industry as parent	-0.709*	(0.361)	-0.306†	(0.175)
Parent ownership	-0.026*	(0.011)	-0.020***	(0.005)
Parent sales	0.032	(0.025)	0.081***	(0.012)
Primary industry	-0.734†	(0.393)	0.394	(0.258)
Manufacturing industry	-0.349	(0.597)	-0.112	(0.194)
Wholesale industry	-0.643	(0.505)	0.204	(0.361)
Host market size	-0.073***	(0.004)	-0.024	(0.070)
Host market potential	0.005	(0.045)	-0.051	(0.051)
Host composite risk	0.042	(0.049)	0.026†	(0.014)
Host political terror	-0.012	(0.462)	-0.019	(0.241)
Home–host diplomacy	-4.703*	(1.876)	-1.311	(1.426)
Home–host BIT	0.414	(0.702)	0.323	(0.597)
Home–host cultural distance	0.201	(0.245)	0.266	(0.177)
Home–host geographic distance	0.244*	(0.098)	0.096†	(0.058)
Peer exits	0.056***	(0.017)	0.023***	(0.006)
Distance-adjusted conflict area(s)	0.156*	(0.062)	0.562	(0.558)
Geographic concentration with home-country peers	1.454*	(0.632)	-0.705**	(0.239)
Geographic dispersion of same-parent peers	-3.819*	(1.694)	0.218***	(0.047)
Constant	-3.499	(5.699)	-4.913**	(1.604)
Number of subsidiary years	1084		4559	
Number of subsidiaries	69		601	
AIC	297.218		915.741	
BIC	377.032		1018.538	
Log likelihood	-132.609		-441.870	

Standardized coefficients are reported, with robust standard errors clustered by country in brackets

†, *, **, *** show significance at the $p < 0.10$, $p < 0.05$, $p < 0.01$, $p < 0.001$, respectively (two-tailed)

Out of the 670 Japanese subsidiaries in our sample, 69 – almost 10% – were located inside a conflict zone. For these 69 subsidiaries located inside a "hot spot," the sign on the dynamic exposure variable is positive and significant (0.156, $p < 0.001$), suggesting that higher dynamic exposure encourages subsidiary exit, supporting Hypothesis 2. Geographic concentration with host-country peers, however, changes sign: such spatial positioning now encourages exit (1.454, $p < 0.05$), which is opposite to what we had predicted in Hypothesis 3. Geographic dispersion with same-parent subsidiaries, on the other hand, now exhibits the sign that we had expected for Hypothesis 4: that is, greater dispersion of the MNE network in the host country increases the likelihood of survival (-3.819, $p < 0.001$). For the 601 subsidiaries not located inside a conflict zone (90% of our sample), the results are similar to those for the full sample, with the exception that the dynamic exposure variable loses statistical significance.

We show the practical significance of these results in Table 7.6, a two-by-two matrix of the focal subsidiary's conflict zone location and its exit-vs-stay decision. Of the 69 subsidiaries located inside a conflict zone, 36 subsidiaries (48%) chose to exit the host country, while 39 (52%) chose to stay. Thus almost half the subsidiaries located inside a conflict zone left the host country. For the 608 subsidiaries located outside a conflict zone, 101 subsidiaries (17%) chose to exit, while 507 (83%) chose to stay. Thus the ratio of exiting to surviving subsidiaries located inside a conflict zone (48%) is almost three times as high as the ratio for those outside a conflict zone (17%), demonstrating the practical significance of Hypothesis 1 – that foreign subsidiary location relative to a conflict zone matters for subsidiary survival.

Table 7.6 also provides interesting information about our main-effect variables. First, mean/average dynamic exposure is much larger for the "inside-zone" subsample than for the "outside-zone" subsample (roughly 0.9 vs 0.2); however, mean exposure varies little for the exit-vs-stay choice (0.90 vs 0.87 inside zone; 0.21 vs 0.25 outside zone). Therefore, while average dynamic exposure is much higher for subsidiaries inside a conflict zone, the variable has little independent impact on the focal subsidiary's exit-vs-stay decision. From this we can conclude that the clear and present danger from locating inside a "hot spot" is sufficient to determine the subsidiary's exit-vs-stay choice.

In terms of geographic concentration with home-country peers, when the focal subsidiary is inside a conflict zone, the mean concentration level for subsidiaries that stay is 0.16, and for subsidiaries that exit is 0.36. This

Table 7.6 Two-by-two matrix of conflict zone location and subsidiary survival

		Exit (non-survival)	Non-exit (survival)	Total
Inside a conflict zone	Number of foreign subsidiaries	36 (48%)	39 (52%)	75 (100%)
	Mean dynamic exposure	0.90	0.87	
	Mean concentration with home-country peers	0.36	0.16	
	Mean dispersion of same-parent subsidiaries	0.01	0.06	
Outside a conflict zone	Number of foreign subsidiaries	101 (17%)	507 (83%)	608 (100%)
	Mean dynamic exposure	0.21	0.25	
	Mean concentration with home-country peers	0.42	0.69	
	Mean dispersion of same-parent subsidiaries	0.40	0.08	
Total	Number of foreign subsidiaries	137	546	683

implies that concentrating with home-country peers inside a conflict zone increases the likelihood of exit, since the mean concentration level for exiting subsidiaries is more than double that for those who stay. When the focal subsidiary is outside a conflict zone, however, the results are reversed: mean concentration with home-country peers is 0.42 for exiting subsidiaries, two-thirds the mean for surviving subsidiaries (0.69). This suggests that concentrating with home-country peers outside a conflict zone does benefit survival. Our results therefore depend on whether the focal firm is inside or outside a conflict zone: concentrating with home-country peers encourages exit for an inside-zone subsidiary; concentrating with peers encourages survival for an outside-zone subsidiary.

Table 7.6 also demonstrates that, when a focal subsidiary is located inside a conflict zone, average geographic dispersion with same-parent subsidiaries is 0.06 for surviving subsidiaries, compared with 0.01 for exiting subsidiaries. This shows the benefits of a dispersed MNE network for survival of subsidiaries located inside a conflict zone: mean dispersion is six times higher for those that survive. For the outside-zone sample the results are reversed: the mean geographic dispersion of the MNE network is 0.40 for exiting subsidiaries, five times higher than for surviving subsidiaries (0.08). Our results therefore depend on whether the focal firm is inside or outside a conflict zone: more dispersed MNE networks encourage survival for an inside-zone subsidiary, but encourage exit for an outside-zone subsidiary.

In order to isolate the effect of being in a conflict zone on subsidiary survival – in addition to conducting *post-hoc* analyses – it is important to construct an appropriate counterfactual by asking the question: *What would have happened to foreign subsidiaries located inside a conflict zone if they had not been located inside a zone (or vice versa)?*[14] Because we cannot observe this counterfactual – firms in reality were either located inside or outside a conflict zone – we use a method called propensity score matching,[15] which generates a hypothetical counterfactual by re-establishing the conditions of a natural experiment with non-experimental data (Heckman, Ichimura, & Todd, 1997; Rosenbaum & Rubin, 1983). Propensity score matching uses a probit equation to define a matched control group, which enables us to overcome the problem of self-selection.[16] The matching estimators from the nearest neighbor matching, kernel, and radius methods generate the impact of being in a conflict zone, or the average treatment effect (ATT) on the treated, defined as the difference between the real and counterfactual outcomes. We estimate the ATT of being located in a conflict zone on foreign subsidiary survival to lie between 1.1 and 2.0, which is statistically significant at the 5% level, a result considered pronounced at the firm level (Chang, Chung, & Moon, 2013). We conclude that location inside a conflict zone significantly increases the probability of foreign subsidiary exit, even after removing self-selection bias.

---

[14] We thank the editors for bringing this point to our attention.

[15] This methodology has been widely used in international economics to evaluate, for example, the effects of exporting and acquisitions on firm performance and returns to scale (Arnold & Javorcik, 2009), and of outward FDI on the decision to invest in tangible assets and R&D at home (Egger & Pfaffermayr, 2004).

[16] A simple comparison between conflict zone and non-conflict zone subsidiaries cannot determine the precise effects of zone location, because the characteristics of the subsidiaries inside conflict zones would have differed from those outside conflict zones before the former were "placed" inside.

Discussion and Conclusions

In this study, we highlight the subnational geographical determinants of foreign subsidiary survival in conflict-prone settings. By examining MNE geography in both its absolute and relative contexts, we establish Beugelsdijk et al.'s (2010) schema of place and space as dimensions that inform MNE strategy in difficult environments. By considering place and space alongside their constituent parts of proximity and distance, expansion and shrinkage, and concentration and dispersion, we show that evaluating geographic exposure to environmental factors is a primary means by which MNEs contextualize strategic decisions.

Because operating in a conflict zone increases a foreign subsidiary's exposure and reduces its chances for survival, we argue that location is as much a subnational decision as it is a country-level decision for the MNE (Cantwell & Mudambi, 2011; Coombs, Mudambi, & Deeds, 2006). Our study points to one of the rarely emphasized downside implications of location: in politically violent countries, it is less advantageous to be an insider than an outsider *vis-à-vis* a conflict zone (Cantwell, 2009; Cantwell & Mudambi, 2011; Eden & Molot, 2002). Our findings with respect to exposure also extend Zaheer and Nachum's (2011) argument that locations do not offer the same benefits to all MNEs, by showing that locations do not pose the same threats to all MNEs.

In addition to static exposure, we introduce to the literature the new concept of dynamic exposure, which we argue varies positively with the number and size of the conflict zones and negatively with the firm's distance from them. This chapter is also the first, to our knowledge, to use Coulomb's law to theorize about and empirically measure the impact on a firm of being exposed to multiple threats. Our modeling of multiple conflict zones captures time–space dynamics that reveal the impact of expanding and shrinking spheres of external threat on firm survival. We show that, in contrast to cultural and institutional distances, which vary slowly over time, geographic distance at the subnational level can quickly rise or fall, with implications for MNE strategy. Moreover, this novel construct illustrates that just as geographic distance suppresses knowledge flows (Audretsch, 1998), greater distance from a conflict zone suppresses subsidiary exposure to threats from that zone. Our approach may prove useful to other researchers in creating more sophisticated cultural and institutional distance measures for the MNE that involve multiple host countries.

Our analysis shows that relative to place, which is passive, space can be defined in terms of social interactions. We conceive of conflicts as socially constructed spaces, and the MNE as a dual organizational form. By orienting peer firms and their interrelationships in spatial conflicts (Beugelsdijk, 2007), and showing that subsidiaries in hostile contexts can leverage proximity to home-country peers to enhance survival prospects, we extend the literature on the competitiveness and innovation-enhancing effects of agglomeration economies (Krugman, 1991). In doing so, we model external threats as both a bottom-up and a top-down phenomenon (Beugelsdijk, 2007), where the interactions between same-country peers jointly determine the exposure and survival odds of each other in the face of exogenous threats. Whereas place denotes the site where top-down violence occurs, space can be construed as the outcome of bottom-up processes to shield geographically against the violence.

However, as our subgroup analysis reveals, the positive influence of concentrating with home-country peers on the focal firm's survival (i.e., Hypothesis 3) is geographically bounded. We find that, if the focal firm is *inside* a conflict zone, concentrating with peers actually *reduces* the probability of subsidiary survival; *outside* a conflict zone, survival probability is *increased* by such concentration. We reasoned in our theoretical development of Hypothesis 3 that geographic concentration generates self-reinforcing agglomeration economies that encourage survival. We also argued that incumbent firms are less likely to leave owing to endowment effects – that is, the greater loss the MNE would face by exiting and leaving the market to its competitors. Moreover, we viewed concentration as generating locational economies of scale, which would encourage staying. Apparently, all three arguments are important only for focal subsidiaries located outside a conflict zone; once inside, the clear and present danger of political conflict overwhelms the positive advantages of concentrating with same-country peers.[17]

[17] We control for the exit of same-country, same-industry peers in the prior year, so that geographic concentration with same-country peers encouraging exit captures other motivations besides peer firm exit.

We also find that geographic dispersion of the MNE's network in the host country has different effects on foreign subsidiary survival (i.e., Hypothesis 4), depending on location. If the focal subsidiary is *inside* a conflict zone, greater dispersion of same-parent subsidiaries *increases* the probability of staying; location *outside* a conflict zone *decreases* survival. We argued that dispersion of the MNE's host-country network meant that sister subsidiaries could provide the focal firm with access to resources, knowledge, and critical support, possibly more readily and quickly than could the parent firm. Sister subsidiaries could also provide a temporary refuge, so that a focal subsidiary might avoid total closure by reducing production and shifting its employees elsewhere in the MNE's in-country network. We therefore expected that a geographically dispersed MNE network would facilitate subsidiary survival.

However, Model 6 in Table 7.5 showed that the sign on geographic dispersion of same-parent subsidiaries was positive and significant (0.181, $p < 0.001$), implying that, in general, greater dispersion hampered subsidiary survival. In attempting to disentangle this counterintuitive result, our *post-hoc* empirical work revealed that "place" mattered: *inside*-zone subsidiaries were more likely to *stay* whereas *outside*-zone subsidiaries were more likely to *leave*, if the MNE network were dispersed.

A possible explanation for this result comes from Chung et al.'s (2008) study of the 1997 Asian economic crisis. They showed that MNE networks, because of their operational flexibility, had a positive impact on foreign subsidiary survival that was stronger during periods of economic crisis. The authors concluded that "a subsidiary network tends to provide more benefits to subsidiaries in economic crisis environments than to those in economically stable environments" (2008: 289). Examples of operational and strategic flexibility during economic crises included the ability to reconfigure operations and shift factors, production and sales from crisis-ridden markets to more lucrative locations. Moreover, the authors found that the greater the ratio of subsidiaries outside a country facing an economic crisis to those inside the country, the more likely were the subsidiaries in the crisis country to be profitable and survive. The explanation was that, when local markets collapsed, the strategic and operational flexibility provided by a widely dispersed network of subsidiaries protected the subsidiaries in the crisis location.

Chung et al.'s (2008) country-level argument can be applied at the subnational level to explain the effects of geographic dispersion of the MNE's network when the focal subsidiary is located inside or outside a conflict zone. The strategic and operational flexibility provided by sister subsidiaries dispersed throughout the host country provides "breathing room" and support to the focal subsidiary in a conflict zone. Rather than exit, the focal subsidiary inside a conflict zone may be able to avoid downside risks by shifting value-chain activities within the MNE network, circumventing the exit decision by escalating its commitment to a high-stake location, and exercising other options provided by a dispersed MNE network (Belderbos & Zou, 2009). When the focal subsidiary is located outside a conflict zone and the MNE's host-country network is geographically dispersed, however, the high cost of coordinating a far-flung network during a political conflict could easily overwhelm the benefits to be derived from operational flexibility. Although the danger inside a conflict zone does not threaten its immediate survival, the focal subsidiary may still face dynamic exposure and the long-term challenge of maximizing upside gains in a conflict-afflicted country. Given these findings, we suggest that place transforms space.

In sum, whereas geographic concentration with home-country peers (neighbors) helps outside-zone subsidiaries to survive, a more dispersed MNE network (far-away siblings) helps inside-zone subsidiaries[18] to survive. Pouder and St John (1996) argue that firms inside and outside innovation clusters differ in their susceptibility to pressures for isomorphism, and their ability to react to industry-wide jolts. We provide empirical evidence that although subsidiaries inside and outside conflict zones differ in their exposure to threats, their survival prospects are contingent on the extent of concentration with home-country peers and dispersion with same-parent subsidiaries. Therefore place – location *vis-à-vis* sources of external threat – may be taken as a given, but space can be leveraged to reduce exposure. Essentially, these notions of space suggest that, rather than being exogenously imposed, geography should be seen as

[18] We also theorized about dispersion as a parent-level phenomenon, but our robustness checks found almost identical results for the effects of dispersion on the focal subsidiary ($\beta = 0.18$ instead of 0.14; $p < 0.001$ for both).

endogenous as subsidiaries continuously redefine their place in the host country through their spatial interdependencies with peers.

Our study makes several contributions to the literature on MNEs in geographic space. First, we develop and test a series of arguments that acknowledge the fundamental nature of the MNE as an organization for which many decisions are inherently locational (McCann & Mudambi, 2004). We demonstrate at the subnational level that geographic concepts such as place and space are central to MNE outcomes, with effects independent of the cultural and institutional distances often studied in the literature. In line with Buckley and Ghauri's (2004) conviction that the management of space by MNEs should be at the forefront of international business research, we develop an actor-centered approach to determine the geographic sources of subsidiary survival in difficult contexts (Beugelsdijk, 2007).

Second, we take a first step in modeling subsidiary responses to geographically defined threats at the street level by measuring their geographic proximity in latitude and longitude coordinates using GIS data. Firm-level studies on the role of firms in space are scarce (Beugelsdijk, 2007), and the majority of these studies are unable to disentangle agglomeration effects and localized inter-organizational linkages (Knoben, 2009). While previous studies have established the impact of external threats on MNE activity at the country level, Beugelsdijk (2007: 182) noted that "blurring macro-level evidence with micro-level arguments about firm strategy may lead to an ecological fallacy, in which global phenomena or data aggregates that are actual representations of lower-level phenomena cannot be generalized to those lower levels." Our novel treatment of external threats at the conflict zone level presents an effective means of gauging strategic choice as a function of MNE positioning in place and space (Beugelsdijk et al., 2010).

Finally, our work contributes to the literatures on political risk and macro-level crises. Even as scholars recognize that exposure to political risk is idiosyncratic across firms, projects, and even product lines (cf. Wells & Gleason, 1995), much of the extant research is at the country level. Rather than attribute firm decisions to macro phenomena, we challenge the space-neutrality of the political risk concept by parceling out the specific threats faced by the MNE, and quantifying the exposure of subsidiaries in geographic terms. We theorized and showed that, beyond a certain threshold, geographic distance from the locus of violence reduces the impact of political conflict on MNE decisions, even when controlling for conflict intensity in terms of battle fatalities. For MNEs in conflict-prone countries, the good news from our analyses is that there are geographical boundaries to political risk (Berman, 2000), a phenomenon that has long been construed as ubiquitous within national confines. Given the similar role of dispersion in MNE exit during economic crises (cf. Chung et al., 2008, 2010), this work highlights parallels to crisis management in MNEs. Our findings shed light on the strategic consequences of MNE location, which have been overlooked in research on political and other macro-level crises.

Our study also has some limitations that can open doors to future research. First, we followed Buhaug and Gates (2002) in conceptualizing conflict zones as circular areas. In reality, conflict zones assume various shapes, and we expect that, in the future, researchers will have better GIS data and methods for taking account of the varying geographic shapes of conflict zones. Despite this limitation, our empirical work breaks new ground by using fine-grained GIS data applied to both firms and contextual events. Another limitation of our paper is that a host country's borders determined our selection of conflict zones; we did not take account of conflicts in neighboring countries. Since "geographic distance can actually be larger within a country than between countries, depending on the exact location of firms" (Beugelsdijk, 2011: 200), in future work we hope to analyze the role of country borders in geographically delimiting conflict zones. A third limitation is the sample restriction to Japanese MNEs. While this was necessary, given the paucity of fine-grained subsidiary data for MNEs from countries other than Japan, it is possible that other data sets (e.g., Swedish or US MNEs) might have sufficient data to enable replication of some of our results. Comparing US and Japanese MNE responses in conflict zones, for instance, would be an interesting way to test the impact of Hofstede's uncertainty and power distance cultural characteristics on foreign subsidiary behavior in politically violent locations.

Because MNEs may learn over time to shield their operations from exposure in a certain locale, future research could also examine the geographic sources of firm resilience as opposed to firm exposure. In addition, while conflicts may be interpreted by inexperienced firms as overwhelming events, MNEs with prior experience in conflict zones may perceive such threats as mere fluctuations in political risk (Delios & Henisz, 2003). There may also, therefore, be value in adopting learning perspectives in the study of exposure to geographically bounded threats.

In conclusion, the geographic domain of the MNE is fundamental not only to its performance, but also to its survival. We have shown in this chapter that in countries with one or even multiple conflict zones, subsidiary survival depends largely on geography – the characteristics both of the place (the conflict) and of the space (distance) between the subsidiary and its peers. Our findings indicate that, in certain situations, far-away relatives (parents and sister subsidiaries) may actually be less helpful than good neighbors (home-country peers) in the face of pressing hardships (cf. Beugelsdijk & Cornet, 2002). By studying MNE exposure to spatially defined threats, we hope to encourage more work on the geographic determinants of firm survival to external threats including but not limited to political conflicts.

Acknowledgements We gratefully acknowledge the encouraging guidance and insightful feedback of the Special Issue Editors, Ram Mudambi and Sjoerd Beugelsdijk, as well as *JIBS* Editor-in-Chief John Cantwell. The chapter has also benefited from the comments and suggestions made by two anonymous *JIBS* reviewers. We also thank the participants and commentators at the *JIBS* Special Issue Conference at Temple University and the Faculty Research Seminar Series at Loyola Marymount University for their helpful input and rich discussions on this topic. The authors are also indebted to Quan Li, who first drew our attention to geographic information systems (GIS) data for conflict zones; Miriam Olivares and Ryan Lee, who helped with the ArcGIS software; and Dan Xie, who helped with the mathematical formulas.

References

Abler, R., Adams, J. S., & Gould, P. (1971). *Spatial organization: The geographer's view of the world.* Prentice Hall.

Adams, J. D., & Jaffe, A. B. (1996). Bounding the effects of R&D: An investigation using matched establishment-firm data. *RAND Journal of Economics, 27*(4), 700–721.

Adger, W. N. (2000). Social and ecological resilience: Are they related? *Progress in Human Geography, 24*(3), 347–364.

Agnew, J., & Duncan, J. (1989). *The power of place: Bringing together geographical and sociological imaginations*. Unwin Hyman.

Allen, L., & Pantzalis, C. (1996). Valuation of the operating flexibility of multinational corporations. *Journal of International Business Studies, 27*(4), 633–653.

Anderson, J. L., Markides, C., & Kupp, M. (2010). The last frontier: Market creation in conflict zones, deep rural areas and urban slums. *California Management Review, 52*(4), 6–28.

Arnold, J. M., & Javorcik, B. S. (2009). Gifted kids or pushy parents? Foreign direct investment and plant productivity in Indonesia. *Journal of International Economics, 79*(1), 42–53.

Audia, P. G., Sorenson, O., & Hage, J. (2001). Tradeoffs in the organization of production: Multiunit firms, geographic dispersion and organizational learning, multiunit organization and multimarket strategy. *Advances in Strategic Management, 18*, 75–105.

Audretsch, D. B. (1998). Agglomeration and the location of innovative activity. *Oxford Review of Economic Policy, 14*(2), 18–29.

Bania, N., Calkins, L., & Dalenberg, D. (1992). The effects of regional science and technology policy on the geographic distribution of industrial R&D laboratories. *Journal of Regional Science, 32*(2), 209–228.

Barney, J. B. (1997). *Gaining and sustaining competitive advantage*. Addison-Wesley.

Baum, A., Garofalo, J. P., & Yali, A. M. (1999). Socioeconomic status and chronic stress: Does stress account for SES effects on health? *Annals of New York Academy of Sciences, 896*(1), 131–144.

Belderbos, R., & Zou, J. (2009). Real options and foreign affiliate divestments: A portfolio perspective. *Journal of International Business Studies, 40*(4), 600–620.

Benito, G. R. G. (1997). Divestment of foreign production operations. *Applied Economics, 29*(10), 1365–1377.

Berman, J. (2000). Boardrooms and bombs: Strategies of multinational corporations in conflict areas. *Harvard International Review, 22*(3), 28–32.

Beugelsdijk, S. (2007). The regional environment and a firm's innovative performance: A plea for a multilevel interactionist approach. *Economic Geography, 83*(2), 181–199.

Beugelsdijk, S. (2011). Liability of foreignness and location-specific advantages: Time, space and relative advantage. In C. G. Asmussen, T. Pedersen,

T. M. Devinney, & L. Tihanyi (Eds.), *Dynamics of globalization, Advances in International Management* (Vol. 24, pp. 181–210). Emerald Group.

Beugelsdijk, S., & Cornet, M. (2002). A far friend is worth more than a good neighbor: Proximity and innovation in a small country. *Journal of Management and Governance, 6*(2), 169–188.

Beugelsdijk, S., & Frijns, B. (2010). A cultural explanation of the foreign bias in international asset allocation. *Journal of Banking and Finance, 34*(9), 1221–1231.

Beugelsdijk, S., McCann, P., & Mudambi, R. (2010). Introduction: Place, space, and organization – Economic geography and the multinational enterprise. *Journal of Economic Geography, 10*(4), 485–493.

Boeh, K. K., & Beamish, P. W. (2011). Connecting flights: The time sink that kills profits. *Harvard Business Review, 89*(12), 30–30.

Boeh, K. K., & Beamish, P. W. (2012). Travel time and the liability of distance in foreign direct investment: Location choice and entry mode. *Journal of International Business Studies, 43*(5), 525–535.

Boulding, K. (1962). *Conflict and defense*. Harper & Row.

Brams, S. J. (1966). Transaction flows in the international system. *American Political Science Review, 60*(4), 880–898.

Buckley, P. J., & Ghauri, P. N. (2004). Globalization, economic geography and the strategy of multinational enterprises. *Journal of International Business Studies, 35*(1), 81–98.

Buhaug, H. (2010). Dude, where's my conflict? LSG, relative strength, and the location of civil war. *Conflict Management and Peace Science, 27*(2), 107–128.

Buhaug, H., & Gates, S. (2002). The geography of civil war. *Journal of Peace Research, 39*(4), 417–433.

Calder, K. (1988). Japanese foreign economic policy formation: Explaining the reactive state. *World Politics, 60*(4), 517–541.

Cantwell, J. A. (2009). Location and the multinational enterprise. *Journal of International Business Studies, 40*(1), 35–41.

Cantwell, J. A., & Mudambi, R. (2011). Physical attraction and the geography of knowledge sourcing in multinational enterprises. *Global Strategy Journal, 1*(3–4), 206–232.

Cantwell, J. A., & Piscitello, L. (2005). Recent location of foreign-owned research and development activities by large multinational corporations in the European regions: The role of spillovers and externalities. *Regional Studies, 39*(1), 1–16.

Chang, S. J., Chung, J., & Moon, J. J. (2013). When do wholly owned subsidiaries perform better than joint ventures? *Strategic Management Journal, 34*(3), 317–337.
Chang, S. J., & Xu, D. (2008). Spillovers and competition among foreign and local firms in China. *Strategic Management Journal, 29*(5), 495–518.
Chung, C. C., & Beamish, P. W. (2005). The impact of institutional reforms on characteristics and survival of foreign subsidiaries in emerging economies. *Journal of Management Studies, 42*(1), 35–62.
Chung, C. C., Lee, S. H., Beamish, P. W., & Isobe, T. (2010). Subsidiary expansion/contraction during times of economic crisis. *Journal of International Business Studies, 41*(3), 500–516.
Chung, C. C., Lu, J. W., & Beamish, P. W. (2008). Multinational networks during times of economic crisis versus stability. *Management International Review, 48*(3), 279–295.
Cleves, M. A., Gould, W. W., & Gutierrez, R. G. (2010). *An introduction to survival analysis using STATA*. STATA Corporation.
Cohen, J. (1988). *Statistical power analysis for the behavioral sciences*. Erlbaum.
Coombs, J. E., Mudambi, R., & Deeds, D. L. (2006). An examination of the investments in US biotechnology firms by foreign and domestic corporate partners. *Journal of Business Venturing, 21*(4), 405–428.
Delios, A., & Beamish, P. W. (2004). Joint venture performance revisited: Japanese foreign subsidiaries worldwide. *Management International Review, 44*(1), 69–91.
Delios, A., & Henisz, W. J. (2003). Political hazards and the sequence of entry by Japanese firms. *Journal of International Business Studies, 34*(3), 227–241.
Delios, A., & Makino, S. (2003). Timing of entry and the foreign subsidiary performance of Japanese firms. *Journal of International Marketing, 11*(3), 83–105.
Dellestrand, H., & Kappen, P. (2012). The effects of spatial and contextual factors on headquarters resource allocation to MNE subsidiaries. *Journal of International Business Studies, 43*(3), 219–243.
Devinney, T. M. (2011). Social responsibility, global strategy, and the MNE: Global monitory democracy and the meaning of place and space. *Global Strategy Journal, 1*(3–4), 329–344.
Dhanaraj, C., & Beamish, P. (2004). Effect of equity ownership on the survival of international joint ventures. *Strategic Management Journal, 25*(3), 295–303.
Dunning, J. H. (1988). The eclectic paradigm of international production: A restatement and some possible extensions. *Journal of International Business Studies, 19*(1), 1–31.

Dunning, J. H. (2009). Location and the multinational enterprise: John Dunning's thoughts on receiving *the Journal of International Business Studies* 2008 decade award. *Journal of International Business Studies, 40*(1), 20–34.
Dutton, J. E., & Jackson, S. E. (1987). Categorizing strategic issues: Links to organizational action. *Academy of Management Review, 12*(1), 76–90.
Eden, L., & Molot, M. A. (2002). Insiders outsiders and host country bargains. *Journal of International Management, 8*(4), 359–433.
Egger, P., & Pfaffermayr, M. (2004). The impact of bilateral investment treaties on foreign direct investment. *Journal of Comparative Economics, 32*(4), 788–804.
Feil, M., Fischer, S., Haidvogl, A., & Zimmer, M. (2008). *Bad guys, good guys, or something in between?* Corporate governance contributions in zones of violent conflict, peace research institute Frankfurt, Report no. 84.
Flowers, E. B. (1976). Oligopolistic reactions in European and Canadian direct investment in the United States. *Journal of International Business Studies, 7*(2), 43–55.
Gallopin, G. C. (2006). Linkages between vulnerability, resilience, and adaptive capacity. *Global Environmental Change, 16*(3), 293–303.
Gartzke, E. (2006). *The affinity of nations index.* http://dss.ucsd.edu/~egartzke/htmlpages/data.html. Accessed 20 June 2012.
Ghemawat, P. (2001). Distance still matters: The hard reality of global expansion. *Harvard Business Review, 79*(8), 137–147.
Gleditsch, S. K., & Weidmann, N. B. (2012). Richardson in the information age: Geographic information systems and spatial data in international studies. *Annual Review of Political Science, 15*, 461–481.
Greve, H. R. (1995). Jumping ship: The diffusion of strategy abandoned. *Administrative Science Quarterly, 40*(3), 444–473.
Head, K., Ries, J., & Swenson, D. (1995). Agglomeration benefits and location choice: Evidence from Japanese manufacturing investments in the US. *Journal of International Economics, 38*(3–4), 223–247.
Heckman, J., Ichimura, H., & Todd, P. (1997). Matching as an econometric evaluation estimator: Evidence from evaluating a job training program. *Review of Economic Studies, 64*(4), 605–654.
Heidelberg Institute for International Conflict Research (HIIK). (2011). *Conflict barometer 2011.* http://www.hiik.de/de/konfliktbarometer. Accessed 28 Aug 2012.
Henisz, W. J. (2000). The institutional environment for multinational investment. *Journal of Law, Economics, and Organization, 16*(2), 334–364.

Henisz, W. J., & Delios, A. (2004). Information or influence? The benefits of experience for managing political uncertainty. *Strategic Organization, 2*(4), 389–421.

Hillman, A. J., & Hitt, M. A. (1999). Corporate political strategy formulation: A model of approach, participation, and strategy decisions. *Academy of Management Review, 24*(4), 825–842.

Hofstede, G. (1980). *Culture's consequences: International differences in work-related values*. Sage.

Hymer, S. H. (1960). *The international operations of national firms: A study of direct investment, Unpublished PhD dissertation (published 1976)*. Sloan School of ManagementMIT.

Ingram, P., & Baum, C. (1997). Opportunity and constraint: Organizations' learning from the operating and competitive experience of industries. *Strategic Management Journal, 18*(Special Issue 1), 75–98.

Kahneman, D., Knetsch, J. L., & Thaler, R. (1991). Anomalies: The endowment effect, loss aversion, and status quo bias. *Journal of Economic Perspectives, 5*(1), 193–206.

Kalyvas, S. (2003). The ontology of political violence: Action and identity in civil wars. *Perspectives on Politics, 1*(3), 475–494.

Kim, T. Y., Delios, A., & Xu, D. (2010). Organizational geography, experiential learning, and subsidiary exit: Japanese foreign expansions in China, 1979–2001. *Journal of Economic Geography, 10*(4), 579–597.

Kim, Y. C., Lu, J. W., & Rhee, M. (2012). Learning from age difference: Interorganizational learning and survival in Japanese foreign subsidiaries. *Journal of International Business Studies, 43*(8), 719–745.

King, G., & Zeng, L. (2001). Logistic regression in rare events data. *Political Analysis, 9*(2), 137–163.

Knickerbocker, F. T. (1973). *Oligopolistic reaction and the multinational enterprise*. Harvard University Press.

Knoben, J. (2009). Localized inter-organizational linkages, agglomeration effects, and the innovative performance of firms. *Annals of Regional Science, 43*(3), 757–779.

Kogut, B., & Singh, H. (1988). The effect of national culture on the choice of entry mode. *Journal of International Business Studies, 19*(3), 411–432.

Krugman, P. (1991). *Geography and trade*. MIT Press.

Lazerson, M. H., & Lorenzoni, G. (1999). The firms that feed industrial districts: A return to the Italian source. *Industrial and Corporate Change, 8*(2), 235–266.

Li, J. (1995). Foreign entry and survival: Effects of strategic choices on performance in international markets. *Strategic Management Journal, 16*(5), 333–352.

Li, Q. (2006). Political violence and foreign direct investment. In M. Fratianni & A. M. Rugman (Eds.), *Research in global strategic management* (Vol. 12, pp. 231–255). Elsevier.

Lorenzen, M., & Mudambi, R. (2013). Clusters, connectivity and catch-up: Bollywood and Bangalore in the global economy. *Journal of Economic Geography, 13*(3), 501–534.

Markusen, A. (1999). Sticky places in slippery space. In T. Barnes & M. Gertler (Eds.), *The new industrial geography* (pp. 98–128). Routledge.

McCann, P. (2011). International business and economic geography: Knowledge, time and transaction costs. *Journal of Economic Geography, 11*(2), 309–317.

McCann, P., & Mudambi, R. (2004). The location decision of the multinational enterprise: Some theoretical and empirical issues. *Growth & Change, 35*(4), 491–524.

McCann, P., & Mudambi, R. (2005). Analytical differences in the economics of geography: The case of the multinational firm. *Environment and Planning A, 37*(10), 1857–1876.

McLeod, J. D., & Kessler, R. C. (1990). Socioeconomic differences in vulnerability to undesirable life events. *Journal of Health and Social Behavior, 31*(2), 162–172.

Miguel, E., Satyanath, S., & Sergenti, E. (2004). Economic shocks and civil conflict: An instrumental variables approach. *Journal of Political Economy, 112*(41), 725–753.

Mowery, D., Oxley, J., & Silverman, B. (1996). Strategic alliances and interfirm knowledge transfer. *Strategic Management Journal, 17*(Winter Special Issue), 77–91.

Mudambi, R., & Swift, T. (2012). Multinational enterprises and the geographical clustering of innovation. *Industry and Innovation, 19*(1), 1–21.

Nachum, L., Zaheer, S., & Gross, S. (2008). Does it matter where countries are? Proximity to knowledge, markets, and resources, and MNE location choices. *Management Science, 54*(7), 1252–1265.

Newson, R. (2004). Generalized power calculations for generalized linear models and more. *Stata Journal, 4*(4), 379–401.

O'Loughlin, J., & Witmer, F. (2010). The localized geographies of violence in the north Caucasus of Russia, 1999–2007. *Annals of the Association of American Geographers, 101*(1), 178–201.

Phelps, N. A., & Fuller, C. (2000). Multinationals, intracorporate competition, and regional development. *Economic Geography, 76*(3), 224–243.

Piscitello, L. (2011). Strategy, location, and the conceptual metamorphosis of the MNE. *Global Strategy Journal, 1*(1), 127–131.

Porter, M. E. (2000). Locations, clusters, and company strategy. In G. L. Clark, M. P. Feldman, & M. S. Gertler (Eds.), *The Oxford handbook of economic geography* (pp. 253–274). Oxford University Press.

Pouder, R., & St John, C. H. (1996). Hot spots and blind spots: Geographical clusters of firms and innovation. *Academy of Management Review, 21*(4), 1192–1225.

Rosenbaum, P., & Rubin, D. B. (1983). The central role of the propensity score in observational studies for causal effects. *Biometrica, 70*(1), 41–55.

Roxburgh, S. (1996). Gender differences in work and well-being: Effects of exposure and vulnerability. *Journal of Health and Social Behavior, 37*(3), 265–277.

Schotter, A., & Beamish, P. W. (2013). The hassle factor: An explanation for managerial location shunning. *Journal of International Business Studies, 44*(5), 521–544.

Slangen, A. H. L., & Beugelsdijk, S. (2010). The impact of institutional hazards on foreign multinational activity: A contingency perspective. *Journal of International Business Studies, 41*(6), 980–995.

Sorenson, O., & Audia, P. G. (2000). The social structure of entrepreneurial activity: Geographic concentration of footwear production in the United States, 1940–1989. *American Journal of Sociology, 106*(2), 424–462.

Sorenson, O., & Stuart, T. E. (2001). Syndication networks and the spatial distribution of venture capital investments. *American Journal of Sociology, 106*(6), 1546–1588.

Starr, H. (2005). Territory, proximity, and spatiality: The geography of international conflict. *International Studies Review, 7*(3), 387–406.

Taylor, P. J. (1999). Places, spaces and Macy's: Place-space tensions in the political geography of modernities. *Progress in Human Geography, 23*(1), 7–26.

Tomz, M. (2001). Relogit: Rare events logistic regressions. http://gking.harvard.edu/category/research-intersts/methods/rare-events. Accessed 20 June 2012.

Turvey, R. (2007). Vulnerability assessment of developing countries: The case of small island developing states. *Development Policy Review, 25*(2), 243–264.

Uppsala. (2011). Conflict data program. http://www.pcr.uu.se/data/. Accessed 31 Oct 2011.

Vergne, J. P. (2012). Stigmatized categories and public disapproval of organizations: A mixed methods study of the global arms industry (1996–2007). *Academy of Management Journal, 55*(5), 1027–1052.
Wallace, J. M., Jr., & Muroff, J. R. (2002). Preventing substance abuse among African American children and youth: Race differences in risk factor exposure and vulnerability. *Journal of Primary Prevention, 22*(3), 235–261.
Wells, L. T., & Gleason, E. S. (1995). Is foreign infrastructure investment still risky? *Harvard Business Review, 73*(5), 44–55.
Zaheer, A., & Hernandez, E. (2011). The geographic scope of the MNC and its alliance portfolio: Resolving the paradox of distance. *Global Strategy Journal, 1*(1–2), 109–126.
Zaheer, S., & Mosakowski, E. (1997). The dynamics of the liability of foreignness: A global study of survival in financial services. *Strategic Management Journal, 18*(6), 439–464.
Zaheer, S., & Nachum, L. (2011). Sense of place: From location resources to MNE locational capital. *Global Strategy Journal, 1*(1–2), 96–108.
Zipf, G. K. (1949). *Human behavior and the principle of least effort*. Addison Wesley.
Zucker, L., Darby, M., & Armstrong, J. (1998). Geographically localized knowledge: Spillovers or markets? *Economic Inquiry, 36*(1), 65–86.

8

Place and Space in Foreign Subsidiary Exit from Conflict Zones: A Commentary

Lorraine Eden

Going Back in Time

Crises and Disruptions in International Business is a timely and important book: the twenty-first century has been filled with regional and global crises and disruptions. International business (IB) scholars have even coined a new acronym, VUCA (volatility, uncertainty, complexity, and ambiguity), to characterize the current disruptiveness of the global economy (Petricevic & Teece, 2019; Buckley, 2020; van Tulder et al., 2020). The article, "Place, Space, and Geographic Exposure: Foreign Subsidiary Survival in Conflict Zones" (Dai et al., 2013) has, I believe, still very

I would like to thank the editors for selecting our JIBS article and for inviting me to write this commentary. I believe our article contributes to the IB literature on many dimensions and am glad to have the opportunity to reflect on these contributions in this commentary. I also thank Li Dai and Paul Beamish for their helpful comments and recollections. The views expressed in this commentary and any errors or omissions are my own.

L. Eden (✉)
Department of Management, Mays Business School, Texas A&M University, College Station, TX, USA
e-mail: LEden@mays.tamu.edu

M. A. Mithani et al. (eds.), *Crises and Disruptions in International Business*, JIBS Special Collections, https://doi.org/10.1007/978-3-030-80383-4_8

much to say about how and why foreign firms respond in different ways when exposed to crises and disruptions.

Let us start with a bit of historical background to the Dai et al. (2013) JIBS article. Li Dai was a first-year doctoral student when she took my doctoral seminar on multinational enterprises and was also assigned to me as a research assistant at Texas A&M University in 2008. Li was interested in global issues, ranging from wars to sister cities, and she and I shared an interest in how geography affects international business (IB). The topic of how and why multinational enterprises (MNEs) exit from conflict zones emerged from our conversations about how to put these issues together for her dissertation.

At the time, Paul Beamish generously offered Li access to his Toyo Keizai (TK) dataset on Japanese MNE parents and their subsidiaries for her dissertation and became an informal member of her committee. Paul had just supervised two dissertations using the TK dataset, which complemented and informed Li's dissertation (Dai, 2012). The first, by Chris Changwha Chung, was on economic crises and three of his articles are cited in Li's dissertation (Chung & Beamish, 2005; Chung et al., 2010; Chung & Song, 2004). The second dissertation Paul supervised, by Kevin Boeh, used a sub-national measure of "place" to specify subsidiary locations; this work was later published in Boeh and Beamish (2012). Paul brought with him deep knowledge of the TK data, having used it in dozens of published articles. He also brought years of real-world knowledge based on interactions with managers, case writing, and professional activities in nearly 90 countries. The three of us have continued to work together on the topic of MNE exit from conflict zones since then, with Li taking the lead role on our joint papers.

There are several innovations in our Dai, Eden and Beamish (2013) JIBS article that remain relevant for today's scholars interested in studying crises and disruptions. These innovations are outlined below.

Vulnerability as a Theoretical Framework

The theoretical framework underlying Li's dissertation was drawn from the literature in economic geography on the topic of vulnerability. Vulnerability is the perceived and actual susceptibility of an entity (e.g., an individual, business, or institution) to a specific threat. While geographers have written extensively on the disruptive impacts of earthquakes and hurricanes, the most useful article for us was Gallopin (2006). Gallopin's interest was rooted in socio-ecological systems and their vulnerability to environmental threats such as earthquakes and hurricanes. His work argued that the vulnerability of a system depended on its exposure to a specific threat and the system's capacity for response (its resilience or ability to bounce back).

Li's dissertation builds on these ideas, hypothesizing that vulnerability depends on three factors: (1) exposure to the threat; (2) what the entity could lose due to the threat (its resources at risk); and (3) the entity's ex ante and ex post coping mechanisms. The actual analogy in the dissertation (see Dai, 2012: 45) is a person's vulnerability to influenza (the flu), as depending on (1) exposure: how many others around you have the flu and how long you are in contact with them; (2) at-risk resources: what you could lose if you caught the flu (e.g., days off sick); and (3) coping mechanisms: ex ante (having had a flu shot) and ex post (aspirin and vitamin C).[1] The dissertation addresses three nested responses of a foreign subsidiary in a conflict zone: (1) whether the subsidiary stays or exits and, if the subsidiary chooses to exit, (2) whether the exit is whole or partial and (3) early or late. Thus, the three decision questions are: go/stay, partial/full, and early/late, with the second and third decisions conditional on the first. While our 2013 JIBS article focuses on the physical (i.e., geographical) exposure as a core component of vulnerability, the full vulnerability model – encompassing a firm's exposure, at-risk resources, and resilience – was later published in Dai, Eden and Beamish (2017).

---

[1] The analogy is appropriate given the current Covid-19 pandemic. I write this commentary at the end of January 2021 in College Station, Texas, going into my 11th month of "sheltering in place" to avoid exposure to the virus, with no clear end date in sight, and sitting somewhere on our local hospital's list of 30,000 registrants waiting for the vaccine.

Linking Vulnerability to Place and Space

In May 2011, while Li was writing her dissertation, there was a Call for Papers for a Special Issue of JIBS on "The Multinational in Geographic Space", guest edited by Ulf Andersson, Sjoerd Beugelsdijk, Ram Mudambi, and Srilata Zaheer. The goal of the Special Issue was to "improve our understanding of the spatial dimension of IB activity and the interaction of location with governance and organization aspects of MNE activity – building on insights from economic and human geography and regional science". We realized that the exposure component of the vulnerability model in Li's dissertation could be the unit of analysis for a paper submitted to the JIBS Special Issue. Li started work on this topic with Paul and me while she was also writing her dissertation. The paper was submitted for the JIBS Special Issue in November 2011 and Li defended and submitted her dissertation in December 2011.

The JIBS article is quite different from Li's dissertation and makes multiple contributions to the IB and economic geography literatures in its own right. I discuss some of these contributions below.

Capturing "Place" Using GIS Coordinates

First, the concepts of "place" and "space" are core concepts used throughout the article. A "place" is a distinct, nonempty, geographic location. A place (e.g., a building or a city) has a physical location with characteristics such as its GIS (geographic information system) coordinates (latitude and longitude) and geographic features (borders, terrain, population). While most IB research views countries as places, our article focuses on two subnational places: the location of the foreign subsidiary and the location of the conflict zone (or zones) in the host country. The place or location of the foreign subsidiary refers to its actual street address, coded into GIS coordinates. When an MNE has more than one subsidiary in a country, the GIS attributes must be captured for each location. In addition, subsidiaries close and new ones open so that the place data for subsidiaries must be calculated each year. To our knowledge, with the exception of Boeh and Beamish (2012), no prior IB research had been carried out at this level of analysis.[2]

Our database for conflict zones, including their geographic characteristics, is regularly used in political science: the UCDP-PRIO Armed Conflict Database maintained by the Uppsala Conflict Data Program and the International Peace Research Institute. The Uppsala database geocodes conflict zones as the smallest circle that surrounds violent events in a given country and year; thus, conflict zones are circles with a center and radius.[3] This measure of place must also be calculated annually because each conflict zone is likely to change over time, becoming more or less violent, and shifting its geographic boundaries.

Distance (Static Exposure) Versus Diversity (Dynamic Exposure)

With geo-coordinates for both the foreign subsidiary and the conflict zone, the distance between the two becomes an obvious proxy for measuring exposure. How close or how far away is the foreign subsidiary from the war zone? The closer the two, the greater the exposure and the more likely that the foreign plant exits. The easiest proxy, which we use in Dai et al. (2013), is simply a zero-one dummy variable to capture whether the subsidiary is inside or outside the conflict zone on an annual basis. More sophisticated calculations, also used in the article, are based on the Great Circle Distance between the plant location and either the perimeter or the center of the conflict zone.

These distance metrics, however, are only capturing part of the story. They measure the *static or dyadic exposure* that one foreign subsidiary faces when located in or near one conflict zone in a given year. However, in a few of the host countries in our dataset there were several conflict

[2] The TK dataset contained a number of foreign subsidiaries without street addresses. Li Dai used the Internet and old news articles to search for, and find, those street addresses, which were then translated into GIS coordinates.

[3] More recent versions of the Uppsala dataset allow conflict zones to have different geographic shapes, which would permit more accurate measures of exposure. See https://www.prio.org/Data/Armed-Conflict/UCDP-PRIO/. The data can be downloaded here: https://ucdp.uu.se/downloads/

zones within the country in the same year. Capturing the combined or *dynamic exposure* that a foreign subsidiary faces when there are multiple conflict zones turned out to be a much more difficult task than measuring the dyadic distance.

I worried about solving this problem for some time and then realized that the problem of a focal place (subsidiary) surrounded by a variety of other places (conflict zones) of different sizes and distances from the focal place was analogous to the solar system and that exposure was akin to gravity – that was as far as my thought experiment could carry us at the time. The answer to the problem came from a serendipitous dinner party in College Station with a group of about twenty theoretical and nuclear physicists from Lawrence Livermore Labs and Sandia, to which I was invited as a spouse (my husband was running the executive education program in the Bush School) in June 2011. At dinner, I posed the problem to the scientists and received an immediate, unanimous response: Coulomb's Law, which provides a mathematical formula for computing the combined gravitational effect (both centripetal and centrifugal/push and pull) of multiple places (planets) on a focal place (planet).[4] I went home and read up on Coulomb's Law.

Equipped with the formula for solving the problem, Li (now a new faculty member at Loyola Marymount University in Los Angeles) went to the UCLA Technology Sandbox, an interdisciplinary computing facility formally known as the UCLA Institute for Digital Research and Education, and enlisted the help of a leading-edge GIS expert to develop measures of dynamic exposure using ArcGIS software. Li's husband, Dan Xie (a theoretical physicist) had collected the GIS coordinates data using street addresses in the TK dataset and did the mathematical calculations to integrate Coulomb's Law. This Commentary gives me the opportunity to thank Dan Xie, the UCLA GIS expert, and the theoretical and nuclear physicists who helped us identify an appropriate measure for capturing dynamic exposure to conflict zones.

Our dynamic exposure variable based on Coulomb's Law, to my knowledge, has not yet been used by other IB scholars, perhaps because

[4] For simple explanations of Coulomb's Law see https://en.wikipedia.org/wiki/Coulomb%27s_law and https://www.physicsclassroom.com/class/estatics/Lesson-3/Coulomb-s-Law

we were not clear enough in our article about the measure's novelty and usefulness. I have recently highlighted the variable in Eden and Nielsen (2020), where Bo Nielsen and I argued that IB researchers have examined IB research questions through four lenses – Difference, Distance, Diversity, and Disparity – roughly in chronological order, starting with difference. "Diversity" – the third "D" – is a newer focus that looks at variations within and across countries, paying attention to the "multiplicity of actors and networks and the multiplexity of their interactions" (Eden & Nielsen, 2020: 1615). Bo and I make the point that Diversity needs new research metrics and methods and refer to Dai et al. (2013)'s method for capturing the multiple exposures faced by one foreign subsidiary that is surrounded by conflict zones of different sizes, at different distances from the subsidiary, at different points in time.

The results of the econometric work in Dai et al. (2013) show that both static exposure and dynamic exposure have separate and negative impacts on the foreign subsidiary's survival. The largest impact comes from simply being located inside a conflict zone – a one standard deviation increase in the odds ratio for static exposure causes a 52% increase in the probability of exit; in turn, we found that for dynamic exposure, the result is a 9% increase in the probability of exit (Dai et al., 2013: 565).[5] In a post hoc analysis, we employ a two-by-two matrix with the location of the foreign subsidiary relative to the conflict zone on one axis and the exit-stay decision on the other axis. We find that 48% of foreign subsidiaries inside a conflict zone leave the country compared with 17% of subsidiaries located in the country but outside the conflict zone.

Capturing "Space" as Peers and Sisters

Turning now to "space" as a construct, the key insight underlying space is that it emphasizes how places are related or linked to one another; that is, "the variety of relationships linking two or more places, examples of

[5] The smaller effect for dynamic exposure may reflect the fact that a subsidiary in a large country with two or more conflict zones may not be located inside the zones. It is the location inside a war zone that drives the exit decision.

which include distance, connectivity or shared ties, and spatial dependence" (Dai et al., 2013: 558). In the article we conceptualize space as the concentration and dispersion of firms in geographic space. We focus on two types of firms: home-country peers and same-parent subsidiaries (sisters). Peers are subsidiaries from the same home country that are unrelated to the focal subsidiary; sisters are related to the focal subsidiary; and both types are located in the same host country and may be inside or outside a conflict zone.[6] Treating space as relationships with peers and sisters enabled us to use insights from the IB and economics literatures to develop hypotheses; e.g., we draw on the concepts of hysteresis, agglomeration economies, herding behavior, interdependence, motivation versus capability, and operational flexibility.

In our empirical work, we use entropy measures of concentration and dispersion (Dai et al., 2013: 563) to capture the peer and sister networks in each country. What we find is that the likelihood of survival for a subsidiary located in a conflict zone is six times higher when there is a dispersed network of sisters in the host country; clearly, the sister network provides resources and coping mechanisms that enable the focal firm to stay. When the focal subsidiary is co-located with peers inside a conflict zone, the subsidiary is more than twice as likely to exit; on the other hand, when the subsidiary and its peers are co-located outside a conflict zone, the focal firm is much more likely to stay (Dai et al., 2013: 571).

Diversity and Econometric Methods

The last contribution of Dai et al. (2013) to the disruption and crises literature that I want to highlight is the "best practice" econometric techniques in this article, which provide a model for other IB researchers.

First, geographers have been modeling the impacts of natural disasters on firms and communities for many years (Adger, 2000, 2006; Gallopin, 2006). Their empirical modeling has typically used regression analysis; however, natural disasters tend not to be normally distributed, because

[6] An obvious extension would have been to include peers from other home countries that are also located in the host country (these data were unavailable to us).

they are more likely to be rare events. Andriani and McKelvey (2007) argue that rare events need Pareto-based statistics (i.e., data points are independent-multiplicative, and distributions are asymmetric with long tails) rather than Gaussian-based statistics (data points are independent-additive with normal distributions). There are specific empirical techniques for modelling rare events; however, few IB scholars are currently using rare-event empirical techniques. Andriani and McKelvey (2007: 1221) argue that they should be, stating that "...there is a far higher probability of fractals, Pareto distributions and power laws in IB than in domestic settings. In short, IB managers face Pareto much more than Gaussian distributions." Here again, our article was a trail blazer, using rare-event logit models to test the likelihood of foreign exit.

Second, our article includes several additional tests to show the practical significance of the results.[7] For example, the rare-event results are presented as logistic regressions using odds ratios to show what would happen if an independent variable varied by one standard deviation. In addition, the two-by-two matrix mentioned earlier, in a post hoc analysis illustrates practical significance.

A third contribution, which also speaks to practical significance but extends past that, is the use of the propensity score matching technique. In another post hoc analysis (Dai et al., 2013: 571), we build a counterfactual model, as recommended in experimental economics, and by our JIBS Special Issue Editors Ram Mudambi and Sjoerd Beugelsdijk. We use propensity score matching to generate a hypothetical counterfactual that mimics a natural experiment with non-experimental data. IB researchers are now urged to do matched control groups to calculate the average treatment effect (the difference between the real and counterfactual outcomes); see, for example, Nielsen et al. (2020) or Reeb, Sakakibara and Mahmood (2012). Our paper was among the earliest JIBS articles to use this experimental technique.

[7] My personal view is that empirical IB research should include a section on the power of the results. An empirical IB article that cannot demonstrate any power or practical significance of its results is basically "dancing on the head of a pin" and provides little information of value to either practitioners or other scholars. The paper may make theoretical contributions, but its empirical work has little impact.

Conclusion

As I have attempted to illustrate in this commentary, Dai et al. (2013) was a true multidisciplinary project. The simplicity of the question – *How does exposure to a conflict zone affect a foreign subsidiary's stay-versus-exit decision?* – was deceptive. To answer the question, we needed to draw on theoretical insights and empirical tools from a variety of disciplines in both the social sciences and physical sciences. Indeed, it "takes a village" (as Li Dai reminded me) to answer a research question that lies at the crossroads of IB, economic geography, political science, and physics.

The article advances our knowledge of "whether, why, how, and when" firms react if they are exposed to specific threats. We theorize and show how place and space affect these decisions, and the differing impacts of static and dynamic exposure. The article also makes a variety of empirical contributions to the IB literature, including (1) using street-level GIS data and ArcGIS software to capture sub-national location and (2) Uppsala data from political science on conflict zones to calculate (3) static exposure, i.e., the distance between a focal firm and a specific threat, and (4) dynamic exposure, i.e., the gravitational push/pull effects of multiple and diverse threats on a focal firm, using Coulomb's Law, and (5) performing a variety of leading-edge econometric tests using rare-event and experimental-economics techniques.

Overall, I hope that my commentary will encourage other IB scholars to work on topics involving disruptions and crises, particularly at the sub-national level. While the research question in Dai et al. (2013) may seem very specific – *Do foreign subsidiaries stay or leave a host country at war?* – the theoretical framework involving vulnerability, exposure, place, and space is widely applicable to a variety of firm decisions characterized by VUCA (volatility, uncertainty, complexity and ambiguity). Predicting and understanding how, when, and why "place" and "space" react to a specific external threat, particularly a rare event threat, is a puzzle worthy of attention by all IB researchers.

References

Adger, W. N. (2000). Social and ecological resilience: Are they related? *Progress in Human Geography, 24*(3), 347–364.

Adger, W. N. (2006). Vulnerability. *Global Environmental Change, 16*(3), 268–281.

Andriani, P., & McKelvey, B. (2007). Beyond Gaussian averages: Redirecting international business and management research toward extreme events and power laws. *Journal of International Business Studies, 38*, 1212–1230.

Boeh, K. K., & Beamish, P. W. (2012). Travel time and the liability of distance in foreign direct investment: Location choice and entry mode. *Journal of International Business Studies, 43*(5), 525–535.

Buckley, P. J. (2020). The theory and empirics of the structural reshaping of globalization. *Journal of International Business Studies*. https://doi.org/10.1057/s41267-020-00355-5

Chung, C. C., & Beamish, P. W. (2005). The impact of institutional reforms on characteristics and survival of foreign subsidiaries in emerging economies. *Journal of Management Studies, 42*, 35–62.

Chung, W., & Song, J. (2004). Sequential investment, firm motives, and agglomeration of Japanese electronics firms in the United States. *Journal of Economics and Management Strategy, 13*(3), 539–560.

Chung, C. C., Lee, S. H., Beamish, P. W., & Isobe, T. (2010). Subsidiary expansion/contraction during times of economic crisis. *Journal of International Business Studies, 41*, 500–516.

Dai, L. (2012). *Caught in the crossfire: Strategies of multinationals in host countries at war*. Department of Management, Texas A&M University.

Dai, L., Eden, L., & Beamish, P. W. (2012). *External threats and MNE strategy: The role of exposure, resources, and coping mechanisms*. Academy of Management Best Paper Proceedings. Boston.

Dai, L., Eden, L., & Beamish, P. W. (2013). Place, space and geographic exposure: Foreign subsidiary survival in conflict zones. *Journal of International Business Studies, 44*(6), 554–578.

Dai, L., Eden, L., & Beamish, P. W. (2017). Caught in the crossfire: Dimensions of vulnerability and foreign multinationals' exit from war-afflicted countries. *Strategic Management Journal, 38*(7), 1478–1498.

Eden, L., & Nielsen, B. B. (2020). Research methods in international business: The challenge of complexity. *Journal of International Business Studies, 51*(9), 1609–1620.

Gallopin, G. C. (2006). Linkages between vulnerability, resilience, and adaptive capacity. *Global Environmental Change, 16*(3), 293–303.

Nielsen, B. B., Welch, C., Chidlow, A., Miller, S. R., Aguzzoli, R., Gardner, E., Karafyllia, M., & Pegoraro, D. (2020). 50 years of methodological trends in *JIBS*: Why future IB research needs more triangulation. *Journal of International Business Studies, 51*(9), 1478–1499.

Petricevic, O., & Teece, D. J. (2019). The structural reshaping of globalization: Implications for strategic sectors, profiting from innovation, and the multinational enterprise. *Journal of International Business Studies, 50*, 1487–1512.

Reeb, D., Sakakibara, M., & Mahmood, I. P. (2012). From the editors: Endogeneity in international business research. *Journal of International Business Studies, 43*, 211–218.

Van Tulder, R., Verbeke, A., & Jankowska, B. (Eds.). (2020). *International business in a VUCA world*. Emerald.

9

Impact of Historical Conflict on FDI Location and Performance: Japanese Investment in China

Gerald Yong Gao, Danny Tan Wang, and Yi Che

Introduction

Foreign direct investment (FDI) is a central motor of economic integration and interdependence among countries in this increasingly globalized world. Its driving forces have attracted extensive attention in the international business field. Prior research has examined the impact of host country specific factors, such as labor cost, infrastructure, and market potential (Dunning, 1998; Narula & Dunning, 2000); industry agglomeration (Chang & Park, 2005; Cheng & Kwan, 2000; Head et al., 1995);

Accepted by Ron Boschma, Guest Editor, on 8 October 2016. This article has been with the authors for two revisions.

G. Y. Gao
Department of Marketing, University of Missouri-St. Louis,
St. Louis, MO, USA

D. T. Wang
Department of Marketing, Hong Kong Baptist University,
Kowloon Tong, Hong Kong

M. A. Mithani et al. (eds.), *Crises and Disruptions in International Business*, JIBS Special Collections, https://doi.org/10.1007/978-3-030-80383-4_9

and institutional environments (Ma & Delios, 2007; Meyer & Nguyen, 2005). Researchers have also adopted a nation-dyadic perspective, using the distance concept to capture differences between home and host countries, including cultural distance (Hofstede, 1980; Kogut & Singh, 1988), economic distance (Tsang & Yip, 2007), geographic distance (Kim et al., 2010; Nachum & Zaheer, 2005), and institutional distance (Kostova & Zaheer, 1999; Xu & Shenkar, 2002). Extending this stream of research, Makino and Tsang (2011) incorporate historically shifting relational factors between countries to demonstrate that historical relations bring enhanced explanatory power for FDI decisions, above and beyond those distance attributes. Thus adopting a historical perspective to *bring history back* into international business research is crucial for generating new insights into existing theoretical frameworks of FDI (Jones & Khanna, 2006). However, given historical relation is a nation-dyadic level construct, little is known whether a home–host country relation exhibits universal or heterogeneous effects across the country's subnational regions.

This oversight is particularly serious in large emerging economies, where substantial diversities and variations in culture, economy, and politics exist across subnational regions (Dow et al., 2016; Ma et al., 2013; Meyer & Nguyen, 2005; Xu, 2011). Because economic and institutional transitions usually introduce changes unevenly across regions in those markets, foreign firms operating there are exposed to differential regulation rules, social norms, and business practices. Therefore it is imperative for researchers to zoom into reveal within-country differences of national-level constructs (Chan et al., 2010; Lorenzen & Mudambi, 2013; Ma et al., 2013). In particular, historical relations are path dependent ties between nations, intertwined with cultural, religious, and political traditions, and affected by local conventions and social norms in different geographic locations (Arikan & Shenkar, 2013; Makino & Tsang, 2011).

Y. Che (✉)
School of Business, East China University of Science and Technology, Shanghai, China

Antai College of Economics and Management, Shanghai Jiao Tong University, Shanghai, China
e-mail: tccheyi@sjtu.edu.cn

For example, according to a study conducted by Chinese Academy of Social Sciences,[1] although national animosity toward Japan exists in China, people's attitudes vary across regions: strong anti-Japanese sentiment marks central and western provinces like Guangxi, Shanxi, and Hubei, however people in coastal areas such as Shanghai and Guangdong hold less hostile attitudes, and some young generations are even Japanophiles. Therefore national-level relations might not be held in a constant form across subnational regions. To enhance our understanding on how home–host country historical relations affect FDI differentially in various regions within a host country, FDI research should move to the next level of refinement of geographic units.

Examining the impact of home–host country historical relations on FDI performance represents another critical issue, as how to achieve better FDI performance remains a central challenge in the international business field (Peng, 2004). Traditional perspectives on determinants of FDI performance include resource-based view (Barney, 1991), industry-based view (Porter, 1980), and institution-based view (Peng et al., 2008). Past studies have identified ways of reducing the liability of foreignness and developing competitive advantages in foreign markets, such as appropriate entry modes and timing (Chang & Rosenzweig, 2001), exploitation of location-specific advantages (Dunning, 1998; Ma et al., 2013), alliances with partners (Lu & Beamish, 2001), and local experience accumulation (Luo & Peng, 1999). Social, cultural, political, and historical factors also play significant roles in determining economic activities and firm behavior (Dai, Eden, & Beamish, 2013; Martin & Sunley, 1996). However, despite their relevance and salience, scant attention addresses non-economic determinants of FDI performance, largely due to the difficulty of modeling such factors (Jones & Khanna, 2006; Martin, 1999). To date, no research has empirically tested the effect of historical relationships on FDI performance.

To address these research gaps, we examine how historical conflict, as a specific manifestation of historical relations between home and host countries, exerts long-term impact on FDI location choices and performance. We use the eight-year Second Sino–Japanese War (1937–1945) as

[1] The details of the 2002 survey by the Chinese Academy of Social Science can be found at http://qk.cass.cn/rbxk/qkml/2002year/6/201303/P020140425560832665895.pdf (in Chinese).

the context of historical conflict of analysis. A severe historical conflict such as a war between countries can create deep antagonism imprinted in citizens' memories of the country victimized by the war. Through assessing the long-term impact of within-country differences of a single war on FDI location choices and performance, this study provides a more rigorous theory testing because it can rule out multiple country- or conflict-level confounding factors. The war-related civilian casualties in different subnational regions of China varied significantly, so we can examine whether the national-level conflict affects FDI differently across regions. The investigation of the performance effect of historical conflict helps broaden existing theoretical perspectives and generates new insights into FDI performance research. Moreover, based on social capital theory and particularly the political capital literature, we propose three political capital accumulation strategies that can remedy the negative impact of historical conflict: host-country state capital involvement, excessive tax payment, and local employment. We posit that these strategies can effectively signal a focal foreign firm's trustworthiness and long-term commitment to the host country, thus mitigating the operational difficulties caused by historical conflict.

We test the hypotheses with a sample of 8646 Japanese FDI in China during 1992–2001. We collected data about civilian casualties in 26 regions[2] (nineteen provinces with Sichuan and Chongqing combined, three municipalities, and four minority autonomous regions) in China as the key independent variable indicating the long-term effect of historical conflict. The findings show that Japanese firms are less likely to invest in Chinese regions that suffered greater civilian casualties during the war. Civilian casualties also negatively affect FDI performance; yet the political capital accumulation strategies in the forms of excessive tax payment and local employment can reduce the negative effect of historical conflict on performance, which provides critical implications for FDI operation in a hostile environment.

[2] We excluded three northeastern provinces, Heilongjiang, Jilin, and Liaoning. They were occupied by the Japanese army in 1931 before the full-scale war and were subject to different colonial strategies. Therefore in the books about losses of China during the war, there was no information about these three regions.

Theory and Hypotheses

Historical Conflict

Historical conflicts include economic and political conflicts, which can escalate into serious military confrontation. Political science and international relations literature has studied historical conflict extensively in terms of its origins, evolution, justifications, and consequences for dyads of adversaries (e.g., Benson, 2004; Hewitt, 2003). A critical issue is how perceptions of fairness emerge during a conflict and subsequently affect interactions between nations (Maoz, 2009). Prior research generally suggests that any reconciliation process is likely to be long and tough, because it requires changes in the conflict ethos, together with building of trust, acceptance, cooperation, and consideration of mutual needs (Bar-Tal, 2000). This process is particularly difficult following severe conflicts (Coleman, 2003; Mitchell, 1981). Moreover, negative sentiment from historical conflicts can pass from generation to generation, hindering the development of bilateral trust and cross-border activities (Arikan & Shenkar, 2013; Guiso et al., 2009).

Previous international economics literature has investigated the impact of historical events on trade between countries. Based on the gravity model of international trade (Tinbergen, 1962), the majority of past studies has focused on determinants such as income, population, contiguity, and distance in shaping the patterns and directions of international trade. Recent studies started to investigate the long-run impact of historical events on trade flows. For example, Berger, Easterly, Nunn, & Satyanath (2013) found that CIA interventions during the Cold War increased the influence of US over foreign governments, which was used to increase US exports to the intervened countries. Head, Mayer, and Ries (2010) investigated the effect of independence on post-colonial trade, and found that it had little short-run effect but led to a significant long-run decline in trade between colonizers and colonies. Glick and Taylor (2010) found large impact of wars on bilateral trade among belligerent nations and neutrals. Guiso et al. (2009)'s study in Europe showed that lower bilateral trust between countries resulted in less trade, portfolio investment, and direct investment in the long-term, and gave rise to entrenched culture bias among conflictive countries.

Animosity

Frequent conflicts between countries often create the sentiment of national animosity, defined as "hostility of mind" (Arikan & Shenkar, 2013), or "remnants of antipathy" (Klein et al., 1998), toward a particular country. These sentiments, if not reconciled, persist over time, because negative memories imprinted in people's minds can be easily provoked with new sets of antagonistic nation-to-nation acts. As it can be rendered by the society and enlarged by the media, national animosity affects people's judgments and finally becomes a part of the country's societal beliefs and culture. Depending on its source, Klein et al. (1998) distinguish two types of animosity as economic- and war-based. Economic animosity stems from trading practices that one country perceives as unfair, unreliability exhibited by a trading partner, or the economic power of a foreign country. While economic animosity often evolves as trading relationships change, war-based animosity tends to be more country-specific and stable over time. Recent studies generally followed this classification, and further evaluated the two types of animosity's behavioral impact across different eras, source countries, target countries, and product categories (for a comprehensive review, see Riefler & Diamantopoulos, 2007).

The marketing and international business literature on animosity mostly focuses on its impact on consumer behavior, with the fundamental premise that animosity's effect on consumers' purchase is independent of their product quality judgment, such that "anger can lead consumers to eschew a country's goods in spite of positive product perceptions" (Klein, 2002: 348). Klein et al. (1998) showed for example that Chinese consumers in Nanjing avoid buying Japanese products, even when the products are comparable or superior to products with other countries of origin. In another study, using the United States and Japan as target countries and the 1997 Asian financial crisis as the backdrop, Leong et al. (2008) discovered that both stable and situational animosity reduce consumers' willingness to buy products from a country they perceive as hostile. Harmeling, Magnusson, and Singh (2015) examined differential responses of agonistic and retreat emotions from animosity and found that consumer anger is related to negative word of mouth and product avoidance whereas fear leads to product quality judgment and product avoidance. Only recently has the effect of animosity been examined at the firm level. Using panel data on firm-level cross-border alliances between nation pairs, Arikan and Shenkar (2013) found that animosity heavily affects the formation and types of firm-level cross-border alliances. The level of animosity between two nations significantly reduces the number and probability of alliance formation of firms within the nation dyad.

Historical Conflict Between China and Japan

The Second Sino–Japanese War[3] started in the aftermath of the Marco Polo Bridge Incident. Its significance is reflected in not only the length (1937–1945), but also the huge casualties and losses. Chinese sources list the total number of casualties at 35 million, largely consistent with estimates from the Historical Society of Japan (1967: 213). Among the total casualties, military casualties account for a small part with the lion's share of losses coming from Chinese civilians (Clodfelter, 2002; Rummel, 1991).

The psychological damage for Chinese people was created by the gross war atrocities and then reinforced by repeated disputes between the two nations regarding Japan's responsibilities. China and Japan normalized their diplomatic relations in 1972; yet the war remains a point of contention and a stumbling block to their bilateral relationship. War-related issues – including controversies about descriptions in Japanese textbooks, Japan's denials of war crimes, visits by top Japanese government officials to the Yasukuni Shrine, and recent provocative actions about Diaoyu/Senkaku Islands – readily stir up Chinese. As a result, roughly 7 out of 10 Chinese people dislike Japan, according to a study conducted by the Pew Research Center.[4]

[3] The First Sino–Japanese War was from 1894 to 1895.

[4] See "Publics of Asian Powers Hold Negative Views of One Another", Pew Research Center, September 21, 2006. www.pewglobal.org/2006/09/21/publics-of-asian-powers-hold-negative-views-of-one-another

The Second Sino–Japanese War is an appropriate setting for examining the long-run impact of a significant historical conflict on FDI location and performance. Because of the vast size of China, large variances exist in our focal variables of interest: civilian casualties and FDI activities. China was never occupied entirely during the war, so subnational regions suffered differently. China's central corridor, from Shanxi and spreading south to Guangxi, passing provinces such as Henan, Hubei, Hunan, and Jiangxi, suffered the most severe attacks because of Japan's intention to establish a military supply line. The Chinese Armies resisted staunchly, incurring significant military and civilian casualties. Other areas experienced varying degrees of loss, depending on their military importance and the contest between the two sides. Japanese FDI activities also vary greatly across regions in China. Despite their political contentions, Japan ranked third among major source countries of FDI in China during 1992–2002, only behind Hong Kong and the US, accounting for 7.8% of the total volume of FDI (Almanac of China's Foreign Economic Relations and Trade, 1993–2003 [query 2]). Japanese investments also have not concentrated in mega-cities like Beijing and Shanghai, but instead exhibit a wide geographic distribution. Therefore we can investigate the relationship between historical conflict and FDI in a realistic, subnational setting.

Previous studies have focused on the effects of economic factors on location choices of Japanese FDI in China. Belderbos and Carree (2002) addressed the role of agglomeration and found that Japanese investments tend to follow early entrants from the same industry or industrial groups, highlighting a strong path dependency effect. Cheng and Stough (2006) showed that national policy incentives, agglomeration, labor and land costs are important determinants of the locations of Japanese greenfield manufacturing firms in China. Fung, Iizaka, and Parker (2002) compared FDI from the US and Japan in China. The results showed that while local GDP and policy variables significantly affect the inflow of investment from both countries, labor quality exerts a larger influence on Japanese FDI. Ma and Delios (2007) showed that Japanese firms tend to choose an economic-oriented rather than a political-oriented city as their investment location, with the consequence of higher survival likelihood in Shanghai than in Beijing. Zhao and Zhu (2000) investigated whether firms with different countries of origin responded dissimilarly to locational factors, and found that Japanese investments favor those areas with low rental costs, abundant human capital, and high export intensity. Zhou, Delios, and Yang (2002) demonstrated an influence of special economic zones and coastal cities on the location choices of Japanese FDI.

While past research has generated important knowledge on the impact of market size, cost of operations, agglomeration, and quality of economic institutions, our study examines the impact of non-economic factors, historical conflict in particular, in accounting for FDI location choices. Dai et al. (2013) examined the effect of contemporary conflict as an important type of non-economic factor. They developed an innovative means of capturing subsidiary static and dynamic exposure to conflict zones and showed that exposure to threats is an important determinant of subsidiary survival. In this study, we extend the investigation on conflict and focus on historical conflict using the Second Sino–Japanese War as the context and link it with FDI location and performance. We demonstrate that repressed war memories can add to distrust and cast a shadow, even after decades-long efforts and bilateral economic cooperation. The particular conflict-induced psychological consequence should only affect foreign investors from the antagonist country.

Historical Conflict and FDI Location Choices

In this study, we propose that the nation-dyadic level historical conflict exhibits variations in different subnational regions and in turn plays a significant role in determining FDI location choices. In the Japan–China dyad, though the war ended more than half a century ago, people from both nations constantly engage in cognition about its causes and other relevant facts, due to the lack of a consensus between the two national governments. This cognitive process can be painful, especially for Chinese people, who suffered extensive violence on their national soil. Over the years, considerable animosity has accumulated and the hostile emotions intertwined with cognitive activities have formed societal beliefs that can serve motivations for ego defense and national pride (Bar-Tal, 2000). The animosity effect is particularly pronounced in areas that suffered severe civilian casualties. Killing and wounding violate the moral code of the sanctity of life, marking an enduring scar on people's memories. Without effective post-war reconciliation, people gradually become socialized to a conflictive ethos, believing in a form of antagonism toward the conflict-evoking country (Arikan & Shenkar, 2013). Japanese firms aiming to enter China make location decisions in the context of this Sino–Japan relation and the long-existing animosity.

We hypothesize that all else being equal, Japanese firms are less likely to invest in regions that suffered greater casualties during the war, because the impact of regional casualties is non-trivial. The greater animosity associated with casualties may lead to higher transaction costs and exchange hazards for Japanese firms, including uncertainty (Luo, 2007), mistrust (Guiso et al., 2009), and perceptions of the likelihood of opportunism of future business partners (Kastner, 2007). In turn, these firms may need to make greater, more credible commitments *ex ante* to signal their goodwill to stakeholders such as consumers, business partners, and local governments. These credible commitments are irrevocable and not transferrable to other investments, and can lose much of the value when the investment relationship ends. *Ex post* governance of Japanese FDI in heavily affected regions also requires more costs to alleviate the heightened risks and exchange hazards. If behavioral opportunism by local partners is a serious threat, Japanese investors need to spend more on monitoring, socialization, or incentive alignment (Wathne & Heide, 2000). Finally, political tensions at the national level easily provoke antagonistic sentiments in areas that experienced heavy historical civilian casualties. Thus Japanese firms must maintain a relatively high level of flexibility and responsiveness, which further increases operating costs. Taken together, regional casualties during the war should constitute a critical historical factor affecting Japanese FDI location choices. Thus we predict:

Hypothesis 1 Japanese firms tend to avoid regions in China that were heavily affected during the Second Sino–Japanese War for FDI locations.

Historical Conflict and FDI Performance

We also expect that animosity, stemming from civilian casualties in a region, affects not only Japanese FDI location choices but also its performance. First, the persistent psychological damage of the war suggests that the greater the civilian casualties during the war, the greater the remaining antipathy toward Japan and Japan-related symbols might be. Thus consumers in regions that experienced heavy civilian casualties hold stronger animosity toward Japanese firms and are more reluctant to purchase products made by Japanese companies (Harmeling et al., 2015; Klein et al., 1998). Second, if employees are socialized through their previous education and experience to hold hostile attitudes toward Japan within an organization, Japanese firms will need to exert extra efforts to align their values, build a psychological infrastructure, and develop trust and cooperative attitudes. All these efforts involve considerable administrative burdens and costs. In turn, Japanese FDI in those regions face more hurdles in achieving better performance, compared with operating in other regions that experienced fewer civilian casualties. Third, deeply negative emotions can extend beyond the individual level to influence organizational behavior (Hutzschenreuter et al., 2007). Trust in local partners usually has a pivotal effect on foreign firms' coordination effectiveness and overall performance (Malhotra & Lumineau, 2011). Perceptions of trustworthiness between business partners from different countries can largely depend on cultural and historical factors (Guiso et al., 2009). If local partners originate from an environment with a strong conflictive ethos, it would be harder for Japanese firms to collaborate with them. Upper echelons theory also suggests that top management's psychological biases greatly affect firms' attitudes and behaviors (Hiller & Hambrick, 2005). Therefore local managers' negative proclivity against Japan might influence their companies' relationships with Japanese firms, causing greater coordination uncertainties and costs.

Despite the fact that local governments usually welcome and support Japanese FDI, we propose that the above operation difficulties pertaining to both individual and organizational levels will cast a negative impact on performance. We thus hypothesize:

Hypothesis 2 Civilian casualties during the Second Sino–Japanese War relate negatively to the performance of Japanese FDI in subnational regions in China.

Political Capital Accumulation Strategies

Firms align their managerial actions with the environmental conditions to improve competitive positions (Child et al., 2003; Reger et al., 1992). Multinational firms in particular can engage in certain strategic responses to the unique business settings in host markets (Regnér & Edman, 2014). In our context, because it is challenging to cope with the hostile environment caused by civilian casualties, Japanese firms can adopt strategies to seek institutional support and enhance their organizational legitimacy. Drawing upon social capital theory, we posit that political capital accumulation strategies can serve such functions. At the firm level, social capital is a collective resource of an organization obtained through network ties, which allow members to access social resources within the network (Burt, 1992; Granovetter, 1985). Political capital of an organization is a specific type of social capital that a firm can acquire through its political affiliations and interactions with dominant political entities (Hillman & Hitt, 1999). It can enhance firms' legitimacy and grant them access to policy information or other valuable resources (Faccio et al., 2006). These benefits may balance the negative effect of historical conflict and make firms less vulnerable to social hostility.

Political capital continues to be a valuable resource for firm operation in emerging economies. Despite the ongoing institutional transition, government influence and intervention remain prevalent. For example, the government still plays a key role in guiding business activities through implementing differential tax, land, and labor policies (Xu et al., 2014a). In other words, the market mechanism and government redistributive mechanism coexist (Li & Zhang, 2007). As long as the government still controls scarce resources including access to finance and key technology, political capital will continue to be a critical resource that firms have high incentives to acquire (Walder, 2002). Furthermore, acquiring political capital helps firms reduce exchange hazard in emerging markets. Business contracts backed by local governments can effectively reduce transaction costs for foreign firms by providing official assurance that the contract terms will be fulfilled in a timely manner (Nee, 1992). Firms can acquire and accumulate political capital with different levels of governments. In the Chinese regulation regime, institutional transition has essentially created a regionally decentralized authoritarian system characterized by institutional polycentrism (Batjargal et al., 2013; Xu, 2011; Xu et al., 2014b). The central government formulates main policies, while regional governments also have great influences on economic activities through implementing national policies with direction and establishing regulation rules locally. Therefore we focus on three types of political capital accumulation strategies with both the central and regional governments, namely host-country state capital involvement, excessive tax payment, and local employment.

At the central government level, Japanese FDI can acquire crucial political capital by getting state capital involved. Through collaborating with state capital, Japanese firms will be able to obtain important institutional support in the market and they are more likely to get favorable treatments in the administration system (Cui & Jiang, 2012). Consequently, political capital from the state enables Japanese FDI to overcome regulatory constraints such as bureaucratic and inefficient procedures that are still hindering business operations in the Chinese market. Furthermore, the high level of government affiliation indicates a high status in the business environment that can foster normative legitimacy and trustworthiness of a focal Japanese FDI (Wang et al., 2012). As a result, the uncertainty, together with the potential bias that customers and business partners may hold toward Japanese FDI, can be alleviated.

Japanese firms can also accumulate important political capital with local governments in subnational regions. In the process of institutional transition in China, the central government has delegated more power including investment approval, land use, and banking to local governments through administrative decentralization (Xu, 2011). Local governments can exercise great discretion initiating changes, coordinating business activities, and enforcing regulation rules regionally (Xu et al. 2014a, b). Given the power of regional governments in influencing economic activities in China, it is critical for foreign firms to engage relationship building with them to acquire political capital. With fiscal decentralization and tax sharing reform started from 1994 in China, tax revenues for the central government have been boosted (Zhang, 2006). Local governments thus face tougher fiscal burden and collecting taxes becomes a top priority (Lin & Liu, 2000). The unique features of the tax system in China often result in substantial variations in firms' actual tax burden. Local governments can impose different levels of taxes and provide additional incentives and reductions to attract foreign investments. In addition, the enforcement of tax laws and rules differs significantly, largely depending on the connection of firms with the governments. Therefore the effective tax rates can be varied for firms operating in the same industry and region (Cai et al., 2011). Tax payments of foreign firms can be a major source for local governments to generate fiscal revenues in subnational regions. Therefore those Japanese firms with higher tax payments are more likely to establish better political connection with local governments, and get institutional support as a reward.

Another way to accumulate political capital regionally is to employ more local workers. Boosting employment is a primary objective of local governments in emerging economies (Sun et al., 2010). For example, the unemployment problem became a serious social issue with the restructuring of state-owned enterprises and layoffs of large numbers of workers in China (Fleisher et al., 2010). Consequently, employment creation becomes one of the most important incentives for local governments to attract FDI. FDI contributes to the host economies with capital and advanced technology injection. Foreign firms usually pay a wage premium for local workers compared with domestic firms in emerging markets, which helps improve living conditions and enhance social stability (Fosfuri et al., 2001). Moreover, local employees of foreign firms can also acquire important foreign human capital, such as advance knowledge and skills (Sofka et al., 2014). Therefore increasing local employment is consistent with regional governments' interest and represents an effective means of signaling foreign firms' long-term commitment to the local market and fostering their trustworthiness with the governments, business partners, and consumers.

Although Japanese firms suffer from animosity and social bias in regions that were heavily affected during the Second Sino–Japanese War, we posit that they can leverage political capital accumulation strategies with both central and regional governments to obtain government support and enhance their legitimacy. Such strategies should mitigate the negative effect of regional casualties on FDI performance. We hypothesize:

Hypothesis 3a The negative performance effect of civilian casualties is weaker for Japanese FDI with Chinese state capital involvement.

Hypothesis 3b The greater the tax paid, the weaker the negative performance effect of civilian casualties on Japanese FDI.

Hypothesis 3c The more local employment generated, the weaker the negative performance effect of civilian casualties on Japanese FDI.

Method

Sample and Variables

We obtained data from the Survey of Foreign-invested Enterprises, conducted by the National Bureau of Statistics of China in 2001, which provides firm-level information about FDI's locations, sales, profits, assets, and employment. The 147,203 foreign-invested enterprises in the survey account for around 75% of all those operating in China, according to the China Statistical Yearbook of 2002. We focused on Japanese firms that invested in China since 1992, the year that FDI in China began to increase substantially, following Deng Xiaoping's South China Tour. After deleting entries with missing values for the key variables, we retained 8646 Japanese FDI invested in China during 1992–2001.

We employed a conditional logit model to study the location choices of Japanese FDI (McFadden, 1974; Hoffman & Duncan, 1988). The dependent dummy variable indicates the province each Japanese firm chose to enter in a specific year. To match the data form requirement of conditional logit models, we rearranged the data structure into a firm-year format to have 224,796 (8646 firms for 26 provinces) observations.

For firm performance, we used return on assets (ROA) as the indicator (Huang et al., 2013).

To measure subnational levels of historical conflict, we used the percentage of civilian casualties (including minor or major wounds and death), defined as the ratio of civilian casualties to the pre-war population across provinces, from the Statistical Abstract of the Republic of China (Chi, 1987). Because this measure originates from historical facts, it is less likely to be affected by endogeneity problems, such as omitted variable biases. As a robustness check, we used the number of wars and property losses as alternative proxies (Chi, 1987; Han, 1946).[5] Figure 9.1 shows the distribution of war atrocities; darker shading corresponds to greater damage during the Second Sino–Japanese War.

We included a number controls that may determine FDI location choices. First, to control for the costs of transportation and infrastructure, we included minimum distance of a province to four major seaports in China (Dalian, Hong Kong, Qinhuangdao, and Shanghai) and highway density[6] (Wei & Wu, 2001). Second, we controlled for firm agglomeration in the same industry, which could exert network externalities (Chang & Park, 2005). Third, to capture the political influence of local policies, we included a dummy variable to indicate whether a province contains a special economic zone that may favor FDI, and the average ratio of a firm's extralegal payment to its total revenue in a province, to account for the impact of property rights protection (Johnson et al., 2002). Fourth, foreign firms typically consider market demand as an important factor of location choices (Helpman et al., 2004), so we included regional gross domestic product as a proxy. Finally, to capture the effect of skilled labor in the region, we controlled for regional education measured by secondary school enrollment rates as a proxy of human capital (Borensztein et al., 1998; Liu et al., 2010). Table 9.1 presents the means, standard deviations, and correlations of all variables.

[5] Wars were more likely to generate media coverage and property losses can capture the locational damage. Thus the inclusion of these two alternative measures help provide a more complete picture of historical conflict.

[6] Transportation infrastructure is an important engine of regional development and can increase urbanization and promote industrial growth, therefore represents a critical factor for FDI location choices (Faber, 2014; Head & Ries, 1996).

Fig. 9.1 War atrocity across China. Notes: this figure illustrates the war atrocity index across provinces in China. This index absorbs the variation of civilian casualty, wars, and property losses using Principal Component Analysis Method. Five levels of shades represent varying levels of war atrocity with a darker shade corresponding to greater war atrocity. The figure using civilian casualty alone for illustration generated similar patterns

In examining the effect of civilian casualties on FDI performance, we examined three moderators: state capital involvement, excessive tax payments, and local employment. State capital is a dummy variable, equal to 1 if a focal Japanese FDI contains an investment from the central government of China and 0 otherwise. To measure tax payments, we employed a two-stage estimation method. In the first stage, we investigated the determinants of firm taxes, using the following estimating equation:

Table 9.1 Descriptive statistics and correlations

	1	2	3	4	5	6	7	8	9	10	11
1 Civilian casualty	1.00										
2 Wars	0.80***	1.00									
3 Property losses	0.40***	0.50***	1.00								
4 Distance	-0.20***	-0.31***	-0.83***	1.00							
5 Infrastructure	0.24***	0.35***	0.48***	-0.56***	1.00						
6 Agg_domestic	0.04***	0.18***	0.64***	-0.50***	0.45***	1.00					
7 Agg_foreign	-0.03***	0.12***	0.64***	-0.59***	0.47***	0.73***	1.00				
8 SEZ	0.01***	-0.05***	0.34***	-0.40***	0.47***	0.60***	0.57***	1.00			
9 PRP	0.06***	0.06***	0.11***	-0.08***	0.13***	-0.01***	-0.01***	-0.01***	1.00		
10 GDP	0.11***	0.28***	0.47***	-0.21***	0.41***	0.72***	0.51***	0.33***	0.13***	1.00	
11 Education	0.03***	0.16***	0.47***	-0.51***	0.32***	0.45***	0.52***	0.30***	0.07***	0.45***	1.00
Mean	1.77	51.50	1.07	2.84	7.72	0.04	0.03	0.38	0.53	0.73	0.89
SD	1.90	56.39	0.95	0.75	0.88	0.04	0.04	0.49	0.42	0.51	0.08

Notes: N = 224,796; $*p < 0.10$; $**p < 0.05$; $***p < 0.01$

$$tax_{fj} = \alpha_j + X'_{fj}\beta + \varepsilon_{fj}, \tag{9.1}$$

where tax_{fj} denotes the taxes paid by firm f in industry j; α_j is a set of industry-fixed effects controlling for time-invariant factors that determine the firm's tax (e.g., industry-specific statutory tax rate); X'_{fj} is a vector of firm characteristics, including total assets, exporting dummy, annual sales, profits, registered equity, and firm age; β is a vector of their coefficient estimates; and ε_{fj} is the error term with *t* distributed asymptotically. After fitting Eq. (9.1) with firm-level data from the industrial census of China in 2000, we obtained all coefficient estimates determining a firm's tax and then we predicted firm taxes for Japanese FDI in 2001. Excessive tax payment was calculated as the ratio of actual firm taxes minus the predicted taxes to firms' total assets. Local employment is measured by the ratio of a firm's total employment minus the number of expatriates to total local labor forces.

For the FDI performance model, we included a set of covariates that potentially affect firm performance. We controlled for exporting as a dummy indicating whether a firm engaged in exporting activities, capital labor ratio, and debt equity ratio at the firm level. Industry level controls include Herfindahl index to capture the degree of competition and agglomeration of both domestic and foreign firms. For regional controls, we included distance to major seaports, a dummy indicating whether a province has a special economic zone, property rights protection, and education.

Models

To test Hypothesis 1, we employed a conditional logit model and analyzed the location choices for Japanese FDI in difference provinces in China (Chang & Park, 2005; McFadden, 1974). Specifically, we expressed firm *f*s location choice function as

$$\pi_{fpt} = \alpha + \beta \times casualty_p + X'_{pt-1}\sigma + \varepsilon_{fpt}, \tag{9.2}$$

where $casualty_p$ denotes civilian casualty in province p, and X'_{pt-1} is the vector of control variables that affect FDI location choices. To alleviate concerns of reverse causality, we measured all independent variables at t - 1. ε_{fpt} is the error term that contains variables that cannot be observed.

The probability that Japanese firm f chooses province p for its FDI can be expressed as

$$\begin{aligned} p_{fpt} &= \Pr\left\{\pi_{fpt} > \pi_{fkt}\right\} \\ &= \Pr\{\left(\varepsilon_{fpt} - \varepsilon_{fkt}\right) \geq \beta\left(casualty_p - casualty_k\right) \\ &\quad + \left(X'_{kt-1} - X'_{pt-1}\right)\sigma\}, p \\ &\neq k. \end{aligned} \tag{9.3}$$

Assuming that ε_{fpt} follows a Type I extreme distribution, p_{fpt} can be written as

$$p_{fpt} = \Pr\left(Y_{ft} = j\right) = \frac{\exp\left(\beta \times casualty_k + X'_{pt-1}\sigma\right)}{\sum_{k \in J} \exp\left(\beta \times casualty_k\right) + X'_{kt-1}\sigma}, \tag{9.4}$$

where J is the set of province choices faced by Japanese firms, and Y_{ft} is a dummy variable that indicates whether Japanese firm f in year t chooses province j. A negative, significant estimate of β suggests that, holding other factors constant, Japanese firms are less likely to locate in provinces with heavy civilian casualties. In addition, Eq. (9.4) can be estimated using maximum likelihood estimation. The maximized log-likelihood function is

$$\ln L = \sum_{f=1}^{n}\sum_{p=1}^{J} d_{fpt} \ln \Pr\left(Y_{ft} = j\right), \tag{9.5}$$

where d_{fpt} equals 1 if $Y_{ft} = j$, and it equals 0 otherwise. We chose β and σ to maximize the log-likelihood ln L.

To test Hypotheses 2 and 3, we used the following estimate:

$$ROA_{fjp} = \alpha + \beta \times Casualty_p + X'\theta + \varepsilon'_{fjp}, \quad (9.6)$$

where ROA_{fjp} represents the return on assets of firm f in industry j and province p; α is the constant; ε'_{fjp} is the error term; and X' is a vector of firm-, industry-, and province-level controls.

Results

Table 9.2 presents our empirical results testing Hypothesis 1. Column 1 includes only control variables in the conditional logit model. Column 2 shows the full model in which civilian casualty was included in addition to the agglomeration and institutional effects, regional attributes, and other conventional determinants. The results show that civilian casualty has a significant effect ($\beta = -0.145$, $p < 0.01$), suggesting Japanese firms tend to avoid regions with heavy civilian casualty. This estimate indicates that one standard deviation increase of civilian casualty (1.9%) in a province will decrease the probability of being chosen as a location by 28%. Thus Hypothesis 1 is supported. For the effects of control variables, Japanese firms choose provinces with low costs (i.e., distance, infrastructure, and agglomeration) to locate while preferring locations with better institutions (i.e., property rights protection) and more market demand (i.e., GDP) to invest; they also choose provinces with more open policies toward foreign firms (i.e., special economic zones) and better human capital (i.e., education). To further examine sub-regional variations of historical conflict on FDI, we collected information on civilian casualties of Shandong province from The List of Victims in Shandong Provinces during Second Sino–Japanese War,[7] complied by the Research Department of Communist Party History in Shandong province, 2014. We conducted analysis at two finer geographic unit levels; prefecture and county.

[7] The data only contained information of deaths of each region during the war. Since no reliable population estimates at prefecture and county levels before the war are available, we normalized civilian deaths by the unit area size following Nunn (2008).

Table 9.2 Conditional logit model of Japanese FDI location in China

	(1)	(2)	(3)	(4)
	Depend variable is a dummy indicating the province that the Japanese firm has chosen			
Civilian casualty		-0.145***		
		(0.014)		
Wars			-3.742***	
			(0.405)	
Property losses				-2.014***
				(0.388)
Distance	-0.470***	-0.530***	-0.537***	-0.719***
	(0.042)	(0.044)	(0.043)	(0.068)
Infrastructure	0.383***	0.364***	0.378***	0.359***
	(0.031)	(0.028)	(0.028)	(0.031)
Agg_domestic	0.106***	0.180***	0.128***	0.149***
	(0.046)	(0.045)	(0.045)	(0.047)
Agg_foreign	0.948***	1.018***	1.061***	0.989***
	(0.031)	(0.031)	(0.033)	(0.032)
Special economic zone	0.409***	0.288***	0.271***	0.364***
	(0.035)	(0.038)	(0.038)	(0.036)
Property right protection	-0.309***	-0.231***	-0.232***	-0.291***
	(0.036)	(0.038)	(0.037)	(0.037)
GDP	0.412***	0.378***	0.400***	0.511***
	(0.041)	(0.039)	(0.039)	(0.045)
Education	3.684***	3.146***	3.314***	3.574***
	(0.305)	(0.297)	(0.303)	(0.307)
Pseudo R square	0.26	0.26	0.26	0.26
Log pseudo likelihood	-20,867	-20,800	-20,820	-20,854
Firms	8646	8646	8646	8646
Location choices	26	26	26	26
Observations	224,796	224,796	224,796	224,796

Notes: *$p < 0.10$; **$p < 0.05$; ***$p < 0.01$. Standard errors are in parenthesis

The estimation results are highly consistent: the coefficient estimates of civilian casualty at both prefecture and county level are negative and significant, suggesting a deterring effect of historical conflict on the location choices of Japanese FDI at sub-provincial level.

The validity of estimates on β relies on the assumption that Japanese army did not encounter more resistance that caused more casualties in regions with certain cultural characteristics, and the war damage has not affected the post-war development and the pattern of investment opportunities for foreign firms. In other words, some omitted factors may be related to civilian casualty while also affect FDI location choices. This possibility can be assessed by estimating the location choices for FDI from countries other than Japan. In addition, previous studies suggest that the distance measures between countries, such as culture, economic, geographic, and institutional distances matter for FDI location choices (Makino & Tsang, 2011). To ensure that our results are robust after incorporating these distances, we controlled for these four types of distances in our models with all foreign firms invested in China included. For the measure of cultural distance, we generated provincial culture measures based on World Values Survey following Beugelsdijk, Maseland, and van Hoorn (2015), and calculated the cultural distance value using foreign countries' scores obtained from Berry, Guillen, and Zhou (2010). Economic distance was constructed as the difference between a province's GDP per capita and those of foreign countries (Berry et al., 2010). Geographic distance denotes the distance between province capital cities of and a specific country, constructed using the Great Circle Distance method. Institutional distance was calculated as the difference of institutional quality of provinces and foreign countries, where province institutions and cross-country institutional quality were extracted from Survey of China's Private Enterprises and Polity IV Project respectively (Acemoglu et al., 2001). Table 9.3 presents the descriptive statistics and correlations of variables for the sample of FDI from all countries. The estimation results reported in column 1 of Table 9.4 suggest that with cultural, economic, geographic, and institutional distances included, we still detected a negative and significant impact of civilian casualty on Japanese FDI locational choices, captured by the interaction between civilian casualty and the Japan dummy.

We employed civilian casualty at province level to measure war damage because the loss of human lives has a profound impact on individuals' emotions and the subsequent formation of animosity toward Japan. To check the robustness of our proxy for war damage and include other causes of citizen animosity during the Second Sino–Japanese War, we used two alternative measures in our analyses: number of wars (i.e., great wars, moderate wars, and skirmishes) and property losses (i.e., movable property and real estate losses) during the war. Estimation results using these proxies are reported in Table 9.4. In all cases, the

Table 9.3 Descriptive statistics and correlations of the overall sample

	1	2	3	4	5	6	7	8	9	10	11	12	13
1 Civilian casualty	1.00												
2 Wars	0.81***	1.00											
3 Property losses	0.41***	0.50***	1.00										
4 Geographic distance	-0.01***	-0.03***	-0.09***	1.00									
5 Cultural distance	0.13***	0.05***	0.18***	-0.15***	1.00								
6 Institutional distance	0.07***	0.06***	0.10***	0.02***	-0.07***	1.00							
7 Economic distance	-0.03***	-0.04***	-0.04***	-0.41***	0.32***	0.03***	1.00						
8 Infrastructure	0.24***	0.35***	0.48***	-0.03***	0.05***	0.12***	-0.14***	1.00					
9 Agg_domestic	0.04***	0.18***	0.64***	-0.05***	0.09***	-0.03***	-0.01***	0.45***	1.00				
10 Agg_foreign	-0.01***	0.04***	0.23***	-0.03***	0.06***	-0.02***	-0.02***	0.18***	0.27***	1.00			
11 SEZ	0.01***	-0.05***	0.33***	-0.02***	0.24***	-0.04***	-0.04***	0.46***	0.60***	0.21***	1.00		
12 GDP	0.11***	0.29***	0.47***	-0.01***	0.01***	0.11***	0.04***	0.41***	0.71***	0.18***	0.33***	1.00	
13 Education	0.03***	0.16***	0.46***	-0.05***	0.20***	0.07***	0.02***	0.33***	0.44***	0.19***	0.30***	0.46***	1.00
Mean	1.77	51.50	1.07	8.82	-3.12	10.89	-10.29	7.73	0.04	0.04	0.38	0.74	0.89
SD	1.90	56.39	0.95	0.68	10.14	14.36	4.35	0.88	0.04	0.14	0.49	0.52	0.08

Notes: N = 778,986; $*p < 0.10$; $**p < 0.05$; $***p < 0.01$

Table 9.4 Location choices of FDI from all countries

	(1)	(2)	(3)
Civilian casualty	-0.011		
	(0.008)		
Civilian casualty × Japan	-0.085***		
	(0.018)		
Wars		0.070	
		(0.265)	
Wars × Japan		-3.125***	
		(0.534)	
Property losses			0.026
			(0.183)
Property losses × Japan			-2.022***
			(0.357)
Geographic distance	-0.651***	-0.771***	-1.194***
	(0.081)	(0.085)	(0.137)
Cultural distance	0.002	0.001	0.002
	(0.002)	(0.002)	(0.002)
Institutional distance	-0.005***	-0.005***	-0.004***
	(0.001)	(0.001)	(0.001)
Economic distance	-0.009	-0.005	0.010
	(0.022)	(0.023)	(0.023)
Infrastructure	0.640***	0.684***	0.685***
	(0.091)	(0.090)	(0.091)
Agg_domestic	3.179***	2.983***	3.319***
	(0.375)	(0.372)	(0.434)
Agg_foreign	8.398***	8.402***	8.408***
	(0.058)	(0.058)	(0.059)
Special economic zone	0.106***	0.109***	0.124***
	(0.030)	(0.031)	(0.029)
GDP	0.323***	0.335***	0.339***
	(0.030)	(0.030)	(0.030)
Education	2.165***	2.200***	2.128***
	(0.206)	(0.207)	(0.214)
Pseudo R square	0.65	0.65	0.65
Log pseudo likelihood	-34,316	-34,313	-34,319
Firms	29,961	29,961	29,961
Location choices	26	26	26
Observations	778,986	778,986	778,986

Notes: $*p < 0.10$; $**p < 0.05$; $***p < 0.01$. Standard errors are in parenthesis

estimate of β is negative and highly significant, suggesting that Japanese firms are less likely to locate in provinces with higher damage during the War. These results imply that our baseline results are robust to alternative proxies for war damage and our selection of civilian casualty as the baseline proxy is not arbitrary.[8] We further estimated the effects of civilian casualty using five major source countries of FDI in China other than Japan, i.e., the US, Germany, France, the UK, and Italy.[9] We did not detect any significant effect of civilian casualty on FDI location choices, which further confirms that civilian casualty only affects FDI from Japan.

Table 9.5 presents the correlation table of the variables used in the performance model. The number of observations dropped to 8259 due to missing values. We reported the performance impact of civilian casualty and the potential moderators on the civilian casualty and FDI performance relationship in Table 9.6. In all columns of Table 9.6, in addition to the regional controls, we further included firm level controls of exporting, capital labor ratio, debt equity ratio, and industry level controls of

Table 9.5 Descriptive statistics and correlations of variables in the performance model

	1	2	3	4	5	6
1 ROA	1.00					
2 Civilian casualty	-0.02**	1.00				
3 State capital	0.02*	0.003	1.00			
4 Tax payment	-0.19***	-0.01	0.03***	1.00		
5 Employment	0.07***	-0.01	0.09***	0.03***	1.00	
6 Export	0.12***	0.03***	0.01	0.13***	0.16***	1.00
7 CLR	0.11***	0.01	0.09***	0.15***	-0.04***	-0.00
8 DER	0.03***	0.01	-0.03**	0.01	0.03***	0.07***
9 Herfindahl Index	0.01	-0.01	0.00	0.00	-0.01	-0.01
10 Agg_domestic	0.06***	0.13***	-0.09***	-0.04***	-0.08***	0.05***
11 Agg_foreign	0.03***	0.30***	-0.06***	-0.03***	0.02	0.12***
12 Distance	-0.02**	-0.25***	0.05***	0.01	-0.06***	-0.10***
13 SEZ	0.05***	-0.21***	-0.09***	-0.02**	-0.08***	-0.01
14 PRP	-0.02**	0.17***	0.01	0.01	-0.00	-0.06***
15 Education	0.04***	-0.05***	-0.03***	-0.01	0.02*	0.07***
Mean	-0.04	1.71	0.10	-0.03	0.05	0.39
SD	0.21	0.95	0.30	0.20	0.18	0.49

Notes: N = 8259; *$p < 0.10$; **$p < 0.05$; ***$p < 0.01$

[8] We standardized the three indictors and compared sizes of the coefficients. Civilian casualty has a larger effect than the other two alternative measures.

[9] We obtained similar results by using top 20 China's major source countries of FDI and these results are available upon request.

Herfindahl index and agglomeration. In column 1, we found a negative and significant effect of civilian casualty on the performance of Japanese FDI ($\beta = -0.605, p < 0.05$), which provides a strong support for Hypothesis 2. We further tested the moderating effects of three political capital accumulation strategies, namely state capital involvement, excessive tax payment, and local employment. We did not detect a significant moderating effect of state capital. Therefore Hypothesis 3a is not supported. The interaction item between excessive tax payment and civilian casualty has a significantly positive effect on FDI performance ($\beta = 0.020, p < 0.01$), supporting Hypothesis 3b. Similarly, the interaction between local employment and civilian casualty yields a significantly positive effect on performance ($\beta = 4.682, p < 0.05$). Therefore Hypothesis 3c is also supported. Taken together, the results suggest that if Japanese firms

7	8	9	10	11	12	13	14	15
1.00								
0.16***	1.00							
0.02	-0.00	1.00						
-0.08***	0.03***	0.00	1.00					
0.03**	0.02**	-0.01	0.43***	1.00				
-0.01	-0.01	0.02*	-0.28***	-0.65***	1.00			
-0.15***	-0.01	0.01	0.55***	-0.16***	0.08***	1.00		
0.01	0.01	0.01	-0.29***	-0.13***	0.18***	-0.21***	1.00	
0.02*	0.01	-0.01	0.43***	0.49***	-0.64***	0.09***	-0.51***	1.00
3.01	0.23	0.27	0.08	0.11	2.16	0.57	0.54	0.98
1.37	0.69	0.17	0.05	0.06	0.49	0.50	0.31	0.02

Table 9.6 Performance model with moderating effects

	ROA						
	(1)	(2)	(3)	(4)	(5)	(6)	(7)
Civilian casualty	−0.605**	−0.613**	−0.614**	−0.626**	−0.819***	−0.579**	−0.472*
	(0.272)	(0.272)	(0.272)	(0.265)	(0.264)	(0.272)	(0.276)
State capital		1.081	1.085				
		(0.765)	(0.766)				
State capital × civilian casualty			0.070				
			(0.748)				
Tax payment				−0.024***	−0.032***		
				(0.001)	(0.001)		
Tax payment × civilian casualty					0.020***		
					(0.002)		
Local employment						6.874***	7.092***
						(1.284)	(1.287)
Local employment × civilian casualty							4.682**
							(2.170)
Firm-level controls							
Exporting	5.216***	5.202***	5.202***	6.606***	6.890***	4.823***	4.815***
	(0.466)	(0.466)	(0.466)	(0.458)	(0.456)	(0.471)	(0.471)
Capital labor ratio	1.778***	1.758***	1.758***	2.296***	2.297***	1.830***	1.837***
	(0.168)	(0.169)	(0.169)	(0.165)	(0.164)	(0.168)	(0.168)
Debt equity ratio	0.050	0.069	0.069	−0.062	−0.081	−0.009	−0.016
	(0.328)	(0.328)	(0.328)	(0.319)	(0.317)	(0.327)	(0.327)
Industry-level controls							
Herfindahl index	1.115	1.110	1.109	1.085	1.068	1.135	1.124
	(1.289)	(1.289)	(1.289)	(1.254)	(1.247)	(1.287)	(1.286)

Agg_domestic	1.446*	1.459*	1.460*	1.299*	1.621**	1.662**	1.635**
	(0.801)	(0.801)	(0.801)	(0.779)	(0.776)	(0.800)	(0.800)
Agg_foreign	0.503	0.540	0.543	0.110	0.062	0.538	0.463
	(0.551)	(0.552)	(0.552)	(0.536)	(0.533)	(0.550)	(0.551)
Region-level controls							
Distance	−0.060	−0.080	−0.076	−0.125	−0.293	0.126	0.058
	(0.720)	(0.720)	(0.721)	(0.701)	(0.697)	(0.719)	(0.720)
Special economic zone	1.989***	2.040***	2.038***	1.995***	1.837***	2.087***	2.167***
	(0.668)	(0.669)	(0.669)	(0.650)	(0.647)	(0.667)	(0.668)
Property right protection	0.795	0.817	0.812	0.993	1.238	0.825	0.822
	(0.935)	(0.935)	(0.937)	(0.910)	(0.905)	(0.933)	(0.933)
Education	3.003	2.635	2.611	5.446	2.644	2.742	1.557
	(15.634)	(15.634)	(15.636)	(15.215)	(15.128)	(15.607)	(15.612)
F Statistics	15.8***	14.69***	13.56***	47.81***	51.14***	18.32***	17.26***
Observations	8259	8259	8259	8259	8259	8259	8259

Notes: $*p < 0.10$; $**p < 0.05$; $***p < 0.01$

contribute to local government revenue and employment at subnational provinces, which is conducive to local public goods, the negative effect of historical conflict on their performance can be mitigated.

Additional Analysis

First, we tested the impact of civilian casualty on Japanese FDI location choices across time by using 5-year intervals (1992–1996 and 1997–2001). The results showed a consistently negative long-term effect of civilian casualty over time. Second, it is important to capture the recent development and trend of Japanese FDI in China. We compiled aggregated province level FDI data to 2013 from the Statistical Yearbooks of China and tested the impact of civilian casualty on FDI inflow into different provinces. The findings were consistent with our results, confirming a persistent effect of civilian casualty on Japanese FDI. Third, the validity of estimates of conditional logit models rests upon the independence from irrelevant alternatives assumption (Hausman & McFadden, 1984). We re-estimated our model using two subsamples without firms located in Shanghai and regions with less than 20 entries; we obtained consistent results. We also tested a nested logit model, which partially relaxes the irrelevant alternatives assumption (Greene, 2008). In the nested logit model, a firm's behavior on location choice was modeled in two steps: a Japanese firm chooses a large region for consideration (e.g., coastal provinces) and then a specific province to locate within this large region. By dividing Chinese provinces into five large regions,[10] we estimated the nested logit mode and obtained robust results, suggesting our original models are not distorted by the assumption of irrelevant alternatives.

[10]To specify the nested logit model, we partitioned our sample (i.e., 26 provinces) into five large regions based on the method of Jin and Qian (1998): coastal provinces (Shandong, Jiangsu, Zhejiang, Fujian, Guangdong, and Hainan), inland provinces (Jiangxi, Nanhui, Hebei, Henan, Shanxi, Hubei, Shaanxi, Sichuan, and Hunan), northwest provinces (Inner Mongolia, Qinghai, Xinjiang, Gansu, and Ningxia), southwest provinces (Yunnan, Guangxi, and Guizhou), and huge cities (Beijing, Tianjin, and Shanghai).

Discussion

Existing research in international business has uncovered the impact of various factors, associated with different economic and policy regimes, on firms' foreign expansion. However, a less understood issue is whether and how historical relations affect FDI activities. In this study, we utilize the context of the Second Sino–Japanese War (1937–1945) to examine the effect of historical conflict on Japanese FDI in China. Using civilian casualties across subnational regions in China, we find that regions that suffered greater damage during the war attract less FDI from Japanese firms. The findings also show that Japanese FDIs located in regions with greater casualties perform worse than those in other regions. Furthermore, we find that political capital accumulation strategies, in the forms of excessive tax payments and local employment, can serve as potential remedies that reduce the negative effect of civilian casualty on performance.

Contributions

This study makes several important contributions to the literature. First, we respond to calls for more fine-grained analyses of within-country differences in international business research (Chan et al., 2010; Lorenzen & Mudambi, 2013; Ma et al., 2013). Specifically, we investigate within-country variations of historical conflict, which is traditionally treated as a host–home country construct, and assess its effects on subnational location choices and performance of FDI. Prior literature generally focuses on country-specific factors as determinants of FDI; but even if the "border effects" assumption of abrupt changes at national frontiers can be valid, it is no longer sufficient (Beugelsdijk & Mudambi, 2013). Instead, the subnational context profoundly affects FDI strategies and thus must be recognized, to reveal the more subtle spatial heterogeneity (Chan et al., 2010). Extending the pioneering work by Makino and Tsang (2011) on historical relations and FDI, our study provides strong evidence of subnational differences in the long-term impact of historical conflict on FDI activities. This approach of focusing on within-country differences of country-level constructs thus adds nuance to our understanding of the effects of historical factors on FDI location decisions and performance. Moreover, our findings demonstrate that political capital accumulation strategies are effective only with local governments, but not with the central government, which provides further evidence that a subnational perspective is critical for investigating firm behavior and strategies in the dynamic environmental conditions in emerging markets.

Second, we extend FDI research by incorporating the influence of historical conflict on FDI performance. Relatively scant attention has been paid to the non-economic determinants of FDI performance (Jones & Khanna, 2006; Martin, 1999). Recent studies start to acknowledge the importance of social, cultural, political, and historical factors. But the ways that history affects international business activities remain unclear (Jones & Khanna, 2006; Makino & Tsang, 2011; Martin, 1999; Martin & Sunley, 1996). We use regional civilian casualties as a proxy for the psychological damage caused by the Second Sino–Japanese War and link it with FDI performance. We demonstrate that repressed war memories can add to distrust and cast a shadow on FDI operation, even after decades-long efforts and continuous economic cooperation. The conflict-induced animosity is persistent, biasing people's judgments and blocking market access of foreign investors from the antagonist country. Our findings reveal the strong influence of local people's post-conflict psychological processes on foreign firms' strategic decisions and performanceoutcomes.

Third, we examine the capacity of political capital accumulation strategies in weakening the negative impact of historical conflict on FDI performance. Political capital can offer firms notable strategic benefits, including access to policy information, legitimacy, and valuable resources that are helpful in overcoming liabilities of foreignness or information asymmetries in foreign markets (Faccio et al., 2006; Hillman & Hitt, 1999). These benefits are particularly relevant in China's regionally decentralized authoritarian system, in which political authorities at the subnational level have significant control over key resources (Xu, 2011). Although acquiring political capital may heighten operational costs, it enables foreign firms to align with the interests of local governments to obtain institutional support, which in turn curtails the negative influence of past conflicts in the local context. Our study thus provides initial, strategic solutions that foreign firms can utilize to mitigate the deterrence effect of historical conflict. These firm-level remedies are highly relevant, considering that many FDI destinations in emerging economies are characterized by turbulent contextual variations (Beugelsdijk & Mudambi, 2013). Our findings shed new light on how foreign firms can adjust their strategic choices in accordance with the unique historical, political, and social backgrounds that mark the various regional markets in host countries.

Implications

Our findings provide important implications for managers and policy-makers. In the global arena, we continue to witness constant conflicts among countries. Firms entering countries or regions with known animosity or conflicts may face increased transaction costs and exchange hazards, and perceive higher likelihoods of opportunism. Managers should not underestimate the negative psychological impact, as sentiments of animosity do not fade away easily.

To mitigate the negative effects of animosity due to historical conflict, foreign companies should seek political capital at the subnational level. In emerging economies such as China, the central government formulates strategic industrial policies, but firm-level performance depends heavily on local governments, which aim to maximize their local fiscal revenues and generate employment opportunities (Sun et al., 2010). Tax payments and local employment opportunities can help foreign firms establish solid relations with local governments. Companies that fail to respect the interests of local governments instead may suffer. This lesson is particularly relevant for Japanese multinationals, which have traditionally tended to work closely with Japanese suppliers rather than locally owned companies to protect their independence (Ravenhill, 1999). In China's auto sector for example, Honda preferred to bring a core group of Japanese suppliers with it to Guangzhou, rather than working with the municipal government to develop indigenous local suppliers in late 1990s. This short-sighted strategic choice made Honda fail to accumulate political capital with local governments, and consequently the company lost its preferential treatment. In contrast, Hyundai in Beijing and Volkswagen in Shanghai have enjoyed more institutional support, including local requirements that every new city taxi must be the companies' car models (Sun et al., 2010). Since 2004, the sales of Honda have lagged behind major competitors, despite its first-mover advantage in China.

We also note several important implications for policymakers. War causes massive collateral damage, including losses of human life and the destruction of physical capital, that are tangible. The psychological and social costs, such as cognitive and emotional damage and the destruction of trusting social relationships, may be more persistent. Policymakers should be aware of the long-run impact of historical conflict when seeking to attract FDI from antagonist countries and accordingly find solutions to reduce this hostility and animosity. For example, during the Asian economic crisis, Japan's initiatives and efforts to absorb imports from struggling Asian nations were applauded by regional and international communities (Leong et al., 2008). Other proactive efforts might include correcting attributions of conflicts, sending aid and trade missions, and encouraging exchange visits by officials, academics, and citizens. Through such efforts, accumulated animosity might be gradually transformed into positive relationships. If China and Japan could turn over a new leaf, their bilateral trade investment might even reach new heights.

Limitations and Future Research

Our study is subject to several limitations that also suggest a variety of directions for future research. First, our measure of war atrocities at the province level may contain an aggregate bias. Continued research could further zoom into investigate within-country differences at a finer geographic level. The sub-provincial results from Shandong represent some initial efforts. Second, we used a firm-year data structure to examine Japanese FDI location choices. Because the database did not contain information about parent firms, we could not investigate sequential entries of the same parent firm. Future studies can further examine whether experience and learning from past entries help Japanese firms deal with the negative impact of historical conflict. Third, the findings document a strong and persistent effect of historical conflict, but our study does not capture consumers' hostile attitudes directly, nor can it describe their shifting cognitive processes over time. It would be worthwhile to examine whether foreign firms can employ strategies to directly mitigate consumers' animosity in regions with heavy civilian casualties. Rigorous qualitative research might help reveal the underlying mechanisms. Finally, our study focuses on political capital accumulation strategies as potential remedies. Establishing strategic alliances with firms from countries that already have bilateral trust with the host country might be another means through which Japanese firms can navigate the hostile environment. Additional studies thus should explore alternative strategies that are beneficial to firm operations in regions and countries where animosity sentiments continue to exist.

Acknowledgements We thank the Editors John Cantwell, Ron Boschma, and three anonymous reviewers for their insightful suggestions. We also appreciate the helpful comments from Ram Mudambi, Shige Makino, Gongming Qian, Xufei Ma, Grazia Santangelo, and participants at the JIBS Special Issue Conference, New Orleans, 2016. Special thanks to Sjoerd Beugelsdijk for the advices on method improvement. Gerald Yong Gao gratefully acknowledges the support from Office of International Studies and Programs at University of Missouri-St. Louis. Yi Che gratefully acknowledges support from the Young Scientists Fund of the National Natural Science Foundation of China (NSFC, Grant No. 71703099) and the Shanghai Pujiang Program (16PJC048).

Appendix: Variable Definitions and Sources

Variable	Definition	Source
Civilian casualty	Ratio of civilian casualties to total population in 1936	A historical account of the surveys of China's losses during the war with Japan; Statistical Abstract of the Republic of China
Wars	Number of major and moderate wars	A historical account of the surveys of China's losses during the war with Japan

(continued)

(continued)

Variable	Definition	Source
Property losses	Log of movable property and real estate per capita	An estimate of China's losses in the war against Japan
Distance	The minimum Great Circle Distance of the province to four major seaports, plus the distance of these sea ports to Japan or each foreign country (unit: km)	The Great Circle Distance method
Infrastructure	Log of the length of highway per square kilometer in a province	China Statistical Yearbook
Agglomeration	Ratio of the number of firms in the same industry-region cell to the national total in the same industry, with domestic and foreign firms calculated separately	Annual Survey of Industrial Firms (ASIF), conducted by National Bureau of Statistics of China (NBSC)
Special economic zone	A dummy variable indicating whether a province contains any special economic zones	Ministry of Foreign Affairs
Property rights protection	Average ratio of a firm's extralegal payment to its total revenue in a province	Survey of China's private enterprises
GDP	Real province gross domestic product with 1992 as the base year	China data online (University of Michigan)
Education	Secondary school enrollment rate at the province level	China Data Online (University of Michigan)
Geographic distance	Log of Great Circle Distance between a Chinese province's capital and a foreign country	The Great Circle Distance method
Cultural distance	Each province culture score minus a foreign country's cultural score	World Values Survey; Mahalanobis Distance (Berry et al., 2010)
Institutional distance	Standardized province measures of institutional quality minus a foreign country's standardized institutional quality score	Survey of China's Private Enterprises; The Polity IV Project
Economic distance	Province GDP per capita minus a foreign country's economic proxy	China Statistical Yearbook; Mahalanobis Distance (Berry et al., 2010)

(*continued*)

(continued)

Variable	Definition	Source
State capital	A dummy variable indicating whether a Japanese FDI contains investments from the Chinese government	Survey of Foreign-invested Enterprises conducted by NBSC
Tax payment	Ratio of extra tax paid by a firm to its total assets	Survey of Foreign-invested Enterprises conducted by NBSC
Local employment	Ratio of number of local workers employed by a firm to local labor forces	Survey of Foreign-invested Enterprises conducted by NBSC
Exporting	A dummy variable equal to 1 if a firm exports and 0 otherwise	Survey of Foreign-invested Enterprises conducted by NBSC
Debt-to-equity ratio	Ratio of debt to firm equity	Survey of Foreign-invested Enterprises conducted by NBSC
Capital labor ratio	Ratio of capital to total employment	Survey of Foreign-invested Enterprises conducted by NBSC
Herfindahl index	Sum of the square of firm market shares in an industry	ASIF conducted by NBSC
Return on assets	Ratio of firm profit to total assets	Survey of Foreign-invested Enterprises conducted by NBSC

References

Acemoglu, D., Johnson, S., & Robinson, J. A. (2001). The colonial origins of comparative development: An empirical investigation. *American Economic Review, 91*(5), 1369–1401.

Arikan, I., & Shenkar, O. (2013). National animosity and cross-border alliances. *Academy of Management Journal, 56*(6), 1516–1544.

Barney, J. B. (1991). Firm resources and sustained competitive advantage. *Journal of Management, 17*(1), 99–121.

Bar-Tal, D. (2000). From intractable conflict through conflict resolution to reconciliation: Psychological analysis. *Political Psychology, 21*(2), 351–365.

Batjargal, B., Hitt, M. A., Tsui, A. S., Arregle, J. L., Webb, J. W., & Miller, T. (2013). Institutional polycentricism, entrepreneurs' social networks and new venture growth. *Academy of Management Journal, 56*(4), 1024–1049.

Belderbos, R., & Carree, M. (2002). The location of Japanese investments in China: Agglomeration effects, keiretsu, and firm heterogeneity. *Journal of the Japanese and International Economies, 16*(2), 194–211.

Benson, M. A. (2004). Dyadic hostility and the ties that bind: State-to-state versus state-to-system security and economic relationships. *Journal of Peace Research, 41*(6), 659–676.

Berger, D., Easterly, W., Nunn, N., & Satyanath, S. (2013). Commercial imperialism? Political influence and trade during the cold war. *American Economic Review, 103*(2), 863–896.

Berry, H., Guillen, M. F., & Zhou, N. (2010). An institutional approach to cross-national distance. *Journal of International Business Studies, 41*(9), 1460–1480.

Beugelsdijk, S., & Mudambi, R. (2013). MNEs as border-crossing multi-location enterprises: The role of discontinuities in geographic space. *Journal of International Business Studies, 44*(5), 413–426.

Beugelsdijk, S., Maseland, R., & van Hoorn, A. (2015). Are scores on Hofstede's dimensions of national culture stable over time? A cohort analysis. *Global Strategy Journal, 5*(3), 223–240.

Borensztein, E., Gregorio, J. D., & Lee, J. W. (1998). How does foreign direct investment affect economic growth? *Journal of International Economics, 45*(1), 115–135.

Burt, R. S. (1992). *Structural holes*. Harvard University Press.

Cai, H., Fang, H., & Xu, L. C. (2011). Eat, drink, firms, government: An investigation of corruption from the entertainment and travel costs of Chinese firms. *The Journal of Law & Economics, 54*(1), 55–78.

Chan, C. M., Makino, S., & Isobe, T. (2010). Does subnational region matter? Foreign affiliate performance in the United States and China. *Strategic Management Journal, 31*(11), 1226–1243.

Chang, S. J., & Park, S. (2005). Types of firms generating network externalities and MNCs' co-location decisions. *Strategic Management Journal, 26*(7), 595–615.

Chang, S. J., & Rosenzweig, P. M. (2001). The choice of entry mode in sequential foreign direct investment. *Strategic Management Journal, 22*(8), 747–776.

Cheng, L. K., & Kwan, Y. K. (2000). What are the determinants of the location of foreign direct investment? The Chinese experience. *Journal of International Economics, 51*(2), 379–400.

Cheng, S., & Stough, R. R. (2006). Location decisions of Japanese new manufacturing plants in China: A discrete-choice analysis. *The Annals of Regional Science, 40*(2), 369–387.

Chi, J. (1987). *A historical account of the surveys of China's losses during the war with Japan*. Academia Historical Press.

Child, J., Chung, L., & Davies, H. (2003). The performance of cross-border units in China: A test of natural selection, strategic choice and contingency theories. *Journal of International Business Studies, 34*(3), 242–254.

Clodfelter, M. (2002). *Warfare and armed conflicts: A statistical reference to casualty and other figures, 1500–2000* (2nd ed.). McFarland.

Coleman, P. T. (2003). Characteristics of protracted, intractable conflict: Toward the development of a metaframework-I. *Peace and Conflict, 9*(1), 1–37.

Cui, L., & Jiang, F. (2012). State ownership effect on firms' FDI ownership decisions under institutional pressure: A study of Chinese outward-investing firms. *Journal of International Business Studies, 43*(3), 264–284.

Dai, L., Eden, L., & Beamish, P. W. (2013). Place, space, and geographical exposure: Foreign subsidiary survival in conflict zones. *Journal of International Business Studies, 44*(6), 554–578.

Dow, D., Cuypers, I., & Ertug, G. (2016). The effects of within-country linguistic and religious diversity on foreign acquisitions. *Journal of International Business Studies, 47*(3), 319–346.

Dunning, J. H. (1998). Location and the multinational enterprise: A neglected factor? *Journal of International Business Studies, 29*(1), 45–66.

Faber, B. (2014). Trade integration, market size, and industrialization: Evidence from China's national trunk highway system. *Review of Economic Studies, 81*(3), 1046–1070.

Faccio, M., Masulis, R. W., & McConnell, J. J. (2006). Political connections and corporate bailouts. *Journal of Finance, 61*(6), 2597–2635.

Fleisher, B., Li, H., & Zhao, M. (2010). Human capital, economic growth, and regional inequality in China. *Journal of Development Economics, 92*(2), 215–231.

Fosfuri, A., Motta, M., & Rønde, T. (2001). Foreign direct investment and spillovers through workers' mobility. *Journal of International Economics, 53*(1), 205–222.

Fung, K. C., Iizaka, H., & Parker, S. (2002). Determinants of U.S. and Japanese direct investment in China. *Journal of Comparative Economics, 30*(3), 567–578.

Glick, R., & Taylor, A. M. (2010). Collateral damage: Trade disruption and the economic impact of war. *Review of Economics and Statistics, 92*(1), 102–127.

Granovetter, M. S. (1985). Economic action and social structure: The problem of embeddedness. *American Journal of Sociology, 91*(3), 481–510.

Greene, W. H. (2008). *Econometric analysis*. Pearson Education.

Guiso, L., Sapienza, P., & Zingales, L. (2009). Cultural biases in economic exchange. *Quarterly Journal of Economics, 124*(3), 1095–1131.

Han, Q. (1946). *An estimate of China's losses in the war against Japan, 1937–1943*. Zhonghua Shuju.

Harmeling, C. M., Magnusson, P., & Singh, S. (2015). Beyond anger: A deeper look at consumer animosity. *Journal of International Business Studies, 46*(6), 676–693.

Hausman, J., & McFadden, D. (1984). Specification tests for the multinomial logit model. *Econometrica, 52*(5), 1219–1240.

Head, K., & Ries, J. (1996). Inter-city competition for foreign investment: Static and dynamic effects of China's incentive areas. *Journal of Urban Economics, 40*(1), 38–60.

Head, K., Ries, J., & Swenson, D. (1995). Agglomeration benefits and location choice: Evidence from Japanese manufacturing investments in the United States. *Journal of International Economics, 38*(3–4), 223–247.

Head, K., Mayer, T., & Ries, J. (2010). The erosion of colonial trade linkages after independence. *Journal of International Economics, 81*(1), 1–14.

Helpman, E., Melitz, M. J., & Yeaple, S. R. (2004). Export versus FDI with heterogeneous firms. *American Economic Review, 94*(1), 300–316.

Hewitt, J. J. (2003). Dyadic processes and international crises. *Journal of Conflict Resolution, 47*(5), 669–692.

Hiller, N. J., & Hambrick, D. C. (2005). Conceptualizing executive hubris: The role of (hyper-) core self-evaluations in strategic decision-making. *Strategic Management Journal, 26*(4), 297–319.

Hillman, A. J., & Hitt, M. A. (1999). Corporate political strategy formulation: A model of approach, participation, and strategy decisions. *Academy of Management Review, 24*(4), 825–842.

Hoffman, S. D., & Duncan, G. J. (1988). Multinomial and conditional logit discrete-choice models in demography. *Demography, 25*(3), 415–427.

Hofstede, G. (1980). *Culture's consequences: International differences in work-related values*. Sage.

Huang, Y., Jin, L., & Qian, Y. (2013). Does ethnicity pay? Evidence from overseas Chinese FDI in China. *Review of Economics and Statistics, 95*(3), 868–883.

Hutzschenreuter, T., Pedersen, T., & Volberda, H. W. (2007). The role of path dependency and managerial intentionality: A perspective on international business research. *Journal of International Business Studies, 38*(7), 1055–1068.

Jin, H., & Qian, Y. (1998). Public versus private ownership of firms: Evidence from rural China. *Quarterly Journal of Economics, 113*(3), 773–808.

Johnson, S., McMillan, J., & Woodruff, C. (2002). Property rights and finance. *American Economic Review, 92*(5), 1335–1356.

Jones, G., & Khanna, T. (2006). Bringing history (back) into international business. *Journal of International Business Studies, 37*(4), 453–468.

Kastner, S. L. (2007). When do conflicting political relations affect international trade? *Journal of Conflict Resolution, 51*(4), 664–688.

Kim, T. Y., Delios, A., & Xu, D. (2010). Organizational geography, experiential learning and subsidiary exit: Japanese foreign expansions in China, 1979–2001. *Journal of Economic Geography, 10*(4), 579–597.

Klein, J. G. (2002). Us versus them, or us versus everyone? Delineating consumer aversion to foreign goods. *Journal of International Business Studies, 33*(2), 345–363.

Klein, J. G., Ettenson, R., & Morris, M. D. (1998). The animosity model of foreign product purchase: An empirical test in the People's Republic of China. *Journal of Marketing, 62*(1), 89–100.

Kogut, B., & Singh, H. (1988). The effect of national culture on the choice of entry mode. *Journal of International Business Studies, 19*(3), 411–432.

Kostova, T., & Zaheer, S. (1999). Organizational legitimacy under conditions of complexity: The case of the multinational enterprise. *Academy of Management Review, 24*(1), 64–81.

Leong, S. M., Cote, J. A., Ang, S. H., Tan, S. J., Jung, K., Kau, A. K., et al. (2008). Understanding consumer animosity in an international crisis: Nature, antecedents, and consequences. *Journal of International Business Studies, 39*(6), 996–1009.

Li, H., & Zhang, Y. (2007). The role of managers' political networking and functional experience in new venture performance: Evidence from China's transition economy. *Strategic Management Journal, 28*(8), 791–804.

Lin, J. Y., & Liu, Z. (2000). Fiscal decentralization and economic growth in China. *Economic Development and Cultural Change, 49*(1), 1–21.

Liu, X. P., Lovely, M., & Ondrich, J. (2010). The location decisions of foreign investors in China: Untangling the effect of wages using a control function approach. *Review of Economics and Statistics, 92*(1), 160–166.

Lorenzen, M., & Mudambi, R. (2013). Clusters, connectivity and catch-up: Bollywood and Bangalore in the global economy. *Journal of Economic Geography, 13*(3), 501–534.

Lu, J. W., & Beamish, P. W. (2001). The internationalization and performance of SMEs. *Strategic Management Journal, 22*(6–7), 565–586.

Luo, Y. (2007). Are joint venture partners more opportunistic in a more volatile environment? *Strategic Management Journal, 28*(1), 39–60.

Luo, Y., & Peng, W. M. (1999). Learning to compete in a transition economy: Experience, environment, and performance. *Journal of International Business Studies, 30*(2), 269–295.

Ma, X., & Delios, A. (2007). A new tale of two cities: Japanese FDIs in Shanghai and Beijing, 1979–2003. *International Business Review, 16*(2), 207–228.

Ma, X., Tong, T. W., & Fitza, M. (2013). How much does subnational region matter to foreign subsidiary performance: Evidence from Fortune Global 500 Corporations' investment in China. *Journal of International Business Studies, 44*(1), 66–87.

Makino, S., & Tsang, E. W. K. (2011). Historical ties and foreign direct investment: An exploratory study. *Journal of International Business Studies, 42*(4), 545–557.

Malhotra, D., & Lumineau, F. (2011). Trust and collaboration in the aftermath of conflict: The effects of contract structure. *Academy of Management Journal, 54*(5), 981–998.

Maoz, Z. (2009). The effects of strategic and economic interdependence on international conflict across levels of analysis. *American Journal of Political Science, 53*(1), 223–240.

Martin, R. (1999). The new 'geographical turn' in economics: Some critical reflections. *Cambridge Journal of Economics, 23*(1), 65–91.

Martin, R., & Sunley, P. (1996). Paul Krugman's geographical economics and its implications for regional development theory: A critical assessment. *Economic Geography, 72*(3), 259–292.

McFadden, D. (1974). Conditional logit analysis of qualitative choice behavior. In P. Zarembka (Ed.), *Frontiers in econometrics* (pp. 105–142). Academic.

Meyer, K. E., & Nguyen, H. V. (2005). Foreign investment strategies and subnational institutions in emerging markets: Evidence from Vietnam. *Journal of Management Studies, 42*(1), 63–93.

Mitchell, C. R. (1981). *The structure of international conflict.* Macmillan.

Nachum, L., & Zaheer, S. (2005). The persistence of distance? The impact of technology on MNE motivations for foreign investment. *Strategic Management Journal, 26*(8), 747–767.

Narula, R., & Dunning, J. H. (2000). Industrial development, globalization and multinational enterprises: New realities for developing countries. *Oxford Development Studies, 28*(2), 141–167.

Nee, V. (1992). Organizational dynamics of market transition: Hybrid forms, property rights, and mixed economy in China. *Administrative Science Quarterly, 37*(1), 1–27.

Nunn, N. (2008). The long-term effects of Africa's slave trades. *Quarterly Journal of Economics, 123*(1), 139–176.

Peng, M. W. (2004). Identifying the big question in international business research. *Journal of International Business Studies, 35*(2), 99–108.

Peng, M. W., Wang, D. Y. L., & Jiang, Y. (2008). An institution-based view of international business strategy: A focus on emerging economies. *Journal of International Business Studies, 39*(5), 920–936.

Porter, M. E. (1980). *Competitive strategy*. Free Press.

Ravenhill, J. (1999). Japanese and US subsidiaries in East Asia: Host economy effects. In D. J. Encarnation (Ed.), *Japanese multinationals in Asia: Regional operations in comparative perspective* (pp. 261–284). Oxford University Press.

Reger, R. K., Duhaime, I. M., & Stimpert, J. L. (1992). Deregulation, strategic choice, risk and financial performance. *Strategic Management Journal, 13*(3), 189–204.

Regnér, P., & Edman, J. (2014). MNE institutional advantage: How subunits shape, transpose and evade host country institutions. *Journal of International Business Studies, 45*(3), 275–302.

Riefler, P., & Diamantopoulos, A. (2007). Consumer animosity: A literature review and a reconsideration of its measurement. *International Marketing Review, 24*(1), 87–119.

Rummel, R. J. (1991). *China's bloody century*. Transaction Publishers.

Sofka, W., Preto, M., & de Faria, P. (2014). MNC subsidiary closures: What is the value of employees' human capital in new jobs? *Journal of International Business Studies, 45*(6), 723–750.

Sun, P., Mellahi, K., & Thun, E. (2010). The dynamic value of MNE political embeddedness: The case of the Chinese automobile industry. *Journal of International Business Studies, 41*(7), 1161–1182.

The Historical Society of Japan. (1967). *Pacific war history* (Vol. 4) (J. Feng, et al. Trans.). The Commercial Press.

Tinbergen, J. (1962). *Shaping the world economy: Suggestions for an international economic policy*. Twentieth Century Fund.

Tsang, E. W. K., & Yip, P. S. L. (2007). Economic distance and the survival of foreign direct investments. *Academy of Management Journal, 50*(5), 1156–1168.

Walder, A. G. (2002). Markets and income inequality in rural China: Political advantage in an expanding economy. *American Sociological Review, 67*(2), 231–253.
Wang, C., Hong, J., Kafouros, M., & Wright, M. (2012). Exploring the role of government involvement in outward FDI from emerging economies. *Journal of International Business Studies, 43*(7), 655–676.
Wathne, K. H., & Heide, J. B. (2000). Opportunism in interfirm relationships: Forms, outcomes, and solutions. *Journal of Marketing, 64*(4), 36–51.
Wei, S., & Wu, Y. (2001). *Globalization and inequality: Evidence from within China* (NBER Working Paper 8611). www.nber.org/papers/w8611
Xu, C. (2011). The fundamental institutions of China's reforms and development. *Journal of Economic Literature, 49*(4), 1076–1151.
Xu, D., & Shenkar, O. (2002). Institutional distance and the multinational enterprise. *Academy of Management Review, 27*(4), 608–618.
Xu, D., Lu, J. W., & Gu, Q. (2014a). Organizational forms and multi-population dynamics: Economic transition in China. *Administrative Science Quarterly, 59*(3), 517–547.
Xu, K., Tihanyi, L., & Hitt, M. A. (2014b). Firm resources, governmental power, and privatization. *Journal of Management*. https://doi.org/10.1177/0149206314546194
Zhang, X. (2006). Fiscal decentralization and political centralization in China: Implications for growth and inequality. *Journal of Comparative Economics, 34*(4), 713–726.
Zhao, H., & Zhu, G. (2000). Location factors and country-of-origin differences: An empirical analysis of FDI in China. *Multinational Business Review, 8*(1), 60–73.
Zhou, C., Delios, A., & Yang, J. Y. (2002). Locational determinants of Japanese foreign direct investment in China. *Asia Pacific Journal of Management, 19*(1), 63–86.

10

Foreign Direct Investment and Military Conflicts: A Commentary

Rakesh B. Sambharya

Introduction: A Complex Relationship Between Historical Conflict and FDI

The significant increase in foreign direct investment (FDI) global outflows from $243 billion in 1990 to $1.314 trillion in 2019 (UNCTAD.org) is mainly attributed to the second wave of globalization. Liberal economic posits that, globalization in the form of increased FDI flows, led to world peace and a greater standard of living in many emerging markets, gained ascendancy. FDI by its very nature is subject to political risk in the host countries in which the multinational enterprise (MNE) operates. Conflicts between states have become an increasingly topical subject of academic research, particularly with respect to their impact on FDI (e.g., Chen, 2017; Gao et al., 2018; Li & Vashchilko, 2010; Oh & Oetzel, 2017). The purpose of this commentary is to examine the notable study by Gao et al. (2018) and to look at research on the relationship

R. B. Sambharya (✉)
School of Business, Rutgers University-Camden, Camden, NJ, USA
e-mail: sambhary@camden.rutgers.edu

M. A. Mithani et al. (eds.), *Crises and Disruptions in International Business*, JIBS Special Collections, https://doi.org/10.1007/978-3-030-80383-4_10

between political conflict and FDI and make suggestions for future research.

One of the problems in the political risk literature is that it mostly examines political risk in isolation and tends to ignore the interdependencies with other types of risk such as economic/financial, technological, ecological, and sociocultural risks. The boundary between political and other risk types is, however, very thin (Boddewyn, 1988). There is a high degree of interconnectedness and interdependence among the various dimensions of risk, largely due to the phenomena of globalization that exists at the sub-national, national, international, and even supranational levels (Sambharya & Rasheed, 2012).

Indeed, there are many types of conflicts that are relevant to FDI flows including military, political, commercial or interstate, extrastate, or intrastate (Chen, 2017). A reasonable assumption is that military conflict may have a negative impact on FDI. Gao et al. (2018) take a historical perspective in examining whether the home–host country relations reveal heterogeneous effects on FDI across the country's subnational regions in the context of Japanese FDI in China. Using civilian casualties across subnational regions in China, Gao et al. (2018) find that regions that suffered greater damage during the war attracted lower levels of FDI from Japanese firms. Namely, Japanese MNEs mitigated the negative effect of civilian casualty on performance by accumulating political capital strategies, in the form of excessive tax payments and local employment. Since there tend to be security alliances amongst different nation states, these treaties and agreements are bound to affect trade and FDI flows as well as lower political risk.

However, the empirical research evidence remains (surprisingly perhaps) mixed and relatively nuanced. In a notable study on manufacturing FDI by U.S. firms entering twenty-four countries over twenty-one years, Nigh (1985) found that inter-nation and intra-nation conflicts reduced U.S. investment whereas inter-nation and intra-nation cooperation increased it. In a gravity model of bilateral investment flows for a sample of 1117 dyads among fifty-eight countries from 1980 to 2000, Li and Vashchilko (2010) found that dyadic military conflict reduced bilateral investment in the high-income and low-income dyads, security alliances stimulated bilateral investment in the high-income and low-income dyads, and neither military conflict, nor security alliances, influenced bilateral investment into the high-income dyads. Furthermore, in a study on the endogenous effects of conflict with FDI inflows, outflows, and stocks in the time period between 1980 and 2000, Bussmann (2010) found the following: fatal conflict reduced FDI inflows and FDI stock; conflict was more likely when the political distance separating the two states was significantly high; trade interdependence reduced the chances that a pair of states would start a conflict; and states that were directly contiguous, were more prone towards conflict. Overall, the abovementioned studies have examined conflict, including military conflict, through a very narrow prism and ignored the various interdependencies with other types of risks that may have been the cause of the conflict in the first place. Amongst them, the Gao et al. (2018) chapter did not examine the geopolitical context in which the Japanese firms were deploying FDI in the subregions that had been affected the most by the war. Perhaps the economic and financial risks were much lower in these subregions along with the benefits of lower cost. Japanese MNEs were potentially lowering their overall political risk by avoiding sophisticated developed coastal regions in China. A relatively more comprehensive global risk model proposed by Sambharya and Rasheed (2012) conceptualizes risk in a holistic and synergistic manner, as explained below.

A New and Expanded Paradigm of Global Risk

One of the issues with any study focusing on one type of risk is that it will examine risk in isolation rather than offering a multidimensional treatment of the phenomenon that is characterized by some level of risk. While each category of risk may have relevance in specific contexts, fewer studies provide a comprehensive assessment of the overall risks faced by the modern MNE. The world today is characterized by an unprecedented level of interconnectedness and interdependence that are manifested in for instance, MNE led global supply chains. Indeed, risks are rarely confined to a nation, an industry, or a firm. Instead, today's risks are systemic, their contagion rapid, and their consequences devastating and unpredictable. Several international business research scholars have already advocated for a more comprehensive approach to the conceptualization of risk (Simon, 1984; Miller, 1992). In particular, Simon (1984) called for widening the scope of the political environment to include the international environment e.g., foreign policies and internal development of nations, and the role of regional and non-governmental organizations; as well as global environmental policies of organizations such as the United Nations and the International Monetary Fund.

In response to the need to better understand risk, together with my colleague – Abdul Rasheed – we developed, some time ago, a comprehensive model of global risk that considers the *interdependence* and *interconnectedness* amongst different risk types (see Sambharya & Rasheed, 2012). In our article, we pointed out five fundamental differences between traditional thinking about political risk and the contemporary way of broadly conceptualizing global risk. First, any conceptualization of type of risk must reflect the global nature of the current environment. Second, the mental models used to conceptualize risk should recognize the multiplicative nature of risk. Third, we should move from discrete analysis of each country as a unit of analysis to the recognition of interconnectedness between countries. Fourth, any analysis of risk needs to change from a linear system of thinking to a non-linear system that acknowledges the more chaotic nature of the contemporary world. Thus, we argue that the Gao et al. (2018) study could have also viewed their research question from a more holistic point of view incorporating interdependencies amongst political, economic, and sociocultural aspects of Japanese FDI in China (which, in turn, represents an opportunity for future research). The utilization of chaos theory, can offer a starting point towards finding an underlying order and structure behind complex events (Thietart & Bourges, 1995). Chaotic systems are highly sensitive to minor differences in initial conditions; the current portfolio approaches to risk management have been mainly based on the idea that risk can be localized, and downside losses can be contained.

We propose that the concept of global risk violates fundamental assumptions underlying much of our thinking about *managing* risk. For a modern MNE, the consequences of the outbreak of a pandemic in China or a financial meltdown in the U.S cannot be contained to those specific countries. When risk is global, the potential downside is a complete breakdown as seen in the ongoing Covid-19 crisis. Fifth, and relatedly, we may all benefit from moving away from equilibrium models to models of reflexivity (Flanagan, 1981) that recognize that social systems are subject to interference by individuals and organizations. This means that the relationship between factors in an environment can change and be altered by the actions of the players themselves. From a reflexivity lens, relationships are viewed as reflexive when causes and effects affect each other, as reflexivity tends to complicate all the traditional roles of classical science i.e., explanation, prediction and control. Thus, the global conceptualization of risk should include several relevant dimensions such as political, ecological, economic/financial and technological, that can have an adverse effect on the establishment of new and ongoing MNE operations.

Risk Interdependence and Interconnectedness: A New Paradigm

Discontinuities are unanticipated events that can suddenly shift the landscape in any business environment. What may be to many the father of management thinking, Peter Drucker (1969) recognized four kinds of discontinuities: new technologies, globalization of the world economy, growth of pluralism, and the spread of knowledge. Due to the speed of change in the contemporary world, a new kind of discontinuity has emerged, which we termed 'interdependence risk' (see Sambharya and Rasheed, 2012). We explain that different types of risks (political, economic, technological, ecological) have become interdependent due to the globalization of finance, spread of information technology, growth of international trade, along with deregulation and privatization. The fundamental characteristic of today's world, we argue, is its interconnectedness and it is manifested within the firm as well through spatially dispersed but tightly coordinated value chains. Therefore, the conceptualization of risk must reflect the global nature of risk (Sambharya & Rasheed, 2012). A relevant example of interdependency is when environmental changes such as climate change, pollution, global immigration or water scarcity are leading to greater mutuality and connectivity in IB. Interdependence arises out of this interconnectedness. I therefore propose that a new risk paradigm should acknowledge the interconnectedness and interdependence amongst risk types.

One important application of the new paradigm that I emphasize here is the connection between ecological risk and political risk. Climate change is a major phenomenon that is already having a huge impact on dislocations, that have led to mass migration, and in some cases, either created conflict or increased conflict. The expected rise in sea levels, extreme droughts, storms, and flooding may lead to security concerns for businesses when people are forced to flee, infrastructure is destroyed, ecosystems fail, agriculture is disrupted, and economic volatility increases; leading even to losses of potential markets.

The stream of research on the relationship between conflict and FDI is relatively new and there are many avenues for further research. Contrary to conventional wisdom, there is FDI even in conflict zones, evidenced by the UNCTAD data that reports how the total stock of FDI in conflict countries was US$169 billion in 2009. This points to the importance of understanding the MNEs themselves. In a study of 693 UK firms in 212 countries over the period 1999–2008, Chen (2017) found that: firm experience with conflict had a horizontal S-shaped relationship with subsidiary profitability, extrastate conflict in the host country was positively related to subsidiary profitability, and the level of engagement of the host country in extrastate conflicts negatively moderated the impact of firm experience with conflict. Driffield, Jones and Crotty (2013) found that, out of 2509 firms (originating from 10 countries), 540 invested in regions with a low level of human development, and which were engaged in some sort of conflict; the authors also found that those MNEs which invested in countries with weaker institutions and fewer concerns about corporate social responsibility were also more likely to invest in conflict regions.

Future Research: Where Next?

We propose as an important area for future research explicitly studying the link between climate change and FDI. As carbon emissions rise to unsustainable levels, there is a real danger of the planet reaching a point of no return, as scientists have been warning for some time now. Unconstrained economic growth has been one of the primary causes for the rise in greenhouse gases and emissions (Kais & Sami, 2016). The only study – to the best of my knowledge – is that by Liobikienė & Butkus (2018) who found that inward FDI stock as a percentage of GDP was not significantly related to greenhouse gas emissions across all types of countries in terms of economic development. Thus, under different stages of economic development, FDI is yet to reach the level at which it significantly contributes to the reduction of greenhouse gas emissions. FDI in the areas of energy efficiency and the share of renewable energy consumption are opportunities form climate change policy and reduced the greenhouse gas emissions.

Another area of research is to further test whether FDI reduces military conflict. Specifically, does FDI lead to improved economic conditions that raise the standard of living and create jobs, thus lowering the conditions for armed conflict? In an empirical study of 147 countries, Mihalache-O'Keef (2018) found that the impact of FDI on conflict was industry-specific; the author found that service sector FDI led to fewer conflicts, extractive sector FDI led to an increase in conflicts, and FDI in the manufacturing sector had a neutral effect. Future research could therefore further examine within-industry differences.

Lastly, we have the inexorable rise of China's outward FDI from $830 million in 1990 to $ 117 billion in 2019 (UNCTAD.org). The Belt and Road Initiative (BRI) started in 2013 as an important policy agenda that has significant foreign policy, economic, legal, and ecological implications. Sutherland, Anderson, Bailey, and Alon (2020) found that countries with fragile institutions attracted higher Chinese FDI and that BRI moderated this link; Chinese FDI may be, at least to some extent, be attracted to countries with weaker institutions that ignore corruption and limit accountability, thus leading to a debt-trap for those under-developed host countries.

In summary, the chapter by Gao et al. (2018) is an excellent depiction of the importance of one type of risk: political risk, which the authors link to historical conflict. Research on conflict and its effects on FDI, however, needs to adopt a broader view of not just examining political risk but a more comprehensive conceptualization of risk itself. Risk needs to be seen as a multidimensional concept that includes the economic/financial, technological, ecological and sociocultural dimensions that exist at the sub-national, national, international and supranational levels. More importantly, different risk dimensions are often interconnected and have their own interdependencies around the dynamics of causes and effects.

References

Boddewyn, J. J. (1988). Political aspects of MNE theory. *Journal of International Business Studies, 19*, 341–363.

Bussmann, M. (2010). Foreign direct investment and militarized international conflict. *Journal of Peace Research, 47*(2), 143–153.

Chen, S. (2017). Profiting from FDI in conflict zones. *Journal of World Business, 52*, 760–768.

Driffield, N., Jones, C., & Crotty, J. (2013). International business research and risky investments an analysis of FDI in conflict zones. *International Business Review, 22*(1), 140–155.

Drucker, P. (1969). *The age of discontinuity: Guidelines to our changing society*. Harper & Row.

Flanagan, O. J. (1981). Psychology, progress, and the problem of reflexivity: A study in epistemological foundations of psychology. *Journal of the History of the Behavioral Sciences, 17*, 375–386.

Gao, G. Y., Wang, D. T., & Che, Y. (2018). Impact of historical conflict on FDI location and performance: Japanese investment in China. *Journal of International Business Studies, 49*, 1060–1080.

Kais, S., & Sami, H. (2016). An econometric study of the impact of economic growth and energy use on carbon emissions: Panel data evidence from fifty-eight countries. Renewable sustainable. *Energy Review, 59*, 1101–1110.

Li, Q., & Vashchilko, T. (2010). Dyadic military conflict, security alliances, and bilateral FDI flows. *Journal of International Business Studies, 41*(5), 765–782.

Liobikienė, G., & Butkus, M. (2018). The challenges and opportunities of climate change policy under different stages of economic development. *Science of the Total Environment, 642*, 999–1007.

Mihalache-O'Keef, A. S. (2018). Whose greed, whose grievance, and whose opportunity? Effects of foreign direct investments (FDI) on internal conflict. *World Development, 106*, 187–206.

Miller, K. D. (1992). A framework for integrated risk management in international business. *Journal of International Business Studies, 23*(2), 311–331.

Nigh, D. (1985). The effect of political events on United States foreign direct investment: A pooled cross-sectional analysis. *Journal of International Business Studies, 16*(1), 1–17.

Oh, C. H., & Oetzel, J. (2017). Once bitten twice shy? Experience managing violent conflict risk and MNC subsidiary-level investment and expansion. *Strategic Management Journal, 38*(3), 714–731.

Sambharya, R. B., & Rasheed, A. A. (2012). Conceptualizing global risk in a changing world: Looking beyond the political dimension. *Organizational Dynamics, 41*, 308–317.

Simon, J. D. (1984). A theoretical perspective on political risk. *Journal of International Business Studies, 15*(1), 123–143.

Sutherland, D., Anderson, J., Bailey, N., & Alon, I. (2020). Policy, institutional fragility, and Chinese outward foreign investment of the belt and road initiative. *Journal of International Business Policy, 3*, 249–272.

Thietart, R. A., & Bourges, B. (1995). Chaos theory and strategy. *Organization Science, 6*(1), 19–31.

UNCTAD.org. Available at: https://unctadstat.unctad.org

Part IV

Climate Change, Climate Risk and MNE Strategy

11

A Perspective on Multinational Enterprises and Climate Change: Learning from "an Inconvenient Truth"?

Ans Kolk and Jonatan Pinkse

Introduction

Sustainability related to multinational enterprises (MNEs) has received increasing attention in the past decade (Lundan, 2004; Rugman & Verbeke, 2001a). In the academic international business literature, a major contribution to a better understanding has originated from Rugman and Verbeke, in a series of publications in the late 1990s (see especially Rugman & Verbeke, 1998, 2000, 2001a). Their attempts to link sustainability to general themes, such as internalization, location-bound and non-location-bound firm-specific advantages (FSAs), competitiveness, public policy and MNE strategy, have been particularly valuable. Considering this work, of which the last publication was written around 2000, there are some obvious areas of further research building on Rugman and Verbeke, all the more because in recent years concern

A. Kolk (✉) • J. Pinkse
University of Amsterdam, Amsterdam Business School,
Amsterdam, The Netherlands
e-mail: akolk@uva.nl

M. A. Mithani et al. (eds.), *Crises and Disruptions in International Business*, JIBS Special Collections, https://doi.org/10.1007/978-3-030-80383-4_11

about MNEs' impact on sustainability issues with a global scope, such as climate change, the hole in the ozone layer and biodiversity loss, has become more pressing than ever before.

Yet the extent to which MNEs are also taking the responsibility to become agents of global change that tackle sustainability issues is still highly debated (Christmann, 2004; Christmann & Taylor, 2001). It is without doubt that MNEs have a huge potential for innovation, which might lead to the development of sustainable products and services (Hall & Vredenburg, 2003). But do MNEs also take the effort to invest in sustainable technologies, and if so how far are they willing to go, if this also means moving away from technologies they are familiar with? This "frontier" of international business research seems very worthwhile pursuing, because it links the sustainability implications of corporate activity and the policy and societal responses engendered by the actual strategic responses of MNEs, particularly the competitive (dis)advantages that may be created (or not) at different locations. It thus sheds light on how a global sustainability issue affects configurations of country-specific and firm-specific advantages, and may incite MNE activities that help shape the (sustainable) future of societies worldwide.

The decision of an MNE to invest in tackling a global sustainability issue can be assessed with Rugman and Verbeke's (1998) resource-based framework on environmental management, which explains the instances when it is likely that MNEs will commit resources to improving environmental performance. They argued that resource commitments to activities such as pollution prevention and waste reduction have a strategic use only if they lead to the creation of "green" FSAs. Whether this is the case depends on the *leveraging potential* of resource commitments and the *flexibility* regarding their reversibility. Leveraging potential indicates whether committing resources to environmental management leads to the creation or improvement of FSAs that simultaneously advance environmental and industrial performance. Rugman and Verbeke (1998) argue that environmental investments have this potential if they enable MNEs to improve performance in existing markets, enter new markets, or boost technological capabilities valuable for the long run. Flexibility, on the other hand, makes it easier for firms to decide upon resource commitments, as mistakes can be corrected. Preferably, firms end up in a green success scenario where resource commitments for environmental improvement have a high leverage potential and are flexible. In many cases, however, environmental investments cannot easily be reversed, and firms run the risk of ending up in a green mistake scenario, in which inflexibility is accompanied by a weak leveraging potential. As a result of this looming danger, firms may be hesitant to engage in this kind of investment. If uncertainties exist in the environmental arena, for example with regard to regulatory instruments, consumer responses and industry standards, firms are likely to postpone decisions until new environmental options are economically superior as well.

Apart from adding insights from the resource-based view by highlighting the instances in which environmental regulation can lead to the development of green FSAs, Rugman and Verbeke (1998) have shown the value of adding country-specific advantages (CSAs). MNEs are confronted not only by the issue of whether or not to develop green FSAs, but also by the fact that environmental regulations differ between the countries in which they operate. Rugman and Verbeke argued that changes in environmental regulations could fundamentally alter CSAs for specific countries. The strategic complexity for MNEs is that they have to combine FSAs and CSAs, which usually means adapting FSAs, to attain optimal FSA–CSA configurations (cf. Rugman & Verbeke, 1992, 2003).

Notwithstanding the contribution of Rugman and Verbeke's (1998) framework to gain insight into the decision of MNEs whether or not to invest in improving environmental performance, and how this differs across countries, it does not tell how MNEs maintain existing FSAs or create new ones for managing a global sustainability issue over time. Assessing the impact of such a global issue on MNE strategy is quite challenging, because it is far more complex than responding to specific local environmental regulation, for example in the case of air pollution or chemical substances laws. The role that a global sustainability issue plays in MNE strategy is not merely a matter of dealing with local regulation, but is usually part of a broader conglomerate of factors involving not only governmental but also societal and market forces, and at different levels, national, regional and/or international. Because of this whole variety of geographically dispersed forces that influence the development of a global sustainability issue, meeting all stakeholder demands essentially forms a moving target for MNEs. What is expected from MNEs constantly changes, because public opinion, regulation, competition and scientific evidence on global sustainability issues usually follow a rather fitful course.

This means that a one-time decision to commit resources does not suffice. Instead MNEs have to constantly adjust their FSAs for deploying these resources, or even create new FSAs to maintain fit with changes in the global sustainability issue. In other words, because MNEs face a moving target they require dynamic capabilities (Teece et al., 1997), and keep modifying and transferring FSAs to stay responsive to issue-relevant CSAs across the globe as well as higher-order learning to keep abreast of future developments that may affect key FSAs (Winter, 2003; Zollo & Winter, 2002). Taking a dynamic capabilities perspective can thus help to uncover whether and how particular global sustainability issues incite MNEs to build green FSAs or reconfigure their key FSAs that are viewed as the main sources of profitability, growth and survival. It provides insight into the strategic changes that MNEs implement to tackle issues of global sustainability, and how these differ between the geographic locations in which an MNE is active.

To examine whether and how particular global sustainability issues induce MNEs to build green or change key FSAs, this chapter focuses on the issue of climate change. Over the past decade this global issue has evolved as the most pressing environmental problem of our time. Particularly as a result of temperature increases, it already affects physical and biological systems by changing ecosystems and causing extinction of species, and will increasingly have a social impact and adversely affect human health (IPCC, 2007). What is more, as a result of the economic costs and risks of extreme weather (Romilly, 2007), climate change could have a severe impact on economic growth and development as well, if no action is taken to reduce emissions (Stern, 2007). Consequently, climate change affects MNEs active in a wide variety of sectors and countries. It is also not a "purely" environmental issue because it is closely linked to concerns about energy security owing to dependence on fossil fuels and oil in particular, and to energy efficiency and management more generally. Over the years, the strategic impact of climate change has been surrounded by great uncertainty (Brewer, 2005) (e.g., uncertainty about type, magnitude, and timing of the physical impact; about the best technological options to address the issue; and about the materialization of public policies). It has been a long time since the first deliberations on regulation of greenhouse gas emissions started, around 15 years ago, until sufficient ratification and thus entry into force of the Kyoto Protocol, in early 2005. The adoption of the Kyoto Protocol in 1997, however, already set some things in motion, such as an emissions trading scheme in the EU (the EU-ETS, which started on 1 January 2005), but for firms the overall policy context has been ambiguous, with a range of national and international initiatives, some binding, others voluntary, and with a multitude of actors involved.

Increasing societal and regulatory attention to the issue has led MNEs to consider how it affects the markets in which they operate, and has engendered a variety of responses, both market and non-market (political) in nature (Kolk & Levy, 2004; Kolk & Pinkse, 2005, 2007; Levy & Kolk, 2002). MNEs clearly show awareness of growing public concerns that have come to the fore in press coverage, but also through popular books and movies on this "inconvenient truth", as one of them was titled. However, because MNEs have been facing a complex international context of continuously changing climate policies, many tend to be cautious in taking steps in one particular direction. They clearly doubt the flexibility of climate-induced investments, and fear making irreversible green mistakes (cf. Rugman & Verbeke, 1998). What is more, tackling climate change effectively might require firms to move away from existing technologies and build new, unrelated FSAs instead. For these reasons, the vast majority have only recently started developing FSAs in response to climate change. Nevertheless, quite a few early movers, particularly in those sectors most confronted by it, have anticipated the ambiguities surrounding climate change by seizing the opportunity to gain a strategic advantage over their rivals (Hoffman, 2005). It is also an issue from which MNEs can learn how to anticipate future developments in a context of uncertainty, and exercise leadership that combines societal and strategic concerns.

To explore in more detail how a global sustainability issue may affect an MNE's FSAs, we examine the existing literature, particularly concerning the nature and geographic location of FSA development, and develop two organizing frameworks, one for each aspect. These are subsequently applied to climate change to indicate what will induce MNEs to develop so-called "climate-induced FSAs". For these sections on firms' actual positions and activities on climate change we have used illustrative information from various sources, including those that have come available through the second cycle of the Carbon Disclosure Project (CDP), published in May 2004. For the CDP, MNEs disclosed wide-ranging information on initiatives currently under way to reduce greenhouse gas emissions. We used the CDP to identify specific cases of MNEs that have become engaged in the development of climate-induced FSAs in whatever form. After that identification we subsequently collected additional archival information about the cases from corporate sustainability reports, research reports from NGOs and carbon consultants, and one international financial newspaper – the *Financial Times*. As the aim of the study is to explore what the response of MNEs to climate change brings in terms of ideas and further research directions regarding FSA development, this empirical information is presented to illustrate the theoretical concepts.

The Nature of Climate-Induced FSA Development

Before we analyze FSA development induced by global climate change, we first give a conceptualization of FSAs and how they compare with capabilities (a concept more often used in strategy). Rugman and Verbeke (1992) have argued that FSAs consist both of proprietary knowledge and of the capability to coordinate and control the geographically spread assets of an MNE. In due course they have rephrased their view on FSAs as "knowledge bundles that can take the form of intangible assets, learning capabilities and even privileged relationships with outside actors" (Rugman & Verbeke, 2003: 127). The FSA concept is thus strongly aligned with that of a capability,[1] which Amit and Schoemaker (1993:

[1] We shall, therefore, in the remainder of the chapter use the terms "FSA" and "capability" interchangeably.

35) defined as "a firm's capacity to deploy resources, usually in combination, using organizational processes to effect a desired end". The added value of Rugman and Verbeke's framework, however, is that it takes note of the consequences of cross-border activities for competitive advantage by putting emphasis on one capability in particular – that is, managing geographically spread assets. MNEs do not only seek to develop FSAs but will also optimize their FSA–CSA configurations by taking the specific conditions of home and host countries into account.

But how will climate change induce MNEs to transform existing FSAs or build new FSAs? Looking at the activities that MNEs initiate in response to a sustainability issue gives insight into the extent to which they change FSAs (cf. Aragón-Correa & Sharma, 2003). Examples of FSA development are product differentiation based on improving environmental quality for which consumers are willing to pay a premium (Reinhardt, 1998) and in-house development of pollution prevention technologies to lower environmentally induced costs (Christmann, 2000). It must be noted, though, that not all environmental management activities lead to a change in an MNE's FSAs. For example, many technologies to control pollution, which have been developed in response to environmental regulation, have a negligible effect on competitiveness (Hart, 1995; Russo & Fouts, 1997). For most issues the impact and type of FSA development depend on the industry in which an MNE is active. Legislation to stop ozone depletion, for example, had a strategic impact on the chemical industry but largely no effect on other industries, because the chemical industry was the main source of the harmful emissions (Levy, 1997). Climate change, on the other hand, is likely to have a strategic impact on the growth, survival and performance of firms across a much wider range of industries, and is more likely to affect activities that form the core business of an MNE (Hall & Vredenburg, 2003).

The impact of climate change is multifaceted in the sense that for MNEs it involves responding to regulatory action as well as to potential market developments and competitor responses (Kolk & Levy, 2004). One factor that determines the impact of climate change is the technological change that its emergence brings about (Hall & Vredenburg, 2003), and the reaction of MNEs to this change (Helfat & Peteraf, 2003). Climate change may lead to technological change for some industries, but for others it will not, and when it does have an effect on technology it may either enhance or destroy the existing capabilities of incumbent firms (Abernathy & Clark, 1985; Tushman & Anderson, 1986). A competence-enhancing discontinuity creates a major change in a firm's technology, which nevertheless still builds on existing capabilities, whereas a competence-destroying discontinuity necessitates firms' developing completely new capabilities as the existing ones have become obsolete (Tushman & Anderson, 1986). Whether a technological change is competence enhancing or destroying thus depends on a firm's existing capabilities (Gatignon et al., 2002). Still, firms have a choice in how to react to technological change (Helfat & Peteraf, 2003): they can, for example, decide to build on existing capabilities, fundamentally change capabilities within the firm, or acquire new capabilities from outside the firm (Gatignon et al. 2002; Lavie, 2006). If the existing FSAs of incumbents still have value even with a change in technology, they can exert considerable influence on the direction in which FSA transformation moves (Helfat & Peteraf, 2003; Rothaermel & Hill, 2005; Tripsas, 1997) and thus also the extent to which climate change is taken on board.

Lavie (2006) developed a framework that is useful for examining the process by which firms adapt their FSAs in response to technological change caused by climate change. The framework presents three capability reconfiguration mechanisms – *capability evolution*, *capability transformation* and *capability substitution* – that represent ways in which incumbents modify existing capabilities when confronted by technological change. Capability evolution is an incremental learning process, which relies on a firm's dynamic capabilities (Lavie, 2006) to accommodate technological change in a competence-enhancing way. Dynamic capabilities refer to the competence of firms to renew the configuration of their FSAs to maintain a fit with a changing business context (Teece et al., 1997), and can be thought of as value-creating processes within an MNE such as product development, strategic decision-making or forging alliances (Eisenhardt & Martin, 2000). Basically, capability evolution does not replace routines, it only modifies and adjusts them by using internal sources of knowledge. As a consequence, path dependencies determine how existing FSAs evolve over time. In other words, through experimentation FSAs change over time, but the way in which they alter depends on a firm's particular history and rigidity of existing FSA configurations (Lavie, 2006). For incumbents, capability evolution may well be the preferred mode of change because it builds on existing FSAs accumulated over time, thus exploiting asset mass efficiencies (Dierickx & Cool, 1989). However, following this route will not necessarily lead MNEs to become agents of global change that significantly improve the condition of the planet because they keep looking at markets of the past instead of the future (Hart, 1995).

The other two mechanisms are more promising in this respect, as they take more note of future contingencies (Lavie, 2006). In the case of capability transformation, existing FSAs are not completely discarded either, but some of the routines that are part of the FSA are modified or newly acquired as a firm opens up to external sources of knowledge. In a transformation process the reconfiguration takes place at the level of the FSA. The FSA maintains its function, but does so in a different way because of the change in underlying routines. An FSA that is formed through transformation thus consists of past as well as new knowledge and skills (Lavie, 2006), and is at the same time competence-enhancing and competence-destroying (Gatignon et al., 2002). Capability transformation is more forward-looking, and involves higher-order learning, as not only some of the routines that form the FSA change but also the dynamic capabilities that shape the FSA (Zollo & Winter, 2002). For example, higher-order learning takes place when MNEs improve understanding of a sustainability issue, which in turn leads to new R&D activities that make production processes less polluting (Sharma & Vredenburg, 1998). FSA transformation holds promise for the role MNEs play in dealing with climate change, because it leaves the function of key FSAs intact while simultaneously enabling them to find ways to help the planet. For MNEs, FSA transformation seems to be a more realistic option than capability substitution, the third reconfiguration mechanism. Capability substitution assumes competence-destroying technological change that causes a firm's whole portfolio of existing FSAs to become obsolete. This means that the configuration of existing FSAs does not alter, but the value of the FSAs disappears (Lavie, 2006). For substitution to take place a firm must acquire a completely new portfolio of FSAs that take the place of the existing one, as no changes are made to the FSAs that lost their value. This basically means that MNEs have to acquire all new FSAs from outside the firm (Lavie, 2006), as it will be difficult – if not impossible – to bring about competence-destroying change from within the firm (Gatignon et al., 2002). A major challenge for MNEs in deciding what course of action to follow is to assess *a priori* the kind of technological discontinuity that climate change will trigger, as its actual impact will be known only in retrospect (Tushman & Anderson, 1986).

How far MNEs are willing to go in taking responsibility for climate change, and to what extent this contributes to competitive advantage, also depends on the potential spillover effects of technological change throughout the value chain (Hall & Vredenburg, 2003). Formulated more broadly, it makes a considerable difference to MNEs whether the issue affects either their upstream (back-end) or downstream (customer-end) activities, or has an impact on the complete value chain all at once (Rothaermel & Hill, 2005; Tripsas, 1997). Depending on the precise impact of climate change, it may induce an MNE to develop FSAs related to upstream activities for production, R&D, and sourcing of raw materials, capital and labor (Rugman, 2005; Rugman & Verbeke, 2004). For example, one possibility is that climate change may lead a firm to create an FSA from developing a climate-friendly technology through upstream R&D activities, which is then commercialized by way of existing downstream FSAs in market-related activities. However, it may also lead to a change in downstream activities for the customer end of the value chain, including sales, marketing, and distribution (Rugman, 2005; Rugman & Verbeke, 2004). By developing green FSAs in downstream activities, such as green marketing, an MNE could not only commercialize existing technologies that have previously unexploited green attributes, but also create an FSA out of a purchased technology. In both instances, the rise of climate change can have a positive impact on MNEs, because they can leverage some of their existing upstream or downstream FSAs, which creates a buffer against competitors (Tripsas, 1997). A more challenging case, however, is when climate change disrupts FSAs throughout the whole value chain. If MNEs are able to adapt both upstream and downstream activities simultaneously, this will contribute more to a sustainable competitive advantage, because such investments will be more difficult to imitate (Verbeke et al., 2006), and lead to higher-order capabilities of combining technological (upstream) and non-technological (downstream) FSAs (Rothaermel & Hill, 2005). However, it will also be riskier for MNEs to accommodate the change, because they cannot leverage existing FSAs and thus open the door to new entrants. Hence MNEs may also have an incentive to attempt to obstruct such a change (Tripsas, 1997).

Figure 11.1 presents a framework that depicts the nature of climate-induced FSA development; it should be noted, though, that this can be applied more broadly as well. The vertical axis refers to the three FSA reconfiguration mechanisms: FSA substitution, FSA transformation, and FSA evolution. This axis measures how radically MNEs change their key FSAs in response to climate change. The three mechanisms form a continuum, where FSA substitution is the most drastic response to external change, followed by transformation and evolution. The horizontal axis corresponds to the value chain orientation of FSA development. It shows whether an MNE changes FSAs related to downstream activities aimed at customers or those related to upstream activities such as sourcing and production. The ensuing matrix sets out six cells in which particular initiatives of MNEs in response to climate change can be positioned, and shows how MNEs adapt their FSAs.

		FSA value chain orientation	
		Downstream FSA	Upstream FSA
FSA reconfiguration mechanism	FSA evolution	1	2
	FSA transformation	3	4
	FSA substitution	5	6

Fig. 11.1 The nature of FSA development

Applying the Framework to MNEs' Climate Activities

A closer look at MNEs' climate activities first shows, as might have been expected in view of their climate impact, that MNEs in the oil and gas, automotive and electric utility industries, in particular, are developing climate-induced FSAs. The currently prevailing technological FSAs of these industries are the main source of carbon emissions, because they rely on the combustion of fossil fuels. But as fossil fuels also form an important part of the production process of many other manufacturing industries (e.g., chemicals, steel, and electronics), climate-induced FSA development is not restricted to MNEs that produce cars, oil and gas, or electricity.

To begin with the car industry, several events can be discerned in this industry that point to developments regarding a change in this industry's key FSAs. Major players in the car industry seem to agree on the idea that hydrogen-powered fuel cells will replace the internal combustion engine in coming decades. The fuel cell vehicle is climate friendly, because it will remove direct carbon emissions from cars.[2] The launch of the fuel cell vehicle would thus mean that car producers could be positioned in cell 4 – upstream FSA transformation – of Fig. 11.1. The technology is aimed at upstream FSAs as it involves changes in R&D and production from modifying the car engine. It is a case of FSA transformation because the FSA portfolio as a whole keeps its function (producing cars); only the underlying routines will change as a result of the fuel cell technology. But why is it taking the car industry so long to commercialize the fuel cell vehicle? One explanation is that, on top of the fact that it is difficult to develop the fuel cell vehicle itself, it also requires a substitution at the customer end of the value chain. The car industry is relying on chemical and energy industries to supply the hydrogen necessary to attract prospective customers. This necessitates a major breakthrough in the production and distribution of hydrogen, which has not occurred yet because it could be a competence-destroying change for suppliers of fossil fuels.

[2] Nevertheless, it must be noted that there may still be some emissions from the production of hydrogen, but this depends on the way it is produced.

As the car industry will not be able to supply the hydrogen itself, it thus faces a major barrier in bringing the fuel cell vehicle to the market.

To overcome this barrier many car firms first invest in so-called transition technologies, which are predominantly competence-enhancing. This serves several purposes: it allows them to satisfy short-term demand for fuel-efficient and climate-friendly cars; it helps in establishing a green brand image (Anderson & Gardiner, 2006); and it creates the asset mass efficiencies (Dierickx & Cool, 1989) necessary to build the fuel cell vehicle.[3] For example, Ford and BMW are developing the hydrogen-powered internal combustion engine, which Ford (2004) views as "a 'bridging strategy' using existing, proven technologies to deliver the environmental benefits of fuel cells at a fraction of the complexity and cost". More accepted, however, is hybrid technology, which is illustrated by the following statement from DaimlerChrysler (2004):

> For the future we view the fuel cell as the technology which has in the long term the most significant potential of reducing the CO_2 emissions of our products. ... Today we focus on three steps to reduce CO_2 emissions: the continuous improvement of conventional combustion engines, the hybrid technology as the bridge between the conventional powertrain and the fuel cell as the most efficient technology for reducing CO_2.

Firms including Toyota, Honda, Nissan, Ford, and General Motors are following a path similar to DaimlerChrysler by offering hybrid cars. However, whereas Toyota and Honda have gained experience by developing the technology in house for almost a decade, others, including Ford and Nissan, have only quite recently licensed the technology from Toyota (Mackintosh, 2004). As a consequence, Ford and Nissan are not likely to create an upstream FSA in developing hybrid cars because they miss out on the asset mass efficiencies, but merely anticipate a short-term increase in demand for fuel-efficient vehicles due to higher fuel prices. This is illustrated by the fact that Nissan has recently ended the license

[3] Although fuel cell and hybrid technology are quite different, investing in hybrid technology does give car firms the building blocks needed for developing the fuel cell vehicle (Anderson & Gardiner, 2006). Future hybrids decouple the mechanical connection between engine and wheels, which is also a requirement for the fuel cell vehicle (Ricardo Consulting Engineers, 2003).

agreement and decided to build its own hybrids instead, because the market for hybrids has surged beyond expectation (Yomiuri Shimbun, 2006).

Toyota's leadership in hybrids is an exemplary case of a firm that has been combining technological and non-technological capabilities. It was the first to develop the hybrid technology, but the technology became a success because Toyota made good managerial decisions (Helfat & Peteraf, 2003) such as licensing the technology, which led others to also offer hybrid cars, thereby creating market acceptance (Spencer, 2003). Toyota has also successfully bet on future contingencies: that is, it anticipated increasing consumer awareness for fuel prices and the environment, which has spurred the demand for fuel-efficient vehicles. Particularly in the US, it has been easier for the Japanese car firms to position themselves as suppliers of fuel-efficient, clean cars, because traditionally they have stronger credentials in the small-car segment (Simon, 2006a). In other words, for the Japanese firms, offering fuel-efficient vehicles merely involves an evolution in downstream FSAs (cell 1): they apply their dynamic capabilities to maintain a fit with a change in consumer preferences in favor of climate-friendly cars. For US firms, on the other hand, it may entail a transformation in downstream FSAs (cell 3): because they are strong in large cars, such as sports utility vehicles, producing small fuel-efficient cars is somewhat competence-destroying.

While most car firms focus on the technological attributes of car engines, thus changing attributes of their product, General Motors, Ford, Volkswagen, Volvo, and DaimlerChrysler also have a fuel strategy. These firms, for example, are contributing to the development of biofuels, by which they aim to create an upstream-oriented FSA. This strategy does not have a large impact on upstream FSAs in R&D and production, because the use of biofuels requires only modest changes to the engine of a car. Its upstream impact may be considerable, though, as car producers try to push new kinds of fuel suppliers for the users of their cars – a shift towards suppliers that produce ethanol and biodiesel instead of petroleum-based fuels, such as the largest US ethanol producer, Archer Daniels Midland (Harvey et al., 2006). Even though it is not expected that these car firms will turn into large-scale biofuels producers themselves, in adapting their cars they will cooperate more with these biofuels suppliers. A fuel strategy can thus be positioned in cell 2: upstream FSA evolution.

Developments in the oil and gas industry more clearly illustrate the trend of firms that will eventually have to go for a competence-destroying FSA substitution of their upstream and downstream activities (cells 5 and 6) through a fundamental change in their portfolio of key FSAs throughout the whole value chain. However, the direction in which this substitution will take place, and the technologies that will prevail in the coming decades, is still unclear. While firms such as BP, ChevronTexaco, ENI, Royal Dutch/Shell, Suncor, and Total are investing in renewable energy sources for the long term, others, including BHP Billiton, ENI, and Royal Dutch/Shell, are also emphasizing the development of hydrogen, which is an energy carrier not an energy source. All these developments require a sharper reconfiguration of the existing FSA portfolio than in the car industry. Not only will the underlying technology of the main product – energy – change, but so too will other downstream processes, such as distribution and sales. For example, a renewable energy source such as solar energy scarcely builds on existing upstream FSAs in R&D and production. Technologically, the production of solar panels is much closer to the semiconductor industry, which has experience with processing silicon, the main raw material for solar panels (Pernick & Wilder, 2007). Similarly, although oil firms are investing in wind power, it is a capital goods producer such as General Electric that has an FSA in producing wind turbines. Moreover, both renewable energy technologies may lead to a system of decentralized energy distribution, and thus threaten centralized energy distribution, currently a key FSA of the oil industry. It is thus not surprising that most of the oil firms are investing in these renewable technologies only marginally. Only BP and Royal Dutch/Shell have been relatively active through some investments in renewable energy, particularly solar power. BP has recently tried to give this business segment an extra impetus by launching its BP Alternative Energy campaign, thus attempting to create a downstream FSA in renewable energy.

Nevertheless, current developments in the oil and gas industry do share some similarities with the car industry: oil and gas firms also invest in competence-enhancing transition technologies, thus choosing an evolutionary path at first. A statement by Royal Dutch/Shell (2004) illustrates the role of transition technologies in the oil industry:

> Given that natural gas has the lowest carbon emissions per unit of energy produced (e.g., electricity) of all the fossil fuels, it offers the world an important bridge to a lower carbon economy as alternative energy technologies are developed and allowed to reach economic maturity.

In the choice for transition technologies many oil and gas firms take their initial FSA configurations as the starting point for the development of climate-induced FSAs, thus showing the importance of path dependencies (cf. Helfat, 1997). MNEs that already have a strong position in the production of natural gas, such as the BG Group, BP, ENI, ExxonMobil, Halliburton, Norsk Hydro, and Royal Dutch/Shell, conceive the changing context due to the emergence of climate change as an opportunity to strengthen this segment of their firms. ExxonMobil (2004) exemplifies this:

> As a leading supplier of clean burning natural gas, ExxonMobil is well positioned to contribute to efforts to address greenhouse gas emissions through fuel switching.

For firms that more heavily rely on the production of coal, climate change is a driver to develop other transition technologies. BHP Billiton and Rio Tinto, which have strong positions in the production of coal, are both investing in clean coal technology and technologies to offset emissions by geological sequestration (the capture and storage of emissions in underground reservoirs). Oil firms such as Statoil and BP have also started to invest in carbon capture and storage, but are doing this cooperatively to spread the risk, thus creating a shared capability instead of an FSA. It thus seems that, although the long-term strategies of oil and gas firms would mean a competence-destroying substitution of the complete FSA portfolio throughout the whole value chain (cell 5), current developments more strongly indicate a competence-enhancing FSA evolution in downstream activities, merely marketing existing activities in gas and renewables more proactively (cell 1).

Whereas current activities in automotives and oil and gas hint at long-run developments whereby MNEs will eventually change (some of) their key FSAs, in other sectors, such as electric utilities, chemicals, electronics, and metals and manufacturing, efforts are focused more on developing green FSAs for the near future. Consequently, firms rely more on existing FSA configurations. They change some routines, and their FSA base slowly evolves in a climate-friendly direction. Electric utilities, for example, are drawing on their key FSAs in the generation, trade and sales of electricity to develop green FSAs. Most utilities are not involved in the development of renewable energy sources themselves, but instead purchase these from technology suppliers such as General Electric (cf. Marcus & Geffen, 1998). However, quite a few, including American Electric Power, CLP Holdings, Endesa, Exelon, Iberdrola, and Scottish & Southern Energy, are expanding generation capacity that is based on renewable energy sources. Such a reconfiguration of energy sources for electricity production can be competence-enhancing, because utilities use their existing downstream FSAs to market energy to end users. Iberdrola (2004), for instance, notes that it has a program for "the promotion of electricity produced from renewable energy sources in the internal electricity market, making electricity users aware of the benefits of renewable energies".

Another recent example of an MNE shifting attention to the green attributes of its technology development is General Electric, with the launch of its Ecomagination campaign. General Electric was already engaged in the development of wind turbines and clean coal technology, but decided to group clean technologies together under one brand (thus creating a green FSA in marketing) and increase investment in these technologies (Harvey, 2005). Depending on the success of marketing its green segment, a conglomerate such as General Electric may eventually expand this strategy further. In other words, even though these firms do not change their key FSAs, they respond to climate change by using their existing key FSAs to develop green FSAs related to successful marketing of the sustainability attributes of their products. Nevertheless, such activities are not necessarily restricted to downstream sales activities, but may also involve a change in upstream production, sourcing, and R&D activities: it can thus put them in cells 1 and 2 simultaneously. Some firms also focus predominantly on sourcing: British Telecom and Du Pont, for example, have decided to source a significant part of their energy consumption from renewable resources. It is arguable whether this leads to an FSA of their own, although some MNEs can undoubtedly put substantial pressure on their suppliers. Du Pont (2004) believes it can have such an impact, and motivates its decision as follows:

> We will source 10% of our global energy use in the year 2010 from renewable resources. We are serious about the need for renewable energy to be a part of our future. We are providing a strong "market signal" that there will be at least one major energy consumer ready to buy; and that we will work with suppliers of renewable energy resources to stimulate their availability at a cost competitive with best available fossil-derived alternatives.

Current evidence on MNEs' climate activities shows that most efforts are still evolutionary, and focus particularly on downstream activities, which means that MNEs market existing products differently, with a stronger focus on green attributes. Nonetheless, this sometimes also entails investments in upstream production and sourcing activities to maintain a fit with green FSAs in sales and marketing. Yet current developments in the car industry do suggest some bolder steps leading to upstream transformation of FSAs, but with mixed success. Whereas hybrids are experiencing a breakthrough, fuel cells are still far from being commercialized. An issue such as global climate change, which has only recently started to attract business attention, clearly does not lead immediately to radical changes such as a competence-destroying substitution of complete FSA portfolios of large MNEs. This is probably still reserved only for small, niche players. In making climate-induced investments, MNEs want to maintain their flexibility to safeguard their organizations against the uncertainties that exist regarding the future of international climate policy. Moreover, the risk of making an irreversible green mistake is quite high, because it is still unclear for many industries which climate-friendly technology will prevail in coming years.

The Geography of Climate-Induced FSA Development

The organizing framework on the nature of FSA development shown in Fig. 11.1 looks at this process at a corporate level. However, this does not mean that the development of FSAs to adapt to climate change occurs only at MNE headquarters, or is implemented uniformly throughout the global organization. As stated in the introduction, the role that climate change plays in MNE strategy is determined by a broad conglomerate of factors involving governmental as well as societal and market forces, working at different geographical levels. There may well be particular geographical factors that are conducive to a climate-induced change in FSAs, but this also means that the change benefits the MNE at a specific location only. In other words, MNEs not only have the option to develop or change FSAs internally, but can also optimize their FSA–CSA configurations by taking the specific conditions of home and host countries into account, so that CSAs form the starting point for FSA development (Rugman & Verbeke, 1992). Climate change thus adds new dimensions to what regionalization or globalization in terms of production and/or sales might mean for an MNE and its network, regarding possible spill-overs of such concerns to other (core) activities and other locations, and how organizational responses are coordinated and controlled (cf. Rugman & Verbeke, 2004).

Climate change creates a geographically dispersed and moving target: while it may form a threat in one location, it can be an opportunity in another. Regardless of whether regional or local characteristics are seen as a potential advantage or disadvantage, liability or risk, geographical differences are something to be faced by MNEs, and those firms that excel in doing this are the ones most likely to develop climate-induced FSAs. Hence learning from climate change does not merely mean that MNEs need dynamic capabilities to cope with technological change; constantly rejuvenating FSAs by being responsive to a wide range of climate-relevant CSAs is what gives them an edge over their competitors. For example, MNEs operating outside their home regions, upstream and/or down-stream, may have difficulty in accommodating host-country concerns and approaches on climate change appropriately, often referred to as the "liability of foreignness" (Zaheer, 1995). If the cost of dealing with host-country concerns becomes so high that it forms a serious threat, an MNE may choose to retire an FSA it once possessed in the host market, or may transfer it to another market (Helfat & Peteraf, 2003). On the other hand, spillover effects can also extend the impact of climate change to firms active in countries without stringent environmental regulations (e.g., in countries that refused to ratify the Kyoto Protocol) (Christmann & Taylor, 2001; Hoffman, 2005). This creates an opportunity for MNEs, because they can replicate, redeploy, or recombine green FSAs built up in countries with strict regulations (Helfat & Peteraf, 2003). Using geographically spread assets proactively in adapting to climate change is a dynamic capability in itself, which complements a change in FSAs in response to climate-induced technological change.

But what kind of geographical factors form climate-relevant CSAs? In general, CSAs are factors such as availability of natural resources, access to markets to sell products and services, factor costs (labor, capital and land), and knowledge-intensive assets such as skilled labor and public infrastructure (Dunning, 1998). These factors form CSAs for all firms investing in a specific country (Makino et al., 2004), and therefore attract MNEs driven by natural resource-seeking, efficiency-seeking, market-seeking or strategic asset-seeking behavior (Dunning, 1993). With the global intentions of the Kyoto Protocol it seemed at first that climate change policy would not result in climate-related CSAs, because it was intended to be quite homogeneous throughout the world. However, in spite of this global agreement, national regulatory responses have varied considerably since 1997, with the EU-ETS and the US rejection of Kyoto as two extremes, leading after all to a wide variety of climate-related CSAs. What is more, many countries in the EU and states in the US even have location-specific climate change regulations such as subsidies to stimulate investments in the development of renewable energy technologies (IEA, 2004).

CSAs are not only a result of a country's regulations; the broader institutional framework also plays a role (Makino et al., 2004). For example, the presence in the local context of a network of other firms or non-profit organizations that are in the process of developing climate-friendly technologies may be complementary to an MNE's own FSA development. Also, consumer awareness of climate change may form a CSA, because it makes them responsive to green marketing campaigns. MNEs may benefit from climate-related CSAs either because they already own facilities in this particular location or because they move to these locations in an effort to seek strategic assets to complement their existing FSAs (Dunning, 1998). For example, strict environmental regulations in the home country may act as a CSA and incite MNEs to develop technologies by which they gain a competitive advantage over their rivals (Porter & van der Linde, 1995).[4] However, host-country locations can also form a potential source of FSAs, as an MNE's subsidiaries may tap into external local knowledge (Almeida & Phene, 2004). The EU emissions trading scheme, for example, has implications for home-region firms in particular, but also (potentially) for "outsiders", host-region MNEs for which the EU is important in terms of production facilities and/or sales (Pinkse, 2007), and/or which compete with EU firms on non-EU markets. The locus (or loci) of origin of FSA development thus depends on the geographic spread of an MNE, as it is partly determined by the "local" institutional context.

MNEs are thus confronted by a wide variety of climate-related CSAs (sometimes even state-specific advantages), which may incite the development of climate-induced FSAs. However, the impact that those climate-related CSAs have on the way MNEs transform existing or develop new FSAs depends to a large extent on the geographical origin of FSA development. If an MNE perceives climate change as a global issue, decision-making power on this issue will be at the level of its headquarters. In this case, an MNE believes that the consequences of climate change will have a significant impact on the firm globally, which is therefore dealt with at the highest management level. Headquarters' support considerably increases the potential that MNEs have for becoming global leaders in tackling climate change. However, since the worldwide institutionalization of climate change policies is still quite fragmented, many

[4] Although it must be noted that this depends partly on the size of the home country. MNEs from small economies are less likely to be affected by home-country regulations than firms from large economies such as the US (Rugman & Verbeke, 1998).

MNEs may also deal with the issue through their regional centers (e.g., decisions to participate actively in the EU-ETS), or national subsidiaries (Husted & Allen, 2006; Rugman, 2005). It then becomes a matter of local responsiveness to climate-related institutional pressures from regulators, NGOs, or the investment community (cf. Brewer, 2005). The more localized the decision is, however, the less likely it is that climate change will have a significant strategic impact on the MNE as a whole, because it will be quite difficult for a local subsidiary to convince MNE headquarters that climate change requires a proactive response. Instead of a global leader, an MNE may then produce local heroes instead.

This is not to say that a local response is of no use at all, however: if through their subsidiaries MNEs are located in countries that have been front runners on climate change, then they have been facing climate-related pressures for a longer period of time already. This may have enabled them to start learning from the issue from an early stage. Therefore, if a country initiates new regulations to curb greenhouse gas emissions, this will probably be a much greater shock to domestic firms than to MNEs. Nonetheless, experience with climate change in a specific location will create a cross-border advantage only if the MNEs are able to transfer FSAs from other locations. Another question relating to the geography of climate-induced FSA development is thus whether MNEs will develop different types of location-bound FSA that fit with the CSAs of individual countries, or non-location-bound FSAs that can be transferred and deployed globally. The peculiarities of MNEs arise particularly from the potential to leverage non-location-bound FSAs. Similar or identical procedures for every subsidiary facilitate the exchange of experiences, breed internal consistency, enable benchmarking, and are clear to outsiders. Some MNEs therefore strive to harmonize their environmental management system and standards at all locations (Christmann, 2004). Yet the situation in specific countries, for example, as a result of stakeholder or government pressure, may create location-bound FSAs as well (related to local responsiveness) (Rugman & Verbeke, 2001b). In some cases these can be used only in the country in question; in others they might help to increase MNEs' competitiveness elsewhere.

The transferability of an FSA typically depends on the attributes of the knowledge bundles that establish it (Singh, 2007): the higher the tacitness of the knowledge, the less transferable it becomes (Kogut & Zander, 1993). A higher level of tacitness may be due to the extent to which an FSA results from linkages with external parties (e.g., governmental bodies, universities, or NGOs). These linkages are in general much better in an MNE's home country (or region), which explains findings that many MNEs are organized on a regional basis (cf. Ghemawat, 2003; Rugman & Verbeke, 2004). Host-country attributes also determine the transferability of an FSA to a foreign location (Cuervo-Cazurra et al., 2007). Transfer of FSAs to relatively "distant" countries (Ghemawat, 2001) in terms of dissimilarity of environmental regulations usually results in higher adaptation costs (in order to realize location-specific "linking" investments) for alignment with the CSAs of these particular host countries (King & Shaver, 2001; Rugman & Verbeke, 2005). Tsai and Child (1997), for example, noted that the transfer of environmental best practices is not always without problems. A global approach to environmental management usually relies on advanced technologies, but successfully implementing these in developing countries can be very expensive, owing to a lack of adequate infrastructure there.

Home- and host-country attributes as well as the nature of the knowledge contained in an FSA together determine whether MNEs develop different types of location-bound FSAs that fit with the CSAs of individual countries, or one non-location-bound FSA that is globally (or regionally) transferable. Although, in the case of climate change, a high potential for transferability can be expected, because most climate-induced FSAs are relevant at many different (or even all) locations where MNEs have production and/or sales, international institutional differences may also lead to typical location-bound FSAs. Figure 11.2 shows a framework that depicts the geography of climate-induced FSA development by combining, on the vertical axis, the location of the decision-making power for climate change and the origin of FSA development – corporate headquarters, regional center, or national subsidiary – with, on the horizontal axis, the transferability of climate-induced FSAs. The framework shows the extent to which it can be expected that an MNE will become a global leader in tackling climate change. If, for example, an MNE initiates investments in non-location-bound FSAs in climate change mitigation from corporate headquarters (cell 2), there is

Origin of FSA development	Transferability of FSAs: Location-bound FSA	Transferability of FSAs: Non-location-bound FSA
Corporate headquarters	1	2
Regional centers	3	4
National subsidiaries	5	6

Fig. 11.2 The geography of FSA development

more potential for a lasting impact on the sustainability of the planet, compared with some local-bound initiatives in distant subsidiaries (cell 5).

Applying the Framework To MNEs' Climate Activities

Looking at MNE's climate activities, it seems that climate-related FSAs have a variety of sources, both geographically and institutionally. MNEs develop FSAs in response to climate-related CSAs, usually of their home country, but sometimes also of one of their host countries. It appears that country-specific climate policies have an effect on MNEs, but not always the desired effect of spurring innovation. In the US, for instance, many firms (particularly electric utilities) are participating in the Environmental Protection Agency's Climate Leaders program. However, currently this merely seems to affect initiatives to set voluntary emission reduction targets rather than FSA development. In the EU, the regional emissions trading scheme is intended to provide a stimulus for firms with energy-intensive activities to become engaged in climate-induced FSA development. Yet it turns out that this scheme particularly influences electric utilities, which by and large do not seem to respond by developing new FSAs either, but instead pass on the costs of their emission allowances to their customers (Hasselknippe & Røine, 2006; Morrison, 2006). It thus seems that country-specific climate change policies are not decisive for MNEs' decision to develop climate-induced FSAs.

However, what also becomes apparent is that, particularly for the purpose of developing climate-friendly technologies, many MNEs seem to prefer to cooperate with external parties. This is in line with what was noted earlier, namely that a country's climate change policy does not determine MNE behavior in isolation; it also depends on the broader institutional framework (Makino et al., 2004). As a consequence, the origin of an FSA does not always depends on the location of corporate headquarters or subsidiaries; it also depends on the location of the external actor – for example, a government agency, university, or other firms – with which an MNE cooperates. For the car industry, for example, one potential reason to opt for cooperation is the fact that pressure to develop these technologies comes from not only the increased attention paid to climate change, but also from the recent surge in oil prices (Mackintosh, 2005a). To reduce the dependence on oil as the primary fuel, car firms spend considerable funds on the development of alternative fuel technologies. Controlling costs is therefore clearly a motive for partnering with other firms. Another potential reason is the uncertainty about which technology will prevail. MNEs may seek to acquire knowledge from external parties, or share knowledge with competitors to build support for their technology in the early stages of FSA development (cf. Spencer, 2003).

To develop new climate-induced FSAs, several MNEs have ties with institutions such as universities and research institutes: Suncor is funding a Clean Energy Laboratory at the University of British Colombia; ExxonMobil is investing in the Global Climate and Energy Project of Stanford University; and ChevronTexaco is co-funding the Massachusetts Institute of Technology's Joint Program on Science and Policy for Global Climate Change. These particular firms are focusing on ties with universities and research institutes in their home country. However, several others are also looking across borders, to affiliate with institutes in host countries. Australian-based Rio Tinto, for example, is participating in the research efforts of the US-based Electric Power Research Institute, and BP (together with Ford) has a partnership with Princeton University, called the Carbon Mitigation Initiative. This initiative has the aim "to resolve fundamental scientific, environmental and technological issues key to public acceptance of carbon management strategies" (Ford, 2004). Technology for carbon capture and storage is one direction in which it is bearing fruit. It must be noted that, for many of these cooperative efforts, the exact goal of linkages with universities and research institutes is not always openly delineated. While such ties can be strategic asset-seeking behavior, and lead to knowledge creation and transfer, the association with respectable institutes and the demonstration of climate change activity cannot be ruled out as (additional) motives for such cooperation.

Cooperation with other firms often has a less ambiguous purpose: this more clearly aims at the development of new technologies. However, whether it also leads to climate-induced FSAs or shared capabilities instead, and at which location(s), depends on the type of partner that is being sought. Many car and oil manufacturers are working together with firms that own a specific technology. This usually includes small, local niche players as well as large global competitors. For example, to develop biofuels, both DaimlerChrysler and Volkswagen are cooperating with Choren industries, a German firm that specializes in gasification technology for the production of energy from biomass. Likewise, Ford and DaimlerChrysler have both entered partnerships with the Canadian niche player Ballard, which has developed fuel cell technology, to further improve fuel cells for use in cars. Two Canadian oil firms, Suncor and Petro-Canada, are working with several local firms to develop an infrastructure for fuel cell vehicles and wind energy, respectively. Because the MNEs engaged in these partnerships are not only collaborators in these particular technologies, but also close competitors, it will be difficult to develop an FSA, as it is inevitable that at least one competitor will own the same technology. There are more opportunities to create an FSA out of collaboration with firms from other industries, because the partners will use the ensuing technology quite differently in their downstream activities. Dow Chemical and General Motors, for example, are working together on the development of fuel cells, but for different purposes.

If climate-related CSAs stimulate upstream FSA development in R&D that translates into new technological capabilities, this would, on the face of it, lead to a position in the right-hand column of Fig. 11.2. It should be relatively easy to transfer a technology to other geographical locations, regardless of whether it originates from corporate headquarters, a regional center, or a national subsidiary. A public-policy-driven CSA, such as a subsidy or tax break for the development of renewable energy technologies, typically has a function only at the start of the life cycle of an FSA, but once the technology becomes incorporated in a firm's products it can be redeployed to other locations (Helfat & Peteraf, 2003), thus creating a non-location-bound FSA. Climate-friendly technologies, such as those related to hydrogen or fuel cells, are no longer of a tacit nature, or tied to external parties such as local governments, and sourcing and production of these technologies can take place anywhere in the world (cf. Rugman & Verbeke, 2004). However, if the CSA continues to be of value further down the FSA life cycle, transferability becomes more difficult. For example, for some specific technologies related to renewable energy, the location of production depends on a country's natural capital. Such geographic site specificity is crucial for hydroelectric and wind power, which require mountainous areas and sufficient wind speed, respectively (Russo, 2003). Such an FSA cannot simply be redeployed, but needs to be recombined with a similar CSA in another geographical location (Helfat & Peteraf, 2003).

The same holds for the development of cars that run on biofuels based on so-called flex-fuel technology, which enables the use of ethanol (a biofuel) as well as gasoline. Car manufacturers including Ford, Fiat, Volkswagen, and General Motors have first introduced this technology in their Brazilian subsidiaries (Johnson, 2006). Since the oil crises in the 1970s the Brazilian government has stimulated local sugar producers to invest in ethanol to reduce dependence on foreign oil, thereby creating a CSA in ethanol. Currently, an FSA in flex-fuel technology is still location-bound in foreign subsidiaries, because the natural resource necessary for this technology is readily available in this specific location. It could thus be positioned in cell 5 of Fig. 11.2. However, after President Bush announced intentions to lower the US's dependence on foreign oil in his 2006 State of the Union address, interest in ethanol as a fuel has also increased in the US (Simon, 2006b), which may form a CSA for the US in coming years. Therefore, for car firms, flex-fuel technology may well become an FSA that moves from cell 5 to cell 3, spanning the whole American continent.

Nevertheless, most technologies for climate-induced FSAs are more likely to depend strongly on CSAs when they have advanced further in the FSA life cycle, and have moved downstream and reached the sales stage. ChevronTexaco (2004), for example, states that:

> We invest in a variety of renewable and alternative energy technologies and believe that those energy sources will be important in the overall mix of energy for the global economy in the future. But widespread application will depend on many factors, including the rate of technological development, market acceptance, and demonstration of economic viability.

A lack of transferability of FSAs is thus not necessarily the result of the tacitness of the knowledge on which they are based, but is instead determined by the ability of MNEs to create market acceptance for new technologies to realize global distribution of sales (Cuervo-Cazurra et al. 2007; Rugman & Verbeke, 2004). In other words, although MNEs may have some influence on market acceptance through marketing campaigns, it depends largely on CSAs related to consumer responsiveness to climate-friendly products and services, and on the availability of the necessary public infrastructure. For example, two main problems related to a successful launch of marketable fuel cell cars are the relatively high costs compared with conventional cars and the lack of a hydrogen infrastructure (Griffiths, 2005). High costs are likely to impede transferability of these cars to low-income countries, and the establishment of a hydrogen infrastructure is necessary in any country where an MNE wants to sell fuel cell cars.[5] Mackintosh (2005b) has formulated this problem of setting up a hydrogen infrastructure as follows:

[5] The high costs of setting up a hydrogen infrastructure are an exemplary case of the difficulties that MNEs face in transferring FSAs, as it requires considerable linking investments to align an FSA with particular host-country CSAs (cf. Rugman & Verbeke, 2005).

> Drivers will not want hydrogen cars until there is a network of filling stations. But no company will invest in filling stations – and hydrogen production – until there is a critical mass of cars.

To find a solution to this problem it appears that MNEs will have to work with other private and public partners to create the necessary infrastructure to bring the fuel cell car to markets worldwide. Activity in this direction can already be observed. Petro-Canada (2004) reports on a collaborative framework for a hydrogen infrastructure, as it is engaged with Ballard Power Systems and Methanex Corporation in a project for a fuel distribution network for hydrogen in Canada. Likewise, Air Products and Chemicals (2004) states that it

> is working with many public, private and governmental organizations to develop and promote the commercialization of hydrogen as a fuel in portable, stationary and transportation fuel markets and is leading the development of hydrogen infrastructure and fuel-handling technologies to enable the commercialization of hydrogen fuel cells.

However, since political relations with the home government are generally much better than with host-country governments (Baron, 1995), downstream FSAs for which sales rely on business–government cooperation are likely to stay bound to the home country or home region (cell 1 or cell 3).

In general, FSAs that rely on organizational capabilities to coordinate and control greenhouse gas emissions are even more problematic to transfer than climate-friendly technologies: not only does such knowledge build on particular CSAs, it is often also of a tacit nature, and organizationally embedded. This is most clearly seen in emissions trading. Currently, an FSA in emissions trading will be difficult to transfer to other affiliates within an MNE, because of the international fragmentation of support for the Kyoto Protocol. A global framework for emissions trading has not yet been established, but remains restricted to regional initiatives. The EU-ETS is the most prominent example, and an FSA based on trading in this scheme is constrained to this region, as it has not yet been linked to other schemes (cell 3). What is more, even though, when new trading schemes are established, MNEs can build on their learning experience with the EU-ETS, this experience may be of limited value. It typically involves tacit, market-specific knowledge such as rules for allocating and trading allowances, which tend to differ considerably, even within the EU (Boemare & Quirion, 2002), and it is by and large organizationally embedded. Successfully trading of emission allowances often depends on good communication between trading and production departments – an organizational capability that cannot be transferred easily. For these reasons, such organizational capabilities cannot be replicated, but need instead to be recombined to fit local conditions (Helfat & Peteraf, 2003). When recombining is perceived as too cumbersome, however, MNEs may restrict trading to the location of their headquarters or particular subsidiaries (cell 1 or cell 5).

To illustrate, Barclays (2004) has been participating in the UK emissions trading scheme (a predecessor of the EU-ETS), but states that it cannot use this experience for the EU-ETS, because participation there is restricted to energy-intensive industries. For similar reasons, Unilever (2004) does not aim to develop a global strategy for emissions trading, but considers it the responsibility of local (or regional) management. Nevertheless, it is notable that some MNEs do seem to have the intention to create a non-location-bound FSA from emissions trading. Several MNEs, including Dow Chemical, Norsk Hydro, Repsol and Royal Dutch/Shell, have established a separate business unit at headquarters that is responsible for participation in emissions trading schemes for the MNE as a whole. These firms thus seem to have the intention to create a non-location-bound FSA in emissions trading (cell 2), and arguably do so because they see possibilities for arbitrage to exploit international differences in emissions trading schemes (cf. Ghemawat, 2003).

On the whole it appears that, with regard to the geography of climate-induced FSA development, MNEs are not positioned in the right-hand column of Fig. 11.2, as stated above, but more often in the left-hand column. There are still many institutional barriers for the transfer of technologies or organizational capabilities (Cuervo-Cazurra et al. 2007), because CSAs play a crucial role in the whole FSA life cycle. Most climate-induced FSAs are therefore likely to stay location-bound, at least for the near future. Only when proper institutional frameworks, such as a hydrogen infrastructure or an emissions trading scheme, are set up on a global scale, will MNEs have the possibility to freely transfer their climate-induced FSAs. This seems to be a problem particularly for transfer of such FSAs to less developed countries, where implementation of such institutions is not to be expected shortly.

Then, again, international transfer of climate-induced FSAs to developing countries may receive an impulse from another institutional arrangement of the Kyoto Protocol – or, that is, one of the Kyoto Mechanisms: the Clean Development Mechanism (CDM). CDM allows countries and firms to take advantage of reductions in emissions resulting from cross-border investments in developing countries (Grubb et al., 1999). As Arquit Nederberger and Saner (2005: 12) explain, CDM gives

> opportunities to technology providers to expand their market for state-of-the-art energy-efficient and climate-friendly technologies to developing countries, which, without CDM financing, may not be commercially viable in a developing country context.

In other words, a country's eligibility for CDM creates a new CSA, to which MNEs can respond by replicating their FSAs from headquarters to this particular location (cell 2 of Fig. 11.2). One example of a firm that has already started to make use of the CDM is the Spanish utility Endesa. Endesa (2006) is the largest privately owned electric utility in Latin America, and is using CDM to transfer some its technologies to this region. Another firm interested in CDM is Nippon Steel (2005: 17):

> Nippon Steel would like to utilize the Kyoto Mechanisms to contribute to a reduction of CO_2 on a global scale through the transfer of its world's top energy conservation and environmental countermeasure technologies.

Conclusion: A Research Agenda

This chapter has argued that a global sustainability issue such as climate change has the capacity to induce MNEs to develop FSAs that not only lead to environmental improvements as such, but may also affect firms' profitability, growth and survival. We have presented two frameworks to analyze the nature and geography of such FSA development. Subsequently, they have been applied to the case of climate change, using illustrative material from MNEs in several global industries. Climate change is an issue that affects a wide range of firms around the world, and which has implications beyond the "pure" environmental dimensions, being linked to energy security and efficiency, and the fate of the planet more broadly. It has become a topic of societal, regulatory and corporate attention in recent years, and has been brought to the fore as an "inconvenient truth" that requires a concerted policy approach. Regardless of one's position in this debate, climate change provides a clear opportunity to consider how (green) FSAs (and FSA–CSA configurations) can develop and change, in a context where there is considerable attention for this topic, not only by environmentalists and policymakers, but also by investors and major multinationals who have become rather active. At the same time, there is also considerable uncertainty and complexity, in view of the diversity of contexts and policy responses, which means that FSAs developed in response to this "moving target" will need constant rejuvenation. The climate change issue can thus give insight into dynamic capabilities, into how MNEs may be able to learn on various fronts, both from the issue itself and from the way in which it is being dealt with in a range of countries and industries. The two frameworks are meant to help identify and understand this, and to reflect on possibilities and barriers, also in anticipating future developments and exercising leadership that reckons with strategic and societal concerns. Managers may want to include this in their consideration of the risks and rewards of investing in FSAs, and policymakers to better understand how CSAs can be shaped and firms be (in)directly induced to invest in FSAs.

The application of the frameworks to the climate change issue showed that MNEs from different industries are developing different kinds of FSA. Moreover, the types of organizational process that are set in motion involve the development of green FSAs for some firms and the change of key FSAs for others. Still we can conclude that, as it currently stands, climate-induced FSA development may lead to a more radical, competence-destroying FSA reconfiguration for a few industries only; most MNEs stay relatively close to their current activities. A strategic reorientation is most likely to occur in the oil and gas and automotive industries, but will not happen in the short run. A reason for this is that MNEs in these industries do not agree on the type of technology that will prevail in coming years, and most firms thus invest first in competence-enhancing transition technologies, thereby still relying on existing FSA configurations.

It can be observed that climate change as a source of competitive advantage is likely to occur in high-salience industries such as those mentioned above – that is, those most confronted by the climate issue. In addition, continuous reflection on FSA development via internal investments (dynamic capabilities) also seems important for firms specialized in goods or services that are instrumental in the mitigation of climate change impacts, or in anticipating, influencing or responding to public policy developments. For the remaining firms, climate change appears not to become a main source of profitability and growth, even though they may obtain legitimacy from acting visibly and credibly in the field of climate change. For them, there is no compelling reason to develop FSAs internally in managing climate change. Their route for addressing the issue is likely to go through external markets: for example, purchasing greener and productivity-enhancing technologies, adopting externally developed tools and routines (such as on mitigation, emissions trading, and measurement instruments), and "outsourcing" certain activities to outsiders (who can, for example, take care of lobbying and stakeholder management). In this situation, FSAs may arise from "internalization arbitrage" (Rugman & Verbeke, 2004; cf. Ghemawat, 2003) in the sense that MNEs obtain advantage from proximity and easy access to multiple external markets that offer such best available practices.

With regard to the geography of climate-induced development, it can be noted that many MNEs still focus on their home regions, for example, when looking for private or public partners with which to interact for the development of new technologies. Region-bound FSA development seems likely in the case of emissions trading, because of the specific location of emissions trading schemes (currently operational on a large scale only in the EU); transferability will also depend on (policy) developments and related opportunities for using these FSAs in other regions. With regard to technological FSAs, a home-region focus may hinder transferability in the later sales stages, but not so much in the early production stages of the FSA development chain.

It should be noted, however, that market responses to global climate change have emerged only recently, which means that our study of climate-induced FSA development could be only exploratory. Further research will be needed, also using other sources of information, when possible, to arrive at a more extensive set of data that allows for an examination of the determinants of such FSA development, and the possible performance implications. The issue of climate change provides a fertile area in which existing international business theories can be tested, and from which new theoretical insights into the dynamics of the interaction between MNEs and their national and international environment can be induced. Climate change particularly illustrates the exact workings of the interactions between FSAs and CSAs. What follows are more concrete research areas for the relationship between climate change and international business.

First, it will be interesting to assess whether transferability pays off throughout the Triad (North America, Europe, and Asia-Pacific) and, if so, under what conditions. For example, will (bi)regional or (semi)"global", or highly internationalized and/or diversified MNEs fare better in this respect? It could be argued that firms internationalize partly to avoid stringent domestic regulation, which means that highly internationalized MNEs have the opportunity to do less about climate change in their host countries. MNEs located in regions of the Triad without stringent climate change regulations (e.g., North America and Asia-Pacific) would thus have the possibility to use their geographical spread to avoid making any changes to their existing FSA configurations. But geographical spread could also motivate MNEs to exploit climate-induced FSAs overseas. In addition, more international firms are also exposed to more diverse public pressures, suggesting that it might be more efficient to have one single "leading edge" strategy towards climate change based on non-location-bound FSAs that encompasses different worldwide standards simultaneously, rather then a range of country-specific responses to each standard/regulation individually.

Second, a related question is what consequences foreign direct investment (FDI) has for emissions in developing countries. Fossil-fuel-based energy use in developing countries such as China and India is on the rise, given their rapid industrialization. At the same time, MNEs are often highly active in these countries by means of FDI. Inward FDI in developing countries is generally believed to be associated with better (more efficient) technologies and production methods. This could lead to spillover effects to local firms, particularly because one of the Kyoto mechanisms – the Clean Development Mechanism – potentially accelerates knowledge transfers to developing countries. It could thus be hypothesized that more inward FDI would reduce emissions. However, factor conditions and regulation could also have induced MNEs to locate their polluting activities in developing countries in order to exploit local circumstances rather than to improve them. In this case, FDI would be associated with higher emissions. It can thus be questioned whether inward FDI by MNEs increases or reduces emissions.

Third, to what extent and under what circumstances do climate change measures affect corporate performance? Organizational activities induced by climate change could present unique FSAs, thus leading to competitive advantages and higher corporate performance, or less ambitiously could result in energy efficiencies that reduce costs. But, on the other hand, measures to deal with climate change may in certain circumstances (depending on for example industry/location/firm-specific aspects) also impose additional costs, which may or may not be worthwhile investments that lead to high returns in the longer run. An additional question that could be asked is what are the sustainability implications of these firms' attempts to address this global problem. Will MNEs be able to contribute in a significant way to the solution for a changing climate?

The exploration of the climate change issue clearly raises a number of questions and several insights into MNE strategy and FSA–CSA configurations that may also be interesting for scholars working on more "mainstream" topics in international business. Climate change is an exemplary, perhaps even unique, issue to investigate how MNEs respond to socially relevant issues of sustainability, because it involves fossil fuel production and consumption. Many MNEs (particularly in energy-intensive industries) recognize the strategic impact and, accordingly, mention activities that seem to hint at initiatives to develop green FSAs or change key FSAs. The study of climate change thus forms a research "frontier" that also clearly illustrates the complexities and societal relevance of international business in the current epoch.

References

Abernathy, W. J., & Clark, K. B. (1985). Innovation: Mapping the winds of creative destruction. *Research Policy, 14*(1), 3–22.

Air Products and Chemicals. (2004). *Air products and chemicals' response to the carbon disclosure project 2*. http://www.cdproject.net. Accessed 8 July 2006.

Almeida, P., & Phene, A. (2004). Subsidiaries and knowledge creation: The influence of the MNC and host country on innovation. *Strategic Management Journal, 25*(8–9), 847–864.

Amit, R., & Schoemaker, P. J. H. (1993). Strategic assets and organizational rent. *Strategic Management Journal, 14*(1), 33–46.

Anderson, M., & Gardiner, D. (2006). *Climate risk and energy in the auto sector*. Ceres.

Aragón-Correa, J. A., & Sharma, S. (2003). A contingent resource-based view of proactive corporate environmental strategy. *Academy of Management Review, 28*(1), 71–88.

Arquit Nederberger, A., & Saner, R. (2005). Exploring the relationship between FDI flows and CDM potential. *Transnational Corporations, 14*(1), 1–40.

Barclays. (2004). *Barclays' response to the carbon disclosure project 2*. http://www.cdproject.net. Accessed 8 July 2006.

Baron, D. P. (1995). Integrated strategy: Market and nonmarket components. *California Management Review, 37*(2), 47–65.

Boemare, C., & Quirion, P. (2002). Implementing greenhouse gas trading in Europe: Lessons from economic literature and international experiences. *Ecological Economics, 43*(2), 213–230.

Brewer, T. (2005). Global warming and climate change: New issues for business strategy, government policy, and research on business–government relations. In R. Grosse (Ed.), *International business and government relations in the 21st century* (pp. 147–170). Cambridge University Press.

ChevronTexaco. (2004). *ChevronTexaco's response to the carbon disclosure project 2*. http://www.cdproject.net. Accessed 8 July 2006.

Christmann, P. (2000). Effects of "best practices" of environmental management on cost advantage: The role of complementary assets. *Academy of Management Journal, 43*(4), 663–680.

Christmann, P. (2004). Multinational companies and the natural environment: Determinants of global environmental policy standardization. *Academy of Management Journal, 47*(5), 747–760.

Christmann, P., & Taylor, G. (2001). Globalization and the environment: Determinants of firm self-regulation in China. *Journal of International Business Studies, 32*(3), 439–458.

Cuervo-Cazurra, A., Maloney, M. M., & Manrakhan, S. (2007). Causes of the difficulties in internationalization. *Journal of International Business Studies, 38*(5), 709–725.

DaimlerChrysler. (2004). *DaimlerChrysler's response to the carbon disclosure project 2*. http://www.cdproject.net. Accessed 8 July 2006.

Dierickx, I., & Cool, K. (1989). Asset stock accumulation and sustainability of competitive advantage. *Management Science, 35*(12), 1504–1511.

Dunning, J. H. (1993). *Multinational enterprises and the global economy*. Addison-Wesley.

Dunning, J. H. (1998). Location and the multinational enterprise: A neglected factor? *Journal of International Business Studies, 29*(1), 45–66.

Eisenhardt, K. M., & Martin, J. A. (2000). Dynamic capabilities: What are they? *Strategic Management Journal, 21*(10–11), 1105–1121.

Endesa. (2006). *2005 sustainability report*. Endesa.

ExxonMobil. (2004). *ExxonMobil's response to the carbon disclosure project 2*. http://www.cdproject.net. Accessed 8 July 2006.

Ford. (2004). *Ford's response to the carbon disclosure project 2*. http://www.cdproject.net. Accessed 8 July 2006.

Gatignon, H., Tushman, M. L., Smith, W., & Anderson, P. (2002). A structural approach to assessing innovation: Construct development of innovation locus, type, and characteristics. *Management Science, 48*(9), 1103–1122.

Ghemawat, P. (2001). Distance still matters: The hard reality of global expansion. *Harvard Business Review, 79*(8), 137–147.

Ghemawat, P. (2003). Semiglobalization and international business strategy. *Journal of International Business Studies, 34*(2), 138–152.

Griffiths, J. (2005, February 8). It's a long and winding road for the car that runs on hydrogen alone. *Financial Times* (p. 11).

Grubb, M., Vrolijk, C., & Brack, D. (1999). *The Kyoto protocol: A guide and assessment*. RIIA/Earthscan.

Hall, J., & Vredenburg, H. (2003). The challenges of innovating for sustainable development. *MIT Sloan Management Review, 45*(1), 61–68.

Hart, S. L. (1995). A natural-resource-based view of the firm. *Academy of Management Review, 20*(4), 986–1014.

Harvey, F. (2005, July 1). GE looks out for a cleaner profit. *Financial Times* (p. 13).

Harvey, F., Cameron, D., & Beattie, A. (2006, June 20). Wind changes in favour of biofuels. *Financial Times* (p. 29).
Hasselknippe, H., & Røine, K. (2006). *Carbon 2006*. Point Carbon.
Helfat, C. E. (1997). Know-how and asset complementarity and dynamic capability accumulation: The case of R&D. *Strategic Management Journal, 18*(5), 339–360.
Helfat, C. E., & Peteraf, M. A. (2003). The dynamic resource-based view: Capability lifecycles. *Strategic Management Journal, 24*(10), 997–1010.
Hoffman, A. J. (2005). Climate change strategy: The business logic behind voluntary greenhouse gas reductions. *California Management Review, 47*(3), 21–46.
Husted, B. W., & Allen, D. B. (2006). Corporate social responsibility in the multinational enterprise: Strategic and institutional approaches. *Journal of International Business Studies, 37*(6), 838–849.
Iberdrola. (2004). *Iberdrola's response to the carbon disclosure project 2*. http://www.cdproject.net. Accessed 8 July 2006.
IEA. (2004). *Renewable energy: Market & policy trends in IEA countries*. International Energy Agency.
IPCC. (2007). *Climate change 2007: Impacts, adaptation and vulnerability*. Cambridge University Press.
Johnson, E. (2006, February 28). Flexibility on fuel gives manufacturers an edge. *Financial Times* (p. 4).
King, A. A., & Shaver, J. M. (2001). Are aliens green? Assessing foreign establishments' environmental conduct in the United States. *Strategic Management Journal, 22*(11), 1069–1085.
Kogut, B., & Zander, U. (1993). Knowledge of the firm and the evolutionary theory of the multinational corporation. *Journal of International Business Studies, 24*(4), 625–645.
Kolk, A., & Levy, D. (2004). Multinationals and global climate change: Issues for the automotive and oil industries. In S. Lundan (Ed.), *Multinationals, environment and global competition* (pp. 171–193). Elsevier.
Kolk, A., & Pinkse, J. (2005). Business responses to climate change: Identifying emergent strategies. *California Management Review, 47*(3), 6–20.
Kolk, A., & Pinkse, J. (2007). Multinationals' political activities on climate change. *Business and Society, 46*(2), 201–228.
Lavie, D. (2006). Capability reconfiguration: An analysis of incumbent responses to technological change. *Academy of Management Review, 31*(1), 153–174.
Levy, D. L. (1997). Business and international environmental treaties: Ozone depletion and climate change. *California Management Review, 39*(3), 54–71.

Levy, D. L., & Kolk, A. (2002). Strategic responses to global climate change: Conflicting pressures on multinationals in the oil industry. *Business and Politics, 4*(3), 275–300.

Lundan, S. (2004). *Multinationals, environment and global competition*. Elsevier.

Mackintosh, J. (2004, March 10). Toyota licenses Ford for hybrid engine patent use. *Financial Times* (p. 31).

Mackintosh, J. (2005a, September 13). Oil prices add to green pressures. *Financial Times* (p. 1).

Mackintosh, J. (2005b, June 8). Hydrogen is new hope to get gas-guzzlers off the road: Ford and BMW are developing an internal combustion engine that will not be dependent on oil. *Financial Times* (p. 20).

Makino, S., Isobe, T., & Chan, C. M. (2004). Does country matter? *Strategic Management Journal, 25*(10), 1027–1043.

Marcus, A., & Geffen, D. (1998). The dialectics of competency acquisition: Pollution prevention in electric generation. *Strategic Management Journal, 19*(12), 1145–1168.

Morrison, K. (2006, April 27). Cloud hangs over emissions scheme. *Financial Times* (p. 41).

Pernick, R., & Wilder, C. (2007). *The clean tech revolution: The next big growth and investment opportunity*. HarperCollins.

Petro-Canada. (2004). *Petro-Canada's response to the carbon disclosure project 2*. http://www.cdproject.net. Accessed 8 July 2006.

Pinkse, J. (2007). Corporate intentions to participate in emission trading. *Business Strategy and the Environment, 16*(1), 12–25.

Du Pont. (2004). *Du Pont's response to the carbon disclosure project 2*. http://www.cdproject.net. Accessed 8 July 2006.

Porter, M. E., & van der Linde, C. (1995). Toward a new conception of the environment–competitiveness relationship. *Journal of Economic Perspectives, 9*(4), 97–118.

Reinhardt, F. L. (1998). Environmental product differentiation: Implications for corporate strategy. *California Management Review, 40*(4), 43–73.

Ricardo Consulting Engineers. (2003). *"Carbon to hydrogen" roadmaps for passenger cars: A study for the department for transport and the department of trade and industry*. Shoreham-by-Sea.

Romilly, P. (2007). Business and climate change risk: A regional time series analysis. *Journal of International Business Studies, 38*(3), 474–480.

Rothaermel, F. T., & Hill, C. W. L. (2005). Technological discontinuities and complementary assets: A longitudinal study of industry and firm performance. *Organization Science, 16*(1), 52–70.

Royal Dutch/Shell. (2004). *Royal Dutch/Shell's response to the carbon disclosure project 2*. http://www.cdproject.net. Accessed 8 July 2006.

Rugman, A. M. (2005). *The regional multinationals: MNEs and "global" strategic management*. Cambridge University Press.

Rugman, A. M., & Verbeke, A. (1992). A note on the transnational solution and the transaction cost theory of multinational strategic management. *Journal of International Business Studies, 23*(4), 761–771.

Rugman, A. M., & Verbeke, A. (1998). Corporate strategies and environmental regulations: An organizing framework. *Strategic Management Journal, 19*(4), 363–375.

Rugman, A. M., & Verbeke, A. (2000). Six cases of corporate strategic responses to environmental regulation. *European Management Journal, 18*(4), 377–385.

Rugman, A. M., & Verbeke, A. (2001a). Environmental policy and international business. In A. M. Rugman & T. L. Brewer (Eds.), *The Oxford handbook of international business* (pp. 537–557). Oxford University Press.

Rugman, A. M., & Verbeke, A. (2001b). Subsidiary-specific advantages in multinational enterprises. *Strategic Management Journal, 22*(3), 237–250.

Rugman, A. M., & Verbeke, A. (2003). Extending the theory of the multinational enterprise: Internalization and strategic management perspectives. *Journal of International Business Studies, 34*(2), 125–137.

Rugman, A. M., & Verbeke, A. (2004). A perspective on regional and global strategies of multinational enterprises. *Journal of International Business Studies, 35*(1), 3–18.

Rugman, A. M., & Verbeke, A. (2005). Towards a theory of regional multinationals: A transaction cost economics approach. *Management International Review, 45*(Special Issue), 5–17.

Russo, M. V. (2003). The emergence of sustainable industries: Building on natural capital. *Strategic Management Journal, 24*(4), 317–331.

Russo, M. V., & Fouts, P. A. (1997). A resource-based perspective on corporate environmental performance and profitability. *Academy of Management Journal, 40*(3), 534–559.

Sharma, S., & Vredenburg, H. (1998). Proactive corporate environmental strategy and the development of competitively valuable organizational capabilities. *Strategic Management Journal, 19*(8), 729–753.

Simon, B. (2006a, August 31). J.D. power says Asian groups poised for more inroads in US automotive. *Financial Times* (p. 21).

Simon, B. (2006b, April 28). Bush and car chiefs to push more ethanol use. *Financial Times* (p. 8).

Singh, J. (2007). Asymmetry of knowledge spillovers between MNCs and host country firms. *Journal of International Business Studies, 38*(5), 764–786.

Spencer, J. W. (2003). Firms' knowledge-sharing strategies in the global innovation system: Empirical evidence from the flat panel display industry. *Strategic Management Journal, 24*(3), 217–233.

Steel, N. (2005). *Sustainability report 2005*. Nippon Steel.

Stern, N. (2007). *The economics of climate change: The Stern review*. Cambridge University Press.

Teece, D. J., Pisano, G., & Shuen, A. (1997). Dynamic capabilities and strategic management. *Strategic Management Journal, 18*(7), 509–533.

Tripsas, M. (1997). Unraveling the process of creative destruction: Complementary assets and incumbent survival in the typesetter industry. *Strategic Management Journal, 18*(S1), 119–142.

Tsai, T., & Child, J. (1997). Strategic responses of multinational corporations to environmental demands. *Journal of General Management, 23*(1), 1–22.

Tushman, M. L., & Anderson, P. (1986). Technological discontinuities and organizational environments. *Administrative Science Quarterly, 31*(3), 439–465.

Unilever. 2004. *Unilever's response to the carbon disclosure project 2*. http://www.cdproject.net. Accessed 8 July 2006.

Verbeke, A., Bowen, F., & Sellers, M. (2006). *Corporate environmental strategy: Extending the natural resource-based view of the firm*. Paper presented at the Annual Meeting of the Academy of Management, Atlanta.

Winter, S. G. (2003). Understanding dynamic capabilities. *Strategic Management Journal, 24*(10), 991–995.

Yomiuri Shimbun. (2006, September 23). *Nissan to end Toyota hybrid tie-up* (p. 1).

Zaheer, S. (1995). Overcoming the liability of foreignness. *Academy of Management Journal, 38*(2), 341–363.

Zollo, M., & Winter, S. G. (2002). Deliberate learning and the evolution of dynamic capabilities. *Organization Science, 13*(3), 339–351.

12

International Business, Climate Change and the Energy Transition: A Commentary on the Importance of Business Models and Digitalization

Ans Kolk and Francesca Ciulli

Introduction

The Covid-19 pandemic has exposed a vulnerability of humankind reminding observers of another crisis they see looming: climate change. As Kumpferschmidt (2020, p. 1397) put it in a reflective piece on SARS-CoV-2, looking back on "A divisive year":

> But a new crisis is coming that scientists have warned and worried about for years—one that is slower, yet even more menacing, and far easier to ignore or deny. "You know the biggest deal of this year?" Hanage [epidemi-

A. Kolk (✉)
Amsterdam Business School, University of Amsterdam,
Amsterdam, The Netherlands
e-mail: akolk@uva.nl

F. Ciulli
Tilburg School of Social and Behavioral Sciences, Tilburg University,
Tilburg, The Netherlands
e-mail: F.Ciulli@tilburguniversity.edu

M. A. Mithani et al. (eds.), *Crises and Disruptions in International Business*, JIBS Special Collections, https://doi.org/10.1007/978-3-030-80383-4_12

> ologist at the Harvard T.H. Chan School of Public Health] asks. "When it comes to climate change we are totally screwed."
>
> There will be no easy scientific fix for global warming. And if this pandemic has shown anything, it is that evidence without action is like a vaccine in a freezer: It is all potential. Scientists knew deaths would follow cases as sure as thunder follows lightning. And yet politicians and ordinary citizens alike found it hard to act until morgues were overflowing. Some refused to acknowledge reality even then. How much harder will it be to act on climate change?

Climate change is, indeed, not new at all, and its causes and (potential) consequences have been studied and discussed for many decades already, with contestation around the problem (the 'science') and the solutions. According to a historical account of a decisive decade (1979–1989), "nearly everything we understand about global warming was understood in 1979" (Rich, 2018). There is wide consensus that, in addition to the effects on biological and physical systems, including changing ecosystems, extinction of species, and more extreme weather, countries around the world face negative implications for health, economic growth and development. Some of these impacts can already be seen and their rapid and possible irreversible aggravation is feared if serious steps to reduce emissions will not be taken soon. Climate change measures have an impact on MNEs active in a wide variety of sectors and countries as they are affected by policies at the local, national and supranational levels. However, absent regulation can also be of influence, as MNEs may suffer from the consequences of climate change. Overall, climate change leads to increased risks of doing business and growing/lasting uncertainty, also for investors, shareholders and (central) banks. At the same time, MNEs can be important actors in furthering a transition to a cleaner and greener economy, with some benefitting more from a move to less/no reliance on fossil fuels, compared to others. To what extent they are vulnerable to climate change and/or can contribute to the energy transition depends heavily on factors such as the specific activities undertaken, locational peculiarities, and the energy base of MNEs' business models.

While climate change had long been studied in the environmental, policy and natural sciences, it took many years before IB scholars joined the debate and started to add important insights on the role of MNEs, considering how MNEs may cause/aggravate the problem and/or help bring solutions closer; and how the issue can affect their strategies, performance and growth. Having followed the evolution of the science and (inter)national politics of climate change since the early 1990s, the first author (Ans Kolk) wrote an initial piece in 1998 (an award-winning essay, in Dutch, submitted to a contest organised in the Netherlands to identify underexposed aspects in international climate research) to explicate the importance of considering the influence of MNE strategies and interests in international policy-making (for the key tenets in English, see Kolk, 2000). While she continued to publish on MNEs' strategic responses to climate change (also with David Levy, and later with her PhD student Jonatan Pinkse, e.g., Kolk & Levy, 2001, 2004; Kolk & Pinkse, 2004, 2005; Levy & Kolk, 2002), the first article in an IB journal only appeared in 2008 (Kolk & Pinkse, 2008), after a plenary pitch by Kolk at the 2005 JIBS/AIB/CIBER Invitational Conference on Emerging Research Frontiers in IB. At that time, the topic of climate change as such was not uncontested given the political ramifications, which might explain, to some extent, why it did not take off easily. Concurrently, her work was directly aimed at advancing IB theory (see further below), also based on an earlier inventory of the complex mix of factors influencing MNEs' responses (see Table 12.1). There are inherent trade-offs and distributional issues involved, but MNEs face the day-to-day reality of consecutive international climate agreements and a pending energy transition, and we will below reflect on the 2008 article in light of the state of the art, to update it to the current business context.

However, this commentary can also be read as a separate piece that introduces new and original ideas building on, and updating, the 2008 article. Subsequent sections deal with, respectively, the recent development from green firm-specific advantages (FSAs) to business model-related specific advantages (BMSAs); the evolution of salience considering sectors, business model (component) and the influence of digitalization; and finally, the locational dimensions, including MNEs' embeddedness in various institutional contexts, and the potential for transferability and recombination of BMSAs. Altogether, a clear and forward-looking agenda

Table 12.1 Factors that influence corporate positions on climate change

Factors	Components
Issue-specific factors	Impact of the issue on sectors, countries, locations Institutional infrastructure for addressing the issue Degree to which issue and regulation are global Complexity and uncertainty associated with the issue
Sector-specific factors	Nature and extent of threat posed by climate change Availability and cost of alternatives Degree of globalization and type of supply chain Political power of the industry Technological and competitive situation Growth and concentration levels
Firm-specific factors	Position within the supply chain; nature of value chain Economic situation and market positioning History of involvement with (technological) alternatives Degrees of (de)centralization and internationalization Availability and type of internal climate expertise Nature of strategic planning process Corporate culture and managerial perceptions Ability to anticipate risks, spread vulnerabilities and manage stakeholders
Country-specific factors	Societal concerns about climate change National policies on climate change National industrial promotion policies Geography / natural capital (e.g., in relation to possibilities for renewables) Societal views on the roles and responsibilities of firms Regulatory culture (litigation or consensus-oriented)

Source: Kolk and Pinkse (2012), p. 474; based on published work from Kolk (et al.) since 1998

for research on international business, climate change and the energy transition, emerges.

From Green FSAs to Climate-Induced BMSAs

The 2008 article introduces two frameworks to explore the nature and geography of climate-induced firm-specific advantages (or more broadly, green FSAs), using illustrative information from the 2003–2005 period. Stemming from Rugman & Verbeke (2003), Kolk and Pinkse (2008,

p. 1362) note that "the FSA concept is strongly aligned with that of a capability". Two main developments since suggest the importance of reflecting on, and updating, the conceptualization of green FSAs. First, recent IB literature on internalization theory points at an increasing divergence between ownership and control (Narula et al., 2019). Notably, technological developments have led IB scholars to place emphasis on the importance of external parties, with the conceptualization of "network advantages" (Banalieva & Dhanaraj, 2019), "ecosystem-specific advantages" (Li et al., 2019), increasing attention also for the recombination and bundling of an MNE's FSAs (Narula et al., 2019) with "complementary assets held by local owners" (Hennart, 2009, p. 1436).

Second, triggered by a rising interest in the "business model" construct in strategic management research (e.g., Massa et al., 2017; Prescott & Filatotchev, 2020), corporate sustainability scholars have supported the adoption of a business model perspective to investigate firms' social and environmental impact. Departing from a focus on specific resources, processes or products, the business model lens captures the integration of sustainability in the whole "design or architecture of the value creation, delivery and capture mechanisms" (Teece, 2010, p. 179) of a firm. It also enables apprehension of the engagement of external parties in the creation of social and environmental value, as highlighted by recent studies on collaborative sustainable business models (Ordonez-Ponce et al., 2020; Pedersen et al., 2020). This is relevant for climate change, as involving and collaborating with multiple external parties, such as customers, suppliers and (non-)governmental organisations, is seen as necessary for effective action (Kolk, 2015; Pinkse & Kolk, 2012a). A body of work exploring sustainable business models, including climate-induced ones, has emerged, for example in the context of electric vehicles (Bohnsack et al., 2014) and energy (Richter, 2013; Tolkamp et al., 2018). This business model view is valuable, because it allows for capturing climate-induced value co-creation and the network of actors involved in attaining the climate and energy-related sustainable development goals (7 and 13).

The article we recently published in JIBS, co-authored with Rene Bohnsack, builds on these trends: by connecting FSAs to the business model construct, it conceptualizes the business model-related specific advantage (BMSA) and investigates it in the context of the energy transition. The BMSA adds to FSAs a "higher-order configurational character", by capturing the bundle of activities that create and capture value and the array of actors contributing to them (Bohnsack et al. 2021). Although the 2008 article did not explicitly adopt a business model lens, it hinted at the need to adopt a more comprehensive perspective that does not just include a change in technology or in marketing, but a transformation that involves different components. In particular, by highlighting that green FSAs may relate to a firm's entire value chain, the 2008 paper suggests that green FSAs may not only be embedded in a specific technology or capability, but also encompass a "configuration" of activities. Yet, this idea was still *in nuce* and the study did not develop it further into a systemic approach to FSA, which the 2021 article proposed with the BMSA concept.

The business model perspective also effectively integrates the dynamic view of FSA proposed by the 2008 article, which underlined that "MNEs have to constantly adjust their FSAs for deploying these resources, or even create new FSAs to maintain fit with changes in the global sustainability issue" (p. 1360). The upper part of Fig. 12.1 (Figure 1 in Kolk and Pinkse, 2008, p. 1364, which is Figure 11.1 in this book) encompasses three main FSA reconfiguration mechanisms, i.e., evolution, transformation or substitution. FSA reconfiguration resonates with the "business model innovation for sustainability" concept, which indicates "innovations that create significant positive and/or significantly reduced negative impacts for the environment and/or society, through changes in the way the organization and its value-network create, deliver value and capture value (i.e., create economic value) [and/] or change their value propositions" (Bocken et al., 2014, p. 44). While business model innovation for sustainability has been overlooked in the IB literature, it is key to appraising a climate-induced BMSA reconfiguration.

Linking Kolk and Pinkse's (2008) JIBS article with the sustainable business model literature and, in particular, with the BMSA concept, leads to a reinterpretation of their Figure 1 (Figure 11.1 in this book). A *new* Fig. 12.1 (which includes the 2008 Figure at the top and our adjusted one below it) has as horizontal axis the "business model components", which, in aggregate, form a firm's BMSA. This dimension builds on the "FSA value chain orientation" of Figure 1 from 2008, but it adds a

		FSA Value Chain Orientation	
		Downstream FSA	Upstream FSA
FSA Reconfiguration Mechanism	FSA Evolution	1	2
	FSA Transformation	3	4
	FSA Substitution	5	6

		Business model components (∑ → BMSA)		
		Value proposition	Value Network	Revenue-cost model
Climate-induced BMSA innovation mechanism	Incremental BMI	1	2	3
	Radical BMI	4	5	6

Fig. 12.1 A reinterpretation of the FSA development through a business model lens. (Source: The upper Figure is taken from Kolk and Pinkse (2008), p. 1364)

configurational element to show that a firm's competitive advantage is not located downstream *or* upstream, but it is embedded in the whole business model architecture. The vertical axis, i.e., "climate-induced BMSA innovation mechanisms" builds on the view, present in the 2008

Figure 1, that the intensity of the FSA transformation that MNEs are prompted to undertake may vary. This dimension thus incorporates the perspective of the (sustainable) business model literature (Foss & Saebi, 2017; Lüdeke-Freund et al., 2016; Wirtz et al., 2016), which sees change as intervening within a system of value creation and capture.

Different categorizations of business model innovation have been developed, e.g., Foss and Saebi (2017, p. 217) denote its scope as "modular" (when changes intervene in one or more business model components) or "architectural" (when the change "affects the business model in its entirety"). We find the incremental versus radical innovation categorization (Egfjord & Sund, 2020; Lüdeke-Freund et al., 2016; Wirtz et al., 2016) most suitable as it captures different configurations of business model innovation, which may involve a limited adaptation of one component and the disruptive change of (an)other one(s). This is in line with the last section of the 2008 article which indicated that few industries will experience a radical, competence-destroying configuration due to climate change.

Refining Salience: The Influence of Business Models and Digitalization

Towards the end of Kolk and Pinkse (2008, p. 1374), the observation was made that the type of industry matters. As elaborated later (Kolk, 2015; Kolk & Mulder, 2011; Kolk & Pinkse, 2012), this involves a distinction between (1) firms operating in "high-salience industries", i.e. whose core activities are directly affected by climate change (policy) and an energy transition; (2) "firms specialized in goods or services that are instrumental in the mitigation of climate change impacts, or in anticipating, influencing or responding to public policy developments"; and (3) the "remaining firms", which are not affected by climate change, but their (early) actions in the climate change realm may subsequently increase their legitimacy and reputation (see Table 12.2).

Interestingly, this distinction can be refined and made more dynamic and up to date by accounting for the large-scale entry of novel digital

Table 12.2 Relevance of climate change for different categories of firms

Category of firms	Impact of climate change issue
Firms in high-salience sectors	Strongly affected in view of energy intensity and dependence Early change in business models might be source of competitive advantage
Firmsspecializedinclimate-Relevant goods and services	Can profit by helping other companies to mitigate their climate change impacts or to anticipate, influence or respond to climate policy
Remaining firms with low-emission activities	No main source of profitability/growth, but may gain legitimacy from acting visibly Can deal with the issue via external markets, possibility for internalization arbitrage

Source: Kolk and Pinkse (2012), p. 475; cf. Kolk (2015); Kolk and Mulder (2011)

Table 12.3 Impact of digitalization on climate induced BMSAs

Category of firms	Impact of climate change issue
Firms in high-salience sectors	Incumbents' business model innovation to reduce climate impact Digital technology MNEs' business model innovation to reduce climate impact Design/adoption of novel business models to provide climate-relevant goods and services
Firms specialized in climate-relevant goods and services	Entry of firms from high-salience sectors Entry of digital technology MNEs Entry of digital technology ventures
Remaining firms with low-emission activities	Minor incremental climate-induced business model innovations

technologies (e.g., digital platforms, Artificial Intelligence (AI), blockchain, cloud computing, big data) and their critical influence on the pathway and speed of the energy transition. As highlighted by ITU (2019), digital technologies "offer solutions to monitor, mitigate and adapt to the impacts of climate change"; they can thus be critical for firms to become "agents of global change" (Kolk & Pinkse, 2008). Digital technologies may also lead to substantially higher energy consumption, thus increasing CO_2 emissions. The interplay between climate change and digitalization has implications for the BMSAs of different actors, summarized in Table 12.3.

Incumbent MNEs in traditionally high-salience sectors are confronted with the need to innovate their existing business models to integrate digital technologies that help curb their carbon emissions and increase energy efficiencies. In the electricity sector, for example, the "Internet of Things" (IoT) enables the monitoring of emissions produced in electricity production and the detection of inefficiencies along the value chain, while machine learning and AI can help optimize energy systems. The most radical BMSA innovation undertaken by incumbents, however, entails becoming active agents in the energy transition by leveraging digital technologies to shift, at least partially, from operating in high-salience sectors to providing climate-relevant goods and services. This is the example of electric utilities that have leveraged digital technologies to design novel business models focused on offering energy efficiency services and devices to their customers. Such BMSA innovation triggered by digitalization (Bohnsack et al., 2021), has had a relevant impact on the location-boundedness of electric utilities' BMSAs in the framework of the energy transition, making them easily transferable and adaptable across countries.

Notably, with the diffusion of digitalization in various domains – which escalated due to Covid-19 – digital technology MNEs are increasingly seen as a high-salience sector given their high energy use. In particular, thriving digitalization is tied to the international proliferation of data centres, which require considerable amounts of energy for their operations and account for "1% of global electricity use in 2019" (IEA, 2020). Large Tech MNEs have expressed their commitment to maximize energy efficiency and use renewables (Facebook, n.d.; Google, n.d.), and mentions to carbon-free or even green data centres abound. The critical role of "Big Tech" MNEs regarding energy consumption is epitomized by Google, "the world's largest corporate purchaser of renewable energy" (Pinchai, 2020). To reduce their environmental impact, digital technology MNEs have to innovate their BMSA, particularly the value network, and to recombine their BMSAs with local assets. Indeed, Google (2020, p. 3) stated that it "[wi]ll need to work with others. Google will only be able to reach 24/7 carbon-free energy in partnership with governments and industry, our customers, and the communities in which we operate". Climate-induced BMSA innovations are more complex for big Tech MNEs whose BMSAs have, besides a data-based component, also a core physical one, like Amazon and Apple. In the case of Apple (n.d.), for example, climate-induced BMSA innovation entails, among others, the design of energy-efficient devices, "transitioning hundreds of [...] manufacturing suppliers to 100% renewable sources of electricity" and the shift to a circular value creation system.

While having to reduce their negative environmental impact, digital technology MNEs have leveraged novel technologies to design climate-relevant value propositions and business models. This is the case of Google and its Nest Learning thermostat, which is based on IoT and AI to help consumers increase energy savings. Nest is just an example of digital solutions that contribute to realise consumers' active engagement in the energy transition, which has been emphasized as a priority by policymakers and practitioners (Accenture & Eurelectric, 2020; European Commission, 2020) (although to what extent this can be done while respecting data privacy remains to be seen). Also notable is Microsoft's recent pledge to become carbon *negative* by 2030 – to achieve this goal, the business model innovations undertaken by the MNE involve, among others, creating "carbon removal technologies" and "co-innovating with customers and partners to develop low-carbon solutions" (Smith, 2020).

Finally, digital ventures with climate-relevant business models have been burgeoning over the last years (Kolk & Ciulli, 2020). New entrants have designed their BMSAs around digital technologies to fight climate change and accelerate the energy transition. An award-winning venture is BL!XT (n.d.), which turned the mechanical circuit breaker into a digital smart device, with the potential to trigger a disruptive transformation in the electricity system and enable a significant reduction of CO_2 emissions. Another awarded venture is Enerbrain (n.d.), which developed an energy retrofit system leveraging IoT, cloud computing, as well as the algorithm designed by Enerbrain, to monitor building parameters (e.g., temperature, humidity and CO_2) in real time and to automatically intervene to improve energy efficiency. These are just some examples to illustrate how a business model perspective and the emergence of digitalization have influenced the sector salience put forward in Kolk and Pinkse (2008).

"Bringing it all together"? On Embeddedness, Transferability and Recombination

A location-related *fil rouge* connects Kolk and Pinkse (2008) with the following works published by Kolk et al. in JIBS, in 2012 and 2021 respectively. The 2008 article introduced the "geography of climate change-induced FSA development", discussing different types of CSAs that may facilitate a climate-induced reconfiguration of FSAs, as well as the CSA pattern which affects FSAs' transferability. Later in 2012, a new paper further reflected on the climate-related institutional dimension affecting green FSAs, by unpacking it into institutional failures and embeddedness (or lack thereof) in home, host and supranational contexts (see Pinkse & Kolk, 2012b). It contended that all these institutional factors can create both opportunities and challenges for climate-induced FSAs. The more recent 2021 article zoomed in on MNEs' host countries and conceptualized "BMSA recombination barriers", as regulatory, infrastructural or market factors, inherent to a foreign location, that hamper the recombination of a firm's BMSA with local assets and applied it to the energy transition (Bohnsack et al., 2021). These studies offer a wealth of possible areas for further research on issues related to the degree and nature of transferability, considering different MNEs, the salience of climate change, and the energy transition for a particular firm and its business model (components).

We note that crucial for studying and understanding climate change and the energy transition are the inherent intricate *locational specificities*. Pinkse and Kolk (2012b) made an important first step by delineating MNEs' "balancing act" regarding their interactions with (non-)market actors in home, host and supranational contexts, exposing multiple types and levels of embeddedness. Interestingly, however, with the progression of climate/energy policy, the local nature of measures that are often taken regardless of national/regional levels (e.g., cities or states within federal systems) – be it emission reduction (stick) or incentives for a transition (carrot) – have become more prominent. Consequently, a fine-tuned analysis of the origin and destination of MNE activity in relation to green market development (see Table 12.4), opportunities for, and/or barriers

Table 12.4 Main institutional factors in relation to green market development

Institutional factors	Possible advantage in green market development	Possible disadvantage in green market development
Provision of public subsidies, knowledge, and infrastructure	Firms may be able to profit if they can utilize corporate political activities and/or institutional entrepreneurship	Foreign firms may not be able to profit if localization clauses hamper leverage of country-specific advantages
Proximity of country to technological frontier	Firms from a technologically leading country on the issue may leverage country-specific advantages	Firms from countries that are not at the technological frontier may be locked in institutional and technological development trajectories
Degree of institutional change	Foreign firms may be able to more easily adjust to new institutional arrangements due to low involvement in past trajectories	Home firms may not be able to adjust to new institutional arrangements due to constraints resulting from high involvement in institutional trajectories
Degree of political contestation of issue	Foreign firms may be able to break more easily with local consensus and leverage country-specific advantages from other locations	Home firms may have difficulty to break with historical positions and suffer from complex domestic debates around the issue
Political stance of country in global issue arena	Firms from a country that supports global climate policy may be able to profit from easier access to supranational stakeholders and spread global norms	Firms from a country that is less favorable to global climate policy may suffer from a liability of origin when operating in countries more supportive of the issue

Source: Pinkse and Kolk (2012b), p. 339

to, recombination is needed, with the role of digital technologies in relation to climate-induced BMSAs deserving special attention. Our most recent article (see Bohnsack et al., 2021) showed that, in the context of the energy transition, electricity firms relying on digital technologies tend to benefit from "limited impediments to BMSA recombination, coupled with low adaptation costs". Indeed, a digital product can be adjusted relatively easily to fit the needs and distinctive features of local markets, and digitalization in general enables interconnections and widespread, in-depth types of "control" that were unthinkable in the "old" electricity system. On the other hand, increased concerns for data protection, safety and ethics, as well as pressures towards techno-nationalism (Petricevic & Teece, 2019), may elicit novel recombination barriers. In summary, this commentary shows that the Kolk and Pinkse (2008) JIBS article on MNEs and climate change has much relevance today, in itself and when extended to cover BMSAs, digital technologies and the energy transition as a whole.

References

Accenture & Eurelectric. (2020). *Seeking shared success: Empowering consumers in the energy transition.*

Apple. (n.d.). *Environment: A planet-size plan.* Available at: https://www.apple.com/environment/

Banalieva, E. R., & Dhanaraj, C. (2019). Internalization theory for the digital economy. *Journal of International Business Studies, 50*(8), 1372–1387.

Bl!XT. (n.d.). *The devil's in the detail.* Available at: https://blixt.tech/the-devil-is-in-the-details/

Bocken, N. M., Short, S. W., Rana, P., & Evans, S. (2014). A literature and practice review to develop sustainable business model archetypes. *Journal of Cleaner Production, 65*, 42–56.

Bohnsack, R., Ciulli, F., & Kolk, A. (2021). The role of business models in firm internationalization: An exploration of European electricity firms in the context of the energy transition. *Journal of International Business Studies, 52*(5), 824–852.10.1057/s41267-020-00364-4

Bohnsack, R., Pinkse, J., & Kolk, A. (2014). Business models for sustainable technologies: Exploring business model evolution in the case of electric vehicles. *Research Policy, 43*(2), 284–300.

Egfjord, K. F. H., & Sund, K. J. (2020). Do you see what I see? How differing perceptions of the environment can hinder radical business model innovation. *Technological Forecasting and Social Change, 150*, 119787.

Enerbrain. (n.d.). *Press kit.*

European Commission. (2020). *Protecting energy consumers*. Available at: https://ec.europa.eu/energy/topics/markets-and-consumers/energy-consumer-rights/protecting-energy-consumers_en

Facebook. (n.d.). *Sustainable data centers*. Available at: https://sustainability.fb.com/innovation-for-our-world/sustainable-data-centers/

Foss, N. J., & Saebi, T. (2017). Fifteen years of research on business model innovation: How far have we come, and where should we go? *Journal of Management, 43*(1), 200–227.

Google. (2020). *24/7 by 2030: Realizing a carbon-free future*. Available at: https://sustainability.google/progress/energy/

Google. (n.d.). *Efficiency*. Available at: https://www.google.com/about/datacenters/efficiency/

Hennart, J. F. (2009). Down with MNE-centric theories! Market entry and expansion as the bundling of MNE and local assets. *Journal of International Business Studies, 40*(9), 1432–1454.

IEA. (2020). *Digitalisation: Making energy systems more connected, efficient, resilient and sustainable*. Available at: https://www.iea.org/topics/digitalisation

ITU. (2019). *Turning digital technology innovation into climate action*. Available at: https://news.itu.int/how-we-can-turn-digital-technology-innovation-into-climate-action/

Kolk, A. (2000). *Economics of environmental management*. Financial Times Prentice Hall.

Kolk, A. (2015). The role of international business in clean technology transfer and development. *Climate Policy, 15*(1), 170–176.

Kolk, A., & Ciulli, F. (2020). The potential of sustainability-oriented digital platform multinationals: A comment on the transitions research agenda. *Environmental Innovation and Societal Transitions, 34*, 355–358.

Kolk, A., & Levy, D. (2001). Winds of change: Corporate strategy, climate change and oil multinationals. *European Management Journal, 19*(5), 501–509.

Kolk, A., & Levy, D. (2004). Multinationals and global climate change: Issues for the automotive and oil industries. In S. Lundan (Ed.), *Multinationals, environment and global competition* (Vol. 9, pp. 171–193). Elsevier, Research in Global Strategic Management.

Kolk, A., & Mulder, G. (2011). Regulatory uncertainty and opportunity seeking: The case of clean development. *California Management Review, 54*(1), 88–106.

Kolk, A., & Pinkse, J. (2004). Market strategies for climate change. *European Management Journal, 22*(3), 304–314.

Kolk, A., & Pinkse, J. (2005). Business responses to climate change: Identifying emergent strategies. *California Management Review, 47*(3), 6–20.

Kolk, A., & Pinkse, J. (2008). A perspective on multinational enterprises and climate change. Learning from an "inconvenient truth"? *Journal of International Business Studies, 39*(8), 1359–1378.

Kolk, A., & Pinkse, J. (2012). Multinational enterprises and climate change strategies. In A. Verbeke & H. Merchant (Eds.), *Handbook of research on international strategic management* (pp. 472–485). Edward Elgar.

Kumpferschmidt, K. (2020). A divisive disease. *Science, 370*(6523), 1395–1397.

Levy, D., & Kolk, A. (2002). Strategic responses to global climate change: Conflicting pressures on multinationals in the oil industry. *Business and Politics, 4*(3), 275–300.

Li, J., Chen, L., Yi, J., Mao, J., & Liao, J. (2019). Ecosystem-specific advantages in international digital commerce. *Journal of International Business Studies, 50*(9), 1448–1463.

Lüdeke-Freund, F., Massa, L., Bocken, N., Brent, A., & Musango, J. (2016). *Business models for shared value*. Network for Business Sustainability.

Massa, L., Tucci, C. L., & Afuah, A. (2017). A critical assessment of business model research. *Academy of Management Annals, 11*(1), 73–104.

Narula, R., Asmussen, C. G., Chi, T., & Kundu, S. K. (2019). Applying and advancing internalization theory: The multinational enterprise in the twenty-first century. *Journal of International Business Studies, 50*, 1231–1252.

Ordonez-Ponce, E., Clarke, A. C., & Colbert, B. A. (2020). Collaborative sustainable business models: Understanding organizations partnering for community sustainability. *Business & Society, 0007650320940241.*

Pedersen, E. R. G., Lüdeke-Freund, F., Henriques, I., & Seitanidi, M. M. (2020). Toward collaborative cross-sector business models for sustainability. *Business & Society, 0007650320959027.*

Petricevic, O., & Teece, D. J. (2019). The structural reshaping of globalization: Implications for strategic sectors, profiting from innovation, and the multinational enterprise. *Journal of International Business Studies, 50*(9), 1487–1512.

Pinchai, S. (2020). *Our third decade of climate action: Realizing a carbon-free future*. Available at: https://blog.google/outreach-initiatives/sustainability/our-third-decade-climate-action-realizing-carbon-free-future/amp/?s=03

Pinkse, J., & Kolk, A. (2012a). Addressing the climate change – Sustainable development nexus: The role of multi-stakeholder partnerships. *Business & Society, 51*(1), 176–210.

Pinkse, J., & Kolk, A. (2012b). Multinational enterprises and climate change: Exploring institutional failures and embeddedness. *Journal of International Business Studies, 43*(3), 332–341.

Prescott, J. E., & Filatotchev, I. (2020). The business model phenomenon: Towards theoretical relevance. *Journal of Management Studies.* https://doi.org/10.1111/joms.12610

Rich, N. (2018, August 1). Losing earth: The decade we almost stopped climate change. *New York Times Magazine* .

Richter, M. (2013). Business model innovation for sustainable energy: German utilities and renewable energy. *Energy Policy, 62*, 1226–1237.

Rugman, A. M., & Verbeke, A. (2003). Extending the theory of the multinational enterprise: Internalization and strategic management perspectives. *Journal of International Business Studies, 34*(2), 125–137.

Smith. (2020). *Microsoft will be carbon negative by 2030.* Available at: https://blogs.microsoft.com/blog/2020/01/16/microsoft-will-be-carbon-negative-by-2030/

Teece, D. J. (2010). Business models, business strategy and innovation. *Long Range Planning, 43*, 172–194.

Tolkamp, J. C. C. M., Huijben, J. C. C. M., Mourik, R. M., Verbong, G. P. J., & Bouwknegt, R. (2018). User-centred sustainable business model design: The case of energy efficiency services in the Netherlands. *Journal of Cleaner Production, 182*, 755–764.

Wirtz, B. W., Pistoia, A., Ullrich, S., & Göttel, V. (2016). Business models: Origin, development and future research perspectives. *Long Range Planning, 49*(1), 36–54.

13

The Impact of Climate Risk on Firm Performance and Financing Choices: An International Comparison

Henry He Huang, Joseph Kerstein, and Chong Wang

Introduction

The effect of climate on economic performance has long been recognized and documented (e.g., Dell et al., 2014; Gallup et al., 1999; Nordhaus, 2006). Studies have generally focused on the economic impact of climatic events on geographic units (countries and municipalities). Concern about worldwide changes in climate has also led to an examination of the impact of the environment on firm valuation (e.g., Beatty & Shimshack, 2010; Chava, 2014; Konar & Cohen, 2001; Matsumura et al., 2014).

Accepted by Gary Biddle, Area Editor, 14 October 2017. This article has been with the authors for three revisions.

H. H. Huang (✉) • J. Kerstein
Sy Syms School of Business, Yeshiva University, New York, NY, USA
e-mail: henry.huang@yu.edu

C. Wang
School of Accounting and Finance, The Hong Kong Polytechnic University, Hung Hom, Kowloon, Hong Kong

M. A. Mithani et al. (eds.), *Crises and Disruptions in International Business*, JIBS Special Collections, https://doi.org/10.1007/978-3-030-80383-4_13

Those studies generally consider regulatory and environmental risks associated with carbon dioxide emissions and other pollutants. We are not aware of any work that directly examines the effect of climate on publicly listed firms. Moreover, few studies have addressed whether and to what extent managers of public firms worldwide weigh the risk of extreme weather shocks when formulating financial policies.[1] Yet managers are likely to be influenced by *climate risk*, that is, losses from major weather events such as storms, floods, and heat waves, because they cannot obtain full insurance coverage against it.[2]

We use a cross-country empirical setting to examine the effect of climate risk on the financing and performance of publicly traded firms around the globe. Our proxy for climate risk is the Global Climate Risk Index (hereafter CRI) compiled and published by the non-profit, non-governmental organization Germanwatch (Kreft & Eckstein, 2014), which provides a quantified measure by country of extreme weather-related economic losses. This measure is also indicative of future extreme weather events (Kreft & Eckstein, 2014). Our study is based on both a long-term CRI score for the years 1993–2012 and seven annual CRI scores for the years 2006–2012. According to Kreft and Eckstein (2014), from 1992 to 2011 extreme weather events led to more than 530,000 casualties and economic losses of over 2.5 trillion USD at purchasing power parity (PPP). There is also anecdotal evidence of significantly negative effects of extreme weather on firm performance. For example, in Hurricane Katrina's aftermath, many chemical firms experienced lower earnings due to surging energy costs and lost production facilities (Reisch, 2005).

Our sample consists of 353,906 firm-years from 55 countries over 20 years from 1993 to 2012. Table 13.1 gives the distribution of firm-years

[1] According to United Nations International Strategy for Disaster Reduction (UNISDR, 2009), risk is the "combination of the probability [of occurrence] of a certain event and its negative consequences."

[2] A large part of the economic damage emanating from extreme weather events is not insured, especially in the case of developing countries (Andersen, 2001; Bals et al., 2006). Catastrophic insurance usually covers only damage to the means of production (e.g., property), not indirect losses such as lost proceeds from property that is destroyed, not losses that other agents may suffer, e.g., loss of supplies from damaged property (Bals et al., 2006). Hence underlying our study is the assumption that firms cannot fully insure against climatic risk. To the extent that they can do so, we anticipate that our findings will be less significant.

Table 13.1 Country-level variable measures by country

Country name	Long-term climate risk index (years 1993–2012)	Annual average number of deaths (years 1993–2012)	Annual average number of deaths per 100,000 inhabitants (years 1993–2012)	Annual average losses in US $PPP (years 1993–2012)	Annual average losses per unit GDP in % (years 1993–2012)	Standard deviation of climate risk index (annual)	Annual average LGDP	Annual average GDP growth	LEG_ ENV	Number of observations (total 353,906 obs.)
Argentina	-88.5	20.60	0.05	533.90	0.12	12.69	8.98	0.07	2.34	705
Australia	-52.2	46.95	0.23	1702.00	0.24	15.03	10.46	0.11	2.57	15,063
Austria	-61.8	26.90	0.33	382.90	0.15	25.36	10.41	0.04	2.22	1253
Bangladesh	-19.7	816.40	0.56	1833.00	1.16	18.69	6.40	0.10	0.19	179
Belgium	-71.5	86.25	0.82	93.55	0.03	12.75	10.39	0.05	2.16	1552
Brazil	-87	154.00	0.09	761.40	0.04	30.46	8.61	0.09	2.22	3483
Bulgaria	-87	7.30	0.09	142.40	0.16	22.58	8.53	0.12	1.66	142
Canada	-102.2	10.90	0.03	861.20	0.08	10.81	10.34	0.07	2.83	12,929
Chile	-106.5	8.60	0.05	132.50	0.07	23.83	8.94	0.09	1.85	1650
China	-42.3	1820.00	0.14	28,927.00	0.49	8.62	7.68	0.17	2.78	25,256
Colombia	-54.2	111.30	0.27	608.10	0.18	23.10	8.18	0.11	1.03	286
Croatia	-59.2	35.15	0.79	86.52	0.13	18.84	9.27	0.06	1.48	261
Czech	-71.2	9.80	0.09	586.40	0.26	21.54	9.22	0.08	0.41	145
Denmark	-115.3	0.80	0.01	215.30	0.13	18.31	10.64	0.04	1.93	1996
Ecuador	-44.3	64.30	0.49	261.70	0.30	32.03	8.24	0.12	2.51	19
Finland	-154.2	0.20	0.00	22.03	0.02	24.27	10.42	0.05	4.08	1856
France	-42.7	959.00	1.59	1623.00	0.09	14.06	10.33	0.04	3.96	9853
Germany	-48	476.30	0.58	2264.00	0.09	11.99	10.37	0.03	2.18	9826

(*continued*)

Table 13.1 (continued)

Country name	Long-term climate risk index (years 1993–2012)	Annual average number of deaths (years 1993–2012)	Annual average number of deaths per 100,000 inhabitants (years 1993–2012)	Annual average losses in US $PPP (years 1993–2012)	Annual average losses per unit GDP in % (years 1993–2012)	Standard deviation of climate risk index (annual)	Annual average LGDP	Annual average GDP growth	LEG_ ENV	Number of observations (total 353,906 obs.)
Greece	-84.3	13.50	0.12	249.90	0.10	26.59	9.96	0.05	1.83	2128
Hong Kong	-175.5	0.00	0.00	0.00	0.00	13.17	10.29	0.04	2.86	3117
Hungary	-68	34.75	0.34	173.90	0.11	7.07	9.05	0.08	3.56	239
India	-74.7	246.20	0.12	744.60	0.09	19.81	7.32	0.14	1.02	3662
Indonesia	-38.5	3142.00	0.30	6236.00	0.26	12.34	6.74	0.12	-0.41	25,747
Ireland	-121.2	2.00	0.05	67.44	0.05	17.78	10.44	0.08	2.91	880
Israel	-121.7	4.35	0.07	39.46	0.03	28.54	10.09	0.08	0.98	2145
Italy	-40.7	1003.00	1.73	1564.00	0.10	18.18	10.25	0.04	0.74	3082
Jamaica	-60.5	4.75	0.18	173.00	0.85	22.58	8.36	0.05	1.51	176
Japan	-92	76.25	0.06	1663.00	0.05	15.34	10.52	0.02	3.19	49,376
Lithuania	-80.5	4.50	0.19	59.53	0.19	26.81	9.15	0.12	3.19	244
Malaysia	-85.2	43.70	0.18	163.80	0.06	24.27	8.68	0.10	1.44	11,095
Mexico	-57.7	140.80	0.14	2377.00	0.19	13.85	8.87	0.07	3.09	1534
Morocco	-86.7	31.50	0.11	111.90	0.11	0.00	7.71	0.08	1.93	540
Netherlands	-74.3	84.65	0.53	151.10	0.03	14.03	10.40	0.05	1.31	2506
New Zealand	-83.3	3.40	0.08	224.70	0.23	19.67	10.08	0.09	2.75	1310
Norway	-134.2	1.55	0.03	50.65	0.02	23.96	10.98	0.08	3.24	2560
Pakistan	-31.8	469.90	0.32	2395.00	0.74	21.08	6.66	0.09	2.11	2257
Panama	-95.3	8.80	0.29	16.26	0.06	18.10	8.88	0.13	-0.87	14

Peru	-63.7	109.20	0.42	171.00	0.09	20.00	8.08	0.10	2.74	819
Philippines	-31.2	643.40	0.79	736.30	0.29	15.92	7.26	0.09	2.04	1625
Poland	-66.5	52.20	0.14	859.00	0.16	22.19	9.17	0.09	1.91	3313
Portugal	-37.3	142.60	1.38	404.90	0.20	30.65	9.68	0.04	2.47	756
Russia	-43.5	2962.00	2.04	1727.00	0.08	28.78	8.85	0.18	3.24	1208
Singapore	-168.5	0.10	0.00	2.48	0.00	19.22	10.41	0.10	3.86	7185
Slovakia	-99.7	4.50	0.08	99.88	0.10	15.39	9.11	0.09	1.58	68
Slovenia	-61.2	11.95	0.60	76.69	0.18	16.53	9.76	0.07	0.60	268
South Africa	-85.7	62.25	0.14	212.90	0.05	13.61	8.44	0.08	1.25	3167
Spain	-48.5	704.70	1.67	783.70	0.07	8.73	9.95	0.05	2.10	1913
Sweden	-129.5	1.25	0.01	138.10	0.05	14.69	10.58	0.05	2.17	4979
Switzerland	-48.5	56.15	0.76	389.20	0.15	20.42	10.82	0.05	2.92	3076
Thailand	-31.5	160.30	0.26	5410.00	1.29	23.00	8.06	0.08	3.04	5230
Turkey	-104.2	40.65	0.06	202.60	0.03	19.69	8.89	0.11	2.45	1523
USA	-44.8	486.10	0.17	38,827.00	0.35	8.42	10.55	0.05	4.28	96,841
United Kingdom	-68.7	117.30	0.20	1415.00	0.08	11.03	10.34	0.05	1.89	21,537
Venezuela	-64	68.90	0.27	344.10	0.11	22.29	8.75	0.14	0.66	135
Vietnam	-24	419.70	0.52	1637.00	0.91	10.61	7.16	0.15	3.11	1197

by country. We control for firm-level factors (e.g., size, age, assets, and growth) and country-level factors (e.g., GDP, GDP growth, and legal environment). As expected, we find that firms in countries with higher climate risk have poorer economic performance as measured by return-on-assets (*ROA*) and cash flows from operations over assets (*CFO*). Moving from the first quartile to the more risky third quartile of the annual CRI score can reduce a firm's *ROA* by 1.8 percentage points. We find also that firms in countries experiencing higher climate risk have more volatile earnings, measured by both accounting earnings and operating cash flows. This is consistent with extreme weather events disrupting business operations and bringing about fluctuations in earnings and operating cash flows.

Next, we examine whether climate risk is anticipated by managers and if it leads them to make changes in financing policies. Diamond (1991) and Bates et al. (2009) find that policies on debt and cash holdings are driven by liquidity concerns. We expect and find that firm managers in environments characterized by higher climate risk are concerned about being able to repay their creditors should an extreme weather event occur that inflicts considerable losses and hence rely less on short-term and more on long-term borrowing. We find that they are also likely to hold more cash and to issue lower cash dividends. These results suggest that firms use financing policies to hedge against operating cash flow volatility and illiquidity due to higher climate risk. However, we also find that the effect of climate risk on firm performance varies across industries, as climate risk has a more negative impact on some than on others.

We conduct an array of robustness tests. To mitigate concern about the omission of country-level control variables, we use the instrumental variable approach and continue to find similar results. We also use propensity scores to match observations on firm characteristics. The results remain robust. They are also robust to other factors such as whether or not the firm has climate risk insurance coverage and whether it is a multinational firm. We also test for alternative measures of climate-related risk, for the exclusion of US firms from the sample, and for the inclusion of CRI sub-indicators one at a time.

Our research makes at least two important contributions. To the best of our knowledge, it is the first study on the direct impact of the risk of major weather events on public firm performance in a cross-country setting. We find that firms in countries that face higher climate risk have significantly lower and more volatile earnings and cash flows. Thus, climate risk represents a significant exogenous source of earnings and cash volatility, along with economy, industry, and accounting factors (e.g., uncertainty surrounding accounting estimates) (Dichev & Tang, 2009; Lipe, 1990). This finding is also relevant to the literature on the effect of earnings volatility on firm operations and valuation (e.g., Francis et al., 2004; Minton & Schrand, 1999; Ronen & Sadan, 1981; Rountree et al., 2008).

Second, we establish a link between global climate risk and firm financing policies. Prior literature shows that liquidity risk affects firm financial policies on debt, cash holdings, and cash dividend issuance (e.g., Bates et al., 2009; Diamond, 1991; Stulz, 1990; Wang, 2012). For example, holding cash can be a risk management tool against cash fluctuations (Bates et al., 2009). Our findings suggest that firms facing higher climate risk have less short-term but more long-term debt, hold more cash, and distribute lower cash dividends. Our results also suggest that holding more cash to create financial slack is one way for firms to maintain organizational resilience to climate risk.

The remainder of the article is organized as follows. We begin the next section with a literature review and then develop hypotheses. We then explain our climate risk measures and describe our sample. Then, we discuss the methodology, give descriptive statistics, and present our analyses on the effect of climate risk on financial performance, earnings volatility, and cash volatility. We present the results of robustness tests in the penultimate section, and our conclusions in the final section.

Literature Review and Hypothesis Development

Effect of Climate Risk on Financial Performance and Earnings Volatility

It has long been recognized that climate can substantially impact a country's economic performance (Dell et al., 2014). For example, Nordhaus (2006) shows that climate is a key variable in explaining per capita income differences between Africa and wealthier regions of the world. One main measure of climate is temperature. Gallup et al. (1999), Bansal and Ochoa (2012), and Dell et al. (2009) show a negative relationship between temperature and economic performance. Specifically, Gallup et al. (1999) and Bansal and Ochoa (2012) find that countries in warmer regions are typically poorer per capita than their counterparts in cooler climates and that their economies and equity markets grow more slowly.[3] Burke et al. (2015) present strong evidence that the productivity of countries increases along with increases in temperature until an annual average temperature of 13 °C, with productivity declining significantly at higher temperatures, suggesting a non-linear relationship between economic productivity and temperature. In a study based on US municipal-level data, Dell et al. (2009) find a negative association between temperature and economic output.[4]

The above studies suggest that ongoing climate change will negatively affect economic activities and outputs as average temperatures rise (IPCC, 2007).[5] Burke et al. (2015) write that by 2100 unmitigated warming could reduce average global income by about 23%, Fuss (2016) that climate change destroys financial assets and disrupts related economic activities, and Covington and Thamotheram (2015) that a diversified global stock portfolio will lose 5–20% of its value if warming reaches 4 °C or more.

The amount of daylight associated with seasonality can also affect human psychology and mood with concomitant effects on economic behavior. For example, Kamstra et al. (2003) find that "seasonal affective disorder" affects stock returns.[6] Hirshleifer and Shumway (2003) find that sunny weather makes traders more upbeat which leads to positive

[3] Bansal and Ochoa (2012) propose that equity returns in countries with higher temperatures (i.e., those closer to the Equator) have a positive temperature risk premium; they also show that increases in global temperature negatively affect the economic growth of countries closer to the Equator.

[4] Albouy et al. (2013) posit that US households prefer a certain temperature level and find a cost of living premium in areas with such levels.

[5] Concern about the effect of rising temperatures is growing. Pal and Eltahir (2016) predict that the temperature in Southwest Asia will rise beyond the habitable level if global warming is left unabated.

[6] Seasonal affective disorder refers to an extensively documented medical condition whereby the shortness of the daylight in fall and winter leads to greater depression and, in turn, heightened risk aversion.

stock returns, and Cao and Wei (2005) that higher temperature is associated with apathy and lower stock returns and lower temperature with aggressiveness and higher stock returns.[7] Similarly, Novy-Marx (2014) points to the effect of New York City temperatures on stock returns.

Prior studies have also examined the effect of extreme weather events on the economy. Kreft and Eckstein (2014) state that global extreme weather events over the 1993–2012 period led to more than 530,000 casualties and over $2.5 trillion in economic losses. Jahn (2013) shows that from 1980 to 2012 the number of extreme weather events and losses from them increased significantly worldwide. Based on the 1970–2002 cross-country data, Yang (2008) shows that stronger storms are associated with higher fatalities and economic losses. Similarly, Hsiang and Narita (2012) show that extreme weather events such as windstorms lead to reduced growth rates as well as economic losses. Based on data from 28 Caribbean nations, Hsiang (2010) finds that while cyclones have a significant negative impact on some industries, they can have a significant positive impact on others, for example, on the construction industry. In a within-country study, Deryugina (2011) finds that government aid mitigates the economic losses from hurricanes and, as a result, there is no significant effect on county-level earnings ten years after their occurrence.[8]

[7] Prior literature tends to treat sunshine and temperature as two distinct weather variables. For example, Howarth and Hoffman (1984) show that skepticism is positively associated with temperature and negatively associated with the amount of sunshine.

[8] Interest in climate change has resulted in a recent strand of studies in this area including some that focus on the impact on firm valuation, as carbon dioxide emissions, hazardous chemicals, and other pollutants may result in onerous regulatory requirements, financial or reputational damage, or costly litigation. Konar and Cohen (2001) show that intangible asset valuation is negatively associated with levels of emitted toxic chemicals, Matsumura et al. (2014) that carbon emissions can negatively affect firm value, and Beatty and Shimshack (2010) that firms suffer from negative market returns when poorly rated on managing (i.e., measuring, reporting, and reducing) greenhouse gas emissions. Based on US evidence, Chava (2014) finds that investors charge firms with higher greenhouse emissions and hazardous chemical discharges more for equity and debt capital. Using a European sample, Tu (2014) finds that firms with better carbon management performance have better share performance. On the other hand, Anderson et al. (2016) document that carbon risk is currently underpriced by financial markets and investors can hedge against climate risks without losing any returns. Finally, Clapp et al. (2015) argue that climate science should play a crucial role in verifying that the "green projects" of firms are climate friendly. However, these studies do not directly study the impact of climate events (as opposed to concerns) on firm valuation and decision-making.

In sum, although many studies have presented evidence of climate and climate-related factors having an economic impact within and across countries, there is a lack of direct evidence of an impact at the firm level, which would be very useful in understanding its impact on managerial decisions and firm performance. Extreme weather can negatively affect firm performance because it can inflict physical damage on firm fixed assets (e.g., property, plant, and equipment), decreasing not only the value of the assets, but also the earnings that might have been generated from them. Given the sometimes significant negative effect of extreme weather conditions on local economies, firm property, and business operations, we present the following hypothesis:

Hypothesis 1

Climate risk is negatively (positively) associated with a firm's financial returns (earnings volatility).

Effect of Climate Risk on Financial Policy

Climate change and increasingly extreme weather necessitate substantial organizational transformations (Wilbanks et al., 2007). A large body of literature addresses the notion of organizational resilience to climate change, which is the ability of an organization to systematically absorb, and recover from, the adverse effects of external environmental disturbance caused by weather extremes (Berkes et al., 2003; Linnenluecke & Griffiths, 2010; Tschakert & Dietrich, 2010). Studies focus mainly on operational resilience to climate change, through relocation of activities, improvements in infrastructure and production techniques, and increased insurance coverage (Berkhout et al., 2006; Hoffmann et al., 2009). Some point to the importance of organizational slack resources, such as backup facilities and financial slack (e.g., Linnenluecke et al., 2008; Vogus & Sutcliffe, 2007; Woods, 2006). However, more studies are needed on financial slack (Linnenluecke & Griffiths, 2010). We expect that firms in countries characterized by extreme weather are more likely to maintain financial slack resources in order to improve organizational resilience to weather extremes.

Effect of Climate Risk on Debt

Given our predicted effects of climate risk (i.e., reducing firm performance and increasing earnings volatility), we expect that firms located where extreme weather events are likely will increase financial slack resources. Debt structure is an important financial policy of this kind. Diamond (1991) posits that firms with high liquidation risk are likely to prefer long-term debt due to short-term illiquidity concerns. Hence, high cash flow volatility and the accompanying liquidation risk are likely to cause firms to take on less short-term debt. In addition, because short-term debt is subject to more frequent renegotiation it is more likely to be negatively affected by liquidity shocks (Custodio et al., 2013). Extreme weather can lead to liquidity shocks, and thus firms in areas characterized by extreme weather may prefer long-term debt to avoid financial constraints.[9]

Based on the above discussion, we present the following hypotheses:

Hypothesis 2
Climate risk is positively associated with firm long-term debt.

Hypothesis 3
Climate risk is negatively associated with firm short-term debt.

Effect of Climate Risk on Cash Holding

The precautionary motive is an important reason for holding cash (e.g., Bates et al., 2009; Huang et al., 2015; Opler et al., 1999). Opler et al. (1999) find that firms are inclined to hold more cash when performance is poor or cash flow volatility is high, suggesting that firms hold more cash to cope with adverse shocks. As country-level climate risk is an adverse shock to firm operation, those in higher climate risk environments have incentives to hold more cash.

---

[9] Atta-Mensah (2016) suggests that countries and firms can issue weather-linked bonds to hedge against volatility due to weather-dependent assets.

Prior studies show that high cash flow volatility leads firms to hold more cash (e.g., by paying lower cash dividends) as a hedge against operational risk (Itzkowitz, 2013; Larkin, 2013; Wang, 2012). For example, Wang (2012) shows that because losing a major customer can lead to a huge drop in cash inflow, firms tend to hold cash as a hedge against that. As we discuss above, climate risk can increase operational risk (e.g., performance volatility) and lead firms to hold more cash.

Based on the above discussion, we present the following hypotheses:

Hypothesis 4
Climate risk is positively associated with cash holding.

Hypothesis 5
Climate risk is negatively associated with cash dividends.

Measurement and Sample Data

Measurement

We use the 2014 Global Climate Risk Index (CRI) compiled and published by Germanwatch to measure climate risk by country.[10] The CRI captures the extent to which countries have suffered direct loss associated with extreme weather-related events such as storms, floods, and heat waves (Kreft & Eckstein, 2014).[11] According to the authors, the CRI is indicative of the severity of the climate risk a country faces in the future due to climate change (Kreft & Eckstein, 2014: 3). The CRI has been widely cited by studies addressing climate change (e.g., Burnell, 2012; Rivera & Wamsler, 2014; Garschagen & Romero-Lankao, 2015), and

[10] Firms in larger countries can possibly move from a country's high-climate risk area to one where the risk is less. That possibility would tend to reduce the robustness of any findings. At the same time, many firms cannot relocate (e.g., some retailers and firms in communication and transportation).

[11] "Geological factors like earthquakes, volcanic eruptions and tsunamis, for which data is also available, are not included as they are not weather-related per se and therefore not climate change-related" (Kreft & Eckstein, 2014: 16).

recent scientific evidence shows that many severe weather events are attributable to climate change (Jahn, 2013; Kreft & Eckstein, 2014).

The CRI has been published annually since 2006, the 2014 edition being the ninth and most recent. There are two sets of CRI scores: annual and long-term. Annual scores are based on data pre-dating by 2 years the edition year. For example, the 2014 edition contains annual scores based on 2012 data. The long-term scores are based on data for a period of 20 years ending 2 years prior to the edition year, e.g., the long-term scores in the 2014 edition are based on the 1993–2012 data. We adopt annual scores from the 2008 to 2014 editions and the 2014 edition long-term scores.[12] That is, we use annual data, 2006–2012, and long-term data for the period 1993–2012.

The CRI is based on the following two absolute and two relative indicators of climate-related risk: (1) number of deaths, (2) number of deaths per 100,000 inhabitants, (3) sum of losses in US$ at purchasing power parity (PPP), and (4) losses per unit of Gross Domestic Product (GDP).[13] A country's index score equals that country's average ranking of all four indicators, absolute indicators (1) and (3) weighting one-sixth each, and relative indicators (2) and (4) weighting one-third each.[14] Lower index scores and the corresponding higher rankings thus indicate greater risk. For example, in the 2014 edition, Honduras has the lowest long-term CRI score of 10.17, derived from the rankings in the four indicators. Honduras is ranked Number 1 on the CRI with the most severe climate-related risk during 1993–2012. Since lower index scores indicate higher climate risk, we multiply the index scores by negative one so that higher scores indicate greater risk. For example, the Honduras score becomes -10.17.

---

[12] We were not able to obtain annual scores from the 2006 and 2007 editions.

[13] Economic losses comprise "all elementary loss events which have caused substantial damage to property or persons" or in other words, direct losses (Kreft & Eckstein, 2014: 16). Indirect losses, i.e., the losses that firms experience due to damaged assets and those of their customers, are not included. However, they are highly correlated to direct losses (Hallegatte, 2008; Kowalewski & Ujeyl, 2012).

[14] Because indicators 3 and 4, sum of losses in US$ at PPP and losses as a percent of GDP, are likely to be affected by the economic size and performance of a country, we control for level and change of GDP in our multivariate regression analysis. Also, according to Kreft and Eckstein (2014: 20), "the indicator 'absolute losses in US$' is identified by purchasing power parity (PPP), because using this figure better expresses how people are actually affected by the loss of one US$ than by using nominal exchange rates."

Data

Table 13.1 shows the number of observations by country. There are a total of 353,906 observations, 27% of which come from the US (96,841 observations). We obtained financial data for these firms from Compustat and country-level institutional data from a number of sources (see the Appendix for details). Following the extant literature (e.g., Masulis & Mobbs, 2014), we exclude the financial and utility industries from our sample since these industries are highly regulated and are quite different from other industries. The country sample size varies between 54 and 55 countries depending on data availability.[15] Table 13.1 presents the descriptive statistics for country-level variables for 55 countries. Vietnam, the Philippines, Thailand, and Portugal have the highest (i.e., the least negative) long-term CRI scores: they suffered the most direct losses from weather-related events over the 1993–2012 time period. For example, in the case of Vietnam the annual average number of deaths is given as 419.70 (0.52 deaths per 100,000 inhabitants) and the annual average loss in purchasing power as $1637 million (0.91% of their GDP). Ecuador has the highest standard deviation of annual CRI (32.03). Norway, Switzerland, Denmark, Sweden, and the US are ranked the highest in terms of GDP, and Russia, China, Vietnam, India, and Venezuela ranked the highest in GDP growth. In terms of legal environment (*LEG_ENV*), the US, Finland, France, Singapore, and Hungary are ranked the highest.

Methodology and Descriptive Statistics

Methodology

We estimate the effect of climate risk on financial performance, on earnings and operating cash flow volatility, and on financial policy using the following specification:

[15] One limitation of this study is that we do not account for how a firm might be affected by climate risk associated with its material operations located overseas.

$$\begin{aligned}
&\text{Financial performance / performance} \\
&\text{financial policy} = \beta_0 + \beta_1 \ \text{Climate Risk} \\
&+\beta_2 ROA / CFO + \beta_3 SIZE + \beta_4 Ln(age) \\
&+\beta_5 Intangible\, Assets + \beta_6 PPE + \beta_7 Total\, Dept \\
&+\beta_8 Sales\, Growth + \beta_9 LGDP + \beta_{10} GDP Growth \\
&+\beta_{11} LEG_ENV + Industry + Year + \varepsilon.
\end{aligned} \tag{13.1}$$

The dependent variables are two measures of financial performance, two of earnings and operating cash flow volatility, and five of financial policies. Financial performance is measured by return-on-assets (*ROA*) and cash flows from operations (*CFO*); hence, *ROA/CFO* is not included in the control variables when testing the effect of climate risk on financial performance. *Earnings Volatility* is the standard deviation of quarterly pre-tax income scaled by total assets over the preceding five fiscal years and *Operating Cash Flow Volatility* is the standard deviation of quarterly cash flows from operations scaled by total assets over the preceding five fiscal years. Financial policy is measured by three measures of debt, *Short-term Debt*, *Long-term Debt*, and *Short and Long-term Debt*, by *Cash Holding* (cash and short-term investment scaled by lagged assets), and by *Cash Dividend* (cash dividend scaled by lagged assets). The variable of interest is *Climate Risk*, measured by annual and long-term CRI scores published by Germanwatch as described previously. The Appendix provides the variable definitions.

We control for firm characteristics including the natural log of assets (*SIZE*), the natural log of firm age (*Ln*(*age*)), intangible assets (*Intangible Assets*), net property, plant, and equipment (*PPE*), *Total Debt*, and *Sales Growth*.

The country-level macroeconomic factors we include in the regression model are log of real GDP per capita (*LGDP*) and annual growth of total GDP (*GDP Growth*), to follow previous study (Kingsley & Graham, 2017). Since CRI is likely to be affected by the size and financial performance of a country's economy, we also use *LGDP* and *GDP growth* to control for these factors. To control for a country's legal environment, we use *LEG_ENV*, the principal component extracted from *COMMON*,

ENFORCE, and *CR*. *COMMON* refers to an indicator by La Porta et al. (1998) that equals one if the legal origin is common law, and zero otherwise; *ENFORCE* is the law enforcement index (from the Economic Freedom of the World 2010 Annual Report) that ranges from 0 to 10, with higher values indicating greater law enforcement. *CR* is an index reflecting creditor rights, which is formed by adding four dummy variables: a dummy equal to one (1) when a country imposes restrictions, such as creditor consent or minimum dividends to file for reorganization; (2) when secured creditors are able to gain possession of their security once a reorganization petition has been approved (no automatic stay); (3) when secured creditors are ranked first in the distribution of proceeds that result from the disposition of the assets of a bankruptcy; and (4) when debtors do not retain the administration of their property pending the resolution of the reorganization. The index ranges from 0 to 4 and is based on La Porta et al. (1998) and Djankov et al. (2007).

Following prior literature (Le & Kroll, 2017; Marano et al., 2017), we control industries and year fixed effects.

Descriptive Statistics

Table 13.2, Panel A shows the descriptive statistics for the sample used for testing for the effect of climate risk on firm performance, earnings volatility, and financial policy.[16] The required data to be included in these tests are available for a total of 55 countries, those listed in Table 13.1. The mean and median annual climate risks are -44.53 and -38.00, respectively, -65.59 for the annual score, and -48.00 for the long-term score. Our sample firms have a median *ROA* of 0.040, a *CFO* of 0.061, a short-term debt of 0.052, cash holdings of 10.4% of assets, and cash dividends of 0.6% of assets. The natural log of their assets (*Size*) is 6.28, the natural log of firm age (*Ln*(*age*)) is 2.197, and sales growth is 7.5%. The median value of the log of a country's per capita GDP (*LGDP*) is 10.36, the median value of *GDP Growth* is 6.3%, and the median score for legal environment (*LEG_ENV*) is 3.039.

[16] We winsorized all the continuous variables at the 1 and 99% levels.

Table 13.2 Descriptive statistics and correlation for variables

Panel A: Descriptive statistics

Variables	Mean	SD	P25	Median	P75	No. of countries	No. of obs.
Climate Risk (Annual)	-44.53	25.11	-63.50	-38.00	-25.17	55	147,223
Climate Risk (Long term)	-65.59	31.21	-92.00	-48.00	-44.83	55	353,906
ROA	-0.005	0.212	-0.018	0.040	0.093	55	353,906
CFO	0.041	0.184	-0.003	0.061	0.127	55	326,087
Earnings Volatility	0.045	0.072	0.010	0.020	0.045	55	218,763
Operating Cash Flow Volatility	0.071	0.075	0.026	0.048	0.085	55	214,647
Short-term Debt	0.111	0.144	0.004	0.052	0.163	55	353,752
Long-term Debt	0.152	0.198	0.001	0.076	0.227	55	353,828
Short and LONG-term Debt	0.272	0.273	0.049	0.214	0.399	55	353,452
Cash Holdings	0.482	1.420	0.034	0.104	0.277	55	351,895
Cash Dividends	0.018	0.031	0.000	0.006	0.021	55	261,581
SIZE	6.532	2.935	4.372	6.280	8.486	55	353,906
Total Debt	0.625	0.411	0.365	0.569	0.774	55	353,906
Ln(age)	2.150	0.729	1.609	2.197	2.639	55	353,906
Intangible Assets	0.100	0.184	0.000	0.011	0.105	55	353,906
PPE	0.346	0.286	0.122	0.281	0.492	55	353,906
Sales Growth	0.188	0.574	-0.041	0.075	0.248	55	353,906
LGDP	9.725	1.339	9.121	10.360	10.590	55	353,906
GDP Growth	0.069	0.094	0.033	0.063	0.115	55	353,906
LEG_ENV	2.834	1.323	2.111	3.039	4.279	55	353,906

Panel B: Climate risk index by continent and year (2006–2012)

Year	Asia	North America	Oceania	Africa	Latin America	Europe
2006	-25.80	-40.55	-39.28	-63.98	-67.12	-51.72
2007	-52.81	-66.29	-41.25	-46.32	-74.45	-65.63

(continued)

Table 13.2 (continued)

Panel A: Descriptive statistics

Variables	Mean	SD	P25	Median	P75	No. of countries	No. of obs.
2008	-40.93	-53.24	-32.90	-22.97	-36.21		-60.70
2009	-44.15	-54.29	-17.04	-55.13	-55.77		-52.29
2010	-51.79	-61.07	-34.51	-56.64	-52.89		-65.76
2011	-37.83	-37.52	-25.65	-64.94	-31.16		-62.20
2012	-57.30	-57.05	-67.30	-53.37	-87.13		-78.63
Mean	-44.37	-52.86	-36.85	-51.91	-57.82		-62.42
SD	9.95	9.67	14.60	13.20	18.63		8.49

Panel C: Pearson correlation

		A	B	C	D	E	F	G	H	I	J	K
Climate Risk (Annual)	A	1										
Climate Risk (Long term)	B	0.699	1									
ROA	C	-0.034	-0.047	1								
CFO	D	-0.024	-0.044	0.647	1							
Earnings Volatility	E	0.046	0.025	-0.470	-0.414	1						
Operating Cash Flow Volatility	F	0.053	0.019	-0.302	-0.326	0.480	1					
Short-term Debt	G	-0.007	-0.029	-0.079	-0.103	0.062	0.067	1				
Long-term Debt	H	0.072	0.079	-0.012	0.016	-0.031	-0.105	0.043	1			
Short and Long-term Debt	I	0.054	0.043	-0.072	-0.048	0.033	-0.031	0.617	0.779	1		
Cash Holdings	J	0.041	0.030	-0.295	-0.360	0.262	0.181	-0.126	-0.096	-0.134	1	
Cash Dividends	K	-0.106	-0.069	0.293	0.294	-0.123	-0.005	0.017	-0.070	-0.018	-0.062	1

Note: All correlations are significant at the $p < 0.05$ level

Panel B of Table 13.2 provides annual CRI scores by continent.[17] They vary over time. For example, in the case of Asia the highest score (-25.80) is in year 2006 and the lowest (-57.30) in year 2012. The mean values for Asia, North America, Oceania, Africa, Latin America, and Europe are -44.37, -52.86, -36.85, -51.91, -57.82, and -62.42 and their standard deviations are 9.95, 9.67, 14.60, 13.20, 18.61, and 8.49, respectively.

Panel C of Table 13.2 provides the Pearson correlations between climate risk and our measures of financial performance, earnings and cash flow volatility, and financing policies. Both annual and long-term climate risk measures are negatively and significantly related to ROA, CFO, short-term debt, and cash dividends and positively related to earnings volatility, operating cash flow volatility, long-term debt, short- and long-term debt, and cash holdings. These univariate correlations are consistent with our hypotheses.

Main Results

Effect of Climate Risk on Financial Performance

Table 13.3 presents the test results relating to the effect of climate risk on financial performance. The sample includes the 55 countries listed in Table 13.1. Columns (1) and (2) show the results using the annual climate risk score with return-on-asset (*ROA*) and cash flow from operation (*CFO*) as the dependent variables. In both columns, we find the coefficients of the annual climate risk score to be significantly negative, indicating that higher climate risk is significantly associated with worse firm performance.[18] For example, in Column (1), the non-transformed coefficient (i.e., all coefficients in Tables 13.3, 13.4, and 13.5 have been multiplied by 100 for exposition purposes) of the annual climate risk is -0.00047 ($p < 0.000$), with the 95% confidence interval of between

[17] To save space, we do not provide the annual CRI by countries where the results are similar.

[18] Results not reported here indicate that both annual and long-term climate risk scores are positively associated with firms having negative extraordinary items and discontinued items.

Table 13.3 Climate risk and firm performance

	(1)	(2)	(3)	(4)
	ROA	*CFO*	*ROA*	*CFO*
Climate Risk (Annual)	-0.047	-0.030		
	(0.003)	(0.003)		
Climate Risk (Long term)			-0.009	-0.008
			(0.002)	(0.002)
SIZE	0.021	0.014	0.020	0.015
	(0.000)	(0.000)	(0.000)	(0.000)
Ln(age)	0.009	0.012	0.013	0.018
	(0.001)	(0.001)	(0.001)	(0.001)
Intangible Assets	0.119	0.122	0.110	0.097
	(0.005)	(0.005)	(0.004)	(0.004)
PPE	0.092	0.120	0.099	0.121
	(0.003)	(0.003)	(0.003)	(0.003)
Total Debt	-0.094	-0.063	-0.089	-0.059
	(0.003)	(0.003)	(0.002)	(0.002)
Sales Growth	0.028	-0.007	0.016	-0.021
	(0.002)	(0.002)	(0.001)	(0.001)
LGDP	-0.021	-0.014	-0.013	-0.004
	(0.001)	(0.001)	(0.001)	(0.001)
GDP Growth	0.055	-0.019	0.068	0.016
	(0.008)	(0.007)	(0.005)	(0.005)
LEG_ENV	0.002	0.008	-0.006	-0.004
	(0.001)	(0.001)	(0.001)	(0.001)
Intercept	0.055	0.009	0.029	-0.033
	(0.011)	(0.010)	(0.008)	(0.007)
Industry/year	Yes	Yes	Yes	Yes
Cluster by firm	Yes	Yes	Yes	Yes
No. of observations	147,223	145,749	353,906	326,087
Adjusted R^2	0.209	0.165	0.182	0.158
F	120.3	98.49	162.6	135.2
No. of countries	55	55	55	55

This table presents the regression results of the impact of climate risk on financial performance. Regressions include year and industry fixed effects. The standard errors reported in parentheses are heteroskedasticity robust and clustered at the firm level. To conserve space, we do not report the coefficient estimates for the industry and year dummies. For exposition purposes, we multiply the coefficients on climate risk by 100. All variables are defined in the Appendix

-0.00053 and -0.00040.[19] This indicates that moving from the first quartile (-63.50) to the third quartile (-25.17) of the annual climate risk score can reduce a firm's *ROA* by 1.8 percentage points.[20] The effect size of the annual climate risk is 0.0027, with the 95% confidence interval of between 0.0022 and 0.0032.[21]

Similarly, in Column (2), the coefficient on the annual climate risk is -0.00030 ($p < 0.000$), with the 95% confidence interval of between -0.00036 and -0.00025. Moving from the first quartile (-63.50) to the third quartile (-25.17) of the annual climate risk score reduces a firm's *CFO* by 1.15 percentage points.[22] The effect size of the annual climate risk is 0.0015, with the 95% confidence interval of between 0.0011 and 0.0019. Columns (3) and (4) show similar results when using long-term climate risk as both coefficients are significantly negative. In sum, consistent with Hypothesis 1, Table 13.3 shows that higher climate risk can have significantly negative economic consequences on firm performance.

Effect of Climate Risk on Earnings Volatility

Table 13.4 shows the results of estimating the relationship between climate risk and earnings volatility. As we do not have the data necessary to calculate earnings volatility for Ecuadorian firms, the sample consists of 54 countries.[23] Columns (1) and (2) show the results for the annual climate risk and Columns (3) and (4) for the long-term climate risk. Results in Columns (1) and (2) indicate that the coefficients for the annual climate risk are significantly positive for accounting earnings volatility (coefficient = 0.0005 and $p < 0.000$) and operating cash flow volatility (coefficient = 0.00016 and $p < 0.000$). The 95% confidence interval of

---

[19] Meyer et al. (2017) point out that it is important to discuss the confidence interval of the coefficient. To save space, we do not provide the confidence intervals in the tables.

[20] It is calculated as follows: (-25.17 - (-63.50)) × (-0.00047) = -0.0108.

[21] Effect size refers to the magnitude of the effects (Ferguson, 2009).

[22] It is calculated as follows: (-25.17 - (-63.50)) × (-0.0003) = -0.0115.

[23] The quarterly pre-tax income (PI) of firms in Ecuador is not given. Thus, we are not able to calculate *Earnings Volatility* for Ecuador and so cannot include Ecuador in our sample, leading to the reduction of sample size from 55 countries in Table 13.3 to 54 countries in Table 13.4.

Table 13.4 Climate risk and earnings volatility

	(1)	(2)	(3)	(4)
	Earnings Volatility	*Operating Cash Flow Volatility*	*Earnings Volatility*	*Operating Cash Flow Volatility*
Climate Risk (Annual)	0.005	0.016		
	(0.001)	(0.001)		
Climate Risk (Long term)			0.001	0.004
			(0.001)	(0.001)
ROA	-0.098		-0.103	
	(0.002)		(0.001)	
CFO		-0.079		-0.075
		(0.003)		(0.002)
SIZE	-0.005	-0.007	-0.006	-0.008
	(0.000)	(0.000)	(0.000)	(0.000)
Ln(age)	-0.004	-0.005	-0.005	-0.002
	(0.001)	(0.001)	(0.000)	(0.000)
Intangible Assets	-0.013	-0.030	-0.010	-0.030
	(0.002)	(0.002)	(0.001)	(0.002)
PPE	-0.017	-0.027	-0.015	-0.026
	(0.001)	(0.002)	(0.001)	(0.001)
Total Debt	0.028	0.024	0.027	0.025
	(0.001)	(0.001)	(0.001)	(0.001)
Sales Growth	0.012	0.010	0.014	0.009
	(0.001)	(0.001)	(0.000)	(0.000)
LGDP	-0.002	-0.004	-0.001	-0.003
	(0.000)	(0.000)	(0.000)	(0.000)
GDP Growth	0.014	0.031	0.028	0.047
	(0.003)	(0.003)	(0.003)	(0.003)
LEG_ENV	0.004	-0.002	0.005	-0.002
	(0.000)	(0.000)	(0.000)	(0.000)
Intercept	0.081	0.166	0.058	0.144
	(0.005)	(0.006)	(0.003)	(0.005)
Industry/year	Yes	Yes	Yes	Yes
Cluster by firm	Yes	Yes	Yes	Yes
No. of observations	117,014	115,170	218,763	212,439
Adjusted R^2	0.278	0.197	0.310	0.203
F	110.3	88.79	203.3	113.6
No. of countries	54	54	54	54

This table presents the regression results of the impact of climate risk on performance volatility. Regressions include year and industry fixed effects. The standard errors reported in parentheses are heteroskedasticity robust and clustered at the firm level. To conserve space, we do not report the coefficient estimates for the industry and year dummies. For exposition purposes, we multiply the coefficients on climate risk by 100. All variables are defined in the Appendix the coefficient is between 0.00026 (0.00013) and 0.00069 (0.00018), when the dependent variable is earnings volatility (operating cash flow volatility). The effect size of annual climate risk is 0.0003 (0.0026), with the 95% confidence interval of between 0.0001 (0.0020) and 0.0005 (0.0032), when the dependent variable is earnings volatility (operating cash flow volatility).

Results in Columns (3) and (4) show that long-term climate risk has an insignificantly positive coefficient for earnings volatility but a significantly positive coefficient for operating cash flow volatility.[24] In sum, consistent with Hypothesis 1, Table 13.4 indicates that higher climate risk is associated with greater earnings volatility and operating cash flow volatility, consistent with extreme weather events disrupting normal operations.

Effect of Climate Risk on Financing Policies

Table 13.5 presents the results of our tests of the relationship between climate risk and a firm's policies on short-term and long-term debt, cash holding, and cash dividends. Panel A uses annual climate risk and Panel B long-term climate risk. In Panel A, Column (1) indicates that annual climate risk is negatively associated with *Short-term Debt* (coefficient = -0.00059, $p < 0.000$), with the 95% confidence interval of between -0.00064 and -0.00054. The effect size of annual climate risk is 0.0083, with the 95% confidence interval of between 0.0074 and 0.0092.

Columns (2) and (3), on the other hand, show that annual climate risk is positively associated with both *Long-term Debt* and *Short- and Long-term Debt*.[25] In Panel B, Columns (1), (2), and (3) show similar results for long-term climate risk. In sum, consistent with Hypotheses 2 and 3, we find climate risk to be associated with higher long-term but lower short-term debt.

---

[24] Rountree et al. (2008) argue that investors are mainly concerned about the cash flow (as opposed to accounting) component of earnings volatility. Moreover, illiquidity issues are usually caused by cash flow volatility, not earnings volatility.

[25] The results indicate that these firms have higher long-term debt and total debt, which is a sign of financial distress (Banerjee et al., 2008) and can be a result of poor earnings performance resulting from extreme weather events.

Table 13.5 Climate risk and financial policy

Panel A: Climate risk (Annual) and financial policy					
	(1) *Short-term Debt*	(2) *Long-term Debt*	(3) *Short and Long-term Debt*	(4) *Cash Holdings*	(5) *Cash Dividends*
Climate Risk (Annual)	-0.059	0.075	0.013	0.364	-0.020
	(0.003)	(0.003)	(0.004)	(0.026)	(0.001)
ROA	-0.127	-0.107	-0.273	-1.703	0.060
	(0.003)	(0.005)	(0.007)	(0.050)	(0.001)
SIZE	0.003	0.008	0.011	-0.037	-0.001
	(0.000)	(0.000)	(0.000)	(0.002)	(0.000)
Ln(age)	-0.012	0.004	-0.007	-0.175	-0.002
	(0.001)	(0.001)	(0.002)	(0.010)	(0.000)
Intangible Assets	0.050	0.266	0.364	-0.385	0.010
	(0.004)	(0.006)	(0.007)	(0.036)	(0.001)
PPE	0.087	0.243	0.371	-0.159	0.006
	(0.003)	(0.005)	(0.006)	(0.034)	(0.001)
Leverage				-0.469	0.005
				(0.020)	(0.001)
Sales Growth	0.013	0.013	0.029	0.122	-0.002
	(0.001)	(0.001)	(0.002)	(0.014)	(0.000)
LGDP	-0.029	0.013	-0.019	0.150	-0.003
	(0.001)	(0.001)	(0.002)	(0.009)	(0.000)
GDP Growth	0.040	-0.085	-0.048	1.180	0.033
	(0.006)	(0.006)	(0.009)	(0.061)	(0.002)
LEG_ENV	0.009	-0.012	-0.001	-0.059	0.001
	(0.001)	(0.001)	(0.001)	(0.007)	(0.000)
Intercept	0.322	-0.110	0.216	0.248	0.046
	(0.012)	(0.014)	(0.020)	(0.094)	(0.003)
Industry/year	Yes	Yes	Yes	Yes	Yes
Cluster by firm	Yes	Yes	Yes	Yes	Yes
No. of observations	147,183	147,202	147,029	146,156	107,824
Adjusted R^2/ Pseudo R^2	0.156	0.239	0.263	0.298	0.177
F/χ^2	132.7	150.2	219.9	77.01	97.92
No. of countries	55	55	55	55	55
Panel B: Climate risk (Long term) and financial policy					

(continued)

Table 13.5 (continued)

	(1) *Short-term Debt*	(2) *Long-term Debt*	(3) *Short and Long-term Debt*	(4) *Cash Holdings*	(5) *Cash Dividends*
Climate Risk (Long term)	-0.040	0.063	0.016	0.115	-0.010
	(0.002)	(0.002)	(0.003)	(0.016)	(0.001)
ROA	-0.128	-0.084	-0.250	-1.491	0.039
	(0.002)	(0.003)	(0.005)	(0.031)	(0.001)
SIZE	0.005	0.006	0.012	-0.025	-0.001
	(0.000)	(0.000)	(0.000)	(0.001)	(0.000)
Ln(age)	-0.008	0.010	0.002	-0.166	-0.001
	(0.001)	(0.001)	(0.001)	(0.006)	(0.000)
Intangible Assets	0.059	0.275	0.389	-0.296	0.009
	(0.003)	(0.005)	(0.006)	(0.025)	(0.001)
PPE	0.084	0.246	0.379	-0.076	0.008
	(0.003)	(0.004)	(0.004)	(0.022)	(0.001)
Leverage				-0.405	0.003
				(0.013)	(0.000)
Sales Growth	0.010	0.012	0.022	0.181	-0.002
	(0.001)	(0.001)	(0.001)	(0.009)	(0.000)
LGDP	-0.027	0.012	-0.017	0.093	-0.003
	(0.001)	(0.001)	(0.001)	(0.005)	(0.000)
GDP Growth	0.003	-0.016	-0.016	0.595	0.023
	(0.004)	(0.004)	(0.006)	(0.033)	(0.001)
LEG_ENV	0.007	-0.005	0.005	-0.008	0.000
	(0.001)	(0.001)	(0.001)	(0.005)	(0.000)
Intercept	0.270	-0.080	0.184	0.318	0.036
	(0.009)	(0.011)	(0.016)	(0.082)	(0.002)
Industry/year	Yes	Yes	Yes	Yes	Yes
Cluster by firm	Yes	Yes	Yes	Yes	Yes
No. of observations	353,752	353,828	353,452	351,895	261,581
Adjusted R^2/ Pseudo R^2	0.141	0.232	0.261	0.234	0.156
F/χ^2	157.0	201.5	314.3	94.86	126.2
No. of countries	55	55	55	55	55

This table presents the regression results of the impact of climate risk on financial volatility. Regressions include the year and industry fixed effects. The standard errors reported in parentheses are heteroskedasticity robust and clustered at the firm level. To conserve space, we do not report the coefficient estimates for the industry and year dummies. For exposition purposes, we multiply the coefficients on climate risk by 100. All variables are defined in the Appendix

In Panel A of Table 13.5, Columns (4) and (5) show that annual climate risk is positively associated with cash holding and negatively associated with cash dividends. The results have economic significance. For example, in Column (4), the coefficient of 0.00364 on the annual climate risk indicates that moving from the first quartile (-63.5) to the third quartile (-25.17) of the annual climate risk score can increase a firm's cash holding by 13.95% of its total assets.[26] Similarly, in Column (5), the coefficient of -0.0002 for annual climate risk indicates that moving from the first quartile (-63.5) to the third quartile (-25.17) of the annual climate risk score can decrease a firm's cash dividend by 0.77% of its total assets.[27] The results in Columns (4) and (5) in Panel B also show that long-term climate risk is also positively associated with cash holding and negatively with cash dividends.[28] These results are consistent with Hypotheses 4 and 5.[29]

Overall, the evidence relayed in Table 13.5 suggests that firms in countries with higher climate risk borrow less short-term and more long-term, hold more cash, and issue lower cash dividends. This is consistent with using extra cash holding to mitigate cash flow volatility that may result from extreme weather events.

Effects of Vulnerable Industries

Different industries have different levels of vulnerability to extreme weather conditions. Climate risk can adversely affect firm profitability in at least two ways. First, extreme weather can inflict physical damage on assets and deprive a firm of potential revenue (Reisch, 2005). According to the Sustainability Accounting Standards Board (2016), Wilbanks et al.

---

[26] It is calculated as follows: (−25.17 − (−63.5)) × (0.00364) = 0.1395.

[27] It is calculated as follows: (−25.17 − (−63.5)) × (−0.0002) = −0.0077.

[28] Our results are robust to controlling for whether a country's company law or commercial code requires firms to distribute certain percentage of their income as dividends (La Porta et al., 1998).

[29] The results in Table 13.5 may be due to extreme weather or to volatility in higher earnings and cash holdings as suggested in Table 13.4. We use path analysis (e.g., Wright, 1934) to examine these potential dependencies where annual extreme weather is treated as the direct path and earnings volatility as the mediated (indirect) path. We find that both direct and mediated paths are significant and positive, indicating that the financing policies are affected by both organizational resilience and earnings volatility.

(2007), and McCarthy et al. (2001), industries with heavy non-deployed and long-lived capital assets are especially vulnerable to these kinds of loss. Industries of this kind include communications, energy (e.g., mining and oil extraction), healthcare, and utilities. Second, extreme weather can disrupt normal operations and lead to operating losses. The SASB (2016) and Wilbanks et al. (2007) show that industries dependent on moderate weather, with both an extended supply chain and a reliance on infrastructure, are likely to see their operations disrupted by extreme climate. Examples of these kinds of industries are agriculture and food manufacturing that depend on land, water, and sun, and industries that provide business services and transportation. There is also support for this view from Fleming et al. (2006), Hsiang (2010), and Challinor et al. (2014). Based on that literature, we consider agriculture, energy (including mining and oil extraction), food products, healthcare, communications, business services, and transportation to be vulnerable industries.[30] *Vulnerable industries* are coded one.

We include the interaction term *Climate Risk (Annual)* × *Vulnerable Industries* in Eq. (13.1) and present the regression results in Table 13.6. Columns (1), (3), (5), (6), (7), (8), and (9) show that the coefficients are generally significant and take the expected sign. Overall, this indicates that the adverse effect of climate risk on reducing ROA, increasing earnings volatility, borrowing less short-term but more long-term, and reducing cash dividends is more pronounced for these vulnerable industries. This industry-specific result provides additional supporting evidence for the link between climate risk and financial performance and financing policies.

Robustness Tests

Instrument Variable Method: Population Density

Because some of the country-level and firm-level variables are difficult to quantify and control, we used an instrumental variable method to re-estimate our models. In that robustness test, we chose population density

[30] We use the Fama–French Industry classification.

Table 13.6 Climate risk and vulnerable industries

	(1)	(2)	(3)	(4)	(5)	(6)	(7)	(8)	(9)
	ROA	*CFO*	*Earnings Volatility*	*Operating Cash Flow Volatility*	*Short-term Debt*	*Long-term Debt*	*Short and Long-term Debt*	*Cash Holdings*	*Cash Dividends*
Climate Risk (Annual)	-0.066	-0.047	0.004	0.012	-0.072	0.053	-0.018	0.294	-0.018
	(0.004)	(0.003)	(0.000)	(0.001)	(0.002)	(0.004)	(0.003)	(0.026)	(0.001)
Vulnerable Industries	-0.007	0.022	0.006	0.003	-0.034	-0.005	-0.039	0.281	0.001
	(0.004)	(0.004)	(0.000)	(0.001)	(0.002)	(0.004)	(0.003)	(0.152)	(0.001)
Climate Risk (Annual) × Vulnerable Industries	-0.021	-0.002	0.002	0.002	-0.017	0.030	0.014	0.351	-0.004
	(0.008)	(0.007)	(0.001)	(0.002)	(0.005)	(0.008)	(0.007)	(0.059)	(0.002)
Control variables	Yes	Yes	Yes	Yes	Yes	Yes	Yes	Yes	Yes
Industry/year	Yes	Yes	Yes	Yes	Yes	Yes	Yes	Yes	Yes
Cluster by firm	Yes	Yes	Yes	Yes	Yes	Yes	Yes	Yes	Yes
No. of observations	147,223	145,749	117,014	115,170	147,008	147,202	147,029	146,156	107,824
Adjusted R^2/Pseudo R^2	0.172	0.128	0.322	0.160	0.120	0.212	0.232	0.299	0.159
F/χ^2	312.7	234.8	2925	348.3	797.9	360.7	1542	75.82	271.6

This table presents the regression results of the impact of climate risk on vulnerable industries. *Vulnerable Industries* is an indicator variable that equals one for Agriculture (Fama–French Industry Code 1), Business Services (Code 34), Communication (Code 32), Energy [Mines (Code 28), Coal (Code 29), and Oil (Code 30)], Food Products (Code 2), Health Care (Code 11), and Transportation (Code 40), and zero otherwise. Regressions include the year fixed effects. The standard errors reported in parentheses are heteroskedasticity robust and clustered at the firm level. To conserve space, we do not report the coefficient estimates for the industry and year dummies. For exposition purposes, we multiply the coefficients on climate risk by 100. All variables are defined in the Appendix as the instrumental variable because it is likely to be highly correlated with climate risk (Albouy et al., 2013), but unlikely to be correlated with our dependent variables. We define *Population Density* as the number of people per square kilometer. We obtained country-year-level data from the World Bank. In the first stage, we regressed *Climate Risk (Long term)* on *Population Density* and on the firm-level control variables included in Eq. (13.1): *SIZE, Ln(age), Intangible Assets, PPE,* and *Sales Growth*. We then computed the fitted value of *Climate Risk (Long term)* and included it in our second-stage regression based on Eq. (13.1). Panel A of Table 13.7 reports the first-stage results. As predicted, the coefficient of *Population Density* is negative and significant ($p < 0.000$), indicating a significantly negative association between population density and climate risk. Panel B of Table 13.6 shows that including fitted *Climate Risk (Long term)* in the second-stage regression does not change our results, and hence that they are unlikely to be driven by omitted country-level variables.

Propensity-Score-Matched Sample

In a second robustness test, we used a propensity-score-matched sample to address the concern, the results of which may be driven by differences in firm characteristics between high-climate risk and low-climate risk groups (Ghoul et al., 2017).[31] We define *High Climate Risk* as firm-year climate risk above the sample median. In the first stage, we regressed our *High Climate Risk* dummy on the firm-level control variables included in Eq. (13.1): *SIZE, Ln(age), Intangible Asset, PPE,* and *Sales Growth*. Panel A of Table 13.8 reports the regression results. We then computed the propensity score for each observation in our sample. We matched each firm-year in the high-climate risk group with the firm-year in the low-climate risk group with the closest propensity score. Panel B of Table 13.8 reports the OLS estimation result of the relationship between climate risk, financial performance, and financing choices using the matched sample under Eq. (13.1). The results are unchanged.

[31] Using propensity-score-matched sample is an effective method to address endogeneity issue in cross-country studies (e.g., Ghoul et al., 2017).

Table 13.7 Climate risk on firm performance and financing choices: Instrument variable method

Panel A: First stage to estimate fitted value of climate risk	
	(1)
	Climate Risk (Long term)
Population Density	-0.167
	(0.000)
SIZE	-0.020
	(0.000)
Ln(age)	0.026
	(0.002)
Intangible Assets	0.010
	(0.006)
PPE	0.021
	(0.005)
Sales Growth	0.019
	(0.001)
Intercept	-0.542
	(0.016)
Industry/year	Yes
No. of observations	353,906
Pseudo R^2	0.394

Panel B: Climate risk and firm performance				
	(1)	(2)	(3)	(4)
	Earnings Volatility	*Operating Cash Flow Volatility*	*Earnings Volatility*	*Operating Cash Flow Volatility*
Fitted Climate Risk (Long term)	-0.056	-0.032	0.006	0.004
	(0.003)	(0.003)	(0.001)	(0.001)
Controls	Yes	Yes	Yes	Yes
No. of observations	353,906	326,087	218,763	212,439
Adjusted R^2	0.184	0.159	0.310	0.203

Panel C: Climate risk and financial policy					
	(1)	(2)	(3)	(4)	(5)
	Short-term Debt	*Long-term Debt*	*Short and Long-term Debt*	*Cash Holdings*	*Cash Dividends*
Fitted Climate Risk (Long term)	-0.043	0.036	-0.011	0.026	-0.009
	(0.003)	(0.003)	(0.005)	(0.022)	(0.001)

(continued)

Table 13.7 (continued)

Controls	Yes	Yes	Yes	Yes	Yes
No. of observations	353,752	353,828	353,452	351,895	261,581
Adjusted R^2/ Pseudo R^2	0.149	0.245	0.263	0.236	0.152

This table presents the OLS estimation results relating climate risk to firm performance and financial policy using instrument variable method. Panel A presents the first-stage OLS model estimation results. Specifically, the dependent variable in the first stage is *Climate Risk (Long term)*. *Population Density* is the number of people (in 1000) per squared kilometer of land area, and Panels B and C report OLS results of examining the relation between the fitted value of *Climate Risk (Long term)* on firm performance and financing choices, respectively. The standard errors reported in parentheses are heteroskedasticity robust and clustered at the firm level. To conserve space, we do not report the coefficient estimates for the industry and year dummies. For exposition purposes, we multiply the coefficients on climate risk by 100. All variables are defined in the Appendix

Table 13.8 Climate risk on firm performance and financing choices: propensity score matching

Panel A: First-stage propensity score matching	
	(1)
	High Climate Risk
SIZE	0.068
	(0.003)
Ln(age)	0.579
	(0.010)
Intangible Assets	-0.118
	(0.034)
PPE	-0.414
	(0.027)
Sales Growth	0.219
	(0.014)
Intercept	1.734
	(0.119)
Industry/year	Yes
No. of observations	167,234
Pseudo R^2	0.143
Panel B: Climate risk and firm performance	

(*continued*)

Table 13.8 (continued)

	(1) *Earnings Volatility*	(2) *Operating Cash Flow Volatility*		(3) *Earnings Volatility*	(4) *Operating Cash Flow Volatility*
High Climate Risk	-0.014	-0.012		0.001	0.003
	(0.003)	(0.002)		(0.001)	(0.001)
Controls	Yes	Yes		Yes	Yes
No. of observations	74,372	74,372		74,372	74,372
Adjusted R^2	0.227	0.185		0.290	0.158
Panel C: Climate risk and financial policy					
	(1) *Short-term Debt*	(2) *Long-term Debt*	(3) *Short and Long-term Debt*	(4) *Cash Holdings*	(5) *Cash Dividends*
High Climate Risk	-0.009	0.050	0.040	0.035	-0.008
	(0.002)	(0.003)	(0.004)	(0.017)	(0.001)
Controls	Yes	Yes	Yes	Yes	Yes
No. of observations	74,372	74,372	74,372	74,372	74,372
Adjusted R^2/ Pseudo R^2	0.165	0.287	0.281	0.170	0.172

This table presents the OLS estimation results relating climate risk to firm performance and financial policy using propensity score matching method. Panel A presents the first-stage Probit model estimation results. Specifically, the dependent variable in the first stage is *High Climate Risk*, an indicator variable that equals one if *Climate Risk (Long term)* is above sample median, and zero otherwise. We regress *High Climate Risk* on firm characteristics and use the estimated coefficients from this first-stage model to compute the propensity score for each observation in our sample. We then match each firm-year that in the high-climate risk group with a firm-year in the low-climate risk group, with the closest propensity score. Panel B reports OLS results of examining the relation between climate risk on firm performance and financing choices, using propensity-score-matched sample. The standard errors reported in parentheses are heteroskedasticity robust and clustered at the firm level. To conserve space, we do not report the coefficient estimates for the industry and year dummies. For exposition purposes, we multiply the coefficients on climate risk by 100. All variables are defined in the Appendix

Insurance Coverage

We used country-level growth in non-life insurance payments as a proxy for country-level insurance coverage (*Insurance*). The data come from Global Insurance Market Trends. In unreported results, we find that the level of insurance coverage is higher for countries with higher climate risk. We then tested whether insurance coverage can mitigate adverse effects of climate risk on firm performance and earnings volatility by interacting country-level insurance coverage with CRI. We find significantly positive coefficients for *ROA* and *CFO* and negative ones for *Earnings Volatility* and *Operating Cash Flow Volatility*. This suggests that insurance coverage can mitigate the adverse effect of climate risk on firm performance and earnings volatility.[32]

CRI for US Multinational Firms

Given the ability of multinational firms to move their operations out of high-climate risk areas, we adjusted the CRI based on the countries where a given multinational is active. Lack of national sales data and segment data for multinationals not headquartered in the US limited somewhat our ability to test firm sensitivity to climate risk. As an alternative approach, we obtained from the Compustat segments database US multinational firm revenue for specific geographic areas. We merged those data with country-year-level CRI and computed the arithmetic average CRI for each firm weighted by its revenue from different countries. We attempted to replicate the previous regressions using this weighted *CRI*. Consistent with our previous results, we find in unreported results a negative impact from climate risk on operating performance measured as CFO and the same impact on financing decisions that we reported earlier.

---

[32] Results are available from the authors.

Alternative Measure of Global Climate Risk

To provide a robustness test for our measure of climate risk, we used another measure of global climate risk. We obtained the Global Climate Report from the National Oceanic and Atmospheric Administration (NOAA) website.[33] The Global Climate Report has included since 2009 a Significant Climate Anomalies and Events section. Based on these data, we created a dummy variable (SCAE), which equals one if a country suffers one or more climatic anomalies or events, and zero otherwise. The variable is not based on the loss of GDP and thus is free of the influence of a country's economic development and performance. We replicated the previous tests using SCAE (instead of CRI). As shown in Table 13.9, the results continue to be robust, suggesting that they are not driven by GDP level or growth.

Other Robustness Tests

We conducted an array of additional robustness tests. The results, which are not reported, are similar. First, we excluded all US observations, which constitute 27% of our sample (see Table 13.1), in order to check that the findings are not US driven. Second, following Edwards (1992), we used country-weighted least squares regression to control for the different weights of countries in the sample. Third, we ran the four indicators of climate risk one at a time (instead of combined). Fourth, we restructured the CRI giving equal weights to its four indicators. Fifth, while Goodwin and Wu (2014) suggest that controlling for country-level fixed effects will reduce the likelihood of observing significant results, we find that including them does not alter our conclusion that climate risk has a profound impact on important financing decisions. Sixth, we measured the climate risk index for the year prior to financial policies. Seventh, we defined the financial crisis period separately for each country based on GDP growth rate

[33] https://www.ncdc.noaa.gov/sotc/global.

Table 13.9 Alternative measure of extreme climate risk – extreme climate events

	(1)	(2)	(3)	(4)	(5)	(6)	(7)	(8)	(9)
	ROA	*CFO*	*Earnings Volatility*	*Operating Cash Flow Volatility*	*Short-term Debt*	*Long-term Debt*	*Short and Long-term Debt*	*Cash Holdings*	*Cash Dividends*
SCAE	-0.007	-0.001	0.004	0.007	-0.030	0.036	0.004	0.168	-0.003
	(0.002)	(0.002)	(0.001)	(0.001)	(0.002)	(0.002)	(0.003)	(0.016)	(0.001)
Control variables	Yes	Yes	Yes	Yes	Yes	Yes	Yes	Yes	Yes
Industry/year	Yes	Yes	Yes	Yes	Yes	Yes	Yes	Yes	Yes
Cluster by firm	Yes	Yes	Yes	Yes	Yes	Yes	Yes	Yes	Yes
No. of observations	85,275	84,447	69,313	68,160	85,238	85,264	85,132	84,656	60,881
Adjusted R^2/ Pseudo R^2	0.176	0.122	0.269	0.201	0.159	0.231	0.251	0.297	0.173
F/χ^2	330.6	230.2	75.34	73.73	106.4	121.2	156.3	59.49	63.84

This table presents the regression results of using an alternative measure of extreme climate risk – extreme climate event. SCAE refers to an indicator variable that equals one if a country suffers one or more significant climate anomalies or events, and zero otherwise. Source: Significant Climate Anomalies and Events, Global Climate Report from National Oceanic and Atmospheric Administration (NOAA). Regressions include the year fixed effects. The standard errors reported in parentheses are heteroskedasticity robust and clustered at the firm level. To conserve space, we do not report the coefficient estimates for the industry and year dummies. For exposition purposes, we multiply the coefficients on climate risk by 100. All variables are defined in the Appendix and find that the results are robust to either interacting financial crisis years with climate risk or dropping financial crisis years from the sample.[34]

Conclusion

Our work contributes to a growing literature on the impact of climate risk on firm decisions. It is one of the first cross-country studies of the direct impact of global climate risk on public firm policies and performance. We provide evidence that managers of public firms across the globe weigh the loss due to extreme weather-related events such as storms, floods, and heat waves, i.e., *climate risk*, when making financing choices. First, as expected, we find that climate risk is negatively associated with firm earnings and positively associated with earnings volatility. This implies that firms cannot fully offset climate risk by insuring against it, either because they are unwilling or unable to do so. We also show that the managers of firms in countries characterized by severe climate risk tend to hold more cash, rely less on short-term and more on long-term borrowing, and pay lower cash dividends. We find similar results using an instrumental variable approach, propensity score matching, path analysis, and an alternative measure of climate risk. Our results are consistent with firms creating financial slack in order to maintain 'organizational resilience' against the threat of climate risk. They are more pronounced in the case of industries that are more vulnerable to climate risk. Our conclusions are invariant to the timing of financial crises that can affect different countries at different times. The strategies documented in our article appear to be consistent with attempts by managers to mitigate the increased volatility and uncertainty of future earnings and cash flows caused by higher climate risk.

[34] For convenience, we use a definition of a recession commonly used in the business press involving a fall in GDP for two successive quarters. [Note that the NBER defines a recession more broadly as "a significant decline in economic activity spread across the economy, lasting more than a few months, normally visible in real GDP, real income, employment, industrial production, and wholesale-retail sales" (NBER, 2008)].

Acknowledgements We thank the valuable comments from the Editor-in-Chief Alain Verbeke, Editor Gary Biddle, the three anonymous reviewers, and the participants of workshop at the University of Kentucky and the Mid-year Conference of International Accounting Section of American Accounting Association. Chong Wang acknowledges the financial support from Hong Kong Polytechnic University Start-up Fund and the National Natural Science Foundation of China (Fund # 71332008).

Appendix

See Table 13.10.

Table 13.10 Variable definitions

Variable	Definition
Climate risk index	
Climate Risk (Annual)	Annual Climate Risk Index from Germanwatch's 2008–2014 editions (for the years 2006–2012) scaled by (-1). Higher score indicates higher Climate risk in the year. Sources: Germanwatch
Climate Risk (Long term)	Accumulated Climate Risk Index from Germanwatch's 2014 edition (covering the years 1993–2012) scaled by (-1). Higher score indicates higher Climate risk from 1993 to 2012. Sources: Germanwatch
High Climate Risk	Indicator variable that equals one if a firm-year's *Climate Risk (Long term)* is higher than the sample median, and zero otherwise. Sources: Germanwatch
SCAE	Indicator variable that equals one if a country suffers one or more climate anomalies or events (SCAE), and 0 otherwise. Source: Significant Climate Anomalies and Events
Financial performance	
ROA	Pre-tax Income (PI) scaled by lagged assets (AT). Sources: Compustat
CFO	Cash flows from operations (OANCF) scaled by total assets. Sources: Compustat
Performance volatility	
Operating Cash Flow Volatility	Cash flow volatility, measured by the standard deviation of quarterly cash flows from operations (OANCF) scaled by total assets (AT) over the preceding five fiscal years. Sources: Compustat

(*continued*)

Table 13.10 (continued)

Variable	Definition
Earnings Volatility	Earnings volatility, measured by the standard deviation of quarterly pre-tax income (PI) scaled by total assets (AT) over the preceding five fiscal years. Sources: Compustat
Financial policy	
Short-term Debt	Short-term debt (DLC), scaled by lagged assets (AT). Sources: Compustat
Long-term Debt	Long-term debt (DLTT), scaled by lagged assets (AT). Sources: Compustat
Short and Long-term Debt	The sum of short- and long-term debt, scaled by lagged assets (AT). Sources: Compustat
Total Debt	Total liability (LT), scaled by lagged assets (AT). Sources: Compustat
Cash Holdings	Cash and short-term investment (CHE), scaled by lagged assets (AT). Sources: Compustat
Cash Dividends	Cash dividends (DVPD), scaled by lagged assets (AT). Sources: Compustat
Country-level control variables	
COMMON	Indicator that equals one if the legal origin is common law, and zero otherwise. Sources: La Porta et al. (1998)
EarnVol	Country-level control variable for earnings volatility. Sources: Compustat
Factor	Principal component of the country's legal tradition (common law versus code law), strength of investor rights, and ownership concentration as developed by La Porta et al. (1998); Legal tradition refers to the indictor variable (COMMON), which equals one if the legal origin is common law, and zero otherwise (La Porta et al., 1998). Investor Rights is measured by an index aggregating the shareholder rights labeled as "anti-director rights." The index is formed by adding 1 when (1) the country allows shareholders to mail their proxy vote to the firm, (2) shareholders are not required to deposit their shares prior to the general shareholders' meeting, (3) cumulative voting or proportional representation of minorities in the board of directors is allowed, (4) an oppressed minorities mechanism is in place, (5) the minimum percentage of share capital that entitles a shareholder to call for an extraordinary shareholders' meeting is less than or equal to 10% (the sample median), or (6) shareholders have preemptive rights that can be waived only by a shareholders' vote. The index ranges from zero to six (La Porta et al., 1998; Djankov et al., 2007). Ownership concentration refers to the average percentage of common shares owned by the three largest shareholders in the 10 largest non-financial, privately owned domestic firms in a given country (La Porta et al., 1998). Sources: La Porta et al. (1998) and Djankov et al. (2007)

Table 13.10 (continued)

Variable	Definition
GDP Growth	Annual growth of total GDP. Sources: International Financial Statistics (IFM)
LEG_ENV	Principal component extracted from COMMON, ENFORCE, and CR. COMMON refers to an indicator that equals one if the legal origin is common law, and zero otherwise. ENFORCE refers to the law enforcement index that ranges from 0 to 10, with higher values indicating greater law enforcement. CR refers to creditor rights, which is formed by adding (1) when the country imposes restrictions, such as creditors consent or minimum dividends to file for reorganization; (2) when secured creditors are able to gain possession of their security once the reorganization petition has been approved (no automatic stay); (3) when secured creditors are ranked first in the distribution of the proceeds that result from the disposition of the assets of a bankrupt firm; and (4) when the debtor does not retain the administration of its property pending the resolution of the reorganization. The index ranges from 0 to 4. Sources: La Porta et al. (1998), Djankov et al. (2007), Economic Freedom of the World
LGDP	Log of GDP per capita, in constant 2000 US dollars. Sources: World Bank
Population Density	People (in 1000) per sq. km of land area. Sources: World Bank
Firm-level control variables	
SIZE ($ million)	The natural logarithm of asset (AT) at the beginning of the year. Sources: Compustat
Total Debt	Total liability, scaled by lagged assets (AT). Sources: Compustat
Intangible Assets	Intangible assets (INTAN), scaled by lagged assets (AT). Sources: Compustat
PPE	Net property, plant, and equipment (PPENT) divided by lagged assets. Sources: Compustat
ROA	Pre-tax Income (PI) scaled by lagged assets (AT). Sources: Compustat
R&D	Research and development expenditures (XRD) scaled by lagged assets (AT). Sources: Compustat
Sales Growth	Sales (SALE) change computed scaled by sales in the last fiscal year. Sources: Compustat
Ln(age)	Natural logarithm of firm age, which is calculated starting from the first year the firm appeared in the Compustat database. Sources: Compustat
Interaction variables	
Vulnerable Industries	Indicator variable that equals one for Agriculture (Fama–French Industry Code 1), Business Services (Code 34), Communication (Code 32), Energy [Mines (code 28), Coal (Code 29), and Oil (Code 30)], Food Products (Code 2), Health Care (Code 11), and Transportation (Code 40), and zero otherwise. Sources: Compustat

References

Albouy, D., Graf, W., Kellogg, R., & Wolff, H. (2013). *Climate amenities, climate change, and American quality of life* (Working paper). Cambridge, MA: National Bureau of Economic Research.

Andersen, T. (2001). *Managing economic exposures of natural disasters: Exploring alternative financial risk management opportunities and instruments* (p. 2001). Natural Disasters Dialogue First Meeting.

Anderson, M., Bolton, P., & Samama, F. (2016). Hedging climate risk. *Financial Analysts Journal, 72*(3), 13–32.

Atta-Mensah, J. (2016). Poverty, climate risk and weather-indexed bonds. *Journal of Mathematical Finance, 6*(2), 275–292.

Bals, C., Warner, K., & Butzengeiger, S. (2006). Insuring the uninsurable: Design options for a climate change funding mechanism. *Climate Policy, 6*(6), 637–647.

Banerjee, S., Dasgupta, S., & Kim, Y. (2008). Buyer–supplier relationships and the stakeholder theory of capital structure. *Journal of Finance, 63*(5), 2507–2552.

Bansal, R., & Ochoa, M. (2012). *Temperature, aggregate risk, and expected returns* (Unpublished working paper no. 17575). National Bureau of Economic Research.

Bates, T., Kahle, K., & Stulz, R. (2009). Why do US firms hold so much more cash than they used to? *Journal of Finance, 64*(5), 1985–2021.

Beatty, T., & Shimshack, J. (2010). The impact of climate change information: New evidence from stock market. *Journal of Economic Analysis and Policy, 10*(1), 1–29.

Berkes, F., Colding, J., & Folke, C. (Eds.). (2003). *Navigating social–ecological systems: Building resilience for complexity and change*. Cambridge University Press.

Berkhout, F., Hertin, J., & Gann, D. M. (2006). Learning to adapt: Organizational adaptation to climate change impacts. *Climatic Change, 78*(1), 135–156.

Burke, M., Hsiang, S. M., & Miguel, E. (2015). Global non-linear effect of temperature on economic production. *Nature, 527*(7577), 235–239.

Burnell, P. (2012). Democracy, democratization and climate change: Complex relationship. *Democratization, 19*(5), 813–842.

Cao, M., & Wei, J. (2005). Stock market returns: A note on temperature anomaly. *Journal of Banking & Finance, 29*(6), 1559–1573.

Challinor, A. J., Watson, J., Lobell, D. B., Howden, S. M., Smith, D. R., & Chhetri, N. (2014). A meta-analysis of crop yield under climate change and adaptation. *Nature Climate Change, 4*(4), 287–291.

Chava, S. (2014). Environmental externalities and cost of capital. *Management Science, 60*(9), 2223–2247.

Clapp, C. S., Alfsen, K. H., Torvanger, A., & Lund, H. F. (2015). Influence of climate science on financial decisions. *Nature Climate Change, 5*(2), 84–85.

Covington, H., & Thamotheram. R. (2015). *The case for forceful stewardship (part 1): The financial risk from global warming* (Working paper). Cambridge University/University of Oxford.

Custodio, C., Ferreira, M., & Laureano, L. (2013). Why are US firms using more short-term debt? *Journal of Financial Economics, 108*(1), 182–212.

Dell, M., Jones, B., & Olken, B. A. (2009). Temperature and income: Reconciling new cross-sectional and panel estimates. *American Economic Review, 99*(2), 198–204.

Dell, M., Jones, B., & Olken, B. A. (2014). What do we learn from the weather? The new climate-economy literature. *Journal of Economic Literature, 52*(3), 740–798.

Deryugina, T. (2011). *The role of transfer payments in mitigating shocks: Evidence from the impact of hurricanes* (Working paper). University of Illinois.

Diamond, D. (1991). Debt maturity structure and liquidity risk. *Quarterly Journal of Economics, 106*(3), 709–737.

Dichev, I., & Tang, V. (2009). Earnings volatility and earnings predictability. *Journal of Accounting and Economics, 47*(1), 160–181.

Djankov, S., McLiesh, C., & Shleifer, A. (2007). Private credit in 129 countries. *Journal of Financial Economics, 84*(2), 299–329.

Edwards, S. (1992). Trade orientation, distortions, and growth in developing countries. *Journal of Development Economics, 39*(1), 31–58.

Ferguson, C. J. (2009). An effect size primer: A guide for clinicians and researchers. *Professional Psychology, 40*(5), 532–538.

Fleming, J., Kirby, C., & Ostdiek, B. (2006). Information, trading, and volatility: Evidence from weather-sensitive markets. *The Journal of Finance, 61*(6), 2899–2930.

Francis, J., LaFond, R., Olsson, P. M., & Schipper, K. (2004). Costs of equity and earnings attributes. *The Accounting Review, 79*(4), 967–1010.

Fuss, S. (2016). Climate economics: Substantial risk for financial assets. *Nature Climate Change, 6*(7), 659–660.

Gallup, J., Sachs, J., & Mellinger, A. (1999). Geography and economic development. *International Regional Science Review, 22*(2), 179–232.

Garschagen, M., & Romero-Lankao, P. (2015). Exploring the relationships between urbanization trends and climate change vulnerability. *Climate Change, 133*(1), 37–52.

Ghoul, S. E., Guedhami, O., & Kim, Y. (2017). Country-level institutions, firm value, and the role of corporate social responsibility initiatives. *Journal of International Business Studies, 48*(3), 360–385.

Goodwin, J., & Wu, D. (2014). Is the effect of industry expertise on audit pricing an office-level or a partner-level phenomenon? *Review of Accounting Studies, 19*(4), 1532–1578.

Hallegatte, S. (2008). An adaptive regional input-output model and its application to the assessment of the economic cost of Katrina. *Risk Analysis, 28*(3), 779–799.

Hirshleifer, D., & Shumway, T. (2003). Good day sunshine: Stock returns and the weather. *Journal of Finance, 58*(3), 1009–1032.

Hoffmann, V. H., Sprengel, D. C., Ziegler, A., Kolb, M., & Abegg, B. (2009). Determinants of corporate adaptation to climate change in winter tourism: An econometric analysis. *Global Environmental Change, 19*(2), 256–264.

Howarth, E., & Hoffman, M. S. (1984). A multidimensional approach to the relationship between mood and weather. *British Journal of Psychology, 75*(1), 15–23.

Hsiang, S. M. (2010). Temperatures and cyclones strongly associated with economic production in the Caribbean and Central America. *Proceedings of the National Academy of Sciences of the United States of America, 107*(35), 15367–15372.

Hsiang, S. M., & Narita, D. (2012). Adaptation to cyclone risk: Evidence from the global cross-section. *Climate Change Economics, 3*(2), 1250011-1–1250011-28.

Huang, T., Wu, F., Yu, J., & Zhang, B. (2015). Political risk and dividend policy: Evidence from international political crises. *Journal of International Business Studies, 46*(5), 574–595.

IPCC. (2007). *Climate change 2007: Synthesis Report, Fourth assessment report (AR4) of the Intergovernmental Panel on Climate Change (IPCC).*

Itzkowitz, J. (2013). Customers and cash: How relationships affect suppliers' cash holdings. *Journal of Corporate Finance, 19*, 159–180.

Jahn, M. (2013). *Economics of extreme weather events in cities: Terminology and regional impact models* (HWWI research paper 143). Hamburg Institute of International Economics.

Kamstra, M. J., Kramer, L. A., & Levi, M. D. (2003). Winterblues: A SAD stock market cycle. *American Economic Review, 93*(1), 324–343.

Kingsley, A. F., & Graham, B. A. (2017). The effects of information voids on capital flows in emerging markets. *Journal of International Business Studies, 48*(3), 324–343.

Konar, S., & Cohen, M. A. (2001). Does the market value environmental performance? *The Review of Economics and Statistics, 83*(2), 281–289.

Kowalewski, J., & Ujeyl, G. (2012). Estimating direct and indirect damages from storm surges: The case of Wilhelmsburg/Hamburg. In F. Klijn & T. Schweckendiek (Eds.), *Comprehensive flood risk management: Research for policy and practice*. CRC Press.

Kreft, S., & Eckstein, D. (2014). *Global climate risk index 2014*. Germanwatch.

La Porta, R., Lopez-de-Silanes, F., Shleifer, A., & Vishny, R. W. (1998). Law and finance. *Journal of Political Economy, 106*(6), 1113–1155.

Larkin, K. (2013). Brand perception, cash flow stability, and financial policy. *Journal of Financial Economics, 110*(1), 232–253.

Le, S., & Kroll, M. (2017). CEO international experience: Effects on strategic change and firm performance. *Journal of International Business Studies, 48*(5), 573–595.

Linnenluecke, M. K., & Griffiths, A. (2010). Beyond adaption: Resilience for business in light of climate change and weather extremes. *Business & Society, 49*(3), 477–511.

Linnenluecke, M. K., Griffiths, A., & Winn, M. I. (2008). *Organizational adaptation and resilience to extreme weather events*. Paper presented at the Annual Meetings of the Academy of Management, Anaheim, CA (Recipient of the Carolyn Dexter Best International Paper Award).

Lipe, R. (1990). The relation between stock returns and accounting earnings given alternative information. *The Accounting Review, 65*(1), 49–71.

Marano, V., Tashman, P., & Kostova, T. (2017). Escaping the iron cage: Liabilities of origin and CSR reporting of emerging market multinational enterprises. *Journal of International Business Studies, 48*(3), 386–408.

Masulis, R., & Mobbs, S. (2014). Independent director incentives: Where do talented directors spend their limited time and energy? *Journal of Financial Economics, 111*(2), 406–429.

Matsumura, E., Prakash, R., & Vera-Munoz, S. (2014). Firm-value effects of carbon emissions and carbon disclosures. *The Accounting Review, 89*(2), 695–724.

McCarthy, J., Canziani, O., Leary, N., Dokken, D., & White, K. (2001). *Climate change 2001: Impacts, adaptation, and vulnerability: Contribution of Working Group II to the third assessment report of the Intergovernmental Panel on Climate Change*. Cambridge University Press.

Meyer, K., Witteloostuijn, A., & Beugelsdijk, S. (2017). What's in a p? Reassessing best practices for conducting and reporting hypothesis-testing research. *Journal of International Business Studies, 48*(5), 535–551.

Minton, B., & Schrand, C. (1999). The impact of cash flow volatility on discretionary investment and the costs of debt and equity financing. *Journal of Financial Economics, 54*(3), 423–460.

National Bureau of Economic Research (NBER). (2008). The NBER's recession dating procedure. *National Bureau of Economic Research*. http://www.nber.org/cycles/jan08bcdc_memo.html

Nordhaus, W. D. (2006). Geography and macroeconomics: New data and new findings. *Proceedings of the National Academy of Sciences of the United States of America, 103*(10), 3510–3517.

Novy-Marx, R. (2014). Predicting anomaly performance with politics, the weather, global warming, sunspots, and the stars. *Journal of Financial Economics, 112*(2), 137–146.

Opler, T., Pinkowitz, L., Stulz, R., & Williamson, R. (1999). The determinants and implications of corporate cash holdings. *Journal of Financial Economics, 52*(1), 3–46.

Pal, J. S., & Eltahir, E. A. B. (2016). Future temperature in southwest Asia projected to exceed a threshold for human adaptability. *Nature Climate Change, 6*(2), 197–200.

Reisch, M. (2005). Katrina's impact: In hurricane's aftermath, chemical firms face higher costs and lower earnings. *Chemical & Engineering News, 83*(38), 8.

Rivera, C., & Wamsler, C. (2014). Integrating climate change adaptation, disaster risk reduction and urban planning: A review of Nicaraguan policies and regulations. *International Journal of Disaster Risk Reduction, 7*, 78–90.

Ronen, J., & Sadan, S. (1981). *Smoothing income numbers: objectives, means, and implications*. Addison-Wesley Publishing.

Rountree, B., Weston, J., & Allayannis, G. (2008). Do investors value smooth performance? *Journal of Financial Economics, 90*(3), 237–251.

SASB (Sustainability Accounting Standards Board). (2016). Climate risk technical bulletin. https://www.eenews.net/assets/2016/10/20/document_cw_01.pdf

Stulz, R. (1990). Managerial discretion and optimal financing policies. *Journal of Financial Economics, 26*(1), 3–27.

Tschakert, P., & Dietrich, K. (2010). Anticipatory learning for climate change adaptation and resilience. *Ecology and Society, 15*(2), 11.
Tu, D. (2014). *Do the stock markets price climate change risks?* (Working paper). HEC. http://www.vernimmen.net/ftp/DoStockMktsPriceClimateChangeRisks_Danni_TU.pdf
United Nations International Strategy for Disaster Reduction (UNISDR). (2009). UNISDR Terminology on Disaster Risk Reduction, Geneva. http://www.unisdr.org/_les/7817UNISDRTerminologyEnglish.pdf.
Vogus, T., & Sutcliffe, K. (2007). Organizational resilience: Towards a theory and research agenda. In *2007 IEEE international conference on systems, man and cybernetics*, Montreal, Quebec (pp. 3418–3422).
Wang, J. (2012). Do firms' relationships with principal customers/suppliers affect shareholders' income? *Journal of Corporate Finance, 18*, 860–878.
Wilbanks, T. J., Romero Lankao, P., Bao, M., Berkhout, F., Cairncross, S., Ceron, J.-P., et al. (2007). Industry, settlement and society. Climate change 2007: Impacts, adaptation and vulnerability. Cambridge: Cambridge University Press.
Woods, D. (2006). Essential characteristics of resilience. In E. Hollnagel, D. D. Woods, & N. Leveson (Eds.), *Resilience engineering: Concepts and precepts* (pp. 21–34). Ashgate.
Wright, S. (1934). The method of path coefficients. *Annals of Mathematical Statistics, 5*, 161–215.
Yang, D. (2008). Coping with disaster: The impact of hurricanes on international financial flows, 1970–2002. *The BE Journal of Economic Analysis & Policy, 8*(1), 1–43.

[illegible]

14

The Impact of Climate Risk on Firm Performance and Financing Choices: A Commentary

Martina K. Linnenluecke

Introduction

Firms are increasingly exposed to the impacts of climate change, and their responses are influenced by a range of factors including political, institutional and stakeholder pressures (e.g., Cadez et al., 2019; Jabbour et al., 2020; Pinkse & Kolk, 2012; Sprengel & Busch, 2011), the perception of risk and opportunities by organizational decision-makers (e.g., Bremer & Linnenluecke, 2017; Pinkse & Gasbarro, 2019; Tisch & Galbreath, 2018), as well as the impacts from adverse conditions in their natural environment (e.g., Rivera & Clement, 2019). Different types of firm responses to climate change have been identified in the literature: those that are "business-as-usual" and climate change inaction; those that correspond to the reduction of climate change (i.e., climate change mitigation); those that correspond to adjustments to a changing physical environment (i.e., climate change adaptation); and those that involve

M. K. Linnenluecke (✉)
Centre for Corporate Sustainability and Environmental Finance, Macquarie University, Sydney, NSW, Australia
e-mail: martina.linnenluecke@mq.edu.au

M. A. Mithani et al. (eds.), *Crises and Disruptions in International Business*, JIBS Special Collections, https://doi.org/10.1007/978-3-030-80383-4_14

different forms of corporate political activities, such as lobbying (e.g., Busch, 2011; Gasbarro & Pinkse, 2016; Gasbarro et al., 2016; Kolk & Pinkse, 2005; Le, 2013; Linnenluecke, Griffiths & Winn, 2013; Slawinski et al., 2017; Winn et al., 2011).

The notable article by Huang, Kerstein and Wang (2017) provides a critical addition to the climate change adaptation stream within an international business context, drawing our attention to the impacts of climate-related risk on financing choices by publicly listed firms. Using a cross-country empirical setting, the authors show that firms in countries with higher climate risk (that is, a higher likelihood of losses from major extreme weather events such as storms, flooding and heat waves) have poorer financial performance as measured by their return-on-assets (ROA) and cash flows from operations over assets (CFO). The authors also find that country-level climate risk is associated with lower and more volatile earnings and cash flows, and that – perhaps expectedly – firms located in regions with higher impacts from severe weather are likely to hold more cash resources as a mechanism to respond to impacts, in addition to holding more long-term debt.

Furthering the Debate on Climate Risk

Huang et al. (2018) is an important starting point for further work on the impact of climate risk on firms and industries more globally. While climate change has been recognized as a distinctive international business issue (Pinkse & Kolk, 2012), international business research is still lagging in terms of fully understanding the impacts of climate change on various countries, regions and supply chains. Initial IB frameworks advocated that MNEs will be exposed to different risk profiles and might be able to benefit from opportunities to develop "green" firm-specific advantages (FSAs) (Kolk & Pinkse, 2008; Romilly, 2007). However, the impacts of different risk profiles and the opportunities to create possible advantages through various firm responses have not yet been fully empirically verified. Some evidence suggests that top MNEs actually show worse environmental performance compared to their peers (Aragón-Correa et al., 2016), and it is unclear how firms are impacted by the costs and benefits of other response options, such as climate adaptation.

Internationally, there is also still limited data that examines local (i.e., firm-level) impacts of climate change on firms across countries. To date, much of the literature has focused on analysing the impacts of climate change on firms in certain regions, or countries, often with a focus on specific sectors or industries (Amelung & Nicholls, 2014; Rivera & Clement, 2019; Rutty et al., 2017). The focus on specific regions, countries and/or sectors is perhaps not surprising given that the impacts of climate change are highly location- and industry-specific, but it also means that we have little aggregate evidence of location-specific impacts of climate change.

The challenges associated with deriving management recommendations for adapting to climate risk become evident when looking at the impacts of climate change even within regions. For instance, and drawing on an example from the sugarcane industry in Brazil, there are substantial regional differences concerning climate change impacts (Linnenluecke et al., 2018; Linnenluecke et al., 2020). For Pernambuco (a northeastern region in Brazil), researchers have concluded that sugarcane yields will be reduced in both the near and distant future due to reduced rainfall levels (de Carvalho et al., 2015). However, in the State of São Paulo (a southeastern region in Brazil) yield increases could be as high as 59–82% by 2090, due to the combined effects of higher air temperatures and higher atmospheric CO_2 concentration (both conducive to sugarcane plant growth), as well as concurrent developments of on-farm management practices (dos Santos & Sentelhas, 2014).

In line with resource- and capability-based theories, such findings could be interpreted to suggest that climate risk responses in the Brazilian sugarcane industry should take place by focusing on areas that have higher natural resource endowments, that production and expansion should mostly take place in southeastern regions to capitalize on yield gains, and that organizations in areas with lower rainfall should focus on the development of capabilities to manage this shortfall (e.g., water storage or irrigation solutions, or financing solution to survive any harvest losses). However, business scholarship cannot confidently adopt any such recommendations without understanding the uncertainties inherent in the underlying scientific results, and also not without clarifying the extent to which scientific results diverge due to the use of different methods, scenarios and models (White et al., 2011). In addition, there are broader effects on local communities and ecosystems, which also need to be considered (Linnenluecke et al., 2018).

What Should Be the Main Focus of Future Research?

In this commentary, I argue for the development of more insights that are capturing both local and regional variability of climate impacts, but are at the same time aggregating findings to answer questions about firm and industry vulnerability as well as adaptation to climate change in an international context. To address uncertainties inherent in the modelling of the potential impacts of climate change, researchers in other disciplines have started to develop more comprehensive protocols (e.g., the Agricultural Model Intercomparison and Improvement Project or AgMIP, see www.agmip.org) to improve study intercomparisons and to reduce prediction uncertainty (Rosenzweig 2014). There are opportunities here for international business scholarship to adopt similar stringent standards for empirical studies, in particular to overcome limitations with existing adaptation studies which often differ in terms of methods, timeframes, regions, and companies investigated (making comparisons more difficult).

At the same time, international business scholarship can also contribute by factoring in global non-linear effects of climate change as well as country-level factors. For instance, prior research has demonstrated a global non-linear effect of temperature on economic production, suggesting that unmitigated warming might reshape the global economy by reducing average global incomes around 23% by 2100 compared to scenarios without climate change (Burke et al., 2015). There is also evidence that country-level factors such as innovation or investments into climate adaptation might mitigate these impacts. Abdelzaher, Martynov and Zaher (2020) analyse the impact of a country's degree of innovation on its vulnerability to climate change in a longitudinal sample of 73 countries over 1998–2013 and find that R&D expenditures as a percentage of GDP (innovation input), openness to trade, and regulatory quality decrease a country's vulnerability to climate change.

Huang et al. (2018) also raised questions about the best financial instruments used to support firm and industry responses to climate risks. The authors find that climate risk is positively associated with earnings volatility and negatively associated with firm earnings, implying that firms might not be able to fully offset climate risk through insurance mechanisms. Future research can investigate if access to financial instruments other than insurance (e.g., instruments that provide direct financing to respond to climate change impacts, or risk management instruments that help to alleviate climate change risks) can effectively assist with climate adaptation. Another question for future research is the level of collective action required to respond to climate change impacts – individual firms might be challenged to respond to regional impacts in the absence of support from municipalities, city level agencies, as well as federal and/or state governments. Importantly, climate change impacts are now becoming "severe, pervasive, and irreversible" (Howard-Grenville et al., 2014: 617), and as such, we require substantially more empirical work that effectively examines the scope of impacts and corporate responses.

References

Abdelzaher, D. M., Martynov, A., & Zaher, A. M. A. (2020). Vulnerability to climate change: Are innovative countries in a better position? *Research in International Business and Finance, 51*, 101098.

Amelung, B., & Nicholls, S. (2014). Implications of climate change for tourism in Australia. *Tourism Management, 41*, 228–244.

Aragón-Correa, J. A., Marcus, A., & Hurtado-Torres, N. (2016). The natural environmental strategies of international firms: Old controversies and new evidence on performance and disclosure. *Academy of Management Perspectives, 30*(1), 24–39.

Bremer, J., & Linnenluecke, M. K. (2017). Determinants of the perceived importance of organisational adaptation to climate change in the Australian energy industry. *Australian Journal of Management, 42*(3), 502–521.
Burke, M., Hsiang, S. M., & Miguel, E. (2015). Global non-linear effect of temperature on economic production. *Nature, 527*(7577), 235–239.
Busch, T. (2011). Organizational adaptation to disruptions in the natural environment: The case of climate change. *Scandinavian Journal of Management, 27*(4), 389–404.
Cadez, S., Czerny, A., & Letmathe, P. (2019). Stakeholder pressures and corporate climate change mitigation strategies. *Business Strategy and the Environment, 28*(1), 1–14.
de Carvalho, A. L., Menezes, R. S. C., Nóbrega, R. S., de Siqueira Pinto, A., Ometto, J. P. H. B., von Randow, C., & Giarolla, A. (2015). Impact of climate changes on potential sugarcane yield in Pernambuco, northeastern region of Brazil. *Renewable Energy, 78*, 26–34.
dos Santos, D. L., & Sentelhas, P. C. (2014). Climate change scenarios and their impact on water balance and sugarcane yield in southern Brazil. *Sugar Tech, 16*(4), 356–365.
Gasbarro, F., & Pinkse, J. (2016). Corporate adaptation behaviour to Deal with climate change: The influence of firm-specific interpretations of physical climate impacts. *Corporate Social Responsibility and Environmental Management, 23*(3), 179–192.
Gasbarro, F., Rizzi, F., & Frey, M. (2016). Adaptation measures of energy and utility companies to cope with water scarcity induced by climate change. *Business Strategy and the Environment, 25*(1), 54–72.
Howard-Grenville, J., Buckle, S. J., Hoskins, B. J., & George, G. (2014). Climate change and management. *Academy of Management Journal, 57*(3), 615–623.
Huang, H. H., Kerstein, J., & Wang, C. (2018). The impact of climate risk on firm performance and financing choices: An international comparison. *Journal of International Business Studies, 49*(5), 633–656.
Jabbour, A., Vazquez-Brust, D., Jabbour, C. J. C., & Ribeiro, D. A. (2020). The interplay between stakeholders, resources and capabilities in climate change strategy: Converting barriers into cooperation. *Business Strategy and the Environment, 29*(3), 1362–1386.
Kolk, A., & Pinkse, J. (2005). Business responses to climate change: Identifying emergent strategies. *California Management Review, 47*(3), 6–20.

Kolk, A., & Pinkse, J. (2008). A perspective on multinational enterprises and climate change: Learning from "an inconvenient truth"? *Journal of International Business Studies, 39*(8), 1359–1378.
Le, J. K. (2013). How constructions of the future shape organizational responses: Climate change and the Canadian oil sands. *Organization, 20*(5), 722–742.
Linnenluecke, M. K., Griffiths, A., & Winn, M. I. (2013). Firm and industry adaptation to climate change: A review of climate adaptation studies in the business and management field. *Wiley Interdisciplinary Reviews: Climate Change, 4*(5), 397–416.
Linnenluecke, M. K., Nucifora, N., & Thompson, N. (2018). Implications of climate change for the sugarcane industry. *Wiley Interdisciplinary Reviews: Climate Change, 9*(1), e498.
Linnenluecke, M. K., Zhou, C., Smith, T., Thompson, N., & Nucifora, N. (2020). The impact of climate change on the Australian sugarcane industry. *Journal of Cleaner Production, 246*, 118974.
Pinkse, J., & Gasbarro, F. (2019). Managing physical impacts of climate change: An attentional perspective on corporate adaptation. *Business & Society, 58*(2), 333–368.
Pinkse, J., & Kolk, A. (2012). Multinational enterprises and climate change: Exploring institutional failures and embeddedness. *Journal of International Business Studies, 43*(3), 332–341.
Rivera, J., & Clement, V. (2019). Business adaptation to climate change: American ski resorts and warmer temperatures. *Business Strategy and the Environment, 28*(7), 1285–1301.
Romilly, P. (2007). Business and climate change risk: A regional time series analysis. *Journal of International Business Studies, 38*(3), 474–480.
Rosenzweig, C., Elliott, J., Deryng, D., Ruane, A.C., Müller, C., Arneth, A., Boote, K.J., Folberth, C., Glotter, M., Khabarov, N. and Neumann, K., 2014. Assessing agricultural risks of climate change in the 21st century in a global gridded crop model intercomparison. Proceedings of the National Academy of Sciences, 111(9), pp. 3268–3273.
Rutty, M., Scott, D., Johnson, P., Pons, M., Steiger, R., & Vilella, M. (2017). Using ski industry response to climatic variability to assess climate change risk: An analogue study in eastern Canada. *Tourism Management, 58*, 196–204.
Slawinski, N., Pinkse, J., Busch, T., & Banerjee, S. B. (2017). The role of short-termism and uncertainty avoidance in organizational inaction on climate change: A multi-level framework. *Business & Society, 56*(2), 253–282.

Sprengel, D. C., & Busch, T. (2011). Stakeholder engagement and environmental strategy – The case of climate change. *Business Strategy and the Environment, 20*(6), 351–364.

Tisch, D., & Galbreath, J. (2018). Building organizational resilience through sensemaking: The case of climate change and extreme weather events. *Business Strategy and the Environment, 27*(8), 1197–1208.

White, J. W., Hoogenboom, G., Kimball, B. A., & Wall, G. W. (2011). Methodologies for simulating impacts of climate change on crop production. *Field Crops Research, 124*(3), 357–368.

Winn, M. I., Kirchgeorg, M., Griffiths, A., Linnenluecke, M. K., & Gunther, E. (2011). Impacts from climate change on organizations: A conceptual foundation. *Business Strategy and the Environment, 20*(3), 157–173.

Part V

The Impact of Crises and Disruptions on Local Market Strategies and Legitimacy

15

Liability of Foreignness, Natural Disasters, and Corporate Philanthropy

Murad A. Mithani

Introduction

Liability of foreignness (LOF), defined as the social and cultural barriers that limit the embeddedness of non-local firms in the host environment, remains a critical concern for multinational enterprises (MNEs) (Zaheer, 1995, 2002). LOF manifests in the form of higher operating costs for MNE subsidiaries relative to domestic firms (Bell et al., 2012). These costs can be particularly significant in emerging economies, whose stakeholders generally have a greater distrust of foreign firms (Kostova & Zaheer, 1999), and especially in newly reformed economies, where direct access to foreign firms is a relatively recent phenomenon (Beugelsdijk & Frijns, 2010). LOF makes it necessary for MNEs to work harder to

Accepted by Mona Makhija, Area Editor, 27 July 2017. This article has been with the author for four revisions.

M. A. Mithani (✉)
School of Business, Rutgers University at Camden, Camden, NJ, USA
e-mail: murad.mithani@rutgers.edu

M. A. Mithani et al. (eds.), *Crises and Disruptions in International Business*, JIBS Special Collections, https://doi.org/10.1007/978-3-030-80383-4_15

legitimize their local presence, and pay greater attention to mechanisms that facilitate social integration (Nachum, 2003). Since philanthropy can be important in minimizing the perceived distance that separates MNEs from domestic firms (Bhanji & Oxley, 2013; Crilly et al., 2016), I argue that it can be used strategically by MNEs to reduce or even eradicate LOF, particularly in the aftermath of national disasters.

I refer to national disaster as one or more disasters (natural or otherwise) that solely or in conjunction have a disproportional impact on the lives and livelihoods of a significant portion of the national population (Glynn et al., 2003; Mitchell, 2006; Roberts, 2010). Such an event destabilizes the social and economic landscape and increases the openness of host communities to external help. It provides an opportunity for non-local firms to build strong local ties. Accordingly, I speculate that in the aftermath of a national disaster, MNEs will exhibit a larger increase in philanthropic contribution than domestic firms and this increase will have a positive effect on the relative performance of MNEs.

To test this hypothesis, I compared the philanthropic contributions of MNEs and domestic firms before and after a national disaster in India. I found that MNEs made larger philanthropic contributions than domestic firms in the aftermath of the disaster, and this difference between MNE and domestic firm philanthropy persisted over time. During this extended period, MNEs were relatively averse to complementing the increase in philanthropy with higher advertising expenditures compared to domestic firms. Moreover, I found that in comparison to domestic firms, there was a large increase in the relative performance of MNEs after the disaster and this increase was strengthened by philanthropic contribution. This suggests that MNEs effectively capitalized on the opportunity presented by the social restructuring that followed the disaster.

My study makes two contributions. First, I show that MNEs use philanthropy strategically, deploying contributions when they can have the largest impact on host communities. These contributions, in turn, mitigate the social and cultural barriers that lead to LOF as demonstrated by the significant improvements in MNEs' relative performance. Thus, I demonstrate that post-disaster philanthropy can serve as a valuable mechanism to mitigate LOF.

Theoretical Development

Disasters and Social Restructuring

Disasters are "collective stress situations" that occur "when many members of a social system fail to receive expected conditions of life from the system. These conditions of life include the safety of the physical environment, protection from attack, provision of food, shelter, and income, and guidance and information necessary to carry on normal activities" (Barton, 1969: 38). Source events for disasters may be political, economic, or natural in origin. In the case of natural disasters, on which this study focuses, the source event can include floods, droughts, earthquakes, and other exogenous shocks. Although the impact domain of a natural disaster is generally limited, one or more disasters can sometimes have a disproportionate impact on the social and the economic environment, creating effects on the lives of a major segment of the national population that last for several years. Such a disaster has nationwide implications, and it can induce significant changes in the social structure of the society (Gilbert, 1998; Kreps, 1985; Quarantelli & Dynes, 1977).

A national disaster and its aftermath increase the community's expectations of support from the immediate environment (Aldrich, 2012). Those who are directly or indirectly affected by the calamity require material, financial, and emotional support to overcome the loss, rebuild their lives, and identify ways to resume day-to-day activities. Personal ties remain the primary source of emotional support; however, the government is typically expected to serve as the major source of financial and material help. Yet governmental institutions are rarely prepared for a major disaster (Drabek & Key, 1976). Often, they are unable to stockpile sufficient resources or build needed skills to deal with calamities, especially in emerging economies where national institutions are typically inefficient and unorganized (Khanna & Palepu, 2013). Once a disaster occurs, this lack of institutional resources increases the need for alternate sources of support, which invokes a reevaluation of social choices and makes it necessary for the community to open itself to dependencies it might previously have resisted (Bates & Peacock, 1993; Horlick-Jones, 1995). The affected communities and others interested in supporting them are driven to seek out individuals and organizations that can help in rescue and relief efforts. This need induces a change in community interactions with the environment, leading to a reevaluation of existing connections and triggering a social restructuring—a change in the configuration of social ties.

The social restructuring that follows a disaster facilitates the legitimization of new social objects (i.e., perceptions, practices, organizations, etc.) that can overcome the negative implications of a disaster. Johnson et al. (2006) explain that the legitimization of new social objects is a gradual process that occurs in four stages: innovation, local validation, diffusion, and general validation. During the first stage, i.e., innovation, a social object that is capable of addressing one or more structural or environmental constraints experienced by the society gains greater visibility. In the second stage, local actors emerge who find the social innovation particularly valuable. These actors become a source of its initial validation. In the third stage, local actors help diffuse the social object to the wider environment. And in the fourth stage, which marks a culmination of the process, the social object becomes validated by the wider society. At this point, the novelty of the social object is replaced by its incorporation into the collective reality. The new social object acquires widespread acceptance and becomes a part of the shared system of belief. Building on this model, I examine how the social restructuring that follows a national disaster can become a foundation for greater local acceptance of MNEs.

Social Spaces and the Legitimation of MNEs

A major disaster can reframe the social perceptions regarding MNEs. The general tendency to view foreign firms as distant, passive, and insensitive to local needs can be replaced by the expectation that MNEs' financial prowess and global experiences make them critical partners for the much needed recovery and relief efforts. It allows MNEs to be viewed as a new social object, framed in terms of their capacity to save and improve lives rather than as a socially or culturally distinct entity that is primarily focused on economic success (Amaeshi et al., 2006). However, the diffusion of this perception among the masses is not immediate. It is often led by the emergence of new social spaces that appear in response to the crisis (Quarantelli, 2000).

Social spaces are a microcosm of values, relationships, and implied or articulated structures (Savage & Silva, 2013). These spaces are not necessarily physical embodiments of preexisting social units, such as the family; rather, they exist as cognitive models for behavioral expectations centered on a shared objective (Pescosolido & Rubin, 2000). A classroom, a church, and an Internet chatroom are all examples of social spaces, as is the line to receive relief goods. The groups that inhabit these spaces develop norms focused on the fulfillment of an underlying goal (Fisher & Naumer, 2006). While these norms are often influenced by the larger society, the relationship is reciprocal; these spaces allow the individuals and groups associated with them the freedom to pursue interests that defy prevailing social orientations, and the values organized within them feed back into the generalized social structure. In other words, social spaces may harbor different sets of values than those accepted by the wider social and cultural environment and they may act as catalysts for changes in the more widely accepted norms (Lefebvre, 2009). In essence, social spaces can be viewed as communal discontinuities that reach out to affect the wider set of relationships prevalent in the society and the effectiveness of these spaces depends on the extent to which they succeed in fulfilling the underlying goals. The primary goal of social spaces that emerge in the aftermath of a major disaster is the identification of urgent needs, facilitation of the flow of material and financial help, and to serve as a point of contact for those who may otherwise have limited access to the region (e.g., Tilcsik & Marquis, 2013: 115). Although the role of these groups diminishes as the community becomes more connected to new partners and the narrative crafted within these spaces is entwined with the communal identity (Chamlee-Wright & Storr, 2011), these groups provide the local validation necessary for MNEs to be viewed as reliable partners and help the diffusion of new ties that go beyond the traditionally accepted interactions (Berkes et al., 2002).

The opening provided by social spaces serves as an avenue for foreign firms to interact with the community in new ways (Oliver-Smith, 1996). Instead of a relationship centered on products and deliverables, local validation makes it possible for MNEs to start building more personal ties. They allow MNEs an opportunity to better understand local preferences, respond in ways that these communities appreciate, and build rapport that can help reduce the social and cultural barriers underlying LOF (Pant & Ramachandran, 2017). With greater diffusion of a renewed perception regarding MNEs, social spaces help ease the apprehensions about foreign entities (Mishina et al., 2012). Even when the role of social spaces is diminished, this validation enables host communities to appreciate a broader engagement with the external environment. Thus, the implications of social spaces continue beyond the immediate aftermath of the disaster. They provide a narrative that eventually becomes part of the communal identity (Chamlee-Wright & Storr, 2011) and strengthens the links between the local environment and the foreign firms.

This development is highly consequential for the community because it allows access to resources that might otherwise not be available, especially resources held by MNEs. MNE involvement has been shown to be an important factor in limiting the ramifications of a major disaster (White & Lang, 2012). MNEs bring important assets to the disaster response effort (Aldrich, 2012; Bhanji & Oxley, 2013; Valente & Crane, 2010), which among other things, include the much needed financial contributions (European Foundation Centre and Council on Foundations, 2007). Thus, social restructuring facilitates the creation of new social spaces that connect communities to MNEs. This connection has benefits in both directions: it helps communities overcome the deficits in recovery and relief operations and it also allows the firms to deploy philanthropic assets effectively for a stronger engagement with the community.

Since global experiences make MNEs more cognizant of the extent to which monetary contributions are essential for a meaningful impact, they are sensitive to the role of philanthropy in the aftermath of a disaster. These insights are less readily available to the domestic firms because large-scale disasters do not typically affect a region very frequently (Webb et al., 2000). This marks a distinction between MNE and domestic firms' philanthropic responses in the aftermath of the disaster. In the following hypotheses, I examine how the choices made by MNEs and domestic firms continue to differ and eventually become a source of a decrease in LOF after a national disaster.

Expansion of Social Ties

In the aftermath of a disaster, domestic firms generally rely on historical ties to understand local needs. Their established networks remain the primary source of communication and engagement. Although the frequency of interaction is likely to increase, it has a limited effect on the nature of existing relationships. In contrast, MNEs, which have less well-developed ties to the community, must look to emergent social spaces to build the knowledge base needed to navigate the social and cultural terrain (Quarantelli, 2000) and know where to direct their philanthropic efforts. This greater MNE engagement with changing social structures leads to both public and private benefits (Baron, 2013; Luo, 2006).

The public benefits emerge from greater local access to the financial and organizational resources held by MNEs, which can enable a more rapid recovery from the disaster and create long-term connections that provide ongoing support to the community. MNEs gain private benefits in the form of a stronger social reputation (Strike et al., 2006), which can help mitigate LOF. However, to gain this benefit, MNEs must take into account two mutually reinforcing considerations. First, a firm's legitimacy within the community is contingent on its responsiveness to the expectations of the new social spaces (Bhanji & Oxley, 2013). These groups not only serve as "reputational intermediaries," connecting the MNE to the rest of the community (Bell et al., 2012), but also help establish the MNE's long-term credibility (Berkes et al., 2002). Thus, it is critical that MNEs respond to emergent social spaces and their norms in a way that nurtures faith in their intentions (e.g., Etzioni, 1975). Particularly in emerging markets, the suspicion with which host communities often view foreign firms makes it necessary for MNEs to demonstrate a very visible philanthropic engagement (Eden & Miller, 2004; Kostova & Zaheer, 1999), both to establish their commitment to providing material help and to allay concerns regarding their lack of local sensitivity (Zhang & Luo, 2013). Second, MNEs operate in multiple markets and thus are less vulnerable to a change in the economic environment of a single host country (Dahan et al., 2006; Geppert et al., 2006). This relative immunity from immediate financial distress makes them less concerned about the viability of the corporation, and hence freer to provide monetary support (Christmann & Taylor, 2001; also see Patten, 2008).

Domestic firms may find it more difficult to take advantage of the social restructuring for a number of reasons. First, their relative lack of experience with disasters is compounded by conflicting expectations. On the one hand, the wake of a disaster brings an overwhelming demand for charitable contribution (Galaskiewicz, 1997). Local ties and domestic shareholding increase the pressure on domestic firms to undertake relief efforts to repair the fabric of the society in which they exist (Babiak & Wolfe, 2006; Muller & Whiteman, 2009). On the other hand, this increased expectation is accompanied by a need for financial restraint (Lines, 2004) since the upending of the local economy also destabilizes the firm. As local markets are materially and symbolically central to domestic firms' operations (Rugman, 2005), the shift in economic sentiment wrought by a disaster and the resulting uncertainty induces in domestic firms a calculus of consequences (Henisz et al., 2014). These firms must contend with greater ambiguity and as a result often delay long-term commercial investments and see a decrease in expectations for financial performance (Berkman et al., 2011; Shan & Gong, 2012). These economic pressures and uncertainties make domestic firms' future relatively unclear (Muller & Kräussl, 2011). Thus, just when corporate philanthropic contribution is most needed, domestic firms are at the most risk (Tilcsik & Marquis, 2013) and thus less able to provide the needed support.

This conflict—between a greater pressure to give and economic conditions that demand greater restraint in giving—makes it likely that, in the aftermath of a major disaster, domestic firms' philanthropic contributions will exhibit a relatively limited increase, even as MNEs increase their contributions more dramatically. Taken together, this confluence of forces suggests the first hypothesis:

Hypothesis 1

Subsequent to a national disaster, the increase in philanthropic contributions will be larger for MNEs than for domestic firms.

Initial Skepticism Towards MNEs

In the wake of a disaster, despite the urgent need for contributions, the wider community may not immediately embrace the ties introduced by the new social spaces (Oliver-Smith, 1996). The social and cultural differences that contribute to LOF, combined with the limited history of interaction, make it difficult for community members to understand the philanthropic motivation of MNEs seeking to connect. While each wave of diffusion of the value of MNE contribution encounters lower resistance, it requires a consistent demonstration of credibility (Johnson et al., 2006). This makes it necessary for MNEs' to ensure that they continue to appear as reliable social partners and their philanthropic choices are visible as a selfless act aimed towards benefiting the local population (Walker & Zelditch, 1993). This suggests that compared to domestic firms, MNEs will not only seek to make larger philanthropic contributions as hypothesized earlier, but they will also be more cautious with complementary choices that can undermine their generosity. One such choice pertains to advertising expenditures. Despite the public benefits of philanthropy, corporate advertisements can make local communities skeptical whether the MNE is acting from a genuine concern or is merely seeking a tool for self-promotion (Fry et al., 1982).

Indeed, MNEs have strong motivation to use their philanthropic work for self-promotion. The promotion of a firms' role in disaster recovery can yield significant social and financial capital; an increase in philanthropy can yield an economic advantage when combined with increased advertising expenditures (Aldrich, 2012). Even when social responsibility is not central to the promotional message, charitable acts are more noticeable for firms that are frequently visible in the media (File & Prince, 1998; Varadarajan & Menon, 1988). This feedback between advertising and philanthropy can be beneficial for a firm's financial performance (Brik et al., 2011; Drumwright, 1996; Servaes & Tamayo, 2013). However, markets are unlikely to respond positively when the social concern is perceived as an ingratiatory tactic (Patten, 2008) or a tool for self-promotion. This effect can be stronger and therefore more alarming for MNEs if local communities come to view their philanthropic contribution as a self-serving goal. MNEs can not only lose the support of social spaces that legitimize their local presence, it may also reinforce the hostility that leads to LOF. Thus, despite the potential benefits of increased advertising investments in conjunction with large philanthropic contributions, global experiences are likely to inform MNEs regarding the negative societal implications of complementarity (Godfrey, 2005; Patten, 2008). Accordingly, MNEs' relatively precarious relationship with the host environment will make them wary of integrating philanthropic choices with promotional activities (see Harjoto & Jo, 2011). At the same time, a lack of complementarity is likely to be reinforced by the difficulty of making large unplanned expenditures in the context of a complex, geographically dispersed organization (Carrigan, 1997; also see Moir & Taffler, 2004: 150). The geographical divide between local operations and the central office limits the firm's flexibility to rapidly escalate monetary commitments (Strike et al., 2006), implying that a sudden increase in philanthropic contributions will require a corresponding curtailment of other expenditures. Given the higher penalty of deceit to which they are subject and the logistical difficulty of escalating spending as a whole, I predict that MNEs will find it convenient to divert their advertising funds to philanthropic aims.[1] It can allow MNEs to abide by the expectations of emergent social spaces and exhibit allegiance to local values and beliefs (see Walker, 2004; Zelditch, 2001). This does not imply that foreign firms will completely avoid promoting their social activities. Rather, I argue that MNEs will exhibit considerable restraint in complementing philanthropic work with promotional ends, and this can manifest either as a decrease or as a relatively limited increase in MNE advertising.

In contrast to MNEs, domestic firms are less concerned about a social backlash from promoting their philanthropic work (Wagner, 2010; also see Surroca et al., 2010). Community stakeholders are generally more willing to accept local producers' efforts to engage as authentic (Crilly et al., 2016); strong local ties can give a domestic firm greater freedom to

[1] My argument for the substitution of philanthropy for advertising expenditure is consistent with evidence that these two expenditure categories are often funded from the same budget (Meyer et al., 2011; Seifert et al., 2004; but also see Smith & Higgins, 2000).

manipulate "its relationships to its own ends" (Bhanji & Oxley, 2013: 297), and allow them to use philanthropy as an investment in self-promotion. Thus, domestic firms are less likely to be inhibited in increasing their advertising expenditures to complement an increase in charitable contributions (Siegel & Vitaliano, 2007; Zhang et al., 2010).

Contrasting pressures and expectations, then, will lead MNEs and domestic firms to treat advertising spending differently in the wake of a disaster. While MNEs are likely to restrain (i.e., either decrease or limit the increase in advertising expenditures) due both to sensitivity to local social concerns and to logistical difficulties, domestic firms will be more free in strengthening an increase in advertising expenditures along with the increase in philanthropic contributions. These differing circumstances lead me to predict that while domestic firms' philanthropy will be complemented by an increase in advertising, in comparison, MNE philanthropy will be accompanied by a relative decrease in advertising expenses:

Hypothesis 2
Subsequent to a national disaster, the difference between MNE and domestic firm philanthropic contributions will be negatively moderated by advertising expenses.

Accumulation of Trust Over Time

Consistent interaction over time generally helps diminish the initial skepticism that inhibits local acceptance of foreign firms and leads to LOF (Zaheer & Mosakowski, 1997). As MNEs demonstrate allegiance to the community's ideals, the local population is likely to find it increasingly easier to trust the firms' intentions. At the same time, in the context of a disaster, the return to normalcy in social spaces can lead to the reestablishment of social and cultural barriers; persistent engagement is required to refresh the social ties established in the disaster period (Mata & Freitas, 2012). I argue that in order to maintain the transition from local to general validation (Johnson et al., 2006), MNEs will sustain an escalated philanthropic commitment for a significant period after a disaster (see Luo, 2006). This extended engagement will ensure that MNEs remain strongly embedded in the social fabric. The continued engagement will provide a further feedback benefit, enabling the firm to develop a deeper understanding of the concerns of local audiences and maintain an avenue for ongoing engagement (Mishina et al., 2012), providing opportunities to continue to diminish LOF. Thus, as the intense need for immediate relief by the community is replaced by an expectation of long-term institutional development (Barton, 1969), MNEs will continue to respond through philanthropic contributions at a higher level than before the disaster (Child & Tsai, 2005; Dahan et al., 2006; Khanna & Palepu, 2013).

As the disaster becomes a distant memory, however, domestic firms have little to gain from continuing to escalate their philanthropic commitments (e.g., Tilcsik & Marquis, 2013). With consumers and the wider society paying less attention to the disaster and its aftermath, a visible philanthropic commitment becomes less valuable for promotion and so loses its strategic value (File & Prince, 1998). Moreover, as governmental agencies become equipped to handle relief activities, there are fewer areas where domestic firms can have a meaningful effect (Henderson, 2007). As a result, the philanthropic commitments of domestic firms are likely to diminish over time (Bin & Edwards, 2009) and these firms will limit further growth in contributions (Glynn, 2008). The difference between MNE and domestic firm philanthropy may not last forever, but, I argue, it will persist for some time after the disaster.[2]

Thus these arguments suggest that while the difference in philanthropic contributions between MNEs and domestic firms will be visible in the immediate aftermath of the disaster when both types of firms are equally likely to be socially engaged. However, this difference will become more significant and it will persist over time as MNEs continue to work to overcome LOF by solidifying general validation while domestic firms see limited benefit from continuing at a heightened level of engagement. These differing motivations lead to my third hypothesis:

[2] I believe that this difference is likely to subside once MNE commitment to institutional development is sufficiently fulfilled or domestic firms come under social pressure to imitate some of the choices of the foreign firms. I come back to this point in the discussion and conclusion section.

Hypothesis 3
Subsequent to a national disaster, the difference between MNE and domestic firm philanthropic contributions will increase and remain persistent over time.

Development of the Potential for Reciprocity

After a disaster, social restructuring increases the philanthropic role of foreign firms and provides an opening for them to engage more productively with local communities. That greater engagement is likely to yield direct benefits, in the form of reductions in the costs typically associated with LOF, such as discriminatory pricing by suppliers, stringent regulatory control by local authorities, and a lack of brand recognition by consumers, as well as a general lack of perceived legitimacy (Eden & Miller, 2004; Mezias, 2002; Zaheer, 1995). Furthermore, this trend is to some extent self-reinforcing. As a higher level of ongoing engagement allows an MNE to understand local expectations more clearly, the firm will become more effective in responding to local social needs (Pearce, 2003). Thus, MNEs' initial validation by emergent social spaces and the subsequent general validation by the wider community can lead to the development of a stronger alignment between MNE commitments and local expectations. The congruence will optimize the social impact of MNEs, giving greater legitimacy to their philanthropic choices (Godfrey, 2005), and further mitigating LOF. It can turn the skeptical local reception into MNEs being viewed as a taken-for-granted social object by the host environment (e.g., Roy, 1999).

On the other hand, domestic firms are not subject to the costs associated with LOF. So, while MNEs may harvest concrete benefits from ongoing philanthropy and growing local acceptance, domestic firms will have to contend with the increased economic pressure and uncertainty generated by the disaster and its aftermath, forces MNEs will be less vulnerable to, both because of their global nature and because of the diminishing cost of doing business engendered by the mitigation of LOF. The joint implication of diminishing legitimacy constraints for MNEs and increasing economic constraints for domestic firms is that MNEs will gain disproportional performance benefits, relative to domestic firms, from the social restructuring that accompanies a disaster. These benefits will mitigate the difference in performance between MNEs and domestic firms.

These predictions offer a direct test of my argument with regard to the effect of social restructuring. If social restructuring increases the openness of host communities to MNE presence, this should lead to a general decrease in LOF. Moreover, since this engagement escalates MNEs' philanthropic commitment and brings the contributing firms in greater contact with the local communities, this in turn implies that MNE philanthropy will accentuate the increase in performance compared to domestic firms after the disaster. This reasoning leads to my final hypotheses:

Hypothesis 4a
Subsequent to a national disaster, there will be an increase in the performance of MNEs compared to that of domestic firms.

Hypothesis 4b
Subsequent to a national disaster, the difference between MNE and domestic firm performance will be positively moderated by philanthropic contributions.

Data and Methods

Empirical Setting

I use the context of India to test my hypotheses. This setting confers three major advantages. First, India's aversion to foreign firms began soon after its independence from the British Empire in 1947 when it adopted a socialist model that focused on the eradication of poverty through an equitable distribution of wealth. In this model, the "royalties and profits collected by the private foreign companies" were viewed as "pure loot" and its first prime minister, Jawaharlal Nehru, even requested the Cabinet to find ways to eliminate such payments (Gopal, 1984: 112). Accordingly, foreign equity investment in a firm operating in India was limited to 40 per cent. This restriction made exports and joint ventures the preferred mode of foreign entry, but many MNEs avoided the Indian market altogether (Panagariya, 2008; Pant & Ramachandran, 2017).[3] Market liberalization reforms starting in 1991 allowed the foreign equity limit to be increased to 51 per cent and eventually higher,[4] but also led to severe criticism from domestic enterprises and affiliated associations. In order to retain their advantage, local producers claimed that foreign firms jeopardize an economy by eliminating local jobs and transferring capital that can be deployed locally into off-shore accounts. The rhetoric of that criticism resonated with the public and it strengthened the view that MNEs are more interested in immediate gains and their presence jeopardizes the traditional values that are integral to the society (Singh, 2005). Although these protests did not deter market reforms, they reinforced the traditional hostility against foreign firms. Thus, while market liberalization has made it possible for MNEs to establish a direct presence in India, LOF remains a critical concern (Jenkins, 1999).

A second benefit of this setting is its salience for the study of the economic and social impacts of natural disasters. Despite its rapid growth, the Indian economy is characterized by weak institutions (Ghoul et al., 2017; Khanna & Palepu, 2013) which are severely tested during natural disasters. Given its geographical size, natural disasters are not a rare occurrence. This frequency allows me to examine post-disaster philanthropy not as a hasty reaction but as a more developed response. A series of such disasters occurred in 2001, beginning with a massive, magnitude 7.7 earthquake in the state of Gujarat on January 26. The earthquake, which lasted for more than two minutes, resulted in the deaths of more than 20,000 people; another 167,000 were injured and approximately 1 million built structures were damaged or destroyed, including more than 11,500 schools, two very large hospitals, more than 1200 clinics, and hundreds of reservoirs that supplied water to urban and rural areas (Asian Development Bank & The World Bank, 2001). The earthquake had a

[3] Regulations on imports and foreign equity went through several changes during this period, but in general remained highly restrictive.

[4] Foreign equity exceeding 51 per cent still requires additional approvals, but the process is relatively simple.

huge economic impact, as reported by the Indian Ministry of Home Affairs, it:

> [E]roded nearly two percent of the GDP of the State of Gujarat—one of the most industrially advanced States in the country … [it] caused nearly ten thousand industrial units to go out of production as it struck the industrial heartland of the State. The total economic loss was assessed at over Rupees five thousand crores [$1.05 billion]. The entire spectrum of industries including the lifeline structures like bridges, roads, power, rail network telecommunication, air control towers and aerodromes suffered damages and hampered restoration and rehabilitation activities. (Issar & Mathur, 2004: 9)[5]

The January earthquake was followed in July and August by devastating flooding in Orissa (now Odisha), a northeastern state; the fifteen floods between July 8 and August 20 were the worst in Orissa's recorded history (BBC, 2001a). They submerged 25 of the state's 30 districts, affected almost 8 million people, and led to agricultural losses valued at 150 billion rupees, or about $3.15 billion (Mirza et al., 2007: 199). Eighty people died (BBC, 2001a). Floods in the state of Bihar, also in August, killed 89 people and affected more than half a million, and resulted in 4.9 billion rupees, or approximately $103 million, in crop damage (Hindu, 2001). A fourth disaster occurred in Andhra Pradesh in October, when heavy rains combined with a cyclonic storm led to the loss of 119 lives and damaged 111,340 houses (National Disaster Risk Reduction Portal; Andhra Pradesh).

These disasters were followed by a massive relief effort that engaged central and state governments; local and international civil society organizations such as the Indian Red Cross Society, Save the Children, Oxfam, and Action Aid; and individuals and corporations (BBC, 2001b). The devastation was widespread as the earthquake and floods hit large

[5] The report further noted that "it was during Bhuj [Gujarat] Earthquake, 2001 that the need for a comprehensive strategy and planning targeted at safeguarding the industrial and lifeline infrastructure was underscored" (Issar & Mathur, 2004: 9). That earthquake and its aftermath led to several major initiatives, including the creation of the National Disaster Management Authority, which has been instrumental in facilitating corporate philanthropic contributions and identifying avenues for long-term engagement by the private sector.

populations in four states, forced the relocation of millions of people for several months, and ruined farmland during the peak agricultural season. The financial impacts reverberated for several years. Several relief organizations, struggling to respond effectively, moved resources across affected regions, overcoming resource constraints in one region by reallocating funds received for the other regions (Indian Red Cross Society, 2002), essentially treating all four events as a single national disaster. I follow suit in my analysis, considering the four disasters as a single crisis event.

A third advantage of the Indian context is the uninhibited access to data on philanthropic contributions. Publicly listed firms in India are required to disclose financial charitable donations in their annual reports. This ensures that all philanthropic contributions of sampled firms are captured and there is no truncation effect, which can be a source of spurious inference.

I limit my focus on financial contributions by publicly listed firms. A major advantage of financial contributions is that they are quantifiable and comparable, offering a common baseline, and because of the difficulties associated with collecting data on and accounting for non-monetary contributions, such as organization-wide goods donation campaigns, crisis response expertise, or paid leave extended to employees for participating in relief activities. Furthermore, financial contributions are the most valuable kind of assistance; they are easy to receive, store, and transmit, and they can be exchanged for whatever goods or services recipients may require, and they provide amplified benefits in the form of economic support for the affected communities, where the funds are spent. As the European Foundation Centre and the Council on Foundations (2007) explain:

> Cash assistance is nearly always preferable to donated goods, because it allows for maximum flexibility to meet the highest priority needs and can be used to purchase required items in the disaster-affected area, thereby boosting the local economy while minimizing transport costs. (p. 14)

Moreover, financial philanthropy is the largest form of corporate social support during disasters (Aeberhard, 2008; European Foundation Centre and Council on Foundations, 2007).

The inclusion of only publicly listed firms in my sample limits an understanding of the behavior of private enterprises. However, listed firms in India are responsible for more than 80 per cent of total corporate taxes, making them highly representative of the overall economy (see Chari & David, 2012; Khanna & Palepu, 2000). Thus, I believe that the tradeoffs I have made are reasonable and my sample offers an effective dataset to compare the philanthropic choices of MNEs with those of domestic firms.

Sample

I collected my data from the Center of Monitoring Indian Economy's (CMIE) Prowess database. This database is widely used by scholars (Khanna & Palepu, 2000; Lamin, 2013; Vissa et al., 2010). It reports the activities of firms specific to their operations in India and allows an effective comparison of the choices made by domestic firms and MNEs. In addition to firm financial indicators, Prowess also captures philanthropic contributions. All values are in millions of Indian rupees, unless otherwise indicated. To distinguish between philanthropic contributions prior and subsequent to the disaster, I chose a four-year interval divided equally around the event: the periods 1999–2000 and 2001–2002. To test my hypothesis regarding temporal persistence of the difference between MNE and domestic firm philanthropy, I extended the sample by an additional two years until 2004. This choice balances proximity with sufficiency of coverage and allows me to examine both immediate and long-term contributions.

During the sample period, one other major disaster affected India. It was a cyclone in 1999 that killed almost 10,000 people in Orissa. However, its impact domain was relatively small, both geographically and in the duration of effect, and the national response did not extend to large parts of the population (Thomalla & Schmuck, 2004). In contrast, the events of 2001 led to extensive calls for government and private intervention. It catalyzed social restructuring and escalated the demand for external help (Issar & Mathur, 2004). To more clearly understand the extent to which the disasters in 2001 were more critical for the country, I compiled the list of all major and minor disasters in India during the sample period (plus one preceding and one following year) to determine the relative change in the difference between MNE and domestic firm philanthropy (Difference-in-Difference or DiD) for each year in the data relative to the previous year. The trend is shown in Fig. 15.1. It illustrates that the difference between MNE and domestic firm philanthropy experienced the most significant change between 2000 and 2001, validating my argument that the national disaster of 2001 had a strong effect on MNE philanthropy. I repeated a similar test for performance (not shown here) and found that the difference between MNE and domestic firm performance also experienced the most dramatic change immediately after the disaster, between 2000 and 2001. Appendix 1 includes a summary of the impact of all major and minor earthquakes and floods in India between 1998 and 2003.

Since the fiscal year for Indian firms ends in March, some immediate relief following the Gujarat earthquake is likely to appear in my baseline

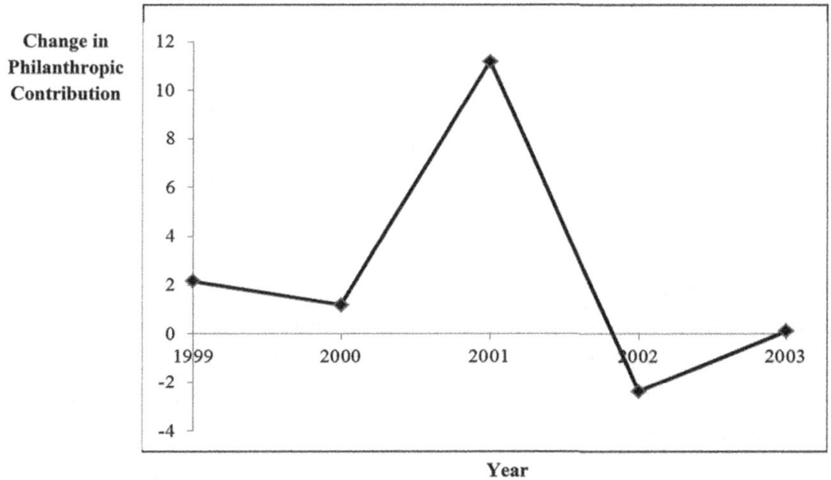

Fig. 15.1 DiD estimates at alternate break points for MNE–domestic firm philanthropy. *Note*: The figure reports change in the philanthropic contributions of MNEs relative to domestic firms in each year (t) relative to the previous year (t - 1). It shows that the largest relative increase in MNE philanthropy occurred immediately after the 2001 national disaster

period, which ends on March 31, 2001 and corresponds to the fiscal year 2000. However, I believe that those amounts represent only the most urgent contributions and the majority of donations are likely to be recorded in later periods. To the extent that some philanthropic contributions may appear in the period preceding March 2001, this raises the baseline effect, making it more difficult to validate my hypotheses and thus yielding a more stringent empirical test.

Measures

Dependent Variables

My measure of *philanthropic contribution* follows that of the Indian Companies Act of 1956 (293B): any "donation, grant, gift, help, assistance, aid, charity, alms, or otherwise, given for any charitable, social, educational, national defence, scientific, purpose or [to] any organisation or activity (formal or informal) having the object of promoting commerce, art, science, religion, charity or other useful object." Thus, I include in the measure all financial charitable donations in the periods of interest, without differentiating disaster-related donations from other philanthropic spending. This decision reflects the nature of the data available in the Prowess database. Although some firms do specify funds spent on disaster-related activities versus other philanthropic efforts in their annual reports, most do not. This limitation is not critical, since my argument is centered on changes in philanthropy that accompany the disaster. As I discuss later, my analytical approach examines this change after controlling for the historical trend in philanthropic contributions.

The research on LOF measures the relative difference between MNE and domestic firm performance in two ways—by comparing the gross profit of a foreign firm relative to the mean gross profit of all domestic firms in the industry (Zaheer, 1995; also see Miller & Parkhe, 2002) and by comparing the performance of a subsample of foreign firms with that of a subsample of domestic firms (Zaheer & Mosakowski, 1997). The latter approach corresponds to the use of a dummy variable that allows the evaluation of firms from one group (i.e., MNEs) relative to firms from the other group (i.e., domestic firms). I combine these approaches and operationalize *relative performance* as the gross profit of a sampled firm relative to the industry[6,7] and in the analytical model, use a dummy variable to distinguish between MNEs and domestic firms. In calculating industry gross profit, I include all domestic firms reported in Prowess and identify the industry boundary corresponding to the four-digit SIC classification commonly used in the United States (e.g., Nachum, 2003; also see Chacar & Vissa, 2005).

Independent Variables

There are several approaches to identify multinational enterprises (Dunning & Lundan, 2008: 3). However, my focus is not simply on establishing a foreign association. Rather, my interest is to identify firms where a foreign corporate entity acts as the controlling body and is actively involved in operations. To establish this, I consulted CMIE staff, who acknowledged that there is no foolproof way of identifying the extent of multinationality for listed firms in India. Based on these discussions, I concluded that the most conservative approach was to restrict the identification of *MNEs* to firms whose proportion of shares held by foreign corporate entities exceeded 50 per cent. This ensured that my sample was restricted to MNEs that are actively controlled by non-domestic corporations. Consequently, firms with a majority of shares held by foreign institutional or individual investors are excluded from the sample. This approach led to the identification of 190 firms, including large, well-known multinationals such as Hindustan Unilever, Procter & Gamble, and GlaxoSmithKline, as well as smaller and less well-known firms.

---

[6] This is necessary because previous studies have measured LOF by comparing the performance of each MNE with the aggregated performance of all domestic firms and have limited their analysis to single industries. Since my empirical approach seeks to make a firm-to-firm comparison across multiple industries, it is necessary to eliminate the industry-level performance effect and then compare, on average, how each MNE performs relative to each of the domestic firms in my sample. Achieving this analysis required a combined approach.

[7] Although research on LOF has preferred the use of the term *performance*, I refer to it as *relative performance* in order to better reflect the theoretical and the operational aspects of the variable.

To ensure a comparable sample of *domestic firms*, I extracted firms whose proportion of shares held by domestic corporate entities exceeded 50 per cent. This resulted in the identification of 660 firms, including firms such as Tata Coffee, Aditya Birla Chemicals, and Advanced Micronic Devices. In total, my sample includes 850 firms with 3118 observations. It extends to 3946 and 4775 observations, respectively, when examining the persistence of the difference between MNE and domestic firm philanthropy (i.e., in the 3rd and the 4th year after the disaster).

To distinguish between the interval prior and subsequent to the disaster, I operationalize *period* as an indicator variable, set at 1 for years 2001 and onwards and 0 otherwise. For the three-way interaction in hypothesis 2, I use the value of *advertising expense* as stated in the annual reports.

Controls

Since philanthropic contributions can be influenced by firm size, I control for the log of *sales* (+1) (Crilly et al., 2016). I also checked by using assets and found the results to be substantively similar. Another important control is the volume of a firm's revenues from foreign markets; considering this factor also controls for domestic multinationals (Chittoor et al., 2009; Michel & Shaked, 1986). I incorporate this control by using the ratio of a firm's *exports to total sales*.

The availability of excess resources, or slack, can also affect philanthropic choices (Brown et al., 2006; Seifert et al., 2004; also see Mata & Freitas, 2012). To capture this, I include both unabsorbed and potential slack. *Unabsorbed slack* is computed as the ratio of current assets to current liabilities, and *potential slack* is the ratio of total debt to equity.[8] Previous studies have found that engagement in R&D can be associated with charitable giving (McWilliams & Siegel, 2000); I control for this effect by capturing R&D expenses. I did not use R&D intensity due to its strong correlation with the slack variables. In addition, it is quite possible that host country experience may affect the implication of my

[8] I did not operationalize a third potential measure of slack, absorbed slack, which includes sales and administrative expenses, due to the absence of a uniform standard for reporting administrative expenses for firms in India.

arguments. I incorporate this possibility by including local *experience* as a control. It is operationalized as the number of years since the firm was incorporated in India. For domestic firms, incorporation generally represents the year of founding. For MNEs, incorporation represents the year in which the firm first started its business in India.

Indian firms are often affiliated with business groups (Khanna & Palepu, 2000; Vissa et al., 2010). As group-level charity may have an effect on affiliated firms' philanthropic contributions, I include a variable *BG philanthropic contribution* to capture the total philanthropic contribution of a business group less that of the focal firm (see Miller et al., 2009).[9]

Since the effect of a disaster may vary across firms, largely due to geographic proximity to the impact zone, and those that are directly affected may exhibit different responses than those that are more geographically distant, I control for location with a dummy variable, *impact zone*, set as 1 for firms with a registered Indian head office in one of the affected cities and 0 otherwise (also see Crampton & Patten, 2008). The proportion of my sample located in affected cities is reported in Appendix 2. I checked this result with an alternate measure that used the state boundary (i.e., Gujarat, Orissa, Andhra Pradesh, or Bihar) to identify the impact zone; this measure yielded identical results. Finally, to control for variations in technology and market, I use industry dummies in all the models (McWilliams & Siegel, 2001).

Table 15.1, which reports the mean values for MNE and domestic firm subsamples across all variables, shows major variations between the two groups of firms. This raises the question of whether there may be systematic differences between MNEs and domestic firms that lead to their philanthropic choices. There are two common approaches to overcome these differences. The first is to create a matched sample with comparable values across at least one of the key variables (e.g., Doukas & Lang, 2003). A second approach is to use an analytical model that controls for subsample differences during estimation, such as the difference-in-difference (DiD) model.

[9]This is a finer-grained measure than the more commonly used binary indicator of business group affiliation. The results are unaffected if I use business group affiliation.

Table 15.1 Subsample means

Variables	MNE	Domestic	*t*-value
Philanthropic contribution	0.24	0.08	0.16**
Advertising expense	24.88	5.58	19.30***
Relative performance	0.04	0.08	−0.04
Sales (Ln)	6.73	5.25	1.48***
Exports/sales	0.17	0.13	0.04***
Unabsorbed slack	1.98	1.46	0.52
Potential slack	8.13	3.10	5.03
R&D expense	4.70	1.11	3.59***
Experience	28.54	25.18	3.36***
BG philanthropic contribution	0.07	0.39	−0.31***
Impact zone	0.04	0.04	−0.01

Note: $^{**}p < 0.01$; $^{***}p < 0.001$

The DiD approach is considered more robust for two principal reasons. First, subsample means are inadequate in capturing underlying differences in panel data. This is because, despite identical means, the variables may experience contrasting trends over time. Second, matched samples require the removal of observations, which not only reduces the sample size but can also introduce a sampling bias. This happens when the mean value of the focal variable in one or both subsamples experiences a drift, which can lead to a failure to represent the associated population parameter (Cram et al., 2009). Given these constraints, I prefer the use of DiD. However, I also validate my findings through a matched sample. To create a matched sample, I mapped each MNE to a domestic firm from the same industry based on sales. Using this approach, I identified 53 MNE–domestic firm pairs with a total of 424 observations (530 observations for the 3rd and 636 observations for the 4th post-disaster year). The results of this analysis, reported in Appendices C and D, are largely consistent with my findings.

Analytical Model

My aim is to compare the philanthropic contributions and performance of MNEs and domestic firms in the period after the disaster relative to their comparative differences prior to the disaster. The DiD model offers the most appropriate estimation technique for this analysis (e.g., Kacperczyk, 2009; Reeb et al., 2012). DiD allows the examination of outcomes associated with a treatment group—i.e., MNEs—relative to a control group—domestic firms. In establishing this comparison, the outcomes are estimated for a significant difference after the focal event to understand whether they exceed the trajectory of their differences prior to the event. This makes it possible for me to infer whether MNE philanthropic contribution and performance differs significantly from that of domestic firms from 2001 onwards relative to the differences between the two groups prior to 2001. DiD offers statistical estimates for treatment and control group differences as a consequence of the event. If philanthropic contribution (or performance) maintains the historical trend and the treatment (MNE) and control (domestic firms) groups do not exhibit any meaningful change, then the estimation model fails to predict a significant effect. If there is a change, but the change in the treatment group is similar to that in the control group, this also leads to a failure to predict a significant effect. The only way to establish significance is for MNEs to exhibit a change in the outcome variable relative to the historical trend that is larger than the relative change exhibited by domestic firms. This eliminates the effect of subsample differences by using both domestic firm and MNE philanthropic history as the baseline effect.

DiD relies on the use of two distinct dummy variables; the significance of the DiD effect is ascertained by the interaction between the two dummies. In my case, these dummies include *period*, which differentiates observations subsequent to the event from those prior to the event, and *MNE*, which separates the treatment group from the control group. A significant interaction between *MNE* and *period* validates the two conditions identified above. This can be seen from the following equation, where y represents the outcome variable (*philanthropic contribution* or *performance*) and β_3 is the coefficient capturing the joint effect of post-disaster implications for MNEs:

$$y = \beta_0 + \beta_1 \times period + \beta_2 \times MNE + \beta_3 \times period \times MNE + \sum \beta_k \times \text{controls} + \varepsilon.$$

The coefficient β_3 is significant only if the outcome variable for MNEs relative to domestic firms (DOM) is significantly different in the period after the disaster (t_2) relative to their difference prior to the disaster (t_1). That is

$$\beta_3(est) = \left(y_{MNE_{t2}} - y_{MNE_{t1}}\right) - \left(y_{DOM_{t2}} - y_{DOM_{t1}}\right).$$

When testing for moderating effects, the focus shifts to the interaction between the two dummies (period and MNE) in the presence of the focal variable (*advertising expense* or *philanthropic contribution*). This approach may be seen as the implementation of two-way fixed effects, across subject groups and across time intervals.

I run the estimation models by accounting for the longitudinal nature of the sample. For this, I use generalized least squares (GLS) models with random effects. These models allow me to account for the effect of multiple observations per firm. Although fixed effects models may also be viable, they exclude variables that are time invariant across the sample period (i.e., MNE), which makes them inappropriate for my analysis. In a separate analysis, I also checked the results using fixed effects and found them to be fully consistent.[10]

Results

Table 15.2 presents the descriptive statistics and first-order correlations. In Table 15.3, I test hypotheses 1 through 3. In models 1–3, I examine the predicted effects for the two years t and $t + 1$ after the disaster relative to the two years prior to the disaster. Model 1 includes only the baseline controls; their effects are consistent with previous research that shows that firms with higher *sales* and *R&D expenses* make larger philanthropic contributions. Model 2 tests the interaction between *MNE* and *period*. The positive and significant effect at $p < 0.05$ shows that the relative increase in *philanthropic contribution* after the disaster is significantly

[10] While the time-invariant variables (including *MNE*) were excluded in this analysis, the interactions produced consistent effects.

Table 15.2 Descriptive statistics and correlations

	Variable	Mean	SD	1	2	3	4	5	6	7	8	9	10	11	12
1	Philanthropic contribution	0.12	1.12												
2	Period	0.51	0.50	0.00											
3	MNE	0.23	0.42	0.06	−0.01										
4	Advertising expense	10.05	101.87	0.22	0.00	0.08									
5	Relative performance	0.07	0.86	0.01	0.01	−0.02	0.04								
6	Sales (Ln)	5.59	2.68	0.12	−0.02	0.23	0.13	0.17							
7	Exports/sales	0.14	0.25	0.00	0.00	0.07	−0.04	0.05	0.13						
8	Unabsorbed slack	1.58	8.12	−0.01	0.02	0.03	−0.01	−0.01	−0.15	0.05					
9	Potential slack	4.27	84.30	0.00	0.01	0.03	0.00	−0.01	0.02	−0.01	−0.01				
10	R&D expense	1.94	15.22	0.21	0.02	0.10	0.32	0.04	0.16	−0.01	−0.01	−0.01			
11	Experience	25.96	20.45	0.02	0.03	0.07	0.10	0.05	0.24	−0.09	−0.07	−0.01	0.11		
12	BG philanthropic contribution	0.32	1.62	−0.01	−0.02	−0.08	−0.01	0.01	0.01	0.00	−0.01	−0.01	−0.02	−0.02	
13	Impact zone	0.04	0.20	−0.02	−0.01	−0.01	−0.02	0.01	0.06	−0.03	−0.02	0.08	−0.03	−0.03	0.08

Note: $N = 3118$; Correlations $\geq |0.05|$ are significant at $p \leq 0.01$

Table 15.3 GLS random effects regression models for philanthropic contribution

	$t+1$			$t+2$	$t+3$
Variable	1	2	3	4	5
MNE × period		10.51*	10.65*	14.86*	21.11*
MNE × period × advertising			−1.08***	−0.89*	−1.53**
MNE		18.12	18.81*	21.76*	24.34*
Period		0.87	0.73	2.00	6.00
Advertising expense			0.61***	0.64***	0.87***
MNE × advertising			0.02	−0.001	0.10
Period × advertising			0.60**	0.22	1.00***
Sales (Ln)	2.88*	2.56*	1.91	1.61	3.29*
Exports/sales	1.02	0.53	2.9	2.11	-11.9
Unabsorbed slack	0.07	0.04	0.03	0.03	0.07
Potential slack	0.0003	−0.002	−0.002	−0.001	−0.002
R&D expense	0.42**	0.40**	0.38**	0.33*	0.40*
Experience	−0.10	−0.11	−0.17	−0.15	−0.14
BG philanthropic contribution	0.17	0.23	0.05	0.16	1.33*
Impact zone	−18.98	−18.5	−16.81	−18.61	−19.06
Industry dummies	Y	Y	Y	Y	Y
Wald χ^2	44.83***	49.93***	146.70***	134.45***	240.71***
R^2	0.11%	0.28%	2.68%	2.06%	3.34%
N	3118	3118	3118	3946	4775

Note: *$p < 0.05$; **$p < 0.01$; ***$p < 0.001$

larger for MNEs than for domestic firms. A unit increase in philanthropic contribution by a domestic firm is matched by about ten times the contribution by a MNE. This supports hypothesis 1.

In model 3, I test for complementarity between *philanthropic contribution* and *advertising expense* subsequent to the disaster. The three-way interaction shows that MNEs that increased their philanthropic contributions exhibit a relatively smaller increase in advertising expenses compared to domestic firms. Interestingly, the analysis also shows that *advertising* is strongly associated with philanthropy, and after excluding MNEs, the sample of domestic firms appears to have complemented the increase in philanthropy with higher advertising expenditures after the disaster (*period × advertising*). However, MNEs that invest more in philanthropy exhibit a marginally smaller increase, almost 50 per cent lower than domestic firms, after taking into account their differences prior to the disaster (*MNE* × *period* × *advertising*). This supports hypothesis 2 at a significance of $p < 0.001$.

An alternative explanation of this effect could be that the limited increase in MNE advertising is associated with the changes in marketing plans. That is, rather than greater sensitivity to local perceptions, MNEs may have decreased advertising due to an overall decrease in marketing activities. I evaluated this possibility by comparing the effect of *advertising expense* to another key component of the marketing budget, *sales and promotional discount*. The benefit of using this variable is that while sales and promotional discounts are coordinated with advertising expenditures for major marketing events, such as product launches, their emphasis on point-of-sale activities is seen by consumers as independent of the corporate brand (DelVecchio et al., 2006). Thus, a change in the marketing plan is likely to diminish the emphasis on advertising as well as on sales and promotional discounts, but a decreased corporate emphasis on self-promotion may only have a constraining effect on advertising. Examining the interactive effect of sales and promotional discounts on post-disaster MNE philanthropy, I found an opposite effect. While MNE advertising shows a negative relationship with philanthropy, MNE sales and promotional discounts show a positive relationship. This confirms that the decrease in MNE advertising after the disaster is independent of changes in other marketing activities, which validates my argument for MNEs' restraint on self-promotion. I have included this test in Appendix 5.

Models 4 and 5 repeat the fully saturated model (model 3) for 3- and 4-year intervals after the disaster, respectively. The consistent and significant increase in the value of the coefficient for *MNE* × *period* supports hypothesis 3. It shows that the difference between MNE and domestic firm philanthropy not only persists but it also widens over time (i.e., in the third and the fourth year after the disaster). For the interactive effect of advertising, the coefficient first increases (3rd year) and then decreases (4th year), which suggests a growing but less consistent restraint in MNEs' self-promotional preferences.

In Table 15.4, I test my final set of hypotheses. Model 1 includes the baseline controls, which show a significant effect for *sales*. Model 2 includes the post-disaster implications for the *relative performance* of MNEs; the positive and significant effect of *MNE* × *period* at $p < 0.05$

Table 15.4 GLS random effects regression models for relative performance

Variable	1	2	3	4
MNE × period		6.70*	7.09**	7.10**
MNE × period × philanthropic contribution			24.76***	24.64***
MNE × period × advertising				0.02
MNE		−22.92***	−23.78***	−23.41***
Period		1.03	1.18	1.17
Philanthropic contribution			2.25*	1.51
MNE × philanthropic contribution			−9.17***	−8.23***
Period × philanthropic contribution			−0.77	−0.76
Advertising expense				0.10**
MNE × advertising				-0.13
Period × advertising				0.01
Sales (Ln)	3.23***	3.72***	3.66***	3.50***
Exports/sales	5.73	6.39	6.80	7.31
Unabsorbed slack	−0.07	−0.05	−0.05	−0.06
Potential slack	−0.002	−0.003	−0.003	−0.003
R&D expense	0.08	0.10	0.09	0.08
Experience	−0.02	−0.04	−0.03	−0.03
BG philanthropic contribution	−0.96	−1.09	−1.08	−1.11
Impact zone	2.51	2.13	2.93	3.14
Industry dummies	Y	Y	Y	Y
Wald χ^2	28.17***	37.53***	78.25***	84.47***
R^2	0.25%	0.50%	1.67%	1.98%
N	3118	3118	3118	3118

Note: $^{*}p < 0.05$; $^{**}p < 0.01$; $^{***}p < 0.001$

supports hypothesis 4a. It shows that the increase in MNE performance was almost 7 times to that of domestic firms after the disaster. It validates my argument that social restructuring mitigates LOF.

Model 3 includes the three-way interaction between *MNE × period* and *philanthropic contribution*. The positive and significant effect at $p < 0.001$ supports hypothesis 4b that philanthropy strengthens the acceptance of MNEs by the host community; after accounting for the mean effect, each additional unit of philanthropic contribution yields around 2 per cent further increase in relative performance. The evidence of social restructuring is also reinforced by the negative significance for *MNE × philanthropic contribution*, which indicates that, in general, MNE philanthropy backfires. That is, in the absence of a crisis, local communities are unlikely to exhibit the openness that contributes to an increase in MNE performance. Accordingly, philanthropy may largely be a cost, and in general, MNEs that do not invest into philanthropy perform better. Model 4 includes the interactive effect of *advertising* and it shows that the *relative performance* effects are persistent despite the lower inclination of MNEs towards self-promotion. I did not hypothesize any relationship between post-disaster MNE advertising and relative performance, and the absence of any effect is not surprising.

Overall, these findings validate the assertion that the social restructuring that accompanies a major disaster leads to an increase in philanthropic contribution by MNEs and an increase in the benefits those contributions provide to MNEs.

Discussion and Conclusion

Natural disasters can wreak havoc on both the physical and the social environment, forcing fundamental social restructuring. This can have large implications for the broadening of ties between MNEs and their host communities. The acute social needs and the social spaces that emerge to support them offer MNEs an opportunity to engage with the local society in a way that may help communities overcome initial skepticism and build trust. The disaster offers a window for MNEs to increase their social engagement, although they are also scrutinized more heavily in terms of their sensitivity to the host environment. In response to the engagement, the host community reduces the social and cultural barriers associated with LOF of the MNE. The result is a mutually beneficial engagement that establishes a new social equilibrium in which foreign firms play a stronger role in social development.

The contrast that we observe between the contributions and performance of MNEs and domestic firms is consistent with my argument that communities continue to differentiate between local and foreign firms in the aftermath of a major disaster, but the nature of this differentiation evolves. Local stakeholders may penalize MNEs for a perceived self-promotional bias but tolerate the same from domestic firms. At the same time, communities appear to confer greater rewards on MNEs for their benevolence but limit support for more economically vulnerable domestic firms. This suggests that local ties are not static; nor are they always favorable to domestic firms. Indeed, the social restructuring associated with disaster reverses the preferential dynamic. Consistent, long-term philanthropic engagement can replenish the ties developed in the aftermath of a disaster, but it is the relative magnitude of contributions that inspires local confidence, yielding greater performance compatibility between MNEs and local communities and ultimately reducing LOF.

This evidence of a more positive relationship between MNEs and host communities reinforces the idea of a growth in mutual dependence between communities and businesses in the wake of a crisis (see McNamara et al., 2015). It also indicates that while local communities are cognizant of MNEs' capabilities, MNEs are also quite aware of their own vulnerability and the need for greater social embeddedness (Granovetter, 1985). Thus, the persistent divide between foreign firms and local communities documented in previous studies (e.g., Amaeshi et al., 2006; Tan, 2009) may not be due to a failure of mutual understanding. Rather, it appears that communities and organizations view social ties as an investment that is difficult to make in the absence of a strong motivator. The shock of a major disaster provides such a justification. This opens up an interesting avenue for further research regarding alternatives to stimulate MNE–community engagement, hopefully in the presence of less extreme conditions than a national disaster (e.g., Mithani, 2016).

A related question pertains to the role of domestic firms. If greater local acceptance of MNEs diminishes the performance superiority of domestic firms, it is quite likely that domestic firms will attempt to create hurdles to make it difficult for MNEs to experience social integration. The context of countries such as India may offer valuable insights in this regard, as market reforms are often accompanied by local initiatives to restrain the influx of foreign equity. It would be an important addition to the literature to understand what social and political actions help local firms maintain or reinforce their domestic superiority. At the same time, my findings for the difference between MNE and domestic firm philanthropy are limited to the four-year period following the disaster. It would be interesting to examine whether MNE–community engagement eventually returns to pre-disaster levels.

Another potential line of research pertains to the effect of business groups. While I found firm-level philanthropy to be associated with business-group contribution only in the long run (i.e., in the 4th year after the disaster), group-level choices showed no effect on firm performance, suggesting a lack of legitimacy spillover across affiliates. In other words, the firms in a business group appear to be on their own when it comes to the local acceptance of MNEs or the competitive deficiencies of domestic firms. More research can help clarify how social restructuring affects the influence of business groups.

A critical limitation of this research pertains to the generalizability of my findings. With the exception of a few studies (e.g., Muller & Whiteman, 2009; Oh & Oetzel, 2011), most of the research on disasters has focused on a single national context. Yet the consistency across findings leads me to believe that my results may not be specific to a single national context. There are likely to be nuances, such as countries where MNEs are more strongly embedded in the local environment or where the effect of advertising may be limited because domestic firms are equally scrutinized in terms of the genuineness of their social intent. I believe that these contextual variations may help extend my findings to provide support for a more generalized theory of corporate social engagement. It can also help bridge my findings with the wider research on the implications of social and cultural differences (Hofstede, 2001).

A second limitation pertains to the causal relationship between disaster and the change in philanthropy and performance. While I have tried to establish the integrity of my findings through several tests, it remains possible that events other than the focal disaster, for example, the changing nature of the economic environment in India which led to a decrease in import restrictions and greater foreign business involvement with local stakeholders, may have also played a role in MNE philanthropy and performance. One way to extend this study would be to parse these differences and understand the extent to which the implications of disaster differ from those arising from the changing nature of the national, and possibly, the global environment. At the same time, it would be interesting to explore alternative approaches that can allow us to establish this causal link more clearly.

Another limitation is that while my use of the Indian context is beneficial in several ways, the country remains exposed to major disasters. While it can make it difficult to establish the persistence of superior MNE contributions, I believe ongoing natural disasters create conditions that enable us to better study firms' philanthropic behavior. They offer an opportunity to examine whether subsequent disasters sharpen the difference between MNE and domestic firm philanthropy (and performance) due to even higher levels of local engagement by foreign firms or minimize the difference because either MNEs fail to sustain their escalated commitment or domestic firms start to match MNE contributions once the economic uncertainty passes. In this regard, an interesting extension would be the use of structuration theory to help understand whether changes in MNEs' social considerations are accompanied by changes in political considerations. Such an approach could help develop a comprehensive understanding of how emergent social spaces and the evolution of wider institutional environments may make philanthropy an even more powerful mechanism to mitigate LOF (Luo, 2006).

Finally, my data are limited to philanthropic contributions. It did not allow me to examine the other ways in which firms support local communities. It is quite possible that domestic firms' stronger local ties may lead them to pay greater attention to non-financial contributions. This implies that the relatively lower magnitude of domestic firm philanthropy may be partly compensated by their greater attention to non-financial recovery and relief efforts. Yet my findings show that performance rewards were relatively smaller for domestic firms, indicating that in the event domestic firms were more vested into non-financial contributions, communities found them to be of relatively limited value. This suggests that financial support may be a more effective mechanism to meet local expectations in the event of a crisis. A second implication of my data is that it did not allow me to observe how philanthropic contributions were deployed. It may be that some of the initial increases in MNE contributions were focused on the development of local services and infrastructure that served as a conduit for future contributions. Further research along these lines offers an opportunity to understand the distinct philanthropic mechanisms and goals that come to the fore in the face of a major disaster.

This study makes several important contributions to the literature. First, I show that MNEs use philanthropy as a strategic tool, giving it greater attention and resources at times when their contributions can be an essential part of social and performance improvements. This finding connects with previous research that suggests the salience of philanthropy for foreign firms with the evidence that shows MNEs to be less benevolent than domestic firms in general (Amaeshi et al., 2006; Campbell et al., 2012; Tan, 2009). I show that MNEs find social restructuring to be critical times for local attention. In addition to shaping the magnitude and timing of contributions, MNEs' global experiences also make them aware of the danger of self-promotion. Despite limiting self-promotion, however, MNEs succeed in achieving significant relative gains in performance as a result of their philanthropic contributions.

My second major contribution is an integration of the research on natural disasters and corporate philanthropy with the research on LOF. In particular, the previous research has viewed social and cultural barriers as largely static (Gaur et al., 2011; Nachum, 2003) and suggested that, to the extent they can be changed, such change can take several decades (Zaheer & Mosakowski, 1997). My findings show that the social restructuring that follows a disaster accelerates this process (see Oliver-Smith, 1996). Thus, in this way the rapid change in local expectations and the associated benefits of social compliance make post-disaster philanthropy a valuable mechanism to achieve greater communal congruence.

In addition, I also contribute to the research on corporate philanthropy by showing that the pessimistic view of MNEs may need to be reassessed in the context of their unique skills and contributions. This connects to the more recent research on political CSR, which suggests a broader conceptualization of the social role of MNEs. The concept of political CSR works from the argument that the failure of emerging market governments to ensure the quality of life of its citizens and the need to satisfy diverse social expectations are pushing MNEs towards more active participation in issues of global governance. This participation is translating into an increased emphasis by MNEs on issues such as poverty reduction, infrastructure development, and disaster relief—fields where political vacuum more than economic expectation is the driving force (Scherer & Palazzo, 2007; Scherer et al., 2009, 2014). My findings are consistent with this line of thinking, showing that MNEs play a more active social role than do domestic firms after a major disaster. In sum, my demonstration of how firms, and in particular MNEs, contribute to social well-being offers a promising avenue to understand the unique social roles corporations may play in their host communities.

Acknowledgements The author would like to thank the area editor, Mona Makhija, the anonymous reviewers, and Ann Mooney Murphy for their extremely valuable feedback.

Appendix 1: The Impact of Natural Disasters (Earthquakes and Floods) in India

Year	Dead + Injured	Dead	Injured	Displaced	Damage (US$)
1998	1368	1368	–	145,000	530,000,000
1999	10,297	9903	394	10,105,400	2,370,000,000
2000	1090	1090	–	3,059,000	415,000,000
2001	187,464	20,628	166,836	4,103,995	2,847,038,928
2002	261	261	–	6,269,498	*No estimates*
2003	429	429	–	3,016,800	55,000,000

Source: Dartmouth Flood Observatory and the National Oceanic and Atmospheric Association

Appendix 2: Proportion of Sample Located in the Impact Zone

City	State	MNE	Domestic	*n*	% Total
Ahmedabad	Gujarat	11	68	79	2.53
Surat	Gujarat	7	8	15	0.48
Jamnagar	Gujarat	8	0	8	0.26
Guntur	Andhra Pradesh	0	8	8	0.26
Chittoor	Andhra Pradesh	0	4	4	0.13
Gandhinagar	Gujarat	0	4	4	0.13
Nellore	Andhra Pradesh	0	4	4	0.13
Patna	Bihar	0	3	3	0.10
Total		26	99	125	4.01

Appendix 3: Subsample Means for Matched Sample

Variables	MNE	Domestic	*t*-value
Philanthropic contribution	0.42	0.38	0.04
Advertising expense	55.07	35.66	19.41
Relative performance	−0.03	0.12	−0.15*
Sales (Ln)	6.67	6.84	−0.16
Exports/sales	0.11	0.13	−0.03
Unabsorbed slack	0.86	0.89	−0.02
Potential slack	2.34	1.23	1.12
R&D expense	8.91	6.93	1.98
Experience	27.54	33.75	−6.21**
BG philanthropic contribution	0.10	0.29	−0.19+
Impact zone	0.02	0.09	−0.07**

Note: +$p < 0.10$; *$p < 0.05$; **$p < 0.01$

Appendix 4: GLS Random Effects Regression Models for Matched Sample

	Philanthropic contribution			Relative performance
Variable	*t* + 1	*t* + 2	*t* + 3	*t* + 1
MNE × period	56.78+	67.94+	82.58+	−2.83
MNE × period × advertising	−3.60**	−3.14*	−5.54**	0.31
MNE × period × philanthropic contribution				26.11**
MNE	2.59	8.74	21.03	−19.50**
Period	1.81	13.79	22.51	0.50
Advertising expense	0.16*	0.15	0.24+	0.03
Philanthropic contribution				−5.11***
MNE × advertising	−0.14	0.78	0.99	−0.08
Period × advertising	1.73**	1.39*	3.04***	−0.07
MNE × philanthropic contribution				3.42
Period × philanthropic contribution				27.66***
Sales (Ln)	17.05	20.20+	24.51+	11.24***
Exports/sales	−3.33	−6.64	−7.01	−9.53

(*continued*)

(continued)

Variable	Philanthropic contribution t + 1	t + 2	t + 3	Relative performance t + 1
Unabsorbed slack	−7.52	−10.17	1.59	−2.99
Potential slack	0.09	0.14	0.18	-0.07
R&D expense	0.24	0.18	0.31	0.26*
Experience	−1.30	−1.41	−1.37	−0.02
BG philanthropic contribution	−0.13	1.15	5.59	−0.21
Impact zone	−26.56	−30.49	−13.2	−7.59
Constant	−67.91	−94.01	−147.94	−65.54*
Industry dummies	Y	Y	Y	Y
Wald χ^2	62.89*	58.20*	70.94**	142.80***
R^2	2.91%	3.61%	6.16%	8.82%
N	424	530	636	424

Note: $^+p < 0.10$; $^*p < 0.05$; $^{**}p < 0.01$; $^{***}p < 0.001$

Appendix 5: GLS Random Effects Regression Model

Variable	Philanthropic contribution
MNE × Period	10.12*
MNE × Period × Advertising	−1.19***
MNE × Period × Sales promotional discount	24.37***
MNE	12.97*
Period	0.48
Advertising expense	0.45***
Sales promotional discount	7.33***
MNE × Advertising	−0.50**
Period × Advertising	0.81***
MNE × Sales promotional discount	4.39
Period × Sales promotional discount	5.03***
Sales (Ln)	1.41
Exports/sales	2.20
Unabsorbed slack	0.04
Potential slack	−0.002
R&D expense	0.60***
Experience	−0.17
BG philanthropic contribution	0.09

(continued)

(continued)

Variable	Philanthropic contribution
Impact zone	−12.20
Industry Dummies	Y
Wald χ^2	1555.22***
R^2	26.35%
N	3118

Note: $^{*}p < 0.05$; $^{**}p < 0.01$; $^{***}p < 0.001$

References

Aeberhard, P. (2008). Expectations are changing for disaster relief. *Nonprofit and Voluntary Sector Quarterly, 37*(1), 17S–24S.

Aldrich, D. P. (2012). *Building resilience: Social capital in post-disaster recovery*. University of Chicago Press.

Amaeshi, K. M., Adi, B. C., Ogbechie, C., & Amao, O. O. (2006). Corporate social responsibility in Nigeria. *Journal of Corporate Citizenship, 2006*(24), 83–99.

Asian Development Bank, & The World Bank. (2001). *Gujarat earthquake recovery program: Assessment report*. World Bank.

Babiak, K., & Wolfe, R. (2006). More than just a game? Corporate social responsibility and Super Bowl XL. *Sport Marketing Quarterly, 15*(4), 214.

Baron, D. P. (2013). *Business and its environment*. Pearson Education.

Barton, A. H. (1969). *Communities in disaster: A sociological analysis of collective stress situations*. Doubleday & Company.

Bates, F. L., & Peacock, W. G. (1993). *Living conditions, disasters, and development: An approach to cross-cultural comparisons*. University of Georgia Press.

BBC. (2001a, July 24). *Fresh floods reported in Orissa*. http://news.bbc.co.uk/1/hi/world/south_asia/1454277.stm

BBC. (2001b, July 22). *Charities plead for India flood aid*. http://news.bbc.co.uk/1/hi/world/south_asia/1450961.stm

Bell, R. G., Filatotchev, I., & Rasheed, A. A. (2012). The liability of foreignness in capital markets: Sources and remedies. *Journal of International Business Studies, 43*(2), 107–122.

Berkes, F., Colding, J., & Folke, C. (2002). *Navigating social-ecological systems: Building resilience for complexity and change*. Cambridge University Press.

Berkman, H., Jacobsen, B., & Lee, J. B. (2011). Time-varying rare disaster risk and stock returns. *Journal of Financial Economics, 101*(2), 313–332.

Beugelsdijk, S., & Frijns, B. (2010). A cultural explanation of the foreign bias in international asset allocation. *Journal of Banking & Finance, 34*(9), 2121–2131.

Bhanji, Z., & Oxley, J. E. (2013). Overcoming the dual liability of foreignness and privateness in international corporate citizenship partnerships. *Journal of International Business Studies, 44*(4), 290–311.

Bin, O., & Edwards, B. (2009). Social capital and business giving to charity following a natural disaster: An empirical assessment. *The Journal of Socio-Economics, 38*(4), 601–607.

Brik, A. B., Rettab, B., & Mellahi, K. (2011). Market orientation, corporate social responsibility, and business performance. *Journal of Business Ethics, 99*(3), 307–324.

Brown, W. O., Helland, E., & Smith, J. K. (2006). Corporate philanthropic practices. *Journal of Corporate Finance, 12*(5), 855–877.

Campbell, J. T., Eden, L., & Miller, S. R. (2012). Multinationals and corporate social responsibility in host countries: Does distance matter? *Journal of International Business Studies, 43*(1), 84–106.

Carrigan, M. (1997). The great corporate give-away: Can marketing do good for the "do-gooders"? *European Business Journal, 9*(4), 40–46.

Chacar, A., & Vissa, B. (2005). Are emerging economies less efficient? Performance persistence and the impact of business group affiliation. *Strategic Management Journal, 26*(10), 933–946.

Chamlee-Wright, E., & Storr, V. H. (2011). Social capital as collective narratives and post-disaster community recovery. *The Sociological Review, 59*(2), 266–282.

Chari, M. D., & David, P. (2012). Sustaining superior performance in an emerging economy: An empirical test in the Indian context. *Strategic Management Journal, 33*(2), 217–229.

Child, J., & Tsai, T. (2005). The dynamic between firms' environmental strategies and institutional constraints in emerging economies: Evidence from China and Taiwan. *Journal of Management Studies, 42*(1), 95–125.

Chittoor, R., Sarkar, M. B., Ray, S., & Aulakh, P. S. (2009). Third-world copycats to emerging multinationals: Institutional changes and organizational transformation in the Indian pharmaceutical industry. *Organization Science, 20*(1), 187–205.

Christmann, P., & Taylor, G. (2001). Globalization and the environment: Determinants of firm self-regulation in China. *Journal of International Business Studies, 32*(3), 439–458.

Cram, D. P., Karan, V., & Stuart, I. (2009). Three threats to validity of choice-based and matched-sample studies in accounting research. *Contemporary Accounting Research, 26*(2), 477–516.

Crampton, W., & Patten, D. (2008). Social responsiveness, profitability and catastrophic events: Evidence on the corporate philanthropic response to 9/11. *Journal of Business Ethics, 81*(4), 863–873.

Crilly, D., Ni, N., & Jiang, Y. (2016). Do-no-harm versus do-good social responsibility: Attributional thinking and the liability of foreignness. *Strategic Management Journal, 37*(7), 1316–1329.

Dahan, N., Doh, J., & Guay, T. (2006). The role of multinational corporations in transnational institution building: A policy network perspective. *Human Relations, 59*(11), 1571–1600.

DelVecchio, D., Henard, D. H., & Freling, T. H. (2006). The effect of sales promotion on post-promotion brand preference: A meta-analysis. *Journal of Retailing, 82*(3), 203–213.

Doukas, J. A., & Lang, L. H. (2003). Foreign direct investment, diversification and firm performance. *Journal of International Business Studies, 34*(2), 153–172.

Drabek, T. E., & Key, W. H. (1976). The impact of disaster on primary group linkages. *Mass Emergencies, 1*(2), 89–105.

Drumwright, M. E. (1996). Company advertising with a social dimension: The role of noneconomic criteria. *The Journal of Marketing, 60*(4), 71–87.

Dunning, J. H., & Lundan, S. M. (2008). *Multinational enterprises and the global economy*. Edward Elgar Publishing.

Eden, L., & Miller, S. R. (2004). Distance matters: Liability of foreignness, institutional distance and ownership strategy. *Advances in International Management, 16*, 187–221.

Etzioni, A. (1975). *Comparative analysis of complex organizations* (Rev. ed.). The Free Press.

European Foundation Centre and Council on Foundations. (2007). *Disaster grantmaking: A practical guide for foundations and corporations*. European Foundation Centre.

File, K. M., & Prince, R. A. (1998). Cause related marketing and corporate philanthropy in the privately held enterprise. *Journal of Business Ethics, 17*(14), 1529–1539.

Fisher, K. E., & Naumer, C. M. (2006). Information grounds: Theoretical basis and empirical findings on information flow in social settings. In A. Spink & C. Cole (Eds.), *New directions in human information behavior* (pp. 93–111). Springer-Kluwer.

Fry, L. W., Keim, G. D., & Meiners, R. E. (1982). Corporate contributions: Altruistic or for-profit? *Academy of Management Journal, 25*(1), 94–106.

Galaskiewicz, J. (1997). An urban grants economy revisited: Corporate charitable contributions in the twin cities, 1979–81, 1987–89. *Administrative Science Quarterly, 42*(3), 445–471.

Gaur, A. S., Kumar, V., & Sarathy, R. (2011). Liability of foreignness and internationalisation of emerging market firms. *Advances in International Management, 24*, 211–233.

Geppert, M., Matten, D., & Walgenbach, P. (2006). Transnational institution building and the multinational corporation: An emerging field of research. *Human Relations, 59*(11), 1451–1465.

Ghoul, S. E., Guedhami, O., & Kim, Y. (2017). Country-level institutions, firm value, and the role of corporate social responsibility initiatives. *Journal of International Business Studies, 48*(3), 360–385.

Gilbert, C. (1998). Studying disaster: Changes in the main conceptual tools. In E. L. Quarantelli (Ed.), *What is a disaster? Perspectives on the question* (pp. 11–18). Routledge.

Glynn, M. A. (2008). Configuring the field of play: How hosting the Olympic Games impacts civic community. *Journal of Management Studies, 45*(6), 1117–1146.

Glynn, S. A., Busch, M. P., Schreiber, G. B., Murphy, E. L., Wright, D. J., Tu, Y., et al. (2003). Effect of a national disaster on blood supply and safety: The September 11 experience. *JAMA, 289*(17), 2246–2253.

Godfrey, P. C. (2005). The relationship between corporate philanthropy and shareholder wealth: A risk management perspective. *Academy of Management Review, 30*(4), 777–798.

Gopal, S. (1984). *Jawaharlal Nehru: A Biography Volume Three 1956–1964*. Harvard University Press.

Granovetter, M. (1985). Economic action and social structure: The problem of embeddedness. *American Journal of Sociology, 91*(3), 481–510.

Harjoto, M. A., & Jo, H. (2011). Corporate governance and CSR nexus. *Journal of Business Ethics, 100*(1), 45–67.

Henderson, J. C. (2007). Corporate social responsibility and tourism: Hotel companies in Phuket, Thailand, after the Indian Ocean tsunami. *International Journal of Hospitality Management, 26*(1), 228–239.

Henisz, W. J., Dorobantu, S., & Nartey, L. J. (2014). Spinning gold: The financial returns to stakeholder engagement. *Strategic Management Journal, 35*(12), 1727–1748.

Hindu. (2001, September 17). *Bihar flood toll mounts to 89*. http://www.thehindu.com/2001/09/17/stories/14172043.htm

Hofstede, G. H. (2001). *Culture's consequences: Comparing values, behaviors, institutions, and organizations across nations*. Sage.
Horlick-Jones, T. (1995). Modern disasters as outrage and betrayal. *International Journal of Mass Emergencies and Disasters, 13*(3), 305–315.
Indian Red Cross Society. (2002, November 20). India Floods 2001: Final Report (appeal no. 21/2001). www.ifrc.org/docs/appeals/21/2001fr.pdf
Issar, R., & Mathur, N. B. (2004). *Disaster risk management and the role of corporate sector: The Indian perspective*. National Disaster Division, Ministry of Home Affairs.
Jenkins, R. (1999). *Democratic politics and economic reform in India*. Cambridge University Press.
Johnson, C., Dowd, T. J., & Ridgeway, C. L. (2006). Legitimacy as a social process. *Annual Review of Sociology, 32*, 53–78.
Kacperczyk, A. (2009). With greater power comes greater responsibility? Takeover protection and corporate attention to stakeholders. *Strategic Management Journal, 30*(3), 261–285.
Khanna, T., & Palepu, K. (2000). Is group affiliation profitable in emerging markets? An analysis of diversified Indian business groups. *Journal of Finance, 55*(2), 867–891.
Khanna, T., & Palepu, K. G. (2013). *Winning in emerging markets: A road map for strategy and execution*. Harvard Business Press.
Kostova, T., & Zaheer, S. (1999). Organizational legitimacy under conditions of complexity: The case of the multinational enterprise. *Academy of Management Review, 24*(1), 64–81.
Kreps, G. A. (1985). Disaster and the social order. *Sociological Theory, 3*(1), 49–64.
Lamin, A. (2013). Business groups as information resource: An investigation of business group affiliation in the Indian software services industry. *Academy of Management Journal, 56*(5), 1487–1509.
Lefebvre, H. (2009). *State, space, world: Selected essays*. S. Elden & N. Brenner (Eds.), G. Moore (Trans). University of Minnesota Press.
Lines, V. L. (2004). Corporate reputation in Asia: Looking beyond bottom-line performance. *Journal of Communication Management, 8*(3), 233–245.
Luo, Y. (2006). Political behavior, social responsibility, and perceived corruption: A structuration perspective. *Journal of International Business Studies, 37*(6), 747–766.
Mata, J., & Freitas, E. (2012). Foreignness and exit over the life cycle of firms. *Journal of International Business Studies, 43*(7), 615–630.

McNamara, P., Pazzaglia, F., & Sonpar, K. (2015). Large-scale events as catalysts for creating mutual dependence between social ventures and resource providers. *Journal of Management (Forthcoming).* https://doi.org/10.1177/0149206314563983

McWilliams, A., & Siegel, D. (2000). Corporate social responsibility and financial performance: Correlation or misspecification? *Strategic Management Journal, 21*(5), 603–609.

McWilliams, A., & Siegel, D. (2001). Corporate social responsibility: A theory of the firm perspective. *Academy of Management Review, 26*(1), 117–127.

Meyer, K. E., Mudambi, R., & Narula, R. (2011). Multinational enterprises and local contexts: The opportunities and challenges of multiple embeddedness. *Journal of Management Studies, 48*(2), 235–252.

Mezias, J. M. (2002). Identifying liabilities of foreignness and strategies to minimize their effects: The case of labor lawsuit judgments in the United States. *Strategic Management Journal, 23*(3), 229–244.

Michel, A., & Shaked, I. (1986). Multinational corporations vs. domestic corporations: Financial performance and characteristics. *Journal of International Business Studies, 17*(3), 89–100.

Miller, D., Lee, J., Chang, S., & Le Breton-Miller, I. (2009). Filling the institutional void: The social behavior and performance of family vs non-family technology firms in emerging markets. *Journal of International Business Studies, 40*(5), 802–817.

Miller, S. R., & Parkhe, A. (2002). Is there a liability of foreignness in global banking? An empirical test of banks' X-efficiency. *Strategic Management Journal, 23*(1), 55–75.

Mirza, M. M. Q., Ahmed, A. U., & Ahmad, Q. K. (2007). *Interlinking of rivers in India: Issues and concerns*. CRC Press.

Mishina, Y., Block, E. S., & Mannor, M. J. (2012). The path dependence of organizational reputation: How social judgment influences assessments of capability and character. *Strategic Management Journal, 33*(5), 459–477.

Mitchell, J. K. (2006). The primacy of partnership: Scoping a new national disaster recovery policy. *The Annals of the American Academy of Political and Social Science, 604*(1), 228–255.

Mithani, M. A. (2016). Innovation and CSR: Do they go well together? *Long Range Planning*. https://doi.org/10.1016/j.lrp.2016.08.002

Moir, L., & Taffler, R. (2004). Does corporate philanthropy exist? Business giving to the arts in the UK. *Journal of Business Ethics, 54*(2), 149–161.

Muller, A., & Kräussl, R. (2011). Doing good deeds in times of need: A strategic perspective on corporate disaster donations. *Strategic Management Journal, 32*(9), 911–929.

Muller, A., & Whiteman, G. (2009). Exploring the geography of corporate philanthropic disaster response: A study of Fortune Global 500 firms. *Journal of Business Ethics, 84*(4), 589–603.

Nachum, L. (2003). Liability of foreignness in global competition? Financial service affiliates in the city of London. *Strategic Management Journal, 24*(12), 1187–1208.

Oh, C. H., & Oetzel, J. (2011). Multinationals' response to major disasters: How does subsidiary investment vary in response to the type of disaster and the quality of country governance? *Strategic Management Journal, 32*(6), 658–681.

Oliver-Smith, A. (1996). Anthropological research on hazards and disasters. *Annual Review of Anthropology, 25*, 303–328.

Panagariya, A. (2008). *India: The emerging giant*. Oxford University Press.

Pant, A., & Ramachandran, J. (2017). Navigating identity duality in multinational subsidiaries: A paradox lens on identity claims at Hindustan Unilever 1959–2015. *Journal of International Business Studies*. https://doi.org/10.1057/s41267-017-0076-x

Patten, D. M. (2008). Does the market value corporate philanthropy? Evidence from the response to the 2004 tsunami relief effort. *Journal of Business Ethics, 81*(3), 599–607.

Pearce, L. (2003). Disaster management and community planning, and public participation: How to achieve sustainable hazard mitigation. *Natural Hazards, 28*(2–3), 211–228.

Pescosolido, B. A., & Rubin, B. A. (2000). The web of group affiliations revisited: Social life, postmodernism, and sociology. *American Sociological Review, 65*(1), 52–76.

Quarantelli, E. L. (2000). Disaster research. In H. E. F. Borgatta & R. J. V. Montgomery (Eds.), *Encyclopedia of sociology* (2nd ed., pp. 681–688). Macmillan.

Quarantelli, E. L., & Dynes, R. R. (1977). Response to social crisis and disaster. *Annual Review of Sociology, 3*, 23–49.

Reeb, D., Sakakibara, M., & Mahmood, I. P. (2012). From the editors: Endogeneity in international business research. *Journal of International Business Studies, 43*(3), 211–218.

Roberts, P. S. (2010). Private choices, public harms: The evolution of national disaster organizations in the United States. In A. Lakoff (Ed.), *Disaster and the politics of intervention* (pp. 41–69). Columbia University Press.
Roy, W. G. (1999). *Socializing capital: The rise of the large industrial corporation in America*. Princeton University Press.
Rugman, A. M. (2005). *The regional multinationals: MNEs and "global" strategic management*. Cambridge University Press.
Savage, M., & Silva, E. B. (2013). Field analysis in cultural sociology. *Cultural Sociology, 7*(2), 111–126.
Scherer, A. G., & Palazzo, G. (2007). Toward a political conception of corporate responsibility: Business and society seen from a Habermasian perspective. *Academy of Management Review, 32*(4), 1096–1120.
Scherer, A. G., Palazzo, G., & Matten, D. (2009). Introduction to the Special Issue: Globalization as a challenge for business responsibilities. *Business Ethics Quarterly, 19*(3), 327–347.
Scherer, A. G., Palazzo, G., & Matten, D. (2014). The business firm as a political actor: A new theory of the firm for a globalized world. *Business & Society, 53*(2), 143–156.
Seifert, B., Morris, S. A., & Bartkus, B. R. (2004). Having, giving, and getting: Slack resources, corporate philanthropy, and firm financial performance. *Business & Society, 43*(2), 135–161.
Servaes, H., & Tamayo, A. (2013). The impact of corporate social responsibility on firm value: The role of customer awareness. *Management Science, 59*(5), 1045–1061.
Shan, L., & Gong, S. X. (2012). Investor sentiment and stock returns: Wenchuan Earthquake. *Finance Research Letters, 9*(1), 36–47.
Siegel, D. S., & Vitaliano, D. F. (2007). An empirical analysis of the strategic use of corporate social responsibility. *Journal of Economics & Management Strategy, 16*(3), 773–792.
Singh, K. (2005). *Foreign direct investment in India: A critical analysis of FDI from 1991–2005*. SSRN Scholarly Paper No. ID 822584. Social Science Research Network.
Smith, W., & Higgins, M. (2000). Cause-related marketing: Ethics and the ecstatic. *Business & Society, 39*(3), 304–322.
Strike, V. M., Gao, J., & Bansal, P. (2006). Being good while being bad: Social responsibility and the international diversification of US firms. *Journal of International Business Studies, 37*(6), 850–862.

Surroca, J., Tribó, J. A., & Waddock, S. (2010). Corporate responsibility and financial performance: The role of intangible resources. *Strategic Management Journal, 31*(5), 463–490.

Tan, J. (2009). Institutional structure and firm social performance in transitional economies: Evidence of multinational corporations in China. *Journal of Business Ethics, 86*, 171–189.

Thomalla, F., & Schmuck, H. (2004). 'We All Knew that a Cyclone Was Coming': Disaster preparedness and the cyclone of 1999 in Orissa, India. *Disasters, 28*(4), 373–387.

Tilcsik, A., & Marquis, C. (2013). Punctuated generosity: How mega-events and natural disasters affect corporate philanthropy in US communities. *Administrative Science Quarterly, 58*(1), 111–148.

Valente, M., & Crane, A. (2010). Public responsibility and private enterprise in developing countries. *California Management Review, 52*(3), 52–78.

Varadarajan, P. R., & Menon, A. (1988). Cause-related marketing: A coalignment of marketing strategy and corporate philanthropy. *Journal of Marketing, 52*(3), 58–74.

Vissa, B., Greve, H. R., & Chen, W.-R. (2010). Business group affiliation and firm search behavior in India: Responsiveness and focus of attention. *Organization Science, 21*(3), 696–712.

Wagner, M. (2010). The role of corporate sustainability performance for economic performance: A firm-level analysis of moderation effects. *Ecological Economics, 69*(7), 1553–1560.

Walker, H. A. (2004). Beyond power and domination: Legitimacy and formal organizations. In C. Johnson (Ed.), *Legitimacy processes in organizations* (pp. 239–271). Emerald Group Publishing.

Walker, H. A., & Zelditch, M. (1993). Power, legitimacy, and the stability of authority: A theoretical research program. In J. Berger & M. Zelditch (Eds.), *Theoretical research programs: Studies in the growth of theory* (pp. 364–381). Stanford University Press.

Webb, G. R., Tierney, K., & Dahlhamer, J. (2000). Businesses and disasters: Empirical patterns and unanswered questions. *Natural Hazards Review, 1*(2), 83–90.

White, S., & Lang, H. (2012). *Corporate engagement in natural disaster response: Piecing together the value chain*. Rowman & Littlefield Publishers.

Zaheer, S. (1995). Overcoming the liability of foreignness. *Academy of Management Journal, 38*(2), 341–363.

Zaheer, S. (2002). The liability of foreignness, redux: A commentary. *Journal of International Management, 8*(3), 351–358.

Zaheer, S., & Mosakowski, E. (1997). The dynamics of the liability of foreignness: A global study of survival in financial services. *Strategic Management Journal, 18*(6), 439–463.

Zelditch, M. (2001). Theories of legitimacy. In J. T. Jost & B. Major (Eds.), *The psychology of legitimacy: Emerging perspectives on ideology, justice, and intergroup relations* (pp. 33–53). Cambridge University Press.

Zhang, J., & Luo, X. R. (2013). Dared to care: Organizational vulnerability, institutional logics, and MNCs' social responsiveness in emerging markets. *Organization Science, 24*(6), 1742–1764.

Zhang, R., Zhu, J., Yue, H., & Zhu, C. (2010). Corporate philanthropic giving, advertising intensity, and industry competition level. *Journal of Business Ethics, 94*(1), 39–52.

16

Liability of Foreignness, Natural Disasters, and Corporate Philanthropy: A Commentary

Murad A. Mithani

Introduction

Organizations are increasingly exposed to natural and man-made disasters (Burke et al., 2015; Mithani, 2020). A major challenge with disasters is the absence of effective insights on logistical, social, and psychological adjustments necessary to mitigate their implications (Mithani, 2020). The difficulty in understanding the implications of a disaster is not just due to the large number of challenges that accompany a disaster but also because knowledge that is relevant for effective management of disasters and recovery is distributed across a number of research areas (Giustiniano et al., 2018; Gligor et al., 2019).

In my study of a national disaster in India (i.e., Mithani, 2017), I bridged the sociological and international business views of organizing in the aftermath of a national disaster. The study was framed around the means through which MNEs legitimize their local presence. Specifically, I argued

M. A. Mithani (✉)
School of Business, Rutgers University at Camden, Camden, NJ, USA
e-mail: murad.mithani@rutgers.edu

M. A. Mithani et al. (eds.), *Crises and Disruptions in International Business*, JIBS Special Collections, https://doi.org/10.1007/978-3-030-80383-4_16

that disasters provide an avenue for MNEs to mitigate their Liability of Foreignness (LOF)—the economic and social constraints that limit their acceptance in the host environment. I built my argument around three main themes: (a) disasters induce social restructuring, (b) social restructuring facilitates the emergence of new social spaces that legitimize difficult to accept ideas and identities, and (c) MNEs more than domestic firms benefit from the emergence of new social spaces, and in turn, from social restructuring. The study showed that while all firms spent more in philanthropy after the disaster than before, for MNEs: the increase in philanthropic contributions was much larger than for domestic firms; their relatively higher level of philanthropy persisted for several years after the disaster; philanthropy was less tied to promotional efforts; and it positively contributed to MNEs' subsequent performance. Thus, post-disaster philanthropy helped mitigate the MNE's liability of foreignness.

In this commentary, I expand upon the above mentioned three themes in light of one major disaster—the Covid-19 pandemic—and incorporate the research that has appeared since then on the subject of crises and disasters. In particular, I discuss how social restructuring, emergent social spaces, and differences between organizational responses have become increasingly important for the study of implications and mitigation strategies in the face of disasters. I then discuss some key questions that remain unanswered, which I propose, are critical to our understanding of the role of domestic and foreign firms in building an effective economic landscape following a major disaster.

Social Restructuring

In the 2017 JIBS paper, I defined social restructuring as a "change in the configuration of social ties". Among other things, it represents changes in the way we connect, communicate, trust, and relate to each other. The recent spread of Covid-19 offers an excellent illustration of social restructuring. It has shown how life-threatening events trigger individual-level cognitive revaluation of how we see ourselves in relation to others (Jaspal & Nerlich, 2020). Despite the personal nature of the revaluation process, societal responses converge to a new mean (Bavel et al., 2020). They produce a systematic shift in priorities (Pinkse & Gasbarro, 2019) that make it less likely for us to accept what we otherwise took for-granted and more likely to acknowledge what appeared inappropriate in the past (Brammer et al., 2020). Although societies vary in the degree of social restructuring, the implications for social change are universal (van Barneveld et al., 2020).

Emergent Social Spaces

A social space is "a microcosm of values, relationships, and implied or articulated structures". Rather than a physical or a structural environment, social spaces encapsulate "cognitive models for behavioral expectations centered on a shared objective". Although there has been considerable work on social spaces that emerge in response to social and political threats such as social movements, protests, mobs, and marches (e.g., Briscoe et al., 2015), we have limited insights surrounding social spaces that emerge in response to a national disaster. In Covid-19, we saw three broad categories of social spaces. The first category represented individuals and groups that demanded fewer restrictions (government or otherwise), the second representing those who favored stronger restrictions, and the third asking for changes in the social and political regime to overcome the challenges highlighted by the other two spaces (Junker, 2020). Thus, social spaces did not just emerge in response to a disaster but also in response to the emergence of other social spaces. The autonomous nature of these groups made it possible for them to organize spontaneously and work towards evolving goals and agendas. This included encouraging distant individuals, groups, and organizations to reinforce their ranks or to mediate with those in power, which is closer to the behavior of political coalitions than of social movements or mobs (Mithani & O'Brien, 2021). Moreover, as some of these spaces disappear, their ideas continue to reverberate across the society. This suggests that they succeeded in achieving their goal (Zajak et al., 2020).

Distinct Organizational Responses

I explained how MNEs and domestic firms viewed a major disaster differently. Although other classifications have also been examined such as proximate versus distant firms (Mithani et al., 2020) or nascent versus experienced owners (Williams et al., 2019), it is now more evident that local institutions also discriminate between firms. For example, in the case of Katrina, Covid-19, and other U.S. disasters, the government has been more responsive to larger and majority-owned businesses than smaller units and minorities, suggesting that distinct organizational responses may complement or even be reinforced by the choices of other influential stakeholders in their environment (Couch et al., 2020).

Unanswered Questions

As I highlighted above, all three themes have become increasingly visible and more salient to our understanding of the economic and social challenges that often follow a disaster. However, the work in this area including my own study has left several fundamental questions unanswered. Foremost, is social restructuring a generic event that changes only in intensity (across disasters and environments) or are there types of social restructuring based on the nature of relationships formed or severed? One possibility is to capitalize on Covid-19—a global shock—to understand if societies responded differently along the magnitude and nature dimensions of restructuring. In addition, does social restructuring affect the values of the society or is it limited to the way extant values manifest in newer relationships? If it's the former, do societies that undergo multiple disasters embrace new moral codes; do we expect to see countries ranking their priorities differently after Covid-19 than before? While it would be easier to examine how societies invest in healthcare after the disaster, measuring a shift in values is significantly more difficult. Perhaps, abnormal changes in values examined through cross-national surveys may help with this endeavour (see also Kim, 2018).

In regard to social spaces, we lack theoretical grounding. Absent a foundation, it is difficult to explain how they differ from social movements, mobs, or coalitions. Is it simply the goal, the desire to mobilize resources, or are there structural differences? Who inhabits these spaces? Do those who interface with local institutions and benefactors, such as politicians working closely with NGOs and corporations, participate in these spaces or act as external facilitators? Moreover, when social spaces disappear, is it because they are not necessary anymore as the society has embraced their goals or because their disappearance becomes a triggering event that increases society's responsiveness to those goals? The latter offers an effective explanation for how the ideas introduced by social spaces tend to diffuse across the broader society.

Lastly, how often do non-economic considerations influence differences in organizational responses to a disaster? When we view relationships as social capital, as I did in the original study, we impose some form of instrumentality; corporate contributions to relief and recovery efforts are in anticipation of economic goals. If that is the case, then who is relatively better-off: firms that benefit from society's trust and legitimation or the society that benefits from firms' willingness to go beyond their legal obligations? Given the social approval that accompanies corporate generosity, who is more responsive: new entrants seeking legitimacy or incumbents preserving legitimacy? To that end, how long does corporate response last? I believe that questions that correspond to managerial intentions and responses are relatively easier to observe than those that correspond to social restructuring or to social spaces. To that end, it may even be easier to start with firm-level insights to develop an understanding of changes in the social environment. For example, if firms exhibit changes in the nature of contributions made after successive disasters, it may be indicative of the shifts in societal expectations. In turn, the actors who connect firms with recipients may reveal the participants who inhabit emerging social spaces.

In sum, the rapid pace of economic, social, and environmental disruptions, have increased both society's expectations from corporations and corporate efforts to win social approval. In this interaction, the three themes that were central to the original study have become increasingly relevant. Evident by this collection, a better understanding of social restructuring, emergent social spaces, and the distinction between corporations in responding to disasters, is starting to receive significant attention. As also argued by other contributors to this book. With more research, I see the promise of a mutually rewarding relationship where firms and the society are not just economic beneficiaries, but valued partners.

References

Bavel, J. J. V., Baicker, K., Boggio, P. S., Capraro, V., Cichocka, A., Cikara, M., et al. (2020). Using social and behavioural science to support COVID-19 pandemic response. *Nature Human Behaviour, 4*(5), 460–471.

Brammer, S., Branicki, L., & Linnenluecke, M. K. (2020). COVID-19, societalization, and the future of business in society. *Academy of Management Perspectives, 34*(4), 493–507.

Briscoe, F., Gupta, A., & Anner, M. S. (2015). Social activism and practice diffusion: How activist tactics affect non-targeted organizations. *Administrative Science Quarterly, 60*(2), 300–332.

Burke, M., Hsiang, S. M., & Miguel, E. (2015). Global non-linear effect of temperature on economic production. *Nature, 527*(7577), 235–239.

Couch, K. A., Fairlie, R. W., & Xu, H. (2020). Early evidence of the impacts of COVID-19 on minority unemployment. *Journal of Public Economics, 192*, 104287.

Giustiniano, L., Clegg, S. R., Cunha, M. P. e., & Rego, A. (2018). *Elgar introduction to theories of organizational resilience*. Edward Elgar Publishing.

Gligor, D., Gligor, N., Holcomb, M., & Bozkurt, S. (2019). Distinguishing between the concepts of supply chain agility and resilience: A multidisciplinary literature review. *The International Journal of Logistics Management, 30*(2), 467–487.

Jaspal, R., & Nerlich, B. (2020). Social representations, identity threat, and coping amid COVID-19. *Psychological Trauma: Theory, Research, Practice, and Policy, 12*(S1), S249.

Junker, Y. A. (2020). On Covid-19, US uprisings, and Black Lives: A mandate to regenerate all our relations. *Journal of Feminist Studies in Religion, 36*(2), 117–129.

Kim, H.-S. (2018). Particularized trust, generalized trust, and immigrant self-rated health: Cross-national analysis of World Values Survey. *Public Health, 158*, 93–101.

Mithani, M. A. (2017). Liability of foreignness, natural disasters, and corporate philanthropy. *Journal of International Business Studies, 48*(8), 941–963.

Mithani, M. A. (2020). Adaptation in the face of the new normal. *Academy of Management Perspectives*, advance online publication 5 June. https://doi.org/10.5465/amp.2019.0054.

Mithani, M. A., Gopalakrishnan, S., & Santoro, M. D. (2020). Does exposure to a traumatic event make organizations resilient? *Long Range Planning*, 102031.

Mithani, M. A., & O'Brien, J. P. (2021). So what exactly is a "coalition" within an organization? A review and organizing framework. *Journal of Management, 47*(1), 171–206.

Pinkse, J., & Gasbarro, F. (2019). Managing physical impacts of climate change: An attentional perspective on corporate adaptation. *Business & Society, 58*(2), 333–368.

van Barneveld, K., Quinlan, M., Kriesler, P., Junor, A., Baum, F., Chowdhury, A., et al. (2020). The COVID-19 pandemic: Lessons on building more equal and sustainable societies. *The Economic and Labour Relations Review, 31*(2), 133–157.

Williams, T. A., Thorgren, S., & Lindh, I. (2019). Rising from failure, staying down, or more of the same? An inductive study of entrepreneurial reentry. *Academy of Management Discoveries, 6*(4), 631–662.

Zajak, S., Stjepandić, K., & Steinhilper, E. (2020). Pro-migrant protest in times of COVID-19: Intersectional boundary spanning and hybrid protest practices. *European Societies, 0*(0), 1–12.

17

International HRM Insights for Navigating the COVID-19 Pandemic: Implications for Future Research and Practice

Paula Caligiuri, Helen De Cieri, Dana Minbaeva, Alain Verbeke, and Angelika Zimmermann

Introduction

COVID-19 altered every person's reality overnight. Individuals, cities, economies, countries, and continents have experienced the shock of lockdown and the fear of unknowing. Managers have had to make many

P. Caligiuri
D'Amore-McKim School of Business, Northeastern University, Boston, MA, USA
e-mail: p.caligiuri@northeastern.edu

H. De Cieri
Monash Business School, Monash University, Caulfield East, VIC, Australia
e-mail: helen.decieri@monash.edu

D. Minbaeva (✉)
Copenhagen Business School, Copenhagen, Denmark
e-mail: dm.si@cbs.dk

M. A. Mithani et al. (eds.), *Crises and Disruptions in International Business*, JIBS Special Collections, https://doi.org/10.1007/978-3-030-80383-4_17

decisions in a very short period of time—decisions about who should stay at work and who should go home; how and where people could be moved into digital space; and what the priorities are and how those priorities can best be communicated to employees. In 2019, Ernst & Young surveyed 500 board members and chief executive officers (CEOs) globally and found that only 20% of the executives surveyed believed their companies were prepared to respond to a large adverse risk (EY, 2020). A few short months later, the COVID-19 pandemic crisis arrived and proved that their concerns were well founded. Concerns related to global supply chain vulnerabilities and financial resilience have come to the fore during the COVID-19 pandemic, along with significant strategic human talent concerns. BCG has called the ongoing COVID-19 pandemic a "people-based crisis." We agree.

The Economist noted that just as the financial crisis in 2007–2009 highlighted the role of talented Chief Financial Officers (CFOs), the COVID-19 pandemic is highlighting the role of Chief Human Resource Officers (CHROs). They wrote:

> When the financial crisis rocked the business world in 2007–2009, boardrooms turned to corporate finance chiefs. A good CFO could save a company; a bad one might bury it. The COVID-19 pandemic presents a different challenge – and highlights the role of another corporate function, often unfairly dismissed as soft. Never before have more firms needed a hard-headed HR boss.

A. Verbeke
Haskayne School of Business, University of Calgary, Calgary, AB, Canada

Henley Business School, University of Reading, Reading, UK

Solvay Business School, Vrije Universiteit Brussel, Brussels, Belgium
e-mail: alain.verbeke@haskayne.ucalgary.ca

A. Zimmermann
School of Business and Economics, Loughborough University, Loughborough, UK
e-mail: a.zimmermann@lboro.ac.uk

> The duties of chief people officers, as human-resources heads are sometimes called, look critical right now. They must keep employees healthy; maintain their morale; oversee a vast remote-working experiment; and, as firms retrench, consider whether, when and how to lay workers off. Their in-trays are bulging. (The Economist, March 24th, 2020)

The COVID-19 pandemic has pushed a massive number of employees, who were already facing stress from the health risk itself, to working from home. Compounding this stressor, many managers are now leading remote teams for the first time. This sudden change has exacerbated the challenges of collaborating and leading from a distance, challenges we in the field of international business (IB) understand well, but that have remained largely unaddressed in management practice. In 2018, RW3 surveyed 1620 employees from 90 countries regarding their experiences working on 'global virtual teams' in multinational enterprises (MNEs). While most of the respondents identified their work on global virtual teams as important for job success, only 22% received training on how best to work in their geographically distributed teams, 90% of which had two or more cultures represented. The picture is not much better at the leadership level. Among the virtual team leaders, only 15% described themselves as "very effective" with less than 20% receiving training on how to lead from a distance (RW3, 2018).

The field of IB has long accounted for the challenges associated with significant global threats and issues concerning geographical distance. From the lens of IB generally, and international human resource management (IHRM) specifically, we can recast the issues emerging from the current COVID-19 pandemic in terms of the existing academic knowledge base. By holding up this theoretical mirror, we can more clearly see the issues and offer insights to MNE managers facing challenges in leading their people through this crisis. In this Editorial, we will distil the knowledge and experience IB scholars, and more specifically IHRM, have accumulated over recent decades to offer some key learnings on managing people from a distance. Our accumulated body of knowledge in IHRM has helped us understand the challenges people face when placed in a wide range of MNE work arrangements, such as expatriate assignments, virtual international work, global project teams, and frequent international travel (Shaffer et al., 2012). This academic knowledge is particularly useful for human resource managers today, as they face new challenges and difficult decisions during this pandemic.

The purpose of this Editorial is not to conduct a comprehensive review of the literature; rather, the goal is to select a few key themes and opportunities for 'quick wins' that could be immediately applied in MNE managerial practice. At the end of this Editorial, we go back to the academic literature and offer suggestions for future research in IHRM. These suggestions represent the topics where practice would be better served from a deeper knowledge base. Thus, our suggestions for future research in IHRM relate to the broader gaps in the IB literature that, if filled, could help answering the next 'big questions' in IB (Buckley et al., 2017).

Handling the COVID-19 Crisis

Insights from IHRM's Selection, Training, and Employee Support Literature

The field of IHRM has long understood that when employees are in novel or uncertain contexts, they experience stress (Anderzén & Arnetz, 1997; Richards, 1996; Stahl & Caligiuri, 2005). To respond to such stress, employees leverage their dispositional traits and coping responses (Shaffer et al., 2006; Stahl & Caligiuri, 2005). Stress affects employees' ability to empathize with others, consider plausible alternatives, remain open-minded, engage in cognitively challenging tasks, and expand one's experiences to learn and grow. As the literature suggests, when individuals encounter periods of stress and anxiety, they have a tendency to seek out and find comfort in the familiar, the people, places, and even food that are the most predictable; this is the reason there are expatriate communities, demographic faultlines, and comfort food in every culture around the world.

The COVID-19 pandemic has produced tremendous novelty and uncertainty which is affecting the mental health of many people around the world (World Health Organization, 2020). Even as the health risks of the pandemic begin to wane in some countries and the probability of a vaccine appears high, the novel ways of working remotely and the fears around the global recession will continue to produce a state of uncertainty. In their stress-induced, cognitively reduced state, employees will have a particularly difficult time working effectively in different countries and with people from different cultures, especially in instances of high unfamiliarity. There is not enough bandwidth, so to speak, for even greater novelty and more uncertainty. Based on knowledge from the IHRM literature, a number of selection, training, and support practices can positively mitigate the concerns at hand.

Selection

IHRM has taught us that some people are naturally better than others at managing stress and uncertainty, enabling them to make better decisions and work more effectively across countries and cultures (Shaffer et al., 2006). Employees with a higher *tolerance of ambiguity* are less likely to experience the negative effects of stress caused by working in a context with greater uncertainty (Frone, 1990). Employees with *resilience* not only bounce back after stressful situations but also find positive meaning from them (Tugade & Fredrickson, 2004). Likewise, employees with natural *curiosity* can adapt better to novel situations, thrive in situations of anxiety and uncertainty, and be more creative and open-minded (Hagtvedt et al., 2019; Kashdan et al., 2013).

During this period of global stress and uncertainty, organizations (and especially MNEs) should select for these three critical, cultural agility competencies: *tolerance for ambiguity, resilience,* and *curiosity* for all employees working multiculturally. Employees working, even virtually, with clients, vendors, or colleagues from different cultures will now, more than ever, need these competencies to be effective. Selection is key. Companies can also use this time to better assess their bench strength for culturally agile talent in order to understand who will be most effective in situations of growing novelty and uncertainty.

Training

Research suggests that a state of anxiety fosters a natural desire for affiliation (Sarnoff & Zimbardo, 1961; Schachter, 1959), especially amongst those who are living the same anxiety-inducing experience (Gump & Kulik, 1997; Schachter, 1959). For global teams in MNEs that have existing familiarity, the COVID-19 pandemic offers an ideal time to foster cross-cultural team cohesion and to validate expectations of reliability since the health-related stress is present everywhere in the world. Training to support relationship formation would be well-received at this time when every team member, irrespective of country, is experiencing a similar stressor. The shared stress, anxiety, and frustrations can create ties that further bind already collegial global teams. This shared experience has the potential to enhance cohesion going forward.

For the many team members who have not yet received cross-cultural training on relationship formation across borders, any lessons learned through training, (if offered today) would land on fertile soil, because team members already have a shared "enemy" in COVID-19. This cross-cultural training in MNEs would help reduce ambiguity for cross-cultural differences by offering skill-building on how to collaborate across cultures; how to actively seek similarities with colleagues from different cultures; how to use technology inclusively; how to set team-level ground rules for communication and work-flow, and the like. This training could also help colleagues from different cultures become mindful of situations where they might be rushing to judgement because of their "reduced bandwidth" state. It could also teach them how to add respectful questioning into cross-cultural work groups to thwart the negative aspects of stereotypes.

Just as the shared stressful experience among colleagues can facilitate their emotional bonding, there are other HRM practices that would land well if offered in this current COVID-19 climate. For example, employees' need for professional growth is likely to strengthen many employees' desire to receive additional training. The psychology literature offers substantial evidence that one of our fundamental human motivators is the need for competence (Deci et al., 2017). During the COVID-19 pandemic, the lack of professional stimulation while working from home is fostering more self-directed knowledge-seeking to satisfy the need to learn, grow, and demonstrate competence. For example, LinkedIn Learning courses have seen a threefold increase in usage since the start of stay-at-home orders (Forbes, 2020). With a growing interest in self-directed learning, companies should actively harness this time to invest in the skill development of employees. At a time when employees' desire to learn, grow, and demonstrate competence is heightened, companies that offer access to, or reimburse, employees' online training achieve a clear win–win; they increase talent capability and, concurrently, foster employee motivation.

Support

In IHRM, we understand how an individual's comfort or fit within a given environment can affect their success, and also that organizational support can positively affect adjustment in a novel environment (Takeuchi et al., 2009). Those who work on global cross-national teams in MNEs face health risks due to requirements to operate across time zones, with flexible schedules, and expectations of availability around the clock (Lirio, 2017). In the ambiguity of both global work and current COVID-19 pandemic, the issues for which support is needed will vary depending on the person's work-life issues, but organizational support remains critical (Kraimer et al., 2001; Shaffer et al., 1999). Companies should offer support practices to help mitigate stress such as webinars on resilience, tutorials on mindfulness (De Cieri et al., 2019), employee assistance programs, and virtual counseling services. These stress-mitigating offerings would be particularly helpful for employees who engage in virtual work at the international level, as they face additional stress.

The world is experiencing a collective state of stress, but the global economy will not pause for employees requiring time to be ready to come out of their comfort zone to work again in different countries and with people from different cultures. More than ever, human resources managers in MNEs need to foster cohesion during this time of uncertainty by using the above selection, training, and support practices.

Insights from IHRM's Management of Health and Safety

The COVID-19 pandemic has brought health and safety issues to center stage and has placed a spotlight on the role of the HRM function in managing the health and safety of the international workforce. While management researchers already know well that employees' health and safety are linked to the demands (such as a heavy workload) and resources (such as a supportive manager) at work, the international HRM field offers specific learnings about managing health and safety for a spatially dispersed and mobile workforce. In IHRM, we understand the challenges of protecting employees, and their families, from injury and illness across national boundaries and in different work arrangements (Gannon & Paraskevas, 2019; Shaffer et al., 2012). Research in IHRM, alongside scholarship in fields such as health and psychology, has shown that globally mobile employees face specific job demands that can affect their health and safety (Anderzén & Arnetz, 1997; Druckman et al., 2014). Frequent travel, high workloads, long work hours, and job pressure lead to negative health consequences (Bader, 2015) and also negatively affect psychological well-being and family relationships (Jensen & Knudsen, 2017). We also know, however, that globally mobile work can be stimulating and rewarding in many positive ways (Ren et al., 2015).

During the pandemic, life has changed a lot for many who were international business travelers and globally mobile employees in MNEs; their current "grounding" may mean they are experiencing a sense of loss. Their frequent travel, hotel accommodation, and business dinners have been replaced by stay-at-home restrictions and virtual meetings. The stress caused by the demands of virtual global work is real; many employees are experiencing long work hours to accommodate time zones and performance challenges in less than ideal remote working conditions. These tangible work challenges all occur with the backdrop of job insecurity and future economic uncertainty. The changed work conditions during the pandemic present new challenges for employees' health and safety.

Communication and Support for Health and Safety

IHRM activities such as international family relocations provide a knowledge base that is of particular value in the pandemic because IHRM is more likely than other functional areas in the MNE or domestic HRM to deal with the interface between employees' professional and private lives (Mayerhofer et al., 2010). We know that understanding work-related demands and resources is important for all managers, and particularly for HR professionals, to support and maintain employees' health and safety. Clear and consistent communication from managers and HR about health risks and available health resources is important. Research on managing expatriate assignments in MNEs shows that communication and support from managers is an important buffer against job stress experienced by employees (Kraimer et al., 2016; Stroppa & Spiess, 2011). This knowledge can be applied to the pandemic situation of working from home. For some people, social isolation as well as uncertainty about their health, job, and future will have a negative impact on their mental health. Any stigma linked to mental health might prevent some employees from seeking help, and MNE senior managers should therefore communicate with empathy, encourage wellness resources, and offer practical support for employees' health and safety.

Flexible Work Arrangements

Many managers will be familiar with flexible work arrangements (FWAs) that formalize where, when, and how employees do their work (Chen & Fulmer, 2018). FWAs, such as flexible scheduling of work and working from home, have been shown to deliver positive benefits for employees' health (e.g., Anderson et al., 2015). IHRM has unique insights into FWAs; for example, people working in global teams are accustomed to working from home and outside standard business hours. IHRM research has highlighted the importance of practices such as FWAs that help MNE employees to maintain their health and wellbeing to cope with the demands of working across geographical and temporal boundaries (Adamovic, 2018).

In response to the COVID-19 pandemic, many MNEs have been forced to rely on one type of FWA: employees working from home. This is a new challenge for many, including IHRM scholars and practitioners. A survey conducted with 800 global HR executives in March 2020 found that 88% of organizations had either encouraged or required employees to work from home during the COVID-19 crisis (Gartner, 2020). Because this shift has been involuntary, continues over a lengthy period, and requires entire households to be house-bound, there is more potential for employees to experience increased work hours, as well as increased work-life conflict. For employees who were globally mobile, and now find themselves working from home during the pandemic, the shift is particularly significant and borders between work and family may require re-negotiation and re-organization.

There are several specific ways by which managers and HR can help their employees to work from home in a safe and healthy manner. There are many simple and cost-effective ways to encourage healthy lifestyle habits. For example, encouraging healthy work practices such as working within regular hours and taking regular work-breaks will help employees to switch off from work (Adamovic, 2018; Chen & Fulmer, 2018). Communicating clearly and managing work expectations will help employees to maintain their family responsibilities. The pandemic offers an opportunity for managers to explore how to implement flexible work arrangements that can enhance the health and safety of employees well into the future, particularly that of globally mobile employees.

Over a decade ago, Collings et al. (2007) identified health and safety as an important area of IHRM practice and pointed out the implications of employee ill-health for organizational performance as well as for the employee and their family. Applying the insights from IHRM to the pandemic situation, managers should give priority to protecting and managing employee health and safety now and in the future. Overall, our goal for employees is not only to protect and manage their health and safety but to enhance positive outcomes such as thriving and engagement with their work.

Insights from International Leadership in MNEs

During this pandemic, leaders in MNEs have needed to make swift decisions with far-reaching consequences, communicate effectively to diverse stakeholders, manage resources judiciously, integrate organizational and local demands, and inspire expectations of reliability via authenticity. The competencies needed for leadership during the COVID-19 pandemic in general are mirroring the competencies of effective leaders in MNEs because the uncertainty, ambiguity, and importance of context are present in both leadership situations.

Those MNE leaders who succeed in situations of novelty typically command three cultural-agility related responses that they can leverage like tools in a toolbox (Caligiuri, 2012; Caligiuri & Tarique, 2016). First, they have the skills *to adapt* to the demands of the context when needed, relying on those familiar with the local context to influence key decisions. Second, they know how *to integrate* diverse perspectives and demands; even when the demands are conflicting, they can work to find an integrated solution. Third, they know when *to provide direction*, even if it is not welcome or popular. A leader's ability to read the demands of the situation and respond, as needed, using the appropriate response out of the three alternatives above, are proving to be especially relevant during the pandemic.

Adaptation

Whether leaders in MNEs adapt to the demands of a situation by wearing a face mask in public during the COVID-19 pandemic, or follow to the tee other local public health recommendations affecting organizational functioning, they are acknowledging that they understand, appreciate, and are willing to abide by the norms of the situation. In some situations (but not all) adapting to the norms of the context will enable leaders to persuade, instill confidence, and influence those whose value system fosters certain behavioral expectations.

Integration

In some circumstances, adaptation is the wrong approach and MNE leaders need to integrate multiple, sometimes conflicting, perspectives to create a course of action. Leaders in MNEs do this when they integrate the cultures represented on their geographically distributed teams. During the COVID-19 crisis we are observing highly effective leaders use the same approach, balancing health demands to protect employees with urgent, firm-level requirements for economic performance.

Direction

In other situations, neither adaptation nor integration is the correct approach. In some cases, a leader will need to decide and "stick by it"—even when the decision is unwelcome or unpopular. During the COVID-19 pandemic, we saw this when business leaders quickly shifted operations, and made difficult decisions to close facilities, lay-off workers, or alter supply chains. In the international leadership context, we see this response used frequently in decisions involving safety standards, codes of conduct, quality standards, fiscal controls, corporate values, and codes of ethics.

During this COVID-19 crisis, we can observe a number of highly effective leaders, setting clear direction, and using their transparency and authenticity to effectively communicate the chosen course of action. These leaders are also acknowledging and communicating the trade-offs necessary to create plans that are responsive to public health concerns and economic imperatives. The ability to use effectively each of the three above responses is a hallmark of good leadership in complex MNEs. The leaders able to navigate the tensions among these three possible responses during the pandemic will likely also be the best MNE leaders going forward.

Insights from the Literature on Virtual International Collaboration

More suddenly and widely than ever experienced before, the COVID-19 crisis has moved collaborative work into the virtual sphere. Large sections of society now find themselves relying exclusively on virtual communication media to complete collaborative tasks. IHRM research teaches us a lot on how managers should support virtual collaborations to facilitate success during the current crisis and beyond. We do not know how long this virtual set-up, spanning the entire world will need to last, but now is a good time for managers to learn from mistakes or at least imperfections in this realm, and to strengthen the quality of virtual work for the future.

The current crisis sheds light on challenges of virtual collaboration that confirm long-standing research insights. For those who had not built strong working relationships before the crisis, working and managing at a distance and through virtual communication media has made it hard to maintain (and even more so to build) strong social ties and networks (Hansen & Lovas, 2004), realistic expectations of reliability (Gibson & Gibbs, 2006) and a team identity (Maznevski et al., 2006), thus impeding a common understanding of norms, goals and tasks as well as effective communication and knowledge sharing (Cramton, 2001; Fulk et al., 2005). Research on global teams tells us that these challenges are amplified when working internationally in MNEs, where boundaries must be crossed between countries, regions, cultures, institutional contexts, firms, and firm units (see Zimmermann, 2011).

As we know from research in IHRM and other disciplines, virtual work also has potential benefits. It can, for example, attenuate the effects of obvious cultural differences in demeanors, reduce misunderstandings due to verbal language struggles and accents, create electronic trails that document decision making processes, and save on meeting time. Moreover, geographic distance is not always a measure of psychological distance, as virtual team members who communicate frequently and share a professional or personal identity can even feel closer to each other than people collaborating face-to-face (O'Leary et al., 2014).

In the current crisis, managers have an exceptional opportunity to learn, or refine means of mitigating the challenges and realizing the potential of virtual working, which may not have been obvious before, in spite of much past work advocating the benefits of the virtual workplace (Illegems & Verbeke, 2003; Verbeke et al., 2008). One prerequisite is to match the type of information and communications technology (ICT) with the focal task (Malhotra & Majchrzak, 2014). For example, asynchronous virtual communication can be most efficient for information gathering whilst regular face-to-face meetings (or in the current situation videoconferences) should be reserved for tasks such as problem solving and comprehensive decision-making that requires synchronous interactions (Maznevski & Chudoba, 2000).

Managers can further support effective virtual working through each stage of the human resource management process (Zimmermann, 2018). The requirement of working over distances should be included in job advertisement and assessment centers, not just for managers but also for technical staff, to attract and select employees who regard this as part of their professional identity (Zimmermann & Ravishankar, 2011). After recruitment, skills of virtual collaboration can be developed through formal training that covers ICT as well as intercultural knowledge and experiential exercises (Li et al., 2013; Sit et al., 2017). As mentioned, cross-cultural training is important for those who work virtually across countries, supporting cross-cultural relationship formation and teamworking skills. On the job, new recruits can early on be given the opportunity to work on virtual teams and visit remote offices to develop an awareness of different cultural and organizational contexts that may cause misunderstandings in the virtual collaboration. Rotational assignments and short-term projects abroad serve to enhance the collaboration in global virtual teams by allowing members to develop a better shared understanding of their tasks, goals, and social norms, and to build stronger social ties and a shared team identity (Zimmermann, 2018). For this purpose, the organizational design must allow for the movement of staff in all geographic directions.

Research on virtual collaboration also suggests what measures managers can take to alleviate obstacles to virtual work; to create a more positive work experience for employees; and to increase employees' motivation to make good on their commitments in the team and the firm. First, managers can facilitate perceived proximity, by allowing employees to communicate frequently and share personal information with remote colleagues, including social media, to help identify personal similarities and to develop stronger relationships (O'Leary et al., 2014). Shared understanding, in turn, must be supported by defining strong shared goals, a clear communication structure, interaction rules, and team member roles (e.g. Earley & Peterson, 2004). To give virtual working skills the attention they deserve, managers should also include employees' effort in virtual communication and teamwork as criteria for employee performance appraisals. The process of virtual working, not just its outcomes, should thus become relevant for rewards and promotion.

Research on MNE headquarters-subsidiary settings alerts us to additional challenges in managing virtual collaborations. In MNEs, employees at headquarters and subsidiaries often compete for interesting tasks and career prospects. Rather than prioritizing headquarters' employees, senior MNE managers need to create a 'combined career pyramid' which balances the career aspirations of headquarters and subsidiary employees. This will help not only to motivate and commit employees at different locations, but also to break down collaboration barriers. For example, in offshoring settings, distributing widely the more attractive tasks and career paths across sites may help alleviate headquarters employees' fears of contributing to the 'offshoring' of their own jobs. The wide distribution of attractive tasks and career paths will make them more willing to provide support to offshore colleagues, which can in turn reinforce offshore employees' work motivation and affective and continuance commitment (Zimmermann & Ravishankar, 2016). Importantly, HR and general managers in the different MNE sites need to work together rather than in silos, so to co-design career paths and achieve better virtual collaboration.

In sum, research on virtual collaborations can teach managers much on how to handle the challenges and reap the benefits of collaborating at a distance, which the COVID-19 crisis has brought to the fore. To cope with virtual collaboration on a large-scale during this crisis, managers must develop and reward employees' virtual collaboration skills, foster perceived proximity, and design ICT, work goals, and the communication structure in a way to foster collaboration. If managers now use the opportunity to take on these insights, they can build their firm's capability of virtual working for the future. In the long run, virtual collaboration skills will become a more important part of employees' professional identity. In an international setting, this also implies that managers in different MNE subsidiaries will need to collaborate to design career paths that balance the aspirations of employees at different sites and foster their motivation to work with each other.

Insights from Global Talent Management

The COVID-19 crisis has stretched organizational resources and has accentuated key organizational capabilities. The crisis has exposed 'holes' in supposed core competencies, both at the individual and collective levels, but it has also revealed new talents. In our conversations with managers[1] we consistently heard the message of some surprising performances, emerging stars, or someone who really showed their new side. These stars are not the usual, more gregarious, employees, but those who tend to be more reserved. This, more introverted group of employees now feels comfortable suggesting new ideas and proposals in the format of virtual meetings (see the benefits of virtual collaboration described in the previous section). The crisis had pushed MNEs to reconsider the key question as to whether they have the right people in the right places. Extant research on Global Talent Management (GTM) has become particularly salient in answering this question. In GTM we have long been arguing the necessity of establishing a differentiated HR architecture for managing talent globally (Minbaeva & Collings, 2013), starting with two key decisions around strategic positions and talent pool.

Strategic Positions

The key point of departure is the focus on strategic positions (Becker & Huselid, 2006), especially those organizational roles that can have an

[1] https://www.linkedin.com/groups/8928700/

above-average impact (Boudreau & Ramstad, 2007). As Minbaeva and Collings (2013) explain, such positions: (1) relate to company strategy and have a direct impact on the effectiveness of strategy implementation; (2) exhibit high variability in the quality of the work completed by the various people occupying these positions; and (3) require unique, firm-specific know-how, tacit knowledge and industry experience that cannot be easily found in the external labor market (see also Evans et al., 2011).

Becker et al. (2009: 51) further explain that the process of identifying strategic positions begins with "the development of a clear statement of the firm's strategic choice (how will we compete?) as well as the firm's strategic capabilities (what must we do exceptionally well to win?)." The answers to these questions will be different after the crisis for each MNE. Hence, what are considered strategic positions must be re-evaluated. In doing so, managers may still be guided by the second and third elements listed above (high variability in performance and unique, firm-specific know how), but the first element may need to be reconsidered. In defining strategic positions, now and in the post-Corona crisis, the emphasis needs to shift from a static and reactive strategy implementation role towards a more agile understanding of positions that have a direct impact on how fast the company can change its direction and adapt to new situations.

Notably, the strategic positions will seldom be at the top of the MNE hierarchy. According to Mark Huselid: "the sorting and selection process used to choose senior executives is very extensive. Each step of this process is based on a variance-reduction system in which poor performers are sorted out or developed into good performers. However, at the bottom and middle of the organization, such variability can still exist."[2] Again, the COVID-19 crisis revealed some unexpected and surprisingly key, pivotal positions.

[2] Professor Mark Huselid (D'Amore-McKim School of Business, Northeastern University, USA). Presentation at the mini-conference on "Human Capital Analytics", Copenhagen Business School, October 2016.

Talent Pool

In GTM, the next step entails the creation of a pool of high-potential talents who can occupy the strategically important positions (see for example Björkman et al., 2013; Collings et al., 2019). Usually, nomination decisions are made by representatives of MNE subsidiaries or subunits, and based on a combination of data on individuals' competencies, past performance, and development potential (Fernandez-Araoz et al., 2017). In the future, the evaluation of potential should also include cultural agility competences as highlighted above: tolerance for ambiguity, resilience, and curiosity.

In the context of the current crisis, the talent pool is changing, expanding and being reconfigured. Handling the crisis has become an overnight stretch assignment and employees' response to this stretch assignment has changed many MNEs' perceptions of their talent pool. With the additional information on how well employees handled the crisis, variance across strategic positions has increased.[3] The current situation will test all previous decisions regarding the leadership pipeline and talent management such that, on the other side of the crisis, the high-potential pool may well consist of a different group of employees.

Prior research has shown the potential correlation between personalities and nominations to the talent pool. For example, Caligiuri (2006) has explained how different personality traits (e.g., extroversion) may be favored in global settings. Mellahi and Collings (2010) have argued that social and geographical distances may lead talented employees in foreign MNE subsidiaries to be in "blind spots" because they are less visible. In contrast, talent located at the headquarters may be more visible to—and more valued by—key decision makers in the MNE. The virtual reality imposed by COVID-19 has had a levelling effect. Introverts have been given an equal chance to participate in the virtual interactions and discussions. Everyone, regardless of location, has had equal access to decision-makers in virtual meetings, and has had an equal opportunity to contribute. The work reality fostered by the COVID-19 pandemic has

[3] As one senior executive explained: "Some 5 s become 9 s, but other 5 s failed to 3 s" (the company is using the performance scale ranging from 1 (min) to 10 (max)).

helped to supersede structural, geographic, and social barriers that previously limited talent management decisions.

In sum, the insights from GTM are especially relevant for companies during the crisis period, and they will be even more relevant in the next stage—the Restart.[4] The crisis has redefined not just where we work but has altered the work we do and how we do it.[5] To succeed in the next 'new normal', MNE senior managers will need to revisit the prevailing definition of talent and their understanding how economic value is created.

Implications for IHRM Research: Looking Beyond the Pandemic

In the first part of this Editorial, we have drawn attention to several key insights from IHRM scholarship that provide the foundation for understanding, interpreting, and addressing COVID-19 related workplace challenges. The insights we have outlined could serve to guide senior MNE managers in HRM and beyond as they address novel, people-related challenges in their organizations. However, the pandemic has also highlighted some gaps in our research: answers to questions we *wish* we had in the academic literature but, to date, do not.

This section of our Editorial turns to recommendations for future IHRM scholarship in the post-pandemic reality. We think that novel and multidisciplinary research will be needed to address the context, processes, and outcomes of work post-pandemic. Below we focus especially on suggestions for research on: (1) how to manage with global uncertainty; (2) how to facilitate global work; and (3) how to redefine organizational performance.

[4] https://www.mckinsey.com/business-functions/strategy-and-corporate-finance/our-insights/the-restart?cid=other-eml-alt-mip-mck&hlkid=17bde39d07df446db8ee005b1edb0404&hctky=9992611&hdpid=d7377876-06d5-4721-83eb-57e9fccaebf4

[5] https://hbr.org/2020/04/how-the-coronavirus-crisis-is-redefining-jobs

Managing with Global Uncertainty

The concept of volatile, uncertain, complex, and ambiguous (VUCA) environments has been recognized for some time (Schoemaker et al., 2018; Van Tulder et al., 2019), yet the health and economic crises resulting from COVID-19 have given the concept further significance. The COVID-19 pandemic has revealed extraordinary vulnerabilities arising from widespread global uncertainty. Uncertainty is no longer the context experienced by just senior MNE leaders involved in managing complex global supply chains, volatile financial markets, and unpredictable geopolitical relationships. Rather, uncertainty has become the context for numerous MNE employees who are working from home for the first time, experiencing job instability and financial insecurity, and worrying about their and their loved ones' health and safety.

The context, as we know in IHRM, sets an important boundary condition in understanding the efficacy of our theories (e.g., Brewster et al., 2016; Cooke, 2018; Cooke et al., 2020) and this context of uncertainty, which has been exacerbated by the COVID-19 pandemic, cannot be ignored. Our view is that IHRM should explore new avenues of managing global uncertainty and that it can thereby contribute to answering some of the 'big questions' in IB (Buckley et al., 2017). While the context of uncertainty has created opportunities for many streams of IB research, we would like to focus on three key ones: *leadership and talent management, collaborating under stress,* and *managing health and safety.*

Leadership and Talent Management

The United States War College was the first institution to coin the term VUCA. For decades, military institutions globally have been developing leaders who could lead through a VUCA reality. Partnering with scholars from the military, future research in IB could advance how leadership styles and behaviors might need to vary during situations of high uncertainty, and how specific interventions might lead to vastly improved outcomes (Adler et al., 2009). This could be especially important when the high uncertainty context creates an emotional fear response, as we saw with some employees who were forced to work without adequate protective equipment during the COVID-19 pandemic. If employees are sensing true fear, a leader's role would be to help employees process the context, allowing the rational response to supplant the emotional response. Universally effective leadership skills might be in play during fear-inducing situations. However, given that both Geert Hofstede and the GLOBE study identified "uncertainty avoidance" as a primary cultural difference, culturally bound leadership styles might be warranted for situations of high uncertainty and fear. Future research should examine this further.

In the case of the COVID-19 pandemic, members on a global team might be experiencing the same tangible level of uncertainty but might have vastly different reactions. Just as uncertainty might be experienced differently across cultures, so might the responses to fear, stress, and anxiety. Thus, future research should examine whether global leaders are able to identify (and respond effectively) across cultures. For example, the same leadership communication to address employees' uncertainty might have differentially effective responses, depending on their cross-cultural context. IB scholars could partner with scholars in neuroscience to understand differences in cross-cultural emotional responses and how to recognize and address these in an international business context.

The ever-growing global uncertainty shapes assumptions beyond talent management, especially with respect to the choice of selection and performance criteria for an MNE's talent pool. Despite recent advances in recognizing the importance of context (Vaiman et al., 2018), the GTM research assumes that what makes talent a talent is universal across cultures and homogeneous for all MNE units. Contrary to this, Morris et al. (2016) identified four types of human capital underlying the talent portfolio of MNEs and explained that different configurations of the talent portfolio tend to be emphasized in different contexts. Future research should examine whether different configurations of the talent portfolio should be emphasized in the context of global uncertainty, and whether different types of human capital could contribute differently to organizational resilience (see next section). In addition, as Minbaeva (2016) points out, what constitutes 'talent' in the fluid context of emerging economies and developing countries differs significantly from the definition of 'talent' in the (comparatively) stable environment of developed economies. Following the traditions of extreme context research (Hällgren et al., 2018), GTM research needs to revisit its assumption that internal MNE talent systems function in a globally uniform way, using a single, standardized understanding of what good performance and high potential entail.

Collaborating Under Stress

The COVID-19 pandemic is a globally shared stress-producing experience which can, according to social psychology, foster a natural desire to connect with others (Gump & Kulik, 1997; Sarnoff & Zimbardo, 1961; Schachter, 1959). Future research should examine whether collaborating through the COVID-19 pandemic has strengthened relationships among colleagues from different cultures or, had the opposite effect, by creating a greater emotional distance because the ability to support one another was limited to virtual interactions filtered through diverse cultural lenses. Delineating the circumstances under which fear facilitates cohesion (or division) among culturally diverse colleagues would be important for generating interventions.

IHRM has long understood that certain competencies affect success when working under stress in different countries and with people from different cultures (Shaffer et al., 2006). Future research should examine the extent to which this new way of collaborating under stress in a context of uncertainty will require additional competencies. In addition to competencies, future research should examine whether employees' experiences have better prepared them to succeed during the COVID-19 pandemic. It might be the case that employees who have lived and worked abroad would be better able to collaborate effectively in a high-uncertainty environment.

Health and Safety

The COVID-19 pandemic has shown that managing employees' health and safety is a key challenge for IHRM, and this is an important component of the grand challenge faced by MNEs in understanding how to deal with social responsibility (Buckley et al., 2017). However, IHRM scholars (and practitioners) are unlikely to command the entire reservoir of requisite knowledge to investigate all the mental, physiological, and even physical problems that employees may experience during and after the pandemic. As for other complex challenges, our understanding of health and safety issues would benefit greatly from multidisciplinary collaboration, particularly with scholars in fields such as health. For example, we could apply health-based knowledge about the long-term health consequences of risk exposure, to investigate the long-term consequences of travel bans and stay at home orders on employees' mental health. IHRM scholars must also broaden their scope of attention. To date, IHRM scholars have largely focused on a narrow range of sub-clinical aspects of psychological well-being and adjustment. Yet, the extreme situation of the pandemic challenges us to support managers who are dealing with health matters that include serious outcomes among employees, including depression, substance abuse, or suicidal ideation, which are already well understood by health scholars. Future research should also give more attention to the positive aspects of global work. While most IHRM research has focused on global work as a context with negative consequences for health and safety, future research could investigate antecedents in global work that lead to positive outcomes such as thriving and resilience (Ren et al., 2015).

Facilitating Global Work

The COVID-19 pandemic has amplified new ways that global work can be accomplished, encouraging us to rethink how MNEs use *global teams and virtual collaboration* and *international assignments*.

Global Teams and Virtual Collaboration

For IHRM, the COVID-19 pandemic has highlighted the importance of how employees can work effectively across borders while remaining at home. The focus on global teams has become particularly salient. With employees sharing the same global stressor, future studies should examine whether their experience of getting through it together has fostered greater cohesion and, if so, whether those MNEs that have spent time to train their employees on cross-cultural virtual collaboration now have global teams with greater expectations of reliability among the members. Working from home has exposed employees' full selves as conference calls are bringing colleagues into each other's homes, possibly seeing each other's pets, children, and home décor. Future studies should examine whether the COVID-19 pandemic has fostered greater global virtual team cohesion by providing visible evidence of each other's true selves.

The crisis also offers a new opportunity to look at the fundamentals of virtual collaboration. IHRM researchers could use the current situation of large-scale virtual working as an 'extreme case scenario' to examine the extent to which virtual collaboration can be effective. They could ask whether the methods that we have derived from virtual collaborations amongst managers or technical experts (e.g., information systems engineers) suffice for achieving effective work in the types of collaborations that were previously not virtual, for example among administration staff inside the MNE.

Future research should thus use the current context of the COVID-19 pandemic to study those who are working from home for the first time. This group would uniquely enable us to examine the cross-national, generational, functional, etc. differences in predicting employees' preferences for working from home in the future, post-pandemic. For example, are relationship-oriented or collectivist cultures more likely to want to return to the workplace? IHRM researchers can also use the extreme case scenario to study the pitfalls and levers of large-scale virtual conferences that have now been held for the first time. Whilst this type of research may bring to the surface new psychological and practical barriers to virtual collaboration, which set its boundaries, it also promises to show how virtual collaboration can be expanded both in scale and scope—to different types of work and forms of collaboration.

So far, insights into virtual collaboration have been gained in different academic disciplines that have largely operated as silos. Besides IHRM and IB, important findings on international or global virtual collaboration stem from the areas of information systems (IS)—which has studied dispersed IS collaborations for a long time—organizational studies, and strategic management. The last two areas have highlighted the role of the organizational and strategic contexts respectively. IHRM researchers, therefore, need to draw on insights from these disciplines to achieve a better understanding of virtual collaboration and practices in order to optimally support these.

International Assignments

With countries' borders closed for fear of the COVID-19 virus spreading further, the idea of an upward trajectory of international assignments seems highly unlikely. Assuming that fewer employees will be sent abroad to live and work in the context of international assignments, future research will need to investigate alternative control MNE mechanisms for subsidiaries, alternatives for developing future global leaders, and alternatives for addressing skill shortages in host countries. For example, could technology-driven control mechanisms successfully replace an expatriate leader sent from headquarters to oversee operations? Could domestic-based experiences in culturally diverse settings also foster cultural agility competencies the way a high-quality international assignment would? Could skills be taught to host country nationals through virtually means, so as to prepare them for anticipated skill shortages in host countries? With fewer expatriates living abroad, those who are sent abroad will need to achieve greater success faster than previous generations of expatriates did because the stakes, so to speak, will be higher. Speed of adjustment for those expatriates who are still going abroad will be of utmost importance.

The expatriate literature has evolved to understand cross-cultural adjustment as an idiosyncratic person–environment relationship based on how people uniquely experience living abroad (Haslberger et al., 2013; Hippler et al., 2014). Various facets of the host country environment—when compared to the home country—are individually determined for their influence on an individual's level of adjustment. For some, the change might be better or worse—or having no real effect. Future research should mirror the approach in the expatriate adjustment literature to determine who is best able to adjust to the various facets of this novel work environment and to what extent the support practices offered have fostered employee adjustment to various facets of work-life during these uncertain times. For example, some employees might have adjusted well to working from home—even preferred it. Others might adjust to working from home only after employer support practices were implemented, such as regular team meetings or training on how to work virtually. The experience of working from home during the pandemic could open new opportunities for IHRM research to examine flexible work arrangements for expatriates. While the IHRM literature has begun to examine flexible work arrangements in the context of global teams (Adamovic, 2018), there has been little attention to date to the FWAs used in other types of international work.

Rethinking how MNEs use *global teams and virtual collaboration* and *international assignments*, could constitute important elements in a reconfiguration of the IHRM function. There is an opportunity for IHRM research to collect relevant and useful evidence to facilitate global work in the future, by examining the role of the IHRM function during and after the crisis. Even large organizations with sophisticated pre-pandemic IHRM policies are likely to be re-writing the rules. For example, as travel restrictions ease, employers and individuals will make decisions about whether, when, and where they feel safe to travel. IHRM scholarship can offer an evidence-base for global mobility policies that will help employees to adjust to new ways of working in teams and the inevitable stress and uncertainty of post-pandemic travel.

Redefining Performance

Minbaeva and De Cieri (2015) wrote about the need for IHRM scholars to rethink their key dependent variable—organizational performance. They referred to enterprise resilience—the ability of an enterprise to respond or "bounce back" from shock events (e.g., Branzei & Abdelnour, 2010; De Cieri & Dowling, 2012)—as an important outcome variable for IHRM in the context of large-scale disasters. The COVID-19 crisis adds to the long list of shock events in the twenty-first century that have included terrorism, corporate scandals, the global financial crisis that began in 2007, natural disasters (e.g., the Indian Ocean tsunami in 2004; the Icelandic volcano eruption in 2010), and environmental disasters (e.g., the BP/Deepwater Horizon oil rig explosion off the US's Gulf Coast) (Minbaeva & De Cieri, 2015). The global pandemic once again stresses the importance of understanding the role of IHRM in building enterprise resilience.

The crisis also brings home the point that sustainability, and more specifically organizations' contributions to the United Nation's sustainable development goals (SDGs), should become a dependent variable in IHRM research. The UN's 17 SDGs, adopted as a non-binding agreement in 2015 by 193 countries, are relevant not only to governments but also to all stakeholders in employment relationships (Fowler & Biekart, 2017; Sachs, 2015; UN General Assembly, 2015). These goals are part of the 'big picture' of global development, with environmental, humanitarian and economic implications. HRM scholars have been criticized for being slow to respond to these goals (Alzola, 2018).

As is the case with other environmental disasters today, the COVID-19 crisis has been directly linked to the unsustainable ways in which humans treat the world's ecosystem (The Guardian, 2020; WWF, 2020). When seen through this (albeit debatable) lens, the COVID-19 crisis should alert us to the need to rethink our working practices to help address environmental sustainability. Unintentionally, IHRM research may in the past have contributed to environmentally unsustainable working practices, e.g., by promoting frequent international travel in instances where such travel could have been easily avoided and replaced by more environment-friendly modes of professional interaction. The current crisis now provides an opportunity for IHRM researchers to guide MNEs towards contributing to achieving the SDGs. They could do this especially by examining how virtual working can be optimized to reduce the extent of commuting and travel. In addition to examining the sustainability of global HR policy and practice, future research could address the SDGs with respect to global health and safety, e.g., by examining how global mobility practices integrate health and safety matters. Specific areas where the IHRM function could demonstrate its relevance might include management of risk exposure in MNE subsidiary locations and travel destinations, anticipative management of emergencies such as medical evacuations, and the reduction of work-related injuries and illnesses.

In the above exposé, we have outlined how IHRM researchers should use the current extreme scenario of virtual working to scrutinize the boundaries of effective virtual collaboration and find means to support it at a broader scale (without compromising on organizational effectiveness or employees' mental health). During the 'lockdown', people have experienced improvements in air quality, noise levels and congestion, and have at the same time tested and practiced their virtual collaboration skills. Through this, many of us may have become more open to the idea of reducing unnecessary travel, which at a larger scale contributes to reducing the environmental destruction that has fed into the crisis itself. Even if unexpected barriers to virtual working surface, IHRM researchers may be more inclined than before to search for new avenues to capitalize on virtual working and to foster sustainable management practices in this realm.

Recognizing that much of the IHRM literature has focused on high-status professional employees, future research should give attention to the MNE's entire workforce and beyond in the context of its CSR strategy, to address the needs of individuals for whom the pandemic has exacerbated conditions of insecurity, disempowerment and vulnerability. This is particularly important given that the SDGs highlight the eradication of extreme poverty and hunger, and reduction of inequality, which are issues that will be exacerbated as we enter a likely post-pandemic global recession. IB needs to better understand the role of globalization from the perspective of job creation and job loss globally. Buckley et al. (2017) have identified the potential for IB scholars to collaborate with scholars in disciplines such as health economics and epidemiology to address grand challenges such as the impact of "poverty and child mortality, on local employees and subsidiaries" (p. 1055). We suggest that IHRM scholars have both a responsibility to join these conversations and an opportunity to contribute their insights about people in the global workforce.

Table 17.1 presents a summary of our suggestions for future IHRM scholarship, informed by our extant knowledge base, our direct learnings from responses to the pandemic and new questions raised by the pandemic as we enter into the post-pandemic 'next normal'.

Table 17.1 Recommendations for Future IHRM Research

	How to manage under global uncertainty (context)	How to facilitate global work (process)	How to redefine performance (outcomes)
During pandemic	What role does communication and support from MNE managers (or lack thereof) play in in the way employees cope with the demands of work during the pandemic? Which bundles/ configurations of IHRM policies and practices are associated with safety and health outcomes, both positive and negative, during the pandemic? Are there culturally nuanced approaches to assuage employees' fears during the pandemic? What can MNEs do to communicate difficult decisions during the pandemic, to help employees better manage expectations and feelings of uncertainty about the future?	How have international work arrangements changed during the pandemic? Has the shared experience of the crisis affected cohesion in global teams, and has virtual team training made a difference? To what extent have the support practices offered, fostered employee adjustment to various facets of work-life during these uncertain times? Which management interventions will be most effective during the pandemic for improving health outcomes for employees?	What matters most at the time of a pandemic, and how can IHRM contribute to it? Which bundles/ configurations of IHRM practices have enabled effective organizational adaptation and prioritization, and which ones have caused organizational failure to respond? How can MNEs recognize and reward leaders who are able to foster a spirit of shared humanity during the pandemic? What can MNEs do within their communities during the pandemic to address growing challenges around food insecurity, mental wellness, and health education?

(*continued*)

Table 17.1 (continued)

	How to manage under global uncertainty (context)	How to facilitate global work (process)	How to redefine performance (outcomes)
General (in the 'new normal')	How is the reality of growing uncertainty reflected in selecting, developing and retaining global talent and international employees? How do leadership styles and behaviors need to vary across cultures under high uncertainty? Under which circumstances does fear facilitate cohesion or division among culturally diverse colleagues? To what extent do new ways of collaborating under uncertainty-induced stress require additional competencies, and how can these be developed? What are the long-term consequences of the COVID-19 pandemic for the mental health of employees? How do global threats change the way we manage the global workforce?	Will global work arrangements in the 'new normal' revert to pre-pandemic patterns or new ones? What are the boundaries to virtual working: Do we need new methods to scale-up virtual collaboration in its different forms? Are there any cross-national, generational, functional, etc. differences in employees' preferences for working from home? Are there alternative control mechanisms for subsidiaries; alternatives for developing future MNE leaders; and alternatives for addressing skills shortages in MNE host countries? Which IHRM practices are associated with the thriving and higher resilience of globally mobile employees? What are the associations between flexible work and organizational outcomes?	What should be the key performance indicators of the IHRM function? How can IHRM help MNEs to build organizational resilience? What is the future role of IHRM in corporate social responsibility? How can IHRM help MNEs contribute to SDGs, including health and safety, and mitigate unintended effects of current practices, such as high-volume global mobility and commuting, on the ecosystem? How can IHRM contribute to addressing the 'grand challenges' and 'big questions' of IB?

Conclusion

Buckley et al. (2017) have pointed out that a "narrow scope of research has potentially hindered IB scholars from studying more impactful research questions" (p. 1048). The same can be said of IHRM. Despite the intrinsic multi-disciplinary nature of the topics in which IHRM scholars are interested, there has been little cross-pollination of ideas and knowledge across disciplines (Andersson et al., 2019). The experience of the COVID-19 crisis has showed again that useful knowledge of IHRM, which could inform and support management practice, remains dispersed and fragmented. There are many reasons for this, yet we cannot answer the 'big questions' unless we share knowledge and collaborate in multidisciplinary research.

This Editorial has hopefully demonstrated that the most useful knowledge for management practice is derived from IHRM research with the following features: multidisciplinary in nature, multi-stakeholder oriented, multilevel, and methodologically pluralist. This is what the future of IHRM should look like, for it to perform a valuable role in IB scholarship (Buckley et al., 2017). The COVID-19 crisis, as a global shock, illustrates once again that IHRM researchers have an opportunity—but also the shared responsibility—to make a difference. They can do so by providing inspired responses, grounded in state-of-the-art scholarly work, to the grand challenges of our time.

Publisher's Note Springer Nature remains neutral with regard to jurisdictional claims in published maps and institutional affiliations.

References

Adamovic, M. (2018). An employee-focused human resource management perspective for the management of global virtual teams. *The International Journal of Human Resource Management, 29*, 2159–2187.

Adler, A. B., Bliese, P. D., McGurk, D., Hoge, C. W., & Castro, C. A. (2009). Battlemind debriefing and battlemind training as early interventions with soldiers returning from Iraq: Randomization by platoon. *Journal of Consulting and Clinical Psychology, 77*(5), 928–940.

Alzola, M. (2018). Decent work: The moral status of labor in human resource management. *Journal of Business Ethics, 147*, 835–853.

Anderson, A. J., Kaplan, S. A., & Vega, R. P. (2015). The impact of telework on emotional experience: When, and for whom, does telework improve daily affective well-being? *European Journal of Work and Organizational Psychology, 24*, 882–897.

Andersson, U., Brewster, C., Minbaeva, D., Narula, R., & Wood, G. (2019). The IB/IHRM interface: Exploring the potential of intersectional theorizing. *Journal of World Business, 54*(5), 100998.

Anderzén, I., & Arnetz, B. B. (1997). Psychophysiological reactions during the first year of a foreign assignment: Results of a controlled longitudinal study. *Work & Stress, 11*(4), 304–318.

Bader, B. (2015). The power of support in high-risk countries: Compensation and social support as antecedents of expatriate work attitudes. *The International Journal of Human Resource Management, 26*(13), 1712–1736.

Becker, B., Huselid, M., & Beatty, R. (2009). *The differentiated workforce: Transforming talent into strategic impact*. Harvard Business Press.

Becker, B. E., & Huselid, M. A. (2006). Strategic human resource management: Where do we go from here? *Journal of Management, 32*, 898–925.

Björkman, I., Ehrnrooth, M., Mäkelä, K., Smale, A., & Sumelius, J. (2013). Talent or not? Employee reactions to talent identification. *Human Resource Management, 52*(2), 195–214.

Boudreau, J. W., & Ramstad, P. M. (2007). *Beyond HR: The new science of human capital*. Harvard Business School Press.

Branzei, O., & Abdelnour, S. (2010). Another day, another dollar: Enterprise resilience under terrorism in developing countries. *Journal of International Business Studies, 41*, 804–825.

Brewster, C., Mayrhofer, W., & Smale, A. (2016). Crossing the streams: HRM in multinational enterprises and comparative HRM. *Human Resource Management Review, 26*, 285–297.

Buckley, P. J., Doh, J. P., & Benischke, M. H. (2017). Towards a renaissance in international business research? Big questions, grand challenges, and the future of IB scholarship. *Journal of International Business Studies, 48*, 1045–1064.

Caligiuri, P. (2006). Developing global leaders. *Human Resource Management Review, 16*, 219–228.

Caligiuri, P. (2012). *Cultural agility: Building a pipeline of globally successful professionals*. Jossey-Bass Publishing.

Caligiuri, P., & Tarique, I. (2016). Cultural agility and international assignees' effectiveness in cross-cultural interactions. *International Journal of Training and Development, 20*(4), 280–289.

Chen, Y., & Fulmer, I. S. (2018). Fine-tuning what we know about employees' experience with flexible work arrangements and their job attitudes. *Human Resource Management, 57*, 381–395.

Collings, D. G., Mellahi, K., & Cascio, W. F. (2019). Global talent management and performance in multinational enterprises: A multilevel perspective. *Journal of Management, 45*(2), 540–566.

Collings, D. G., Scullion, H., & Morley, M. J. (2007). Changing patterns of global staffing in the multinational enterprise: Challenges to the conventional expatriate assignment and emerging alternatives. *Journal of World Business, 42*, 198–213.

Cooke, F. L. (2018). Concepts, contexts, and mindsets: Putting human resource management research in perspective. *Human Resource Management Journal, 93*, 184–201.

Cooke, F. L., Wood, G., Wang, M., & Veen, A. (2020). How far has international HRM travelled? A systematic review of literature on multinational corporations (2000–2014). *Human Resource Management Review, 29*, 59–75.

Cramton, C. D. (2001). The mutual knowledge problem and its consequences for dispersed collaboration. *Organization Science, 12*, 346–371.

De Cieri, H., & Dowling, P. J. (2012). Strategic human resource management in multinational enterprises: Developments and directions. In G. Stahl, I. Björkman, & S. Morris (Eds.), *Handbook of international HRM research* (2nd ed., pp. 13–35). Edward Elgar.

De Cieri, H., Shea, T., Cooper, B., & Oldenburg, B. (2019). Effects of work-related stressors and mindfulness on mental and physical health among Australian nurses and healthcare workers. *Journal of Nursing Scholarship, 51*(5), 580–589.

Deci, E. L., Olafsen, A. H., & Ryan, R. M. (2017). Self-determination theory in work organizations: The state of a science. *Annual Review of Organizational Psychology and Organizational Behavior, 4*, 19–43.

Druckman, M., Harber, P., Liu, Y., & Quigley, R. L. (2014). Assessing the risk of work-related international travel. *Journal of Occupational and Environmental Medicine, 56*(11), 1161–1166.

Earley, C., & Peterson, R. S. (2004). The elusive cultural chameleon: Cultural intelligence as a new approach to intercultural training for the global manager. *Academy of Management Learning and Education, 3*(1), 100–115.

Evans, P., Pucik, V., & Björkman, I. (2011). *The global challenge* (2nd ed.). McGraw-Hill/Irwin.

EY. (2020, April 20). *Global board risk survey, EY*. https://www.ey.com/en_us/news/2020/04/nearly-80-percent-of-board-members-felt-unprepared-for-a-major-risk-event-like-covid-19-ey-survey. Accessed 15 May 2020.

Fernandez-Araoz, C., Roscoe, A., & Aramaki, K. (2017). Turning potential into success: The missing link in leadership development. *Harvard Business Review, 95*(6), 86–93.

Forbes. (2020, May 7). Pandemic spike in AI learning – And what it means for schools. *Forbes.com*. https://www.forbes.com/sites/tomvanderark/2020/05/07/pandemic-spike-in-ai-learning–and-what-it-means-for-/#771cf7df5079. Accessed 15 May 2020.

Fowler, A., & Biekart, K. (2017). Multi-stakeholder initiatives for sustainable development goals: The importance of interlocutors. *Public Administration and Development, 37*, 81–93.

Frone, M. (1990). Intolerance of ambiguity as a moderator of the occupational role stress–strain relationship: A meta-analysis. *Journal of Organizational Behavior, 11*(4), 309–320.

Fulk, J., Monge, P., & Hollingshead, A. B. (2005). Knowledge resource sharing in dispersed multinational teams: Three theoretical lenses. In D. L. Shapiro, M. A. Von Glinow, & J. L. Cheng (Eds.), *Managing multinational teams: Global perspectives* (pp. 155–188). Elsevier/JAI Press.

Gannon, J., & Paraskevas, A. (2019). In the line of fire: Managing expatriates in hostile environments. *The International Journal of Human Resource Management, 30*(11), 1737–1768.

Gartner. (2020). *Gartner HR survey reveals 88% of organizations have encouraged or required employees to work from home due to coronavirus*. https://www.gartner.com/en/newsroom/press-releases/2020-03-19-gartner-hr-survey-reveals-88–of-organizations-have-e. Accessed 15 May 2020.

Gibson, C. B., & Gibbs, J. L. (2006). Unpacking the concept of virtuality: The effects of geographic dispersion, electronic dependence, dynamic structure, and national diversity on team innovation. *Administrative Science Quarterly, 51*, 451–495.

Gump, B. B., & Kulik, J. A. (1997). Stress, affiliation, and emotional contagion. *Journal of Personality and Social Psychology, 72*, 305–319.

Hagtvedt, L. P., Dossinger, K., Harrison, S., & Huang, L. (2019). Curiosity made the cat more creative: Specific curiosity as a driver of creativity. *Organizational Behavior and Human Decision Processes, 150*, 1–13.

Hällgren, M., Rouleau, L., & de Rond, M. (2018). A matter of life or death: How extreme context research matters for management and organization studies. *Academy of Management Annals, 12*, 111–153.

Hansen, M. T., & Lovas, B. (2004). How do multinational companies leverage technological competencies? Moving from single to interdependent explanations. *Strategic Management Journal, 25*(8/9), 801–822.

Haslberger, A., Brewster, C., & Hippler, T. (2013). The dimensions of expatriate adjustment. *Human Resource Management, 52*(3), 333–351.

Hippler, T., Caligiuri, P. M., & Johnson, J. E. (2014). Revisiting the construct of expatriate adjustment. *International Studies of Management and Organization, 44*(3), 8–24.

Illegems, V., & Verbeke, A. (2003). *Moving towards the virtual workplace: Managerial and societal perspectives on telework*. Edward Elgar.

Jensen, M. T., & Knudsen, K. (2017). A two-wave cross-lagged study of business travel, work–family conflict, emotional exhaustion, and psychological health complaints. *European Journal of Work and Organizational Psychology, 26*(1), 30–41.

Kashdan, T., Sherman, R., Yarbro, J., & Funnder, D. (2013). How are curious people viewed and how do they behave in social situations? From the perspectives of self, friends, parents, and unacquainted observers. *Journal of Personality, 81*(2), 142–154.

Kraimer, M., Bolino, M., & Mead, B. (2016). Themes in expatriate and repatriate research over four decades: What do we know and what do we still need to learn? *Annual Review of Organizational Psychology and Organizational Behavior, 3*, 1.1–1.27.

Kraimer, M. L., Wayne, S. J., & Jaworski, R. A. (2001). Sources of support and expatriate performance: The mediating role of expatriate adjustment. *Personnel Psychology, 54*(1), 71–99.

Li, M., Mobley, W. H., & Kelly, A. (2013). When do global leaders learn best to develop cultural intelligence? An investigation of the moderating role of experiential learning style. *Academy of Management Learning and Education, 12*, 32–50.

Lirio, P. (2017). Global boundary work tactics: Managing work and family transitions in a 24–7 global context. *Community, Work & Family, 20*, 72–91.

Malhotra, A., & Majchrzak, A. (2014). Enhancing performance of geographically distributed teams through targeted use of information and communication technologies. *Human Relations, 67*(4), 389–411.

Mayerhofer, H., Müller, B., & Schmidt, A. (2010). Implications of flexpatriates' lifestyles on HRM practices. *Management Revue, 21*(2), 155–173.

Maznevski, M. L., & Chudoba, K. (2000). Bridging space over time: Global virtual team dynamics and effectiveness. *Organization Science, 11*, 473–492.

Maznevski, M. L., Davison, S. C., & Jonsen, K. (2006). Global virtual team dynamics and effectiveness. In G. K. Stahl & I. Björkman (Eds.), *Handbook of research in international human resource management* (pp. 354–384). Edward Elgar.

Mellahi, K., & Collings, D. G. (2010). The barriers to effective global talent management: The example of corporate élites in MNEs. *Journal of World Business, 45*(2), 143–149.

Minbaeva, D. (2016). Contextualizing the individual in international management research: Black boxes, comfort zones and a future research agenda. *European Journal of International Management, 10*(1), 95–104.

Minbaeva, D., & Collings, D. G. (2013). Seven myths of global talent management. *The International Journal of Human Resource Management, 24*(9), 1762–1776.

Minbaeva, D., & De Cieri, H. (2015). Strategy and IHRM. In D. G. Collings, G. Wood, & P. Caligiuri (Eds.), *The Routledge companion to international human resource management* (pp. 13–28). Routledge.

Morris, S., Snell, S., & Björkman, I. (2016). An architectural framework for global talent management. *Journal of International Business Studies, 47*(6), 723–747.

O'Leary, M. B., Wilson, J. M., & Metiu, A. (2014). Beyond being there: The symbolic role of communication and identification in perceptions of proximity to geographically dispersed colleagues. *MIS Quarterly, 38*(4), 1219–1243.

Ren, H., Yunlu, D. G., Shaffer, M. A., & Fodchuck, K. M. (2015). Expatriate success and thriving: The influence of job deprivation and emotional stability. *Journal of World Business, 50*, 69–78.

Richards, D. (1996). Strangers in a strange land: Expatriate paranoia and the dynamics of exclusion. *International Journal of Human Resource Management, 7*(2), 553–571.

RW3. (2018). *2018 trends in high-performing global virtual teams*. RW3.

Sachs, J. D. (2015). Achieving the sustainable development goals. *Journal of International Business Ethics, 8*(2), 53–62.

Sarnoff, I., & Zimbardo, P. G. (1961). Anxiety, fear, and social affiliation. *Journal of Abnormal and Social Psychology, 62*, 356–363.

Schachter, S. (1959). *The psychology of affiliation: Experimental studies of the sources of gregariousness*. Stanford University Press.

Schoemaker, P. J. H., Heaton, S., & Teece, D. (2018). Innovation, dynamic capabilities, and leadership. *California Management Review, 61*, 15–42.

Shaffer, M. A., Harrison, D. A., & Gilley, K. M. (1999). Dimensions, determinants, and differences in the expatriate adjustment process. *Journal of International Business Studies, 30*, 557–581.

Shaffer, M. A., Harrison, D. A., Gregersen, H., Black, J. S., & Ferzandi, L. A. (2006). You can take it with you: Individual differences and expatriate effectiveness. *Journal of Applied Psychology, 91*(1), 109–125.

Shaffer, M. A., Kraimer, M., Chen, Y.-P., & Bolino, M. (2012). Choices, challenges, and career consequences of global work experiences: A review and future agenda. *Journal of Management, 38*, 1282–1327.

Sit, A., Mak, A. S., & Heill, J. T. (2017). Does cross-cultural training in tertiary education enhance cross-cultural adjustment? A systematic review. *International Journal of Intercultural Relations, 57*, 1–18.

Stahl, G., & Caligiuri, P. M. (2005). The relationship between expatriate coping strategies and expatriate adjustment. *Journal of Applied Psychology, 90*(4), 603–616.

Stroppa, C., & Spiess, E. (2011). International assignments: The role of social support and personal initiative. *International Journal of Intercultural Relations, 35*(2), 234–245.

Takeuchi, R., Wang, M., Marinova, S. V., & Yao, X. (2009). Role of domain-specific facets of perceived organizational support during expatriation and implications for performance. *Organization Science, 20*(3), 621–634.

The Guardian. (2020). *Coronavirus: 'Nature is sending us a message', says UN environment chief.* https://www.theguardian.com/world/2020/mar/25/coronavirus-nature-is-sending-us-a-message-says-un-environment-chief#maincontent. Accessed 11 May 2020.

Tugade, M. M., & Fredrickson, B. L. (2004). Resilient individuals use positive emotions to bounce back from negative emotional experiences. *Journal of Personality and Social Psychology, 86*(2), 320–333.

UN General Assembly. (2015). *Transforming our world: The 2030 agenda for sustainable development.* United Nations.

Vaiman, V., Sparrow, P., Schuler, R., & Collings, D. G. (Eds.). (2018). *Macro talent management. A global perspective on managing talent in developed markets.* Routledge.

Van Tulder, R., Verbeke, A., & Jankowska, B. (2019). *International business in a VUCA world: The changing role of states and firms.* Emerald Publishing Limited.

Verbeke, A., Schulz, R., Greidanus, N., & Hambley, L. (2008). *Growing the virtual workplace: The integrative value proposition for telework*. Edward Elgar Publishing.

World Health Organization. (2020). *Physical and mental health key to resilience during COVID-19 pandemic*. http://www.euro.who.int/en/health-topics/health-emergencies/coronavirus-covid-19/statements/statement-physical-and-mental-health-key-to-resilience-during-covid-19-pandemic. Accessed 15 May 2020.

WWF. (2020). *To prevent the next pandemic, we must transform our relationship with nature*. https://medium.com/@WWF/to-prevent-the-next-pandemic-we-must-transform-our-relationship-with-nature-c42ce9dffc62. Accessed 15 May 2020.

Zimmermann, A. (2011). Interpersonal relationships in transnational, virtual teams – Towards a configurational perspective. *International Journal of Management Reviews, 13*(1), 59–78.

Zimmermann, A. (2018). Managing virtual talent. In D. G. Collings, H. Scullion, & P. M. Caligiuri (Eds.), *Global talent management* (pp. 210–228). Routledge.

Zimmermann, A., & Ravishankar, M. N. (2011). Collaborative IT offshoring relationships and professional role identities: Reflections from a field study. *Journal of Vocational Behavior, 78*(3), 351–360.

Zimmermann, A., & Ravishankar, M. N. (2016). A systems perspective on offshoring strategy and motivational drivers amongst onshore and offshore employees. *Journal of World Business, 51*(4), 548–567.

18

The Impact of COVID-19 on International HRM Research and Practice: A Commentary

Kamel Mellahi and David G. Collings

Introduction

The JIBS editorial "International HRM insights for navigating the COVID-19 pandemic: Implications for future research and practice" (Caligiuri et al., 2020) was a timely and important contribution to our understanding of the impact of COVID-19 on international human resource management (HRM) research and practice in the early stages of the pandemic. It was published on June 2nd, 2020 when there were approximately 6.3 million cases and 380 thousand deaths globally (CNN, 2020). The paper brought together a diverse and impressive author team,

K. Mellahi (✉)
Centre for Responsible Business, Dubai Chamber of Commerce, Dubai, UAE
e-mail: Kamel.Mellahi@Dubaichamber.com

D. G. Collings
Dublin City University Business School, Dublin City University, Dublin, Ireland
e-mail: david.collings@dcu.ie

M. A. Mithani et al. (eds.), *Crises and Disruptions in International Business*, JIBS Special Collections, https://doi.org/10.1007/978-3-030-80383-4_18

including three current or former JIBS Senior Editors and the current Editor-in-Chief. The team's breadth and depth of expertise is reflected in a rich review of decades of research in IB and specifically international HRM around lessons for managing people at a distance. Their authors' objective—identifying themes that would offer quick wins and which could be immediately applied in MNE practice—appears to be achieved in the piece.

Caligiuri et al.'s (2020) review of the relevant literature covers five main themes in international HRM practice and offers insights around each of these themes: (1) selection, training and employee support; (2) management of health and safety; (3) international leadership in MNEs; (4) virtual international collaboration; and (5) global talent management. In each of these five research areas, key insights from the literature are summarised with a particular focus on the implications of international HRM practice for COVID-19, these themes have merit and relevance to MNEs globally. Reflecting on Caligiuri et al.'s (2020) contribution nearly a year since the paper was written, when global cases have increased to 112 million with some 2.5 million recorded deaths, we argue, provides an opportunity to reflect on the contribution of the paper and start a discussion on the potential avenues which future research could usefully pursue in order to further deepen our understanding of the considerable impact of COVID-19 on international HRM practice. It also highlights the pace of change during the pandemic and how much things have changed across the globe in less than a year.

Caligiuri et al. (2020) Key Themes Revisited

In this commentary, we note that the discussion on the management of health, safety and wellbeing is particularly important in the context of the management of the pandemic on a global scale. There is now little doubt concerning the significant impact of COVID-19 on employee health and wellbeing (see also Agarwal, 2021; Carnevale & Hatak, 2020). This has brought the consideration of employee health and wellbeing to the fore for international HR leaders (Collings, Nyberg, et al., 2021). Indeed, despite calls in the international HRM literature as early as fifteen years ago for greater consideration of employee health and safety in the context of international assignments (Collings et al., 2007), it is a topic that has been severely neglected in the international HRM literature (De Cieri & Lazarova, 2021; Van De Voorde et al., 2012). Thus, employee health, safety and wellbeing in general, are areas which call for significant research efforts over the coming years. In calling for more research on the issue of employee health and wellbeing across international contexts, we echo Holmes et al.'s (2020) view that the issue of health and wellbeing can only be understood through a multidisciplinary lens with participation from various research communities incorporating facets ranging from *inter alia*, psychology, psychiatry, medicine, behavioural and social sciences disciplines.

Our understanding of the issues raised by Caligiuri et al. (2020) in their paper has advanced in the months since the manuscript was published. For instance, there has a been a flurry of papers on working from home and virtual collaboration (notably, see: Waizenegger et al., 2020). This emerging body of literature suggests that many forms of virtual collaboration worked well during COVID-19 while other forms were relatively less effective. At the same time, we found that virtually all of the studies that have been published on international HRM during COVID-19 are small scale surveys or rely on limited case studies. This is important because the impact of COVID-19 on international HRM is significant and requires a rethink of some of our current knowledge. Additionally, even if practices were effective in the short term, we require a better understanding of the long-term implications and the tensions that may arise between working from home and working on site, and the variations of changes in work practices for different employee groups (Collings, Nyberg, et al., 2021).

Furthermore, this reshaping of the boundaries between work and place may potentially also shift the global talent landscape. For example, it may be possible for MNEs to tap into spatially diverse talent without the requirement for offices in those locations or the requirement for this talent to relocate to sites where MNE units are located. This could have significant implications for global talent markets, as cities become less central and providing significant opportunities for more regional development as individuals could, at least for the most part, work virtually and contribute to regional economies.

However, working from home raises a number of interdisciplinary issues and most likely affects employees of MNEs differently. It is therefore important to understand how remote work is being experienced across countries, including disparities between wealthier and poorer countries as well as within disadvantaged communities. For instance, working from home may be particularly challenging in these countries owing to poor infrastructure such as broadband access, potentially amplifying concerns around employee inclusion. These contexts may, in turn, lead to feelings of professional and social isolation. Additionally, whether working remotely will impact negatively on career progression for these dispersed employees is another important question. The challenges faced by employees in progressing their careers from less central subsidiaries have already been highlighted (Collings et al., 2019). Many of these issues have been amplified by the pandemic. We argue that research needs to draw on theories from diverse fields to fully understand how working remotely impacts work practices and subsidiary performance across international contexts. Importantly, we acknowledge that our plea for interdisciplinary research to study emerging international HRM issues such as working from home, employee health, safety and wellbeing across international context is not an entirely new one. Dunning and colleagues made such a plea more than three decades ago (Dunning, 1989; see also Chabowski et al., 2017). Indeed, given the interdisciplinary nature of international business, JIBS has always positioned itself as an interdisciplinary journal (Cantwell & Brannen, 2011) and, we argue, is likely to be an important outlet for the dissemination of international HRM research. Thus, we call for large-scale and longitudinal studies to better understand the issues raised in the Caligiuri et al. (2020) JIBS article. Next, we discuss how research and practice may move on from overly focusing on firm tactical responses to the changes driven by the pandemic towards developing more strategic and longer-term responses, whilst ensuring effective tactical considerations together with the much-needed temporary solutions.

Moving from the Tactical to the Strategic

Given that Caligiuri and colleagues' article was written in the early stages of the pandemic, it is understandable that they were largely focused on tactical responses to the pandemic in the context of international HRM. The paper captures a number of these tactical considerations very well. Indeed, we know from research on previous crises such as the great recession that tactical HR responses can be hugely valuable. For example, Roche and Teague (2012) highlighted the positive impact of HR's recognized unique operational competencies, such as short-term retrenchment measures, in aiding organisations navigate the great recession. However, such tactical responses can only offer temporary solutions.

Considering the HR implications of the pandemic through a paradox lens, Collings, Nyberg, et al. (2021) argue that many HR responses have resulted in temporary solutions to immediate challenges which are unlikely to offer long term solutions. They argue that without embracing the underlying paradoxes underlying these challenges, contradictions will resurface, highlighting the interrelatedness and persistence of the underlying tensions (Smith & Lewis, 2011). In this context, a paradox is defined as contradictory, yet interrelated elements that exist simultaneously and persist over time (Smith & Lewis, 2011: 382). Paradoxes emerge when beliefs or assumptions held by organisational leaders fail to keep pace with external changes (Cannon, 1996), and there is little doubt that the pandemic has challenged MNEs significantly in this regard. This will challenge leaders in MNEs as solely operational focus cannot generate sustainable outcomes, suggesting that the most effective HR leaders and international HRM functions will better balance shorter-term tactical activities with those activities carrying greater strategic influence (Collings, Nyberg, et al., 2021). As the longer-term implications of COVID-19 on international HRM are better understood, research should again adopt a longitudinal approach and a more ambitious research programme that moves beyond isolating the impact of specific international HRM practices on key outcomes, and by capturing both the individual and the organisational levels of analysis.

Conclusion

Caligiuri and colleagues' paper was a timely and important contribution to our understanding of the early impact of COVID-19 from an international HRM perspective. It accurately identifies many of the key challenges that international HR leaders faced at this time and highlighted some particularly important questions for international HRM research. In this short commentary on their article, we pointed to the key contributions of the paper and highlighted some next steps for advancing research in international HRM in the context of the COVID-19 pandemic and beyond.

References

Agarwal, P. (2021). Shattered but smiling: Human resource management and the wellbeing of hotel employees during COVID-19. *International Journal of Hospitality Management, 93*, 102765.

Caligiuri, P., De Cieri, H., Minbaeva, D., Verbeke, A., & Zimmermann, A. (2020). International HRM insights for navigating the COVID-19 pandemic: Implications for future research and practice. *Journal of International Business Studies, 51*, 697–713.

Cannon, T. B. (1996). Welcome to the revolution: Managing paradox in the 21st century. Pitman.

Cantwell, J., & Brannen, M. Y. (2011). Positioning JIBS as an interdisciplinary journal. *Journal of International Business Studies, 42*, 1–9.

Carnevale, J. B., & Hatak, I. (2020). Employee adjustment and well-being in the era of COVID-19: Implications for human resource management. *Journal of Business Research, 116*, 183–187.

Chabowski, B. R., Samiee, S., & Hult, G. T. M. (2017). Cross-national research and international business: An interdisciplinary path. *International Business Review, 26*(1), 89–101.

CNN. (2020, June 2). Coronavirus News. Available at: https://edition.cnn.com/world/live-news/coronavirus-pandemic-06-02-20-intl/index.html. Accessed 22 Feb 2021.

Collings, D. G., Mellahi, K., & Cascio, W. F. (2019). Global talent management and performance in multinational enterprises: A multilevel perspective. *Journal of Management, 45*(2), 540–566.

Collings, D. G., Nyberg, A. N., Wright, P. M., & McMackin, J. (2021). Leading through paradox in a Covid-19 world: Human resources comes of age. *Human Resource Management Journal.* https://doi.org/10.1111/1748-8583.12343

Collings, D. G., Scullion, H., & Morley, M. J. (2007). Changing patterns of global staffing in the multinational enterprise: Challenges to the conventional expatriate assignment and emerging alternatives. *Journal of World Business, 42*(2), 198–213.

De Cieri, H., & Lazarova, M. (2021). "Your health and safety is of utmost importance to us": A review of research on the occupational health and safety of international employees. *Human Resource Management Review, 31*(4), 100790.

Dunning, J. H. (1989). The study of international business: A plea for a more interdisciplinary approach. *Journal of International Business Studies, 20*(3), 411–436.

Holmes, E. A., O'Connor, R. C., Perry, V. H., Tracey, I., Wessely, S., Arseneault, L. et al. (2020). Multidisciplinary research priorities for the COVID-19 pandemic: A call for action for mental health science. *The Lancet Psychiatry*. Available at: https://www.thelancet.com/journals/lanpsy/article/PIIS2215-0366(20)30168-1/fulltext

Smith, W. K., & Lewis, M. W. (2011). Toward a theory of paradox: A dynamic equilibrium model of organizing. *Academy of management Review, 36*(2), 381–403.

Teague, P., & Roche, W. K. (2012). Line managers and the management of workplace conflict: evidence from Ireland. *Human Resource Management Journal, 22*(3), 235–251.

Van De Voorde, K., Paauwe, J., & Van Veldhoven, M. (2012). Employee well-being and the HRM–organizational performance relationship: a review of quantitative studies. *International Journal of Management Reviews, 14*(4), 391–407.

Waizenegger, L., McKenna, B., Cai, W., & Bendz, T. (2020). An affordance perspective of team collaboration and enforced working from home during COVID-19. *European Journal of Information Systems, 29*(4), 429–442.

Part VI

Conclusion

19

Moving Forward in a Post-COVID World

Jonathan P. Doh and Mirko H. Benischke

Introduction

The global economy and the national economies that comprise it have experienced multiple crises over the past four decades. These include several economic crises (the Mexican Peso Crisis of 1994, the East Asian Financial Crisis of 1997–1998, the dot.com crises of 2001, the global financial crisis of 2007–2008 and the related European debt crisis, and, most recently the economic crisis brought about by the COVID-19 pandemic) and pandemics (the ongoing HIV-AIDS pandemic, the swine flu pandemic of 2009–2010, the multiple Ebola virus epidemics, and the current COVID-19 pandemic). In addition, many nations and regions

J. P. Doh (✉)
Villanova School of Business, Villanova University, Villanova, PA, USA
e-mail: jonathan.doh@villanova.edu

M. H. Benischke
Rotterdam School of Management, Erasmus University, Rotterdam, Netherlands
e-mail: benischke@rsm.nl

M. A. Mithani et al. (eds.), *Crises and Disruptions in International Business*, JIBS Special Collections, https://doi.org/10.1007/978-3-030-80383-4_19

have faced countless natural disasters and armed conflicts. Although there is wide variation in the nature, duration, scope, and impact of these crises, they all have some common effects that include social and economic disruption at multiple levels and, in many cases, substantial disturbance to cross-border trade and coordination of multinational enterprises' (MNE) foreign operations and supply chains.

International business (IB) scholarship has been concerned with crises and disruptions since its inception. In the past, IB scholars were primarily focused on more incremental, or at least less volatile change such as political risk and MNE-host government relations (e.g., Hymer, 1976), as well as the phenomenon of the obsolescing bargain, whereby the focus was on the interaction and power dynamics between the MNE and its various host governments (Vernon, 1971). More recently, as this volume underscores, IB research has become interested in the more dramatic and immediate changes in the form of natural disasters, wars, and insurrection (e.g., Oetzel & Getz, 2012), what some have referred to as non-ergodic changes (Cantwell et al. 2010) in which the future cannot be extrapolated from the past. The COVID-19 pandemic is but one illustration of this type of disruption.

One recurring theme in research on crises and disruption relates to the constructs of risk and uncertainty. In this regard, IB scholars have sometimes differentiated between the two concepts, with some, for example, conceptualizing a higher probability of unfavorable policy changes either as political risk (e.g., Delios & Henisz, 2000) or political uncertainty (e.g., Slangen, 2013; Williams et al., 2017). These studies either suggest that risk and uncertainty are different concepts—including the possibility that uncertainty and risk are dependent on each other-, or that risk and uncertainty sit on the opposite ends of a continuum. As a consequence, we now have different conceptualizations of the relationship between uncertainty and risk, which has particularly important implications for IB research.

In this concluding commentary, we introduce a framework for consideration of crises and disruptions though the lens of risk and uncertainty. We outline four potential relationships between these two constructs. We then use these four relationships to situate some of the original contributions to *JIBS* included in this collection. We leverage this paradigm to explore the relevance and efficacy of the current IB theoretical and empirical toolbox to examine contemporary crises and employ those reflections to draw some inspiration for future research in this area. Specifically, we will use two contemporary crises to explore IB theory and method—one that constitutes a disruption that is more akin to uncertainty (the COVID-19 pandemic) and another that reflects a more traditional conceptualization of risk (global climate change). For each, we will offer suggestions for how IB scholarship could be employed to inform these crises, given their differing character, constituencies, and temporal horizon. We focus especially on the impact of these events on global nonmarket strategy (GNMS), a topic that has gained increasing interest in IB, and that is also reflected in the articles and commentaries in this volume. We argue that IB scholarship must broaden its theoretical scope and widen its empirical toolkit to offer substantive, relevant, and material insights into contemporary global grand challenges, including those that concern risk and crises.

Crises and Disruption Through the Lens of Risk and Uncertainty

Although this collection is primarily organized by research that focuses on (1) exogenous external pressures surrounding crises and disruption and (2) how crises and disruption (and stakeholder influences) affect performance, these studies might also be classified by the primary qualities of risk and uncertainty associated with the disruptions they explore. Unlike much of contemporary IB research in which the constructs of risk and uncertainty are applied almost interchangeably (López-Duarte & Vidal-Suarez, 2010), most of the studies included in this collection provide a relatively clear and unambiguous perspective on how these concepts are used. At the same time, we have noticed that the studies included in this book vary in their conceptualization of the relationship between risk and uncertainty, with the main difference being whether risk and uncertainty are treated as separate constructs or not. In total, we have identified four distinct categories that reflect how IB scholars included in

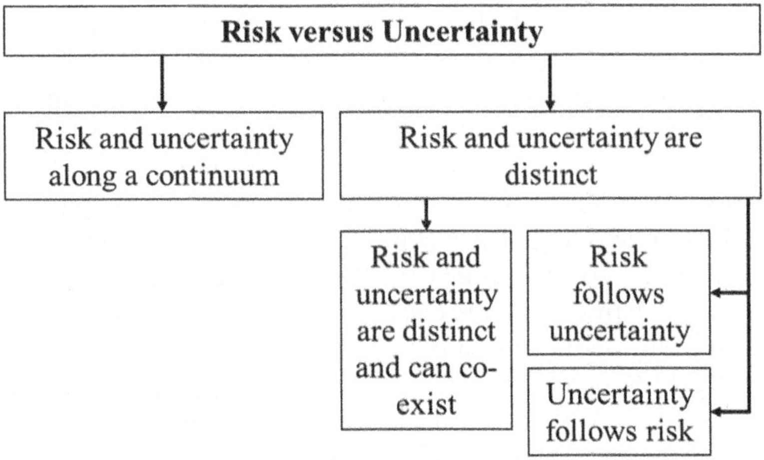

Fig. 19.1 Different Conceptualizations of Risk versus Uncertainty (adapted from Samson et al., 2009)

this collection, but also more generally, have treated the relationship between the risk and uncertainty in their research (see Fig. 19.1). Drawing on the distinction between risk and uncertainty, we acknowledge that the phenomena investigated in these articles likely incorporate aspects of both risk and uncertainty, albeit in different forms.

Category 1: Risk (Uncertainty) Can Be Defined as Uncertainty (Risk)

A number of scholars characterize risk and uncertainty along a continuum as opposed to using a binary classification, i.e., they define uncertainty as risk, and vice versa. Interestingly, these studies assume that both risk *and* uncertainty are quantifiable. An example of this perspective is the study by Weiner (2005), which explores the role of derivative trading during the Gulf Crisis of 1990–1991. He implies that risk as a result of the crisis is defined in terms of the uncertainty of a financial loss. Based on the analysis of the international oil market during the crisis, Weiner (2005) concludes that trading activities themselves during the crisis did not contribute to increased levels of volatility in the oil market. Along similar lines, Huang, Kerstein and Wang (2018) define risk as the uncertainty of economic losses from climate change. Their treatment of the risk-uncertainty concepts is consistent with the findings they report, and specifically the notion that firms located in countries characterized by a higher probability of such losses experience lower earnings and more volatile earnings.

Category 2: Risk and Uncertainty Are Distinct, and They Can Co-Exist

Among those that treat risk and uncertainty as distinct constructs, a set of scholars assume that they are independent from each other and that risk and uncertainty co-exist. One study that implicitly assumes that risk and uncertainty can co-exist is that by Mithani (2017). A particularly insightful finding from this study that supports this notion is that, following a natural disaster, domestic firms are confronted with increased levels of uncertainty, whereas foreign firms face higher levels of risk. Another relevant example is the editorial written by Caligiuri et al. (2020). They develop novel insights into how the field of international human resource management can contribute to conversations about how employees respond to contexts characterized by risk or uncertainty. Specifically, they acknowledge that the COVID-19 crisis has resulted in situations in which employees are confronted with both risk and uncertainty at the same time. The authors provide important guidance concerning how IB scholars can shed light on the heterogeneity across employees as to the amount of risk and uncertainty they perceive, as well as how MNEs can contribute to resolving situations perceived as uncertainty and risky.

Dai, Eden, and Beamish (2013) also speak to that perspective by demonstrating that a foreign subsidiary's geographic location determines whether a violent conflict creates risk or uncertainty. Specifically, foreign subsidiaries that are located outside of conflict zones are more likely to perceive violent conflicts as risk that can be managed, using appropriate measures. In contrast, subsidiaries within conflict zones—and those with an overall greater dynamic exposure to political conflict—may experience these conflicts as uncertainty. Managing such an uncertainty context is often too costly, and hence subsidiaries with greater exposure to conflict are more likely to exit. As such, the study by Dai et al. (2013) contributes to our understanding of how geographic proximity to a geographically confined shock will determine whether such a shock will result in a risk or uncertainty context, implying that, although different subsidiaries will perceive the conflict as either a source of risk or of uncertainty, both can co-exist.

Category 3: Risk and Uncertainty Are Distinct, and Moreover, Risk Follows Uncertainty

Alternatively, it has been assumed or argued that uncertainty and risk can occur in sequence with an initial event that is subject to high uncertainty evolving into high risk. Such a sequential process is often invoked by IB scholars who suggest that high uncertainty can be addressed through certain management strategies, resulting in a risk context. Examples of this perspective include Oetzel and Getz (2012), who show that MNEs are more likely to strategically respond to violent conflict as pressures from internal and external stakeholders increase. The authors further document the distinct strategic responses that MNEs adopt in to the face of different types of stakeholder pressures. A key insight that emerges from their study is that the presence of uncertainty alone may not be sufficient to prompt strategic responses, as such a substantive response necessitates active pressures by internal and external stakeholders. Gao, Wang and Che (2018) describe another situation in which some firms have turned uncertainty into risk. While the initial conflict, which was the Second Sino–Japanese War, undoubtedly resulted in substantial uncertainty—and the fact that the war remains a point of contention (as reflected in the continued animosity between the two nations) means that such a level of uncertainty may persist -, Gao et al. (2018) find that Japanese firms that have proactively deployed non-market strategies to accumulate political capital have been able to turn uncertainty into risk.

Category 4: Risk and Uncertainty Are Distinct, and Uncertainty Follows Risk

Furthermore, the relationship between risk and uncertainty can also reverse such that a situation initially viewed as risky can devolve into one of uncertainty. In this collection, Kolk and Pinkse (2008) describe a scenario in which risk can turn into uncertainty. Focusing on the topics of sustainability and climate change, they argue that unless MNEs invest substantial amounts of corporate resources into improving their environmental performance, they will face a future state characterized by increasing levels of uncertainty. The framework developed by Kolk and Pinkse (2008) also explicates the indirect channels through which MNEs are vulnerable to the physical impact that climate change promises to bring forth, further contributing to a transition from a state of risk to one that is akin to uncertainty.

Overall, the original contributions to *JIBS* included in this collection highlight the important role that risk and uncertainty concepts play in contemporary IB research. At the same time, we emphasize that there are substantial differences in the treatment of these concepts, specifically with regards to how the relationship between uncertainty and risk is conceptualized. One possible explanation for this divergence may relate to the underlying IB phenomenon and associated research questions that are studied. In this regard, our framework explicates the different ways in which IB scholars can think about the relationship between risk and uncertainty. We strongly believe that these approaches are not mutually exclusive, yet our categorization suggests that it is important that IB scholars explicate how they treat the relationship between risk and uncertainty in their research. Moreover, this observation also suggests that there is a need to put the relationship between risk and uncertainty front and center of IB research, especially when studying society's grand challenges. In order to facilitate such research, we will now use two contemporary crises to explore IB theory and method and offer suggestions for how IB researchers could inform these crises, with a focus on the different ways in which risk and uncertainty may relate to one another.

The COVID-19 Pandemic as a Context for Exploring Global Crises

Among the many impacts and reverberations, the COVID-19 pandemic and its social and economic consequences have underscored the need for management scholars to address bigger, bolder, and broader research questions. Indeed, management scholars have been challenging the management research community to tackle what are increasingly termed "grand challenges" i.e., those complex, multi-level, multi-actor issues such as climate change, inequality, mass migrations and health crises (c.f. Howard-Grenville, 2021; Buckley et al., 2017). Many of these challenges have been exacerbated and aggravated by COVID-19; for example, according to the United Nations, an additional 207 million people globally could be pushed into extreme poverty due to the pandemic (United Nations, 2021a).

The COVID-19 pandemic is, in some ways, a classic case of an "exogenous shock" crisis that was (mostly) unforeseen, unfolded in ways and directions that were not accurately predicted, and, perhaps most importantly, metastasized in unexpected forms with associated impacts that went well beyond initial expectations. As such, it initially represented a sort of "Knightian" uncertainty, in that establishing probability distributions around its trajectory and impacts was extraordinarily difficult; indeed, early estimates about the impact of COVID-19 vastly underestimated even the probability distributions, with the ultimate magnitude of its effects turning out to be outside most of those distribution estimates. Over time, as more information became public, and our understanding of the nature of this pandemic increased, many firms have been able to quantify the threat the pandemic poses to their operations and adopted more traditional risk management strategies. Moreover, the effects of the pandemic have unfolded at multiple levels: global, national and local as well as in specific industry sectors and global supply chains.

At the national level, there has been considerable variation in the nature, extent, and specific approaches various countries have taken to combatting the pandemic. China and many other East Asian countries have successfully impeded the spread of the virus, while others, including the United States and most European, Latin American and African countries, have struggled to implement a coordinated approach to contain community transmission. In other words, while some countries have been able to turn uncertainty into risk, others have not been able to do so as successfully. What explains these differences? What might IB scholars offer to inform and explain these observed differences in responses to a crisis?

A starting point would be to understand national responses to the COVID-19 pandemic through the lens of national culture. East Asian countries have higher power distance, are more collectivist and exhibit longer-term orientation compared to their Western counterparts (Hofstede, 1980, 2001; House et al., 2004). For instance, in countries with high power distance, such as China, South Korea, Taiwan, Japan, Singapore, and other Asian countries, citizens readily followed orders or had to face the consequences of noncompliance, sometimes severe. In Western countries, there was considerable pushback against the imposition of restrictions. Further, in individualist societies like many Western cultures, people tend to look after themselves and their direct family. In contrast, in collectivist societies people take care of the broader group in exchange for loyalty and reciprocity. In Asian countries' response to COVID-19, there is an intrinsic expectation that individuals will put collective interests first. For example, in many Asian countries, wearing masks was from the start considered a civic duty and failure to do so was viewed as a violation of a collective norm (although many of those countries had already adopted such practices due to the previous SARS epidemic). Societies that have longer-term orientations tend to encourage short-term sacrifice in order to secure a more positive future. In Asian (versus Western) countries' coronavirus responses, communities have been willing to incur short-term pain in exchange for longer-term gains, such as being able to resume normal activities. These core cultural differences, in turn, can shape political-economic systems. Western—especially Anglo-American—approaches to capitalism often emphasize individual agency and responsibility over collective agreement and commitment.

In terms of global coordination, most countries have struggled to respond effectively to the multiple waves of the outbreak, partly because there has been little global coordination among states, something that IB scholars who have studied coordination between and among global firms and value chains should be in a strong position to inform. At the industry level, specific sectors have been especially upended, including travel, hospitality, and commercial real estate. Relatedly, COVID-19 is simultaneously generating both centripetal and centrifugal effects. The pandemic is exposing and reinforcing interdependencies among countries; sectors (business, government, civil society); groups; and individuals. At the same time, it is also exacerbating divisions and differences in the form of economic and medical nationalism at the global and national level, pressures to source regionally or locally, rising inequalities, and other forms of separation. IB scholars interested in broader debates about the efficacy and potential shortcomings of economic globalization should—and are—contributing to discussion and reflection as to what the pandemic and its impact means for the future of globalization. In a recent study, Contractor (2021), for example, offers a robust defence of globalization in the post-COVID environment, strongly arguing that "we need globalization more than ever."

As in other large-scale global crises, the pandemic has had immediate, profound, and highly disruptive short-term impacts, while at the same time unleashing longer-term—and less well-understood—impacts. Many of these have already been well documented, such as the fact that the pandemic has reinforced and accelerated extant trends (flexible work arrangements, e-commerce, digitalization) while stalling or reversing others (growth of business travel, increased global migration) (c.f. Ancona et al., 2021; Foss, 2021). In IB, the focus has been directed mainly at impacts on global value chains (Kano & Oh, 2020) and on global strategy and coordination more generally (Verbeke & Yuan, 2021).

In our view, the pandemic and its consequences for economics, society, and organizations offers an interesting "natural experiment" for the study of crises and their effects on IB, multinational management, and wider questions related to global governance. Broadly, IB scholars need to be in a better position to help inform higher-level impacts of this crisis and be able to apply more flexible and malleable approaches to it. On one end of the spectrum, IB scholars should be more directly engaged in questions related to global coordination and collaboration around the distribution of personal protective equipment (PPE), antigen testing and vaccines. While this global level of analysis is typically beyond the scope of IB scholars, many counterparts in international political economy, an area closely related to IB, are well equipped to tackle such questions. Indeed, the topic of "global governance" is one that has occupied considerable attention in political science and to a lesser extent management studies, but (perhaps surprisingly) not so much in IB scholarship (for a notable exception, see Doh et al., 2015).

Importantly, we make the point that the COVID-19 crisis offers an example of a crisis that has evolved from uncertainty to risk, providing a unique laboratory to study more carefully the relationship between the two concepts. As such, the pandemic provides a unique context for applying IB theory and concepts, especially in the area of global nonmarket strategy (GNMS), to a number of important questions. First, the pandemic constitutes another example of the periodic resurgence of governmental action and activities in the face of crises and disruption. As was the case with the financial crisis, governments have rapidly and aggressively reasserted their centrality in issues of economic and even business decision-making. MNEs are dealing with a wide range of governmental policies and regulations with respect to business operations, employment policies, and customer interactions, and seeking to benefit from the massive fiscal infusions in many jurisdictions, as reflected by the unprecedented $1.9 trillion coronavirus relief and recovery bill implemented in the United States in early 2021. Concurrently, many tech companies—notably Facebook and Twitter—are grappling with their roles and responsibilities regarding the posting of misleading and inflammatory content in the face of a political "crises" in the United States and elsewhere.

In the face of crises, scholars of GNMS should therefore continue to focus on important questions related to the role of private, government, and nongovernmental actors in response to the pandemic or other such crises. Many of the public health responses to the pandemic included organizations from all three of these sectors and many involved partners from multiple countries, reflecting a form of cross-sectoral collaboration that may be especially effective in the face of a rapidly spreading pandemic. Specifically, of the more than 175 vaccine development efforts underway, including 33 in human trials, many involved cross-national and/or cross-sectoral cooperation, including the Pfizer Inc.-BioNTech vaccine; the Oxford-AstraZeneca vaccine; and the GeoVax-BravoVax vaccine. While IB scholars have begun exploring how organizations from different sectors respond to crises and disruption, such as in the wake of natural disasters, little IB research has focused on these international/cross-sectoral medicine-development initiatives. In our view, this would be among the most fruitful directions for IB research related to the COVID-19 pandemic, and one that can be extended to other types of exogenous crises and disruptions.

Climate Change and Global Crises and Disruptions

In some ways, the climate crisis is quite distinct from the COVD-19 pandemic because it has been in the works for decades, if not centuries. At the same time, however, it also reflects some of the same qualities as the pandemic, although extended out over a longer time horizon. Much of the work on climate change in the IB context has focused on translating the uncertainty associated with climate change into quantifiable risk that can be managed, hence the reference to "climate risk" in the Huang et al. (2018) article. The distinction between risk and uncertainty also becomes salient in the excellent insights from Martina Linnenluecke in her commentary (see Chap. 14). As Linnenluecke observes, organizational responses to climate change can take the form of mitigation (reducing, containing or capturing carbon through governmental policies) or adaptation (adjusting and modifying operations, practices or products to offset or counter the impact of climate change). In this regard, mitigation responses are often framed from a risk perspective, whereas adaptation responses more often reflect decision-making under uncertainty.

Moreover, while both mitigation and adaptation can be advanced by governments, private organizations or both, large-scale mitigation efforts generally require coordination among states, such as in the Paris Climate Accord, whereas adaptation efforts can occur at lower levels, including by individual organizations. Similarly, IB scholars have begun to embrace topics related to the global natural-human environment nexus, including climate change. As a multi-actor, multi-level phenomenon, climate change does pose challenges for IB scholars, but ones that are worth addressing (Doh et al., 2019). Indeed, we believe that, while global efforts to mitigate climate change remain critical, it has become increasingly clear that they are unlikely to be completely successful. To date, the preponderance of natural and social science research has focused on mitigation, as has the relatively limited management and IB research. As a result, MNEs adaptation strategies in response to the physical impact promised by climate change are grossly understudied. From a risk-management and risk-response perspective, we argue that climate change adaptation is a particularly important topic for IB scholars interested in crises and disruption, to understand the relationship between risk and uncertainty and how it affects MNE strategy and outcomes.

Consequently, we believe that a systematic IB research program on climate change adaptation is not only needed given the importance of the phenomenon itself—the United Nations estimates that an investment of 1.5 trillion euros in adaptation measures will be needed to avoid 6 trillion euros in climate change-related costs (UN, 2021b)—but also because existing theory is ill adapted to explain MNE adaptation to climate change. Namely, climate change and its effects are often temporarily and spatially distant from their anthropogenic causes, with the physical consequences thus being unevenly distributed across geographical regions in terms of both magnitude and type of impact. Such impact heterogeneity is qualitatively different from that observed in relation to other shocks. The heterogeneity in climate change impacts therefore makes it difficult for MNEs to quantify the threat that climate change directly or indirectly poses to their operations.

Moreover, the transformation of the physical landscape that is directly associated with a changing climate has implications for where and how MNEs operate, how they transport goods, and what contingencies they must make in light of disruptions caused by the changing climate (Doh et al., 2019). This is particularly relevant for companies that rely on the land, marine, or riparian waterways, such as agribusinesses, mining, minerals, and petrochemical companies, but also for processed food and beverage MNEs such as Unilever, Nestle and Procter & Gamble. Additionally, unlike in other adaptation contexts in which resilient organizations may be able to recover and return to stability, many MNEs may not enjoy such a recovery or future state of stability when confronted with the physical changes associated with climate change. Whereas we have seen increasing attention being paid to climate change adaptation in the public domain, this has not been mirrored in the business community (Doh et al., 2019). As a case in point, in 2020, a survey revealed that CEOs did not perceive climate change and environmental damage as a top ten threat to their organization's future growth prospects (PwC, 2020). This indicates that, while managers often publicly comment on the importance of climate action, research shows that many organizations continue to translate climate change into business as usual (Wright & Nyberg, 2017).

The lack of organizational attention to climate change is concerning as it suggests that, in fact, many managers operate under the false assumption that routine adaptation responses may suffice to address climate changes. Moreover, the lack of urgency with which business leaders prepare their organizations for the physical impact of climate change is particularly disturbing given the central role organizations play in the functioning of society at large. Overall, from a risk-management and risk-response as well as a broader societal perspective, climate change adaptation is an important topic for IB scholars interested in crises and disruption, primarily because it highlights the complex relationship between risk and uncertainty; a theme shared by the studies on crises and disruption included in this collection of notable JIBS articles.

For example, to what extent do multinationals coordinate and integrate their global climate change adaption strategies and to what extent are they developed and implemented among countries/subsidiaries? Furthermore, how do commodity-dependent companies such as food and beverage MNEs (Nestle, Unilever, P&G) and retailers (H&M, Starbucks) plan for changing activities such as growing, production, and supply of the commodities on which they depend? Looking at these and other examples, it appears to be important for future scholarship in IB to develop insights that capture both local and regional variability of climate impacts, but are, at the same time, aggregating findings to answer questions about firm and industry vulnerability and adaptation to climate change in an international context. In other words, IB scholars need to develop a voice in the evolving discourse about climate change adaptation, as a particularly relevant dimension of possibly the most consequential shock with which we will be confronted.

Future Scholarship at the Intersection of International Business and Crises and Disruption

This collection of *JIBS* articles related to crises and disruption underscores the important dynamic among firms, crises and disruption, and the global business environment. Each of the contributions and the accompanying commentaries offer important and relevant insights into the nexus of multinational strategy and decision-making in response to risks and uncertainties emanating from various political, geographic, societal and cultural contexts. In this commentary, we have suggested that different conceptualizations of risk and uncertainty may lend themselves to different approaches to study crises and disruption in IB.

We propose that future research should consider the range of antecedents to crises and disruption, the variety of responses by firms to those stimuli, potential mediating or moderating impacts, and the interaction between various types of crises and disruption. We believe that a particularly fruitful lens to study crises and disruptions is to emphasize the relationship between risk and uncertainty, a relationship that can be conceptualized in many ways. For example, we know that economic vulnerability can contribute to political crises, and that political crises can exacerbate economic disruption. Similarly, climate change and risk may have some impact on the ability of firms to respond to economic challenges brought about by COVID-19, in the same way in which climate risk can also aggravate the potential of countries and organizations to respond to natural disasters. An important theme that warrants attention is also the heterogeneity with which the consequences these shocks have been experienced across and within organizations, countries and regions. There is a real concern that while some MNEs have benefited or will benefit from the COVID-19 pandemic, this crisis has eradicated decades of progress on poverty reduction in the developing world. Given the interconnectedness of the global economy, IB scholars should contribute to conversations about the role of business in society in the post-pandemic era.

We conclude by asserting that the IB discipline is uniquely positioned to contribute to the discourse on crises and disruptions in social science research given the nature of MNEs and their interactions with multiple, global stakeholders. In our commentary, we also recognized that IB scholars have not always fully incorporated the reality that MNEs operate in a volatile, uncertain, complex and ambiguous world. The immediate threat of the COVID-19 pandemic and the longer-term challenge of global climate change are only two examples that underscore the profound impact that such shocks can have on MNEs and the social and economic environment in which they operate. In the end, the core purpose and aspiration of international business as an increasingly important field of research is to contribute to a "more prosperous, just, and sustainable world" (Academy of International Business, 2021).

References

Academy of International Business (AIB). (2021). AIB's *Mission-vision-values statements*. https://aib.msu.edu/aboutAIBmission.asp. Accessed 19 Apr 2021.

Ancona, D., Bresman, H., & Mortensen, M. (2021). Shifting team research after COVID-19: Evolutionary and revolutionary change. *Journal of Management Studies*. https://doi.org/10.1111/joms.12651

Buckley, P. O., Doh, J. P., & Benischke, M. (2017). Towards a renaissance in international business research? Big questions, grand challenges, and the future of IB Scholarship. *Journal of International Business Studies, 48*(9), 1045–1064.

Caligiuri, P., De Cieri, H., Minbaeva, D., et al. (2020). International HRM insights for navigating the COVID-19 pandemic: Implications for future research and practice. *Journal of International Business Studies, 51*, 697–713.

Cantwell, J., Dunning, J., & Lundan, S. (2010). An evolutionary approach to understanding international business activity: The co-evolution of MNEs and the institutional environment. *Journal of International Business Studies, 41*(4), 567–586.

Contractor, F. (2021). The world economy will need *even more* globalization in the post-pandemic decade. *Journal of International Business Studies*. https://doi.org/10.1057/s41267-020-00394-y

Dai, L., Eden, L., & Beamish, P. (2013). Place, space, and geographical exposure: Foreign subsidiary survival in conflict zones. *Journal of International Business Studies, 44*, 554–578.

Delios, A., & Henisz, W. J. (2000). Japanese firms' investment strategies in emerging economies. *Academy of Management Journal, 43*, 305–323.

Doh, J. P., McGuire, S., & Ozaki, T. (2015). Back to the great illusion? Global governance and international nonmarket strategies for the 21st century – Introduction to the special issue. *Journal of World Business, 50*(2), 256–261.

Doh, J. P., Tashman, P., & Benischke, M. H. (2019). Adapting to grand environmental challenges through collective entrepreneurship. *Academy of Management Perspectives, 33*(4), 450–468.

Foss, N. J. (2021). The impact of the Covid-19 pandemic on firms' organizational designs. *Journal of Management Studies*. https://doi.org/10.1111/joms.12643

Gao, G. Y., Wang, D. T., & Che, Y. (2018). Impact of historical conflict on FDI location and performance: Japanese investment in China. *Journal of International Business Studies, 49*, 1060–1080.

Hofstede, G. (1980). *Culture's consequences: International differences in work-related values*. Sage Publications.

Hofstede, G. (2001). *Culture's consequences: Comparing values, behaviors, institutions, and organizations across nations* (2nd ed.). Sage Publications.

House, R. J., Hanges, P. J., Javidan, M., Dorfman, P. W., & Gupta, V. (2004). *Culture, leadership, and organizations: The GLOBE study of 62 societies*. Sage Publications.

Howard-Grenville, J. (2021). Grand challenges, Covid-19 and the future of organizational scholarship. *Journal of Management Studies*. https://doi.org/10.1111/joms.12647

Huang, H. H., Kerstein, J., & Wang, C. (2018). The impact of climate risk on firm performance and financing choices: An international comparison. *Journal of International Business Studies, 49*, 633–656.

Hymer, S. H. (1976). The international operations of national firms: A study of direct foreign investment. Cambridge, MA: MIT Press.

Kano, L., & Oh, C. H. (2020). Global value chains in the post-Covid world: Governance for reliability. *Journal of Management Studies, 57*, 1773–1777.

Kolk, A., & Pinkse, J. (2008). A perspective on multinational enterprises and climate change: Learning from "an inconvenient truth"? *Journal of International Business Studies, 39*, 1359–1378.

López-Duarte, C., & Vidal-Suarez, M. M. (2010). External uncertainty and entry mode choice: Cultural distance, political risk and language diversity. *International Business Review, 19*(6), 575–588.

Mithani, M. A. (2017). Liability of foreignness, natural disasters, and corporate philanthropy. *Journal of International Business Studies, 48*, 941–963.

Oetzel, J., & Getz, K. (2012). Why and how might firms respond strategically to violent conflict? *Journal of International Business Studies, 43*, 166–186.

PricewaterhouseCoopers (PwC). (2020). *23rd Annual Global CEO Survey: Navigating the Rising Tide of Uncertainty*. https://www.pwc.com/gx/en/ceo-survey/2020/reports/pwc-23rd-global-ceo-survey.pdf. Accessed 6 Mar 2021.

Samson, S., Reneke, J. A., & Wiecek, M. M. (2009). A review of different perspectives on uncertainty and risk and an alternative modeling paradigm. *Reliability Engineering & System Safety, 94*(2009), 558–567.

Slangen, A. H. L. (2013). Greenfield or acquisition entry? The roles of policy uncertainty and MNC legitimacy in host countries. *Global Strategy Journal, 3*, 262–280.

United Nations (UN). (2021a). *Impact of COVID-19 on the sustainable development goals*. Available at https://sdgintegration.undp.org/accelerating-development-progressduring-covid-19. Accessed 15 Feb 15.

United Nations (UN). (2021b). *Adaptation gap report 2020*. United Nations Environment Programme.

Verbeke, A., & Yuan, W. (2021). A few implications of the COVID-19 pandemic for international business strategy research. *Journal of Management Studies*. https://doi.org/10.1111/joms.12665

Vernon, R. (1971). *Sovereignty at Bay*. Basic Books.

Weiner, R. (2005). Speculation in international crises: Report from the Gulf. *Journal of International Business Studies, 36*, 576–587.

Williams, C., Lukoianova, T., & Martinez, C. A. (2017). The moderating effect of bilateral investment treaty stringency on the relationship between political instability and subsidiary ownership choice. *International Business Review, 26*, 1–11.

Wright, C., & Nyberg, D. (2017). An inconvenient truth: How organizations translate climate change into business as usual. *Academy of Management Journal, 60*(5), 1633–1661.

Index[1]

[1] Note: Page numbers followed by 'n' refer to notes.

M. A. Mithani et al. (eds.), *Crises and Disruptions in International Business*, JIBS Special Collections, https://doi.org/10.1007/978-3-030-80383-4

The manufacturer's authorised representative in the EU is Springer Nature Customer Service Centre GmbH, Europaplatz 3, 69115 Heidelberg, Germany. If you have any concerns regarding our products, please contact ProductSafety@springernature.com

Printed and bound by CPI Group (UK) Ltd, Croydon, CR0 4YY
22/09/2026
02220984-0014